THE
Little Norton Reader

50 ESSAYS FROM THE FIRST 50 YEARS

THE
Little Norton Reader

50 ESSAYS FROM THE FIRST 50 YEARS

Melissa A. Goldthwaite

Saint Joseph's University

W. W. Norton & Company
New York • London

W. W. Norton & Company has been independent since its founding in 1923, when William Warder Norton and Mary D. Herter Norton first published lectures delivered at the People's Institute, the adult education division of New York City's Cooper Union. The firm soon expanded its program beyond the Institute, publishing books by celebrated academics from America and abroad. By mid-century, the two major pillars of Norton's publishing program—trade books and college texts—were firmly established. In the 1950s, the Norton family transferred control of the company to its employees, and today—with a staff of four hundred and a comparable number of trade, college, and professional titles published each year—W. W. Norton & Company stands as the largest and oldest publishing house owned wholly by its employees.

Editor: Marilyn Moller

Project Editors: Shuli Traub, Katie Callahan

Copyeditor: Katharine Ings

Marketing Manager: Megan Zwilling

Photo Editor: Stephanie Romeo

Design Director: Rubina Yeh

Permissions Manager: Megan Jackson

Composition: Westchester Book Group

Associate Editor: Ariella Foss

Senior Production Supervisor: Ashley Horna

Editorial Assistant: Claire Wallace

Managing Editor: Marian Johnson

Photo Researcher: Fay Torresyap

Book Designer: Pamela L. Schnitter

Permissions Clearing: Margaret Gorenstein

Manufacturing: R.R. Donnelley—Harrisonburg

Permission to use copyrighted material is included in the credits section of this book, which begins on page 506.

Library of Congress Cataloging-in-Publication Data
The little Norton reader : 50 essays from the first 50 years / [compiled by] Melissa Goldthwaite, St. Joseph's University. — First edition.
pages cm
Includes bibliographical references and index.
ISBN 978-0-393-26582-8 (pbk.)
1. Essays.   I. Goldthwaite, Melissa A., 1972–
PN6142.L57 2016
808.84—dc23   2015033632

W. W. Norton & Company, Inc., 500 Fifth Avenue, New York, N.Y. 10110
www.wwnorton.com
W. W. Norton & Company Ltd., Castle House,
75/76 Wells Street, London W1T 3QT

1 2 3 4 5 6 7 8 9 0

Preface

The Little Norton Reader began as a book to commemorate the fiftieth anniversary of *The Norton Reader.* No other composition reader has lived such a long life, so it's a moment to celebrate! But as I began to study the many editions of the *Reader* and noted how much they revealed about the essay as a genre, the book quickly became something more than just commemorative:

It's organized chronologically to showcase how the essay and the issues that matter to students have both changed and remained the same over time. Opening with a journal entry by Ralph Waldo Emerson praising the language of "truckmen and teamsters" and concluding with a blog post by Dennis Baron about how *Facebook* offers a choice of fifty-eight genders but only "the same three tired pronouns," this collection explores the power of language and writing not only to express identity but also to change hearts and minds. *It includes some writing by students,* acknowledging that excellent writing is often done by students. *And it's a "little" Norton Reader,* something instructors have asked for, offered at the low price students want and need.

The pleasures of putting together a collection that celebrates fifty years of *The Norton Reader* are many: to reflect on which essays have lasted and why, to imagine the new voices that will shape composition readers in the next fifty years, to discover essays in older editions that will speak to students today, and to consider how both the essay and the teaching of writing have developed over time. And one more thing, of course: to create a much smaller book while still maintaining the breadth and depth for which *The Norton Reader* is known.

In "The Essay Canon," Lynn Z. Bloom argues that "No matter where an essay first appeared—in the *New Yorker* or a little magazine or on a newspaper's op-ed page—if it is to survive in the hearts and minds" of American readers "it must be reprinted time and again" in a composition reader (401). For Bloom, the criterion for whether an essay should be canonized was not how many times it had been cited by other academics, but how often it had been anthologized in composition readers. Bloom identifies a canon of 174 authors—and notes that twenty-five of them were anthologized for the first time in *The Norton Reader*. Many of the authors introduced in those early editions remain in the book today, even as it continues to introduce excellent new writing to new generations of teachers and students.

Bloom goes on to discuss the pedagogical, academic, and financial concerns that affect whether an essay is anthologized and can become "a candidate for canonicity"—explaining that the essay must first "satisfy the anthologist's criteria for teachability; then it must balance intellectually, politically, and rhetorically with the rest of the book; it must contribute aesthetically; and its permission-to-reprint must be affordable" (413). All these elements have influenced which essays have come and gone from *The Norton Reader* over the years—and have shaped this fiftieth anniversary edition as well.

The selections included in *The Little Norton Reader* celebrate the "staying power" of many beloved essays. At the same time, they show the diversity of authors and topics taught in writing classes over time. Thirteen of Bloom's "canonical" authors appear in this short collection, including eight of the top ten—Joan Didion, Martin Luther King Jr., George Orwell, Lewis Thomas, Henry David Thoreau, Mark Twain, E. B. White, and Virginia Woolf—as well as many newer authors and essays that instructors have identified as favorites (Sherman Alexie's "Superman and Me," Alison Bechdel's "Fun Home," and Joey Franklin's "Working at Wendy's," for example). Close study of past editions also prompted the inclusion of several readings rarely if ever anthologized in another composition reader—Gertrude Stein's "Poetry and Grammar," Vertamae Smart-Grosvenor's "The Kitchen Crisis," and D. Keith Mano's "How to Keep from Getting Mugged."

When I began reading early editions of *The Norton Reader*, I expected the essays to be fairly traditional and to demonstrate the clarity and correctness valued by writing teachers. But what I found surprised me: *The Norton Reader* wasn't nearly as traditional as I thought it had been.

Consider, for example, Gertrude Stein's essay "Poetry and Grammar." One of only ten pieces by female authors included in the first edition, her essay contained sentences such as this one: "Beside being able to be mistaken and to make mistakes verbs can change to look like themselves or to look like something else, they are, so to speak on the move and adverbs move with them and each of them find themselves not at all annoying but very often very much mistaken." I understood why the editors included it; indeed other selections in the book suggested they valued both poetry and grammar. But here was a writer who *broke* many rules of grammar. Still, the editors took this essay and its style seriously: one study question asked how "Miss Stein's prose style" differed from more conventional styles—and prompted students to consider what might be lost if her writing were more conventional. In fact, Stein's use of repetition and lack of standard punctuation create a memorable rhythm—and her less-than-grammatical sentences help students reflect on when and for what purpose it is appropriate to break traditional rules of grammar and punctuation. These questions are as relevant today as they were fifty years ago.

If I was surprised to find Gertrude Stein in the first edition, I was astonished to see Vertamae Smart-Grosvenor in the 1973 edition—and to see that her last name wasn't included; she was just "Verta Mae," one of the first African American women to appear in *The Norton Reader*. She capitalizes none of her sentences, indents none of her paragraphs, and—like Stein—pushes against conventions of grammar and punctuation. In terms of content, she critiques instant food, tying its invention to race and even slavery, writing that "white folks . . . had to invent instant food because the servant problem got so bad that their women had to get in the kitchen herself with her own two little lily white hands. it is no accident that in the old old south where they had slaves that they was eating fried chicken, coated with batter, biscuits so light they could have flown across the mason dixon line if they had wanted to." Like Stein, Smart-Grosvenor pays attention to rhythm, encouraging readers to "rap" her essay.

Then there's D. Keith Mano's essay, which first appeared in *Playboy*. If you could imagine a comic book bubble over my head when I made that discovery, it wouldn't even contain words—just the punctuation missing from Stein's essay: !?!?!?! In this humorous how-to piece, Mano uses short, direct sentences—"Sing aloud. Mutter a lot. Preach Jesus."— and slang, telling readers to "walk gas-fast" and "book it, baby." Students may not recognize all of Mano's slang, but his play with language and attention to sound will be familiar to anyone who attends poetry slams or other oral performances. As with Stein and Smart-Grosvenor, Mano's arguments and use of style give contemporary readers and writers much to think about and learn from.

Other essays will prompt students to reflect on the ways technology shapes reading, writing, and other forms of communication. Nicholas Carr's article on whether *Google* is making us stupid; Judith Newman's personal narrative about Siri; and Dennis Baron's blog entry on *Facebook*, gender, and pronouns all demonstrate the purposes—and peculiarities— of different genres of communication. Students can benefit from making connections among earlier and more contemporary genres of writing—to compare the conventions of email and *Facebook* with those of Garrison Keillor's letters and postcards, for example, or to consider whether sites like *Tumblr*, *Pinterest*, or *Instagram* share any similarities with the notebooks Joan Didion describes. Reading the older and newer essays together will help students move beyond questions about whether technology makes us smart or stupid—and to think about how it affects the ways we communicate and live.

With its chronological organization, *The Little Norton Reader* invites teachers and students to examine the ways nonfiction prose, especially the essay, has developed over time. The book begins with journal entries from Emerson and Thoreau, two of the earliest American essayists; continues with well-known essays by Orwell, White, Woolf, and many others; and ends with a relatively new genre that has become a kind of public journal: a blog post. From Emerson's journal on the power of language, even usage that's "clean contrary to our grammar rules," to Baron's blog post on gender and pronouns and the continued power of the "grammar gods," it's clear that language and identity are connected—even if the questions and concerns about both change with time.

This short collection can also be used to teach a range of nonfiction genres—arguments, cultural analyses, how-to essays, journals, letters, literacy narratives, lyric essays, memoirs, op-eds, profiles, reflections, and more. The Index of Genres lists the readings that demonstrate commonly assigned genres; this will, I hope, prompt readers to reflect on the advantages and purposes of various genres. Journals and letters, for instance, may exhibit a writer's interests and concerns and provide a space for developing those concerns with a defined audience in mind. Memoirs, literacy narratives, lyric essays, and reflections allow writers to expand their audience as they share significant experiences that influence identity, beliefs, and political actions. Op-eds and other kinds of arguments help writers persuade readers to take action or make a change. Each of these genres encourages—and helps—writers to develop their craft and ideas—and to share their thoughts, experiences, and positions with others.

The Little Norton Reader can also be used for courses that focus on particular themes and issues. The Index of Themes will help instructors choose readings on topics and issues that interest students. A course might be organized, for instance, by units on food, class, home and family, and nature and the environment. Another course might be organized around race and ethnicity, language and communication, media and technology, and gender. The themes offered in this index allow for myriad combinations that help readers make connections among different time periods, social contexts, and topics.

In addition to a range of genres and themes, this book includes essays that demonstrate different modes of development. The Index of Rhetorical

Modes categorizes essays that use nine common methods: description, comparison and contrast, and so on. Some essays appear in more than one category, of course, showing students that writers often use more than one rhetorical mode when developing an essay. For example, in "The Clan of One-Breasted Women," Terry Tempest Williams combines narration and argument; in "On Dumpster Diving," Lars Eighner combines definition and classification; and nearly all narratives also include description. From the descriptive memoirs of Maya Angelou, Langston Hughes, and Dylan Thomas to Alison Bechdel's graphic memoir, students can see how sensory details, once expressed in words alone, may now be conveyed in images.

The Norton Reader has always focused on excellent writing, and *The Little Norton Reader* acknowledges that excellent writing is often done by student authors. An album of four student essays includes exemplary writing in frequently assigned genres: a rhetorical analysis, an argument, a personal narrative, and a profile. Two of the essays were runners-up for the Norton Writer's Prize, an annual contest for which teachers can nominate their students' writing. The rhetorical analysis, written by one of my students, is about Terry Tempest Williams's "The Clan of One-Breasted Women," a reading included in the book. I hope these essays will inspire students to seek a broader audience for their writing; to revise and submit their best work to contests, newspapers, and literary magazines; or even to create their own blogs.

May this mix of old and new—canonical essays by well-known writers to award-winning student writing, journals to blogs, a memoir about holidays to an analysis of hunger, an argument about guns to a mixed-genre piece on wild tongues—provide inspiration for thoughtful, lively discussion and models for writing worth reading and celebrating. Here's to another fifty years.

WORK CITED

Bloom, Lynn Z. "The Essay Canon." *College English* 61.4 (1999): 401–30. Print.

Highlights of *The Little Norton Reader*

- **Fifty excellent essays by a variety of authors:** classic (Zora Neale Hurston, George Orwell), contemporary (Nicholas Carr, Alison Bechdel), favorites from the past (Gertrude Stein, Aldo Leopold), and new favorites (Lynda Barry, Judith Newman)—all chosen for writing that inspires students to think, respond, and write.

- **Four exemplary essays written by students,** including a rhetorical analysis, an argument, a personal essay, and a profile.

- **A flexible organization that supports a number of different teaching approaches,** with indexes that organize the essays by genre, rhetorical mode, and theme.

- **User-friendly apparatus:** headnotes provide context about the authors and essays, and study questions focus on key aspects of the readings and prompt written response.

- **A small trim size**—small enough that students will bring the book with them to class.

- **A low price**—and because the readings all come from *The Norton Reader,* the book that's introduced millions of students to the essay as a genre, *The Little Norton Reader* offers the unusual combination of high quality and a low price.

Acknowledgments

In autumn of 2012, Howard Dinin and I were browsing the shelves of a bookstore in Philadelphia. Just after we left the store, he handed me a bag with a thick book inside, a gift: a copy of the first edition of *The Norton Reader*. After looking at the cover art (an image of Yale's Beinecke Library), I turned to the copyright page: 1965. I quickly calculated the publication date for the fourteenth edition and realized its release would mark the fiftieth anniversary of the book.

I'm grateful to Howard not only for the gift of that first edition, which led to this celebratory collection, but for the many ways he supports my work. No matter where we are—Pennsylvania, New Hampshire, or Provence—he makes sure I have an internet connection, a scanner, and a space to work. He provides sustenance and conversation. He also subscribes to numerous journals and magazines, some of which I've drawn from in making nominations for *The Norton Reader*. As I finished the work on *The Little Norton Reader*, he made daily trips to our favorite French bakery so I could start each day of writing with a *chausson aux pommes*.

An excellent editor is also a collaborator, and Marilyn Moller has collaborated with me on every part of this book: the initial idea, proposal, contents, headnotes, questions, indexes, and more. From face-to-face meetings in New York and Tampa to phone calls and emails at all times of the day and night, she has worked with me to shape this collection. I'm grateful for her hard work, expertise, and friendship.

I'm also grateful to Ariella Foss and Claire Wallace, who tracked down every edition of *The Norton Reader* for me; they both helped with the research and attention to details that made this book possible. Ariella, the house editor for the fourteenth edition of *The Norton Reader*, has gone above and beyond in ways too numerous to mention. I owe thanks to many others who contributed to this book: Megan

Jackson and Margaret Gorenstein secured permissions; Susanna Moller provided the beautiful art that helped shape Carin Berger's fanciful cover design and Pamela Schnitter's charming interior design—in close collaboration with Rubina Yeh and Debra Morton Hoyt, our most creative design directors. Thanks also to photo editors Stephanie Romeo and Fay Torresyap—and especially to our outstanding project editors, Shuli Traub and Katie Callahan, and our excellent production supervisor, Ashley Horna.

When I told my friend Libby Jones that I was an editor for *The Norton Reader*, her face brightened as she told me about her first time teaching composition—and how she used the first edition of the *Reader*. She remembered so many details and conveyed such enthusiasm. I'm delighted she was willing to write about that experience.

I'd like to acknowledge all the editors of *The Norton Reader*, past and present, who have made that book what it is today: something worth celebrating. Although I never met Art Eastman, the original general editor, I've come to admire him by reading his work and learning more about how he led a team of editors for nearly three decades.

My respect and gratitude go especially to Linda Peterson. I have admired her leadership and intelligence for many years. She was, for me, the model general editor, keeping the editorial team on task, providing guidance, and doing a great deal of work behind the scenes. When I started my work as general editor of the fourteenth edition, she provided advice and folders full of information (including her review of the seventh edition, reports, and correspondence) that gave me a deeper understanding of the history of *The Norton Reader*. I didn't anticipate that she would not live to see the published *Little Norton Reader* or the fourteenth edition of the book she shaped in so many ways.

I thank Joan Hartman and the later editors who built expertly on the foundation established by Art Eastman, Caesar Blake, Hubert

English Jr., Alan Howes, Robert Lenaghan, Leo McNamara, and James Rosier. Even before she joined the team as an editor, Joan was instrumental in increasing the number and range of essays by women and writers of color; she also encouraged a strong focus on student writing.

I'm also grateful to the current editorial team: John Brereton, Joe Bizup, and Anne Fernald, who—with different interests and areas of expertise—continue to find excellent nonfiction worth reading and teaching.

Finally, to the authors whose work is included, to the instructors who've taught with *The Norton Reader*, and to the students who read and write and re-read and revise—thank you. Your work makes mine possible.

                                                    Melissa A. Goldthwaite

Celebrating Fifty Years

A Brief History of *The Norton Reader*

> A good anthology, like a good banquet, offers food for every
> taste, and all of it high quality.
> —ARTHUR EASTMAN, from his preface to the first edition

November 1962. Professor Arthur Eastman was sitting in his office at
the University of Michigan—a room with bookshelves on three sides,
two ashtrays, the musty smell of cigarettes and old books. That morning, Eastman met with Norton traveler Howard Sims, who told him
that W. W. Norton & Company was looking to publish some books
for composition courses. Sims explained that they were thinking of
anthologies that would cover "the entire field of writing, with a separate
book on each genre—poetry, prose, drama, fiction, all that'" (Sabine 5).
Eastman had no interest in editing such a book and proposed instead
"'an anthology of expository prose, a long volume, very long, to fit a whole
range of teacher interests'" (5). Norton, which had in 1962 published
its first Norton anthology, *The Norton Anthology of English Literature*,
quickly saw the potential in Eastman's approach. Jack Neill, the head
of the college division at Norton, began working on the contract.

Eastman recruited his editors following the model of the Norton
anthologies, that is, by assembling a large team to ensure varied interests
and tastes. A week after Sims's visit, Eastman, Caesar Blake, Hubert
English Jr., Alan Howes, Robert Lenaghan, Leo McNamara, and James
Rosier—all then teaching at the University of Michigan—signed a
contract for *The Norton Reader* (22). All were professors of literature,
most of whom regularly taught composition and were members of

Michigan's Freshman English Committee, working to find more effective ways of teaching composition.

At the time, in the early 1960s, first-year composition—then called freshman English—was taught primarily by professors and graduate students trained in literature. According to Albert Kitzhaber, in a 1963 book about the teaching of first-year writing, the purpose of college composition was to teach students to "write with ease, precision, and correctness" and to "focus the student's attention on fundamental principles of clear thinking and the clear and effective written expression of that thinking" (2, 3). Kitzhaber's study, based on analysis of ninety-eight courses from 1961 to 1962, revealed a diversity of approaches, with courses focusing on everything from grammar and mechanics to literature, "Great Books" to logic, or even propaganda analysis (12–13).

Kitzhaber also noted that the textbooks for these courses were "likely to be among the poorest, the least scholarly, that the student will encounter" (15). He critiqued the readers in particular as merely "springboards for discussions of things in general . . . cut-and-paste affairs that can ill sustain a course of true college grade" (16). He pointed further to the "extraordinary number of these collections on the market" and how they "come and go with extraordinary rapidity" (17).

Eastman and his colleagues had been dissatisfied with "the crop of new readers available," and they wanted to offer something different: "works from the past as well as the present, foreign as well as native, long as well as short, light as well as serious, and in addition, those kinds of literature—journals, letters, characters, apothegms, parables— that are first cousins . . . to the essay."

They also sought to create a book that would appeal to a range of teacher and student interests, an anthology that would, in Eastman's words, be "like a good banquet," with "food for every taste, and all of it high quality." To achieve these goals, Eastman established a process for choosing readings. Each editor nominated ten to twelve readings, which were then reviewed by two other editors; if they both voted "yes," the piece was likely to be included. In the case of one "yes" and one "no," the reading went to another editor for review, or the general editor broke the tie. This process continued for two more rounds with different editors.

To give a sense of how these editors were thinking about that first edition, here's what one of them said: "You're going to go for a few red-hot seventeenth-century pieces. You're not trying to be fair to the centuries to achieve equal or proportional representation, but Plato is going to get a word and Aristotle and Jesus and guys like that" (Sabine 13). Indeed, "guys like that" did get a word—as did Emerson, Thoreau, Orwell, Bacon, Hazlitt, Carlyle, Lamb, and many others. Of the 220 readings included in the first edition, only ten were by women, including a selection from Katherine Mansfield's journal; a few letters by Margaret Culkin Banning and Emily Dickinson; and essays by Hannah Arendt, Edith Hamilton, Margaret Mead, Gertrude Stein, and Roberta Wohlstetter. The only essay by a writer of color was James Baldwin's "Stranger in the Village."

The final table of contents featured eleven thematic chapters, some with subsections of prose forms: "Journals" in the chapter on "Personal Reports," "Apothegms" in the one on "Government," and so on. Eastman explained the organization this way:

> They begin with personal experience, turn to the equipment and training with which a person confronts and masters experience— his language, his education, his mind; then look broadly outward at certain insistent concerns of our civilization—manners and marriage, discrimination, poverty, the machine; and develop, finally, along the great traditional lines of a liberating education— art, morality, politics, history, science, religion.

The book included some glosses and contextual notes—and some readings had study questions—but Eastman feared that further help would be intrusive, reasoning that teachers "tend to like to go by their own paces along roads of their own choosing."

Writing instruction came at the end of the book in "A Compendious Rhetoric and Rhetorical Index," which provided guidance for developing a thesis statement, using rhetorical methods to support the thesis, and paying attention to style. These guidelines were also linked to examples from the readings.

Through attention to selection and organization, Eastman and his colleagues created an anthology of excellent writing, one that was better than just a "cut-and-paste affair," that linked reading with writing, that prompted discussion of much more than "things in general"—a book that would last.

Much has changed in *The Norton Reader* since that first edition. New editors from different generations and schools—some with degrees in literature, others in creative writing or rhetoric and composition—have introduced new readings and pedagogical approaches. This anthology has changed with the times to include more diverse authors, topics, themes, and genres; to pay more attention to the writing process; and to focus on the ways new technologies shape reading and writing.

Diversity of Authors

Do you have a policy concerning selections by and about women in composition texts? Do you think you should?
—JOAN HARTMAN, from a letter to publishers

In the 1960s and early 1970s, calls for women's rights and civil rights were much in the news: Betty Friedan wrote *The Feminine Mystique*, published by Norton in 1963; Congress passed the Civil Rights Act in 1964 and the Voting Rights Act in 1965; the National Organization for

Women was founded in 1966. Protests, marches, civil disobedience. Laws were changing, making discrimination on the basis of race and gender illegal. But not everyone agreed on the best way to enact such changes—or that change was even necessary.

Just as social change does not happen overnight, neither do changes in textbooks. The second edition of *The Norton Reader* included a few more women (Jane Jacobs, Diana Trilling, Virginia Woolf) and one more African American (Martin Luther King Jr.) but most of the essays were still written by white men. Between the second and third editions, though, universities began to change. The first Black Studies program began at San Francisco State in 1968. CUNY instituted its open admissions policy in 1970, welcoming a wider and more diverse population. That same year, Women's Studies programs were established at San Diego State and SUNY–Buffalo. And change came as well to the third edition of the *Norton*, thanks in part to Joan Hartman, a professor of English at the College of Staten Island.

As a member of the MLA Commission on the Status of Women in the Profession, Hartman wrote to the major publishing houses, including Norton, asking about their policies concerning the inclusion of women in composition texts. Recognizing the need for more diversity in *The Norton Reader*, Art Eastman invited Hartman to nominate essays written by women. Her nominations helped increase the number of female authors to twenty-seven in the third edition, adding Joan Didion, Emma Goldman, Pauline Kael, Adrienne Rich, Simone Weil, and many others.

This third edition also welcomed a number of African American writers: Maya Angelou, Eldridge Cleaver, W. E. B. Du Bois, Ralph Ellison, George L. Jackson, Toni Morrison, Vertamae Smart-Grosvenor, and others. It's worth noting that these authors spoke to different audiences and took different positions. Angelou praised the sustaining power of "preachers, musicians and blues singers." Smart-Grosvenor critiqued those who would "rap for hours" about the feminine mystique and black power but didn't recognize the importance of food and cooking. Jackson, a member of the Black Panthers, concluded his "Letter from Soledad Prison" by proclaiming "Power to the People"—a letter that directly followed the "Letter from Birmingham Jail," in which Martin Luther King Jr. signed off with "Yours for the cause of Peace and Brotherhood."

Over time, attention to diversity has continued to evolve. In his preface to the sixth edition (1984), Eastman noted that women writers discuss "a far wider range of topics than matters exclusively female" and that writers from other countries "speak to issues far less national than broadly human," signaling a move beyond seeing writers as representatives of a particular gender, ethnicity, place, or kind of experience. This new perspective helped expand the range of voices, and by the seventh edition (1988), the book included forty-one essays by women as well as works by S. I. Hayakawa, N. Scott Momaday, Gloria Naylor, Ngũgĩ wa Thiong'o, Richard Rodriguez, and other African American, Native American, Asian American, and Chicano authors.

In addition to adding new writers and perspectives, the editors continually reconsidered readings already in the book. When Linda Peterson, who became an editor of *The Norton Reader* in the eighth edition, reviewed the seventh edition, she critiqued the bias of some chapters and selections, noting, for example, that the "Mind" chapter had only male authors. Come the eighth edition, that chapter was gone. And consider the uproar over Wayne Booth's essay "Is There Any Knowledge That a Man *Must* Have?" Booth first thought feminist critics were "over-reacting," but after thinking about it, he added the following in a footnote:

> Once I reread the essay carefully . . . I discovered, with some shock, that the women had a right to complain. Though I had been thinking of both men and women as I wrote, I had simply failed to consider how my language would strike female readers,

consciously or unconsciously, or how it might encourage males
to see themselves as the real center of all thought about education. My excuse now is only that I wrote before the feminist
critique of language had got well under way, and that I was an
author who badly needed that critique.[1]

By the ninth edition (1996), however, Booth's essay was no longer
included. Not all readers, though, agreed with the feminist critiques.
One professor, in a letter to Norton in the late 1980s, worried that
Norton would come under the "pernicious pressure of radical feminists." He complained, that he'd "seen their influence on textbooks
already," and believed it was "narrow, ideological, unscholarly and full
of special pleading," continuing, "I urge you, sir, to come against the
manipulative aggression of the feminists" (qtd. in Sabine 35). A decade
later, one teacher requested that Booth's essay be reinstated, arguing
that "its thesis becomes ever increasingly important to the products of
the computer generation for whom electronic gadgets are all" (personal
correspondence, files of Linda Peterson), demonstrating again the ways
concerns shift over time.

Questions of diversity were not limited to gender, race, and ethnicity.
The ninth edition featured several authors writing about living with disease or disability: Nancy Mairs on multiple sclerosis, Alice Walker on
blindness, Michael Lynch on AIDS, Maggie Helwig about eating disorders. These pieces were added just two years after the first Disability
Studies program was instituted at Syracuse University in 1994 and six
years after the Americans with Disabilities Act was passed in 1990.

---

1. In the materials that Linda Peterson gave me when I became general editor, I found
exchanges between Eastman, Booth, and the other editors on the controversy that led
to the footnote, including a letter sent to Norton that pointed to Booth's "macho style"
that said, "My God, imagine trying to teach a human being who doesn't have a penis;
what folly!" (qtd. in Sabine 61).

The editions published in the 1990s and early 2000s brought new emphasis on multiculturalism, at a time when more colleges were establishing offices of multicultural affairs. Writers such as Gloria Anzaldúa in "How to Tame a Wild Tongue," Maxine Hong Kingston in "Tongue-Tied," and Richard Rodriguez in "Aria" showed different perspectives on language and culture. These pieces, in the same chapter as John Tierney's "Playing the Dozens," Patricia Williams's "The Death of the Profane," and Gloria Naylor's "Mommy, What Does 'Nigger' Mean?" showed not only the importance of language and identity but also the challenges of communication. Many essays seemed simultaneously to value home cultures and to recognize that cultures and values change over time—changes that can be both painful and liberating, marked by both gains and losses.

As the twenty-first century has progressed, there seems to be a growing awareness of the realities of intersectionality—that gender, sexuality, class, culture, language, disability, and other aspects of identity interact. Although an author might emphasize only one of these aspects, the realities of individual lives are far more complicated. In the fourteenth edition (2016), readings such as Gwendolyn Ann Smith's "We're All Someone's Freak" and Jaswinder Bolina's "Writing Like a White Guy" reflect that complexity.

For each team of editors, the question of diversity and how it is represented in the book is significant. One of the advantages of a long volume designed to appeal to a range of interests is the space for inclusivity; still, space and resources are not limitless, and the editors have to decide what to include—and what to leave out. Each generation of editors, including the present one, has its own expertise, concerns, and blind spots. With each edition, we find room for change and improvement—and for bringing in new voices that challenge us to examine the past as well as to look forward, to see the world and its inhabitants anew.

Readings: Something Old, Something New

A vital culture is constantly in motion. The interests of readers
change with the times. Essays which stood at the forefront of
student concern only a few years ago, now seem dated, calling
for us to address new issues and to reinforce old ones, always
with one prime prerequisite—quality.

—ARTHUR EASTMAN, from his preface to the sixth edition

While certain topics and themes remain from edition to edition, the
essays that address them change over time. Compare, for example,
Allan Seager's "The Joys of Sport at Oxford," a 1962 narrative about one
student's experience rowing and swimming at a British university, to
David Halberstam's "Jordan's Moment," a journalistic profile of Michael
Jordan leading the Chicago Bulls to an NBA championship in 1998. Or
read Charles Lamb's "A Dissertation upon a Roast Pig," first published
in 1822, and get lost in his elevated language: "Pig—let me speak his
praise—is no less provocative of the appetite, than he is satisfactory to
the criticalness of the censorious palate." Then read Vertamae Smart-
Grosvenor's "The Kitchen Crisis," a 1970 manifesto against instant
food, urging readers, "PRO TECT YO KITCH'N." Something for every
taste, indeed.

Beyond taste, such differences illustrate, though, that the dic-
tion, focus, and conventions of writing—from paragraph length to
punctuation—sometimes evolve slowly, other times dramatically. And
writing, even on the same topics—sports or food—looks very different
depending on author, era, purpose, and genre.

Given that interests of readers do, indeed, change over time, roughly
a third of the essays are new in each edition. Some new selections are
chosen to introduce specific genres—Michael Lewis's sportswriting or
Alison Bechdel's graphic memoir, for example. Other selections may
be added to highlight particular topics or important perspectives on

historic events. In the latest edition, for example, we include President Barack Obama's eulogy for Reverend Clementa Pinckney. We also sometimes feature clusters of essays that reflect concerns of the times: animal rights, AIDS, 9/11, binge drinking, environmental issues, and so on.

Although much has changed over the past fifty years, it's important to acknowledge what has lasted: eight readings—yes, all by men, but also vastly different in purpose and genre—have appeared in every edition of *The Norton Reader*:

E. B. White's "Once More to the Lake"
James Baldwin's "Stranger in the Village"
Niccolò Machiavelli's "The Morals of the Prince"
Henry David Thoreau's "The Battle of the Ants"
Thomas Jefferson's "The Declaration of Independence"
Abraham Lincoln's "Second Inaugural Address"
Jonathan Swift's "A Modest Proposal"
Plato's "The Allegory of the Cave"

Why have these selections lasted? And why might they matter to students today? Even though White's reflection on returning to a camp in Maine was first published in 1941, and recalls his childhood memories from 1904, the themes of change and timelessness still resonate with readers today, and his sensory descriptions of the lake model a kind of writing students can learn from.

"Stranger in the Village" begins with a glimpse of life in a tiny, isolated Swiss village, a setting where Baldwin's presence as a black American makes him, at first, an unfamiliar outsider—not merely a stranger, but wholly alien. Using this unique circumstance as pretext, Baldwin shifts the focus and expands on the larger issue of black-white relations in America, reflecting on "the rage of the disesteemed." From our present-day vantage, we recognize his prescience in analyzing the enduring issues of race in America: domination, identity, and the difference between citizen and visitor. Baldwin's insights remain thought-provoking as racial injustices endure.

"The Declaration of Independence" is included not just for the quality of its writing but also because it still inspires students to reflect on the multiple ways one sentence has been interpreted, revised, and used in various contexts for different purposes for more than 200 years: "We hold these truths to be self-evident, that all men are created equal, that they are endowed by their Creator with certain unalienable Rights, that among these are Life, Liberty, and the pursuit of Happiness."

As for "The Morals of the Prince," Lincoln's "Second Inaugural Address," "The Battle of the Ants," "The Allegory of the Cave," and "A Modest Proposal," they all provide examples of different genres, as well as material that helps students interrogate current political positions and philosophical viewpoints. And in a time when satire as seen in the *Onion* and on the *Daily Show* shapes responses to current events, an understanding of satire and other methods of making arguments remains relevant.

Although only a small number of selections have been published in *every* edition, many other essays have been included in *almost* every edition. Selections by Zora Neale Hurston, Annie Dillard, Brent Staples, Joan Didion, Scott Russell Sanders, Martin Luther King Jr., George Orwell, and Langston Hughes are perennial favorites, assigned year after year. These essays encourage readers to reflect on their identities, to question their behaviors and allegiances, and to think about the basis for their beliefs—from parental values to religion, to race to the expectations of others. And new selections and authors—Eula Biss, Roxane Gay, Tim Kreider, and many others—help readers see those familiar favorites in a different context, perhaps prompting reflection on what has changed and what remains the same.

A Range of Nonfiction Genres

It is far easier to say what the essay is not than to say
what it is. . . .
—from "Notes on Reading and Writing,"
in the seventh edition

From "Journals" and "Letters" to "Op-eds" and "Cultural Analysis," *The Norton Reader* has always had sections on a number of prose forms. Over the years, various prose forms have come and gone: "Letters" and "Characters"[2] were removed from the third edition "for want of use," and "Op-eds" were introduced in the tenth edition. Initially, prose forms were treated as subsections of thematic chapters: "Parables," for example, began as a subset of the "Science" chapter, was later expanded to "Fables and Parables" and moved to the "Literature and the Arts" chapter—and then ceased to be its own section, though the chapter on "Philosophy and Religion" now includes a Zen parable and one from Jesus.

In recent editions, these prose forms have been presented in their own chapters, no longer subsets of thematic chapters. One reason for this shift is to emphasize the connections between specific themes and genres. In fact, the titles of some chapters have even been changed to emphasize genre—for example, the chapter once titled "People, Places" is now called "Profiles," a genre composition instructors often assign. Another example of a shift from theme to genre is the chapter "Cultural Analysis," once called "Signs of the Times." Embedded in this new title is a widely taught approach to both reading and writing: analysis.

---

2. As a prose form, "characters" were short profiles of certain types of people. In the first edition, these included, among others, a coward, a harlot, a flatterer—and, no joke, a fair and happy milkmaid.

Increased Attention to Writing

How a reader might link reading and writing has exercised my
imagination throughout my rereading of the *Norton*.
—LINDA PETERSON, from a review of the seventh edition

As a text for composition classes, *The Norton Reader* has always paid
attention to writing, but as composition pedagogies have developed,
the support for student writing provided in this book has increased.

The first six editions included a chapter originally called "A Compendious Rhetoric and Rhetorical Index" at the end of the book. Organized
in three parts—"Saying Something That Matters," "The Means of Saying It," "And the Style"—it included instructions on writing thesis-
driven essays, marshalling evidence, drawing conclusions, and paying
attention to style. Renamed "Notes on Composition" in the second edition, this chapter remained in the book for four more editions.

Some of the readings were followed by study questions—mainly reading comprehension, though other questions asked students to find evidence
to support or refute a thesis or to compare two selections. By the seventh
edition the study questions had a new dimension, inviting students to practice different kinds of writing and to engage with the readings by writing in
different ways. This edition also offered a new chapter on reading and writing that "explicitly yet informally [coached] young readers in analyzing the
processes of writing and reasoned response." This chapter, written by Robert Hosmer, took a decidedly different approach and tone from Eastman's.
Whereas Eastman emphasized "the hard labor of writing," saying, for
instance, that "no worthwhile thesis comes without work," Hosmer told
students not to "despair," acknowledging that all writers make mistakes
and encouraging them not to be "crippled by unrealistic expectations"—
either their own or their instructor's. This new chapter also focused on
writing as a process—one that involved invention, drafting, and revising—
an established concept in composition pedagogy at the time.

The seventh edition was reviewed by Linda Peterson, director of the Bass Writing Program at Yale and president of the Council of Writing Program Administrators. Critiquing "the failure to connect the kinds of essays contemporary writers produce with the kinds of essays students might try," Peterson argued that study questions should not only focus on an essay's subject but should also ask students to do the kind of writing and analyses that an essay models. This critique led to further changes in the writing prompts and helped make *The Norton Reader* a book that would inspire students not just to analyze essays they read but to practice the kinds of writing they were reading: personal essays, nature writing, op-eds, analyses, and many other genres.

The writing instruction has been expanded in subsequent editions, providing additional guidance on determining purpose and writing for a specific audience, on choosing a genre and deciding which rhetorical methods of development to use to support a claim, on acknowledging the words and ideas of others, and more—all things that address the WPA Outcomes and that help students "learn to analyze rhetorical situations, identify genre conventions, and understand how genres shape reading and writing."

Attention to How Technologies Shape Reading and Writing

> For some time now, students have been writing for peers
> outside of class and for larger communities as well. . . . creating
> discussion boards, blogs, wikis, websites, and other new genres.
> —from the introduction to the thirteenth edition

Technology has dramatically changed the ways we read, research, write, revise, and even think about composing. When the first edition of *The Norton Reader* was published in 1965, there was no internet, and there were no personal computers, smartphones, e-readers, or online courses. Whereas early editions asked students to focus on close reading of texts, later editions also ask for collaboration and research. And students are expected not only to research books and periodicals but also to conduct interviews and to consult and analyze databases, websites, films, podcasts, photographs, archives, and more.

Many teachers today are likely to assign multimodal reading and writing projects, ones that require an ability not only to analyze and write text but also to understand and include appropriate visuals or audio. For both reading and writing, students have access to more information and have more choices in terms of genre, format, design, and media than ever before. With so many genres available, which ones do we choose to write and for what purposes? How do we choose from such a range of sources—images, sounds, printed words—and use them effectively, persuasively, and responsibly?

Such questions have shaped writing instruction—and the selections and chapters included in *The Norton Reader*. The fourteenth edition includes a new chapter, "Media and Technology," opening with Nicholas Carr's provocative essay "Is Google Making Us Stupid?" The chapter includes a range of perspectives on the ways technology is affecting our lives, from Judith Newman's personal narrative about the relationship between her son and Siri to Tasneem Raja's argument that coding is the new literacy, one that should be taught more widely in schools.

Technology has shaped *The Norton Reader* in other ways as well. Consider the prevalence of images. The first edition had one essay that included a map, another with some tables, a third with a few drawings; the fourteenth edition includes a wide range of photographs, drawings, maps, graphs, and more. Sometimes an image supports or illustrates a point made in writing; other times it might challenge the reader's understanding of the text; still other times, it might evoke an emotion or other response independent of the written words. Selections such as Scott McCloud's from *Understanding Comics* and Alison Bechdel's from *Fun Home* depend as much on visual information as on written text.

Other selections include audio and video. For example, Annie Leonard's "The Story of Bottled Water," included in the fourteenth edition as an annotated script, also appears as an eight-minute film online. In its film format, it's part animation, part speech. But the text version includes yet another dimension: footnotes that reveal the extensive research involved in creating the film and its argument. We hope students will read the text and view the film.

A print anthology, of course, has its limits. It can't include audio files or active hyperlinks. The fourteenth edition, therefore, is available as an e-book. We also offer a companion website that allows teachers and students to search for and sort readings by theme, genre, keyword, medium, and date. Still, we believe there are advantages to sitting down with a print book—pleasure from reading without the distraction of ads, videos, animations, news tickers, links, or automatic alerts. And so we offer you both: a beautiful print anthology and the convenience of reading it on a digital device.

Then and Now

> Excellence would be their pillar of smoke by day,
> of fire by night.
> —ARTHUR EASTMAN, from his preface to the eighth edition

I conclude as I began, by quoting Art Eastman—here, with an allusion to a verse from Exodus. What was Eastman's intention? Was he being ironic, replacing "the LORD" with "excellence"? Or was he serious? To claim "excellence" without defining it, as none of the editors (including me) has been able to do, might be like trusting a cloud or spirit as guide. To shape and reshape a book over time requires faith in collaboration, a belief that excellence can be achieved when writers, editors, publishers, teachers, and students work together. And there's a kind of faith in hoping that this collaboration will continue—in whatever form it takes—for another fifty years or more.

Although much has changed in the decades since work on the first edition of *The Norton Reader* began, the current editors share the same commitment held by the original team: to work collaboratively to find and present excellent writing. This task, however, is not without its challenges. The cost of permissions, for example, rises with each new edition. Consider this: several readings in the fourteenth edition of *The Norton Reader* cost more to reprint individually than the entire budget for the 220 readings in the first edition. Dramatically increasing permissions fees (sometimes a fee will increase 100 percent from one edition to another) make it impractical—even impossible—to reprint certain essays.

Still, the process of choosing readings hasn't changed, except that the editors have moved from planning new editions at Art Eastman's kitchen table to sharing ideas in a conference room at Norton's New York office. And instead of sending materials by mail, we share files electronically using Dropbox. But wherever we are and no matter what mediums we use to communicate, we continue to work together, valuing the work of those who came before us, even as we try to offer something new.

A half-century ago, Arthur Eastman compared a good anthology to a banquet. He acknowledged in his preface to the first edition that some pieces may be "better than others" and that "undoubtedly some fall short of the highest mark," but he also affirmed what I believe to be true of every edition: that although times and tastes change, "*The Norton Reader* offers very little that is not very good." And much of it is positively delicious. Welcome to the table.

WORKS CITED

Kitzhaber, Albert R. *Themes, Theories, and Therapy: The Teaching of Writing in College.* New York: McGraw-Hill, 1963. Print.

Sabine, Gordon. *Memoir of a Book: The Norton Reader.* Ann Arbor: University of Michigan Library, 1993. Print.

Bell-Bottoms, English 101, and *The Norton Reader*

LIBBY FALK JONES

September 1968. My first day as a teacher: English 101, Composition, at the State University of New York at Stony Brook. My section, one of fifty-odd, met in the Light Engineering Building; Stony Brook was a science-emphasis institution, boasting multiple engineering buildings, but only one building to house all of the humanities. Still, the faculty had decided that all first-year students should "develop abilities in expository and argumentative writing . . . and gain practice in the logical and clear expression of ideas and the exposition of facts and opinion," as the English 101 catalogue description proclaimed. The task of developing and teaching composition fell naturally to those of us in English. As a second-year graduate student, I was raring to go.

I wore, I'm sure, my 1960s bell-bottom cords, an oxford cloth shirt, and boots; I carried a handful of white index cards with my first-day notes. Barely six years older than the students who turned to greet me as I came into the room, I held tight to my new authority; I would ask my students to address me as Mrs. Jones and I'd call them "Mr." and "Miss." My role, as I understood it, was to stimulate students' intellectual excitement about reading and writing—and to teach them the skills of analysis and expression. I was a woman with a mission, and in addition to my academic title and my index cards, I carried with me one other badge of authority, a kind of secret weapon: the first edition of *The Norton Reader*. Though I knew that this book would be valuable for my students, I didn't know then that I would cut my teeth on it as a writing teacher, that the *Norton* would help shape my teaching philosophies and practices.

English students and professors at the time bandied about theories of literature, not of composition. And though change was in the air (the next year, the department would offer a seminar in the theory and practice of teaching composition), in 1968, I was pretty much on my own. It was assumed then that learning to write meant reading models of good writing, learning to make arguments about readings, and supporting claims with textual references. Thomas Rogers, Director of Composition and my personal mentor, modeled the kind of classroom inquiry I aimed for. I'd studied eighteenth-century literature with Tom the previous year, and had observed his undergraduate literature class, so I was deeply familiar with his pedagogy. He posed open-ended questions about texts, urged respondents to support their points with references to specific passages, and never gave the class any "right" answers. I had seen how a group of students working together could challenge one another and tease out meaning even from difficult texts, yielding ample material to be pursued in individual expository and argumentative essays, the frequent "short papers" English 101 students were expected to write. How best to offer instructors and students the intellectual grist for such writing? A reader, of course.

A month before, I'd stood in the English Department's office, pondering the two readers from which teaching associates could choose. I hefted both volumes, scrutinized contents, and flipped pages. No contest: *The Norton Reader* was small but rich, compact enough to slide easily into a book bag, extensive enough at 1221 pages to include voices and ideas for a lifetime, not just a semester, of learning. Its pages were solid enough to receive (and preserve!) underlining and penciled marginal notes, but thin enough that it was only a little more than an inch thick and weighed less than two pounds. I was later to discover as well that the binding was solid. Nearly a half-century later, my copy shows only a little fraying on the front spine of the bright orange cloth cover.

I liked the *Norton's* organization—with pieces on subjects from education to ethics to history, civilization, science, and the arts—and the clusters of readings written in particular prose forms, among them journals, letters, and fables. I knew my writing students would bring diverse academic and personal interests, and I wanted to be sure that reading and writing assignments would invite everyone in. In choosing the *Norton*, I'd also been swayed by my colleagues' preferences. My best friend in graduate school, Barbara Leuthner, who already had a year of teaching under her belt, had told me she'd share some assignments. Indeed, she recently reminded me that at that time, everyone in Stony Brook's English Department—from teaching associates to full professors—taught composition, mostly using *The Norton Reader*. If Professors Alfred Kazin, Richard Levin, and Homer Goldberg liked the book, how could I go wrong? The department had even developed an informal instructor's manual through word-of-mouth recommendations about provocative readings and successful assignments.

I still recall some of my favorite assignments from the *Norton*. Asking my students to compare Jonathan Edwards's sermon, "Sinners in the Hands of an Angry God," with the priest's sermon from James Joyce's *A Portrait of the Artist as a Young Man* elicited insightful analyses of subject and style. Another comparison, of Margaret Culkin Banning's "Letter to Susan" with Lord Chesterfield's "Letter to His Son," asked students to analyze each writer's arguments, use of evidence, and tone—and I found that these letters to young people from different eras still spoke to my students' sensibilities. I lifted another assignment straight from my Boswell-Johnson course with Tom Rogers: to analyze Samuel Johnson's thesis and structure in his *Rambler* piece "On Self-Love and Indolence." That had been my graduate class's opening inquiry, one which rewarded careful reading of topic sentences as well as attention to sequences of reasoning and kinds of evidence. It was Barbara who directed me to essays in the *Norton* related to the 1964 murder of Kitty Genovese in

Queens: the *New York Times* story "37 Who Saw Murder Didn't Call the Police," Stanley Milgram and Paul Hollander's analysis of what would come to be called the "bystander complex," and Milgram's earlier study on behavioral obedience. These materials—timely and geographically relevant—led students to probing causal analyses. And finally, perhaps my all-time favorite writing assignment—breathtaking in its demand for both imagination and logic—was to apply the principles described by Thomas Henry Huxley in "The Method of Scientific Investigation" to James Thurber's fable "The Glass in the Field," arguing that the swallow was either foolish or wise.

The Norton Reader spurred my own intellectual development as well. I had entered graduate English studies with a B.A. in history and a background in journalism and technical writing; there was lots of literature I hadn't read. *The Norton Reader* introduced me to texts that would become formative, almost mythic, in my personal and scholarly growth. These included E. B. White's "Once More to the Lake," which still speaks to me now as movingly as it did almost five decades ago; Bruno Bettelheim's "A Victim," which introduced me to the concept of the self-fulfilling prophecy; and Jonathan Swift's brilliantly ironic argument, "A Modest Proposal." My years of teaching critical writing and thinking as well as my work with faculty across the curriculum have been helped immensely by William Perry's distinction between "bull" and "cow" ("Examsmanship and the Liberal Arts: A Study in Educational Epistemology"), precursor to his theories of cognitive stage development. I credit the *Norton* as well for deepening my understanding of some pieces I'd already come to love: Thurber's fables, especially "The Unicorn in the Garden," and the preface to Joseph Conrad's *The Nigger of the "Narcissis,"* a piece that Reynolds Price, my own first-year writing instructor at Duke University, had claimed was the most useful guide for fiction writers he'd ever encountered.

Its role in shaping readers and writers has propelled the *Norton* through fourteen editions to this milestone fiftieth anniversary. *The*

Little Norton Reader is a perfect way to celebrate. These fifty selections testify to the enduring life of the essay; to its marvelous range of subject, shape, tone, and style; to its ability to shout, whisper, illuminate, stir to action. Readers will each have their own favorites; writers may benefit especially by reading fruitful pairings or clusters. A. Bartlett Giamatti's "The Green Fields of the Mind" (1977), for example, plays productively off of White's "Once More to the Lake" (1941). Mark Twain's "Advice to Youth" (1882), William Zinsser's "College Pressures" (1979), and Lynda Barry's "The Sanctuary of School" (1992) will speak to students of all ages. By reading George Orwell's "Shooting an Elephant" (1936), Langston Hughes's "Salvation" (1940), and Judith Ortiz Cofer's "More Room" (1990), writers can explore the implications of personal choices within larger social contexts. Try coupling Virginia Woolf's reflection "The Death of the Moth" with Annie Dillard's argument on the importance of seeing ("Sight into Insight") or David Foster Wallace's lobster with Sandra Steingraber's tuna fish to explore rhetorical purposes and techniques; Chang-rae Lee's depiction of his mother with Scott Russell Sanders's portrait of his father; Gertrude Stein and Martin Luther King Jr. for stylistic virtuosity. Almost a century of commentary on race relations emerges through reading Zora Neale Hurston's "How It Feels to Be Colored Me" (1928) alongside Eula Biss's "Time and Distance Overcome" (2009), especially by bringing in the essays by James Baldwin, Martin Luther King Jr., Maya Angelou, Vertamae Smart-Grosvenor, Alice Walker, Brent Staples, and Henry Louis Gates Jr.

My advice to writers for engaging with *The Little Norton Reader*? As you read and reread this rich collection, keep your writer's notebook by your side, à la Joan Didion. You'll fill it with quotations, comments, memories, maybe even some postcards (Garrison Keillor) or blog posts (Dennis Baron)—and, in time, with essays of your own.

Berea, Kentucky

May 2015

Contents

"... if you want to really hurt me, talk badly about my language.
Ethnic identity is twin skin to linguistic identity—I am my language."

"I do not wish to compete for a trophy in suffering. I am only trying to
understand the corrosive mixture of helplessness, responsibility, and
shame that I learned to feel as the son of an alcoholic."

"Tolerating blind obedience in the name of patriotism or religion
ultimately takes our lives."

"Consider that it is now normal for North American women to have
eating disorders."

"We need to write, otherwise nobody will know who we are."

"Mamá could tell you the history of each room in her *casa*,
and thus the genealogy of the family along with it."

"I was with my teacher, and in a while I was going to sit at my desk,
with my crayons and pencils and books and classmates all around me,
and for the next six hours I was going to enjoy a thoroughly secure,
warm and stable world. It was a world I absolutely relied on."

"Ban the damn things. Ban them all. You want protection? Get a dog."

"I began scavenging by pulling pizzas out of the Dumpster behind a pizza delivery shop. In general, prepared food requires caution, but in this case I knew when the shop closed and went to the Dumpster as soon as the last of the help left."

"The kitchen was permanent, irredeemable, irresistible kink. Unassimilably African. No matter what you did, no matter how hard you tried, you couldn't de-kink a person's kitchen."

"[My mother] was the house accountant, the maid, the launderer, the disciplinarian, the driver, the secretary, and, of course, the cook. She was also my first basketball coach."

"EARLY GREEK WRITING RAN IN LINES ALTERNATING FROM LEFT TO RIGHT AND RIGHT TO LEFT THIS CONVENTION . . ."

"I read books late into the night, until I could barely keep my eyes open. I read books at recess, then during lunch, and in the few minutes left after I had finished my classroom assignments."

"Buzz Peterson . . . was watching Game Six with his wife, Jan, at their home, in Boone, North Carolina. In the final minute of the game, Jan turned to him and said, 'They're going to lose.' . . . 'Don't be too sure,' [he told her.] 'Michael's got one more good shot at it.'"

"Once you know what the story is and get it right—as right as you can, anyway—it belongs to anyone who wants to read it."

An Album of Writing by Students   465

"I swear that it's the butter that makes everything taste so good."

"Walking into M & M Pawnshop feels like walking into Home Depot, Toys "R" Us, Best Buy, Zales Jewelers, Sports Authority, and Petco all at once."

RALPH WALDO EMERSON

The Language of the Street

1840

RALPH WALDO EMERSON (1803–1882) wrote essays, poetry,
and lectures, collected in *Essays: First Series* (1841), *Nature:
Addresses and Lectures* (1849), and several other books.
Emerson is seen as the father of Transcendentalism, an
American philosophical and political movement that encouraged individualism over conformity, and the search for one's
"original relation to the universe." This selection is drawn
from Emerson's June 24, 1840, journal entry. In the full entry,
he also reflects on how other writers—Carlyle, Plutarch,
Montaigne, Milton, Goethe, and others—use language.

THE LANGUAGE OF THE STREET IS ALWAYS STRONG. WHAT can describe the folly and emptiness of scolding like the word *jawing*? I feel too the force of the double negative, though clean contrary to our grammar rules. And I confess to some pleasure from the stinging rhetoric of a rattling oath in the mouth of truckmen and teamsters. How laconic and brisk it is by the side of a page of the *North American Review*. Cut these words and they would bleed; they are vascular and alive; they walk and run. Moreover they who speak them have this elegancy, that they do not trip in their speech. It is a shower of bullets, whilst Cambridge men and Yale men correct themselves and begin again at every half sentence.

Thinking about the Text

1. What does Ralph Waldo Emerson mean by the "language of the street"? Who, according to Emerson, speaks this language? Who does not?

2. Emerson points to the communicative power of words and constructions that may not follow conventional rules of grammar or speech but are nonetheless effective. For example, he mentions "the force of the double negative." Are there any kinds of speech that do not follow conventional rules that you find especially powerful or effective? If so, what are they—and what makes them so compelling?

3. Listen carefully to a group of people speaking and jot down any words, phrases, and constructions they use that stand out to you. Then write a short essay in which you analyze how the language is used and why it's particularly effective (or not).

HENRY DAVID THOREAU

Observation

1854

HENRY DAVID THOREAU (1817–1862) composed essays and poems. Best known for *Walden; or, Life in the Woods* (1854), he also wrote *Resistance to Civil Government, or Civil Disobedience* (1849), *Walking* (1861), and many other books on nature, philosophy, and politics. Thoreau's writing has been included in every edition of *The Norton Reader*. This selection is from Thoreau's journal entry from May 6, 1854.

THERE IS NO SUCH THING AS PURE *OBJECTIVE* OBSERVATION. Your observation, to be interesting, *i.e.* to be significant, must be *subjective*. The sum of what the writer of whatever class has to report is simply some human experience, whether he be poet or philosopher or man of science. The man of most science is the man most alive, whose life is the greatest event. Senses that take cognizance of outward things merely are of no avail. It matters not where or how far you travel—the farther commonly the worse—but how much alive you are. If it is possible to conceive of an event outside to humanity, it is not of the slightest significance, though it were the explosion of a planet. Every important worker will report what life there is in him. It makes no odds into what seeming deserts the poet is born. Though all his neighbors pronounce it a Sahara it will be a paradise to him; for the desert which we see is the result of the barrenness of our experience. No mere willful activity whatever, whether in writing verses or collecting statistics, will produce true poetry or science. If you are really a sick man, it is indeed to be regretted, for you cannot accomplish so much as if you were well. All that a man has to say or do that can possibly concern mankind, is in some shape or other to tell the story of his love—to sing, and, if he is fortunate and keeps alive, he will be forever in love. This alone is to be alive to the extremities. It is a pity that this divine creature should ever suffer from cold feet; a still greater pity that the coldness so often reaches to his heart. I look over the report of the doings of a scientific association and am surprised that there is so little life to be reported; I am put off with a parcel of dry technical terms. Anything living is easily and naturally expressed in popular language. I cannot help suspecting that the life of these learned professors has been almost as inhuman and wooden as a rain-gauge or self-registering magnetic machine. They communicate no fact which rises to the temperature of bloodheat. It doesn't all amount to one rhyme.

Thinking about the Text

1. Throughout this selection, Henry David Thoreau repeats references to being "alive." What are the qualities of a person who, according to Thoreau, is alive?

2. Trace Thoreau's uses of contrast in this selection (subjective/objective
   observation, poetic/scientific language, sickness/wellness, etc.). What
   is his purpose in using these contrasts?

3. Thoreau writes that he is put off by "dry technical terms" and
   instead advocates "popular language." Do you agree that popular
   terms are preferable to technical ones? Should informal language be
   acceptable in academic discourse? Write an essay in which you argue
   for or against the use of informal language in academic discourse.

MARK TWAIN

Advice to Youth

1882

MARK TWAIN (1835–1910), the pen name of Samuel Clemens, wrote novels, short stories, and essays, which were often humorous and satirical. He is best known for his novels *The Adventures of Tom Sawyer* (1876) and *The Adventures of Huckleberry Finn* (1885). Selections by Twain have been included in every edition of *The Norton Reader*. Twain delivered "Advice to Youth" as a lecture in 1882, demonstrating humor throughout—especially when he instructed his audience: "Always obey your parents, when they are present."

BEING TOLD I WOULD BE EXPECTED TO TALK HERE, I inquired what sort of a talk I ought to make. They said it should be something suitable to youth—something didactic, instructive, or something in the nature of good advice. Very well. I have a few things in my mind which I have often longed to say for the instruction of the young; for it is in one's tender early years that such things will best take root and be most enduring and most valuable. First, then, I will say to you, my young friends—and I say it beseechingly, urgingly—

Always obey your parents, when they are present. This is the best policy in the long run, because if you don't they will make you. Most parents think they know better than you do, and you can generally make more by humoring that superstition than you can by acting on your own better judgment.

Be respectful to your superiors, if you have any, also to strangers, and sometimes to others. If a person offend you, and you are in doubt as to whether it was intentional or not, do not resort to extreme measures; simply watch your chance and hit him with a brick. That will be sufficient. If you shall find that he had not intended any offense, come out frankly and confess yourself in the wrong when you struck him; acknowledge it like a man and say you didn't mean to. Yes, always avoid violence; in this age of charity and kindliness, the time has gone by for such things. Leave dynamite to the low and unrefined.

Go to bed early, get up early—this is wise. Some authorities say get up with the sun; some others say get up with one thing, some with another. But a lark is really the best thing to get up with. It gives you a splendid reputation with everybody to know that you get up with the lark; and if you get the right kind of a lark, and work at him right, you can easily train him to get up at half past nine, every time—it is no trick at all.

Now as to the matter of lying. You want to be very careful about lying; otherwise you are nearly sure to get caught. Once caught, you can never again be, in the eyes of the good and the pure, what you were before. Many a young person has injured himself permanently through a single clumsy and illfinished lie, the result of carelessness born of incomplete training. Some authorities hold that the young ought not to lie at all. That, of course, is putting it rather stronger than necessary; still, while I cannot go quite so far as that, I do maintain, and I believe I am right, that the young ought to be temperate in the use of this great art until practice and experience shall give them that confidence, elegance, and precision which alone can make the accomplishment graceful and profitable. Patience, diligence, painstaking attention to detail—these are the requirements; these, in time, will make the student perfect; upon these, and upon these only, may he rely as the sure foundation for future eminence. Think what tedious years of study, thought, practice, experience, went to the equipment of that peerless old master who was able to impose upon the whole world the lofty and sounding maxim that "truth is mighty and will prevail"—the most majestic compound fracture of fact which any of woman born has yet achieved. For the history of our race, and each individual's experience, are sown thick with evidence that a truth is not hard to kill and that a lie told well is immortal. There is in Boston a monument of the man who discovered anaesthesia; many people are aware, in these latter days, that that man didn't discover it at all, but stole the discovery from another man. Is this truth mighty, and will it prevail? Ah no, my hearers, the monument is made of hardy material, but the lie it tells will outlast it a million years. An awkward, feeble, leaky lie is a thing which you ought to make it your unceasing study to avoid; such a lie as that has no more real permanence than an average truth. Why, you might as well tell the truth at once and be done with it. A feeble, stupid, preposterous lie will not live two years—except it be a slander upon somebody. It is indestructible, then, of course, but that is no merit of yours. A final word: begin your practice of this gracious and beautiful art early—begin now. If I had begun earlier, I could have learned how.

Never handle firearms carelessly. The sorrow and suffering that have been caused through the innocent but heedless handling of firearms by the young! Only four days ago, right in the next farmhouse to the one where I am spending the summer, a grandmother, old and gray and sweet, one of the loveliest spirits in the land, was sitting at her work, when her young grandson crept in and got down an old, battered, rusty gun which had not been touched for many years and was supposed not to be loaded, and pointed it at her, laughing and threatening to shoot. In her fright she ran screaming and pleading toward the door on the other side of the room; but as she passed him he placed the gun almost against her very breast and pulled the trigger! He had supposed it was not loaded. And he was right—it wasn't. So there wasn't any harm done. It is the only case of that kind I ever heard of. Therefore, just the same, don't you meddle with old unloaded firearms; they are the most deadly and unerring things that have ever been created by man. You don't have to take any pains at all with them; you don't have to have a rest, you don't have to have any sights on the gun, you don't have to take aim, even. No, you just pick out a relative and bang away, and you are sure to get him. A youth who can't hit a cathedral at thirty yards with a Gatling gun in three-quarters of an hour, can take up an old empty musket and bag his grandmother every time, at a hundred. Think what Waterloo would have been if one of the armies had been boys armed with old muskets supposed not to be loaded, and the other army had been composed of their female relations. The very thought of it makes one shudder.

There are many sorts of books; but good ones are the sort for the young to read. Remember that. They are a great, an inestimable, an unspeakable means of improvement. Therefore be careful in your selection, my young friends; be very careful; confine yourselves exclusively to Robertson's Sermons, Baxter's *Saint's Rest, The Innocents Abroad,* and works of that kind.

But I have said enough. I hope you will treasure up the instructions which I have given you, and make them a guide to your feet and a light to your understanding. Build your character thoughtfully and painstakingly upon these precepts, and by and by, when you have got it built, you will be surprised and gratified to see how nicely and sharply it resembles everybody else's.

Thinking about the Text

1. What kind of advice is Mark Twain actually giving? Is he being ironic? What does he want youth to do—or not do?

2. What kind of relationship between youth and authority figures does Twain portray? Cite passages from the text to support your answer. Do you think Twain sees himself as an authority figure in giving advice to youth? Point to passages in his text to support your answer.

3. Write your own "advice" speech. It can be serious or satirical—or a mix of the two. Make your audience clear in your title: for example, "Advice to the Elderly," "Advice to Teachers," "Advice to High School Seniors," and so on.

ZORA NEALE HURSTON

How It Feels to Be Colored Me

1928

ZORA NEALE HURSTON (1891–1960) wrote fiction, nonfiction, poetry, and plays. Though best known for her novel *Their Eyes Were Watching God* (1937), Hurston published widely in the other genres as well. "How It Feels to Be Colored Me" was first published in the *World Tomorrow* (1928), a magazine founded by the Fellowship of Reconciliation, a religious group devoted to nonviolence.

I AM COLORED BUT I OFFER NOTHING IN THE WAY OF extenuating circumstances except the fact that I am the only Negro in the United States whose grandfather on the mother's side was not an Indian chief.

I remember the very day that I became colored. Up to my thirteenth year I lived in the little Negro town of Eatonville, Florida. It is exclusively a colored town. The only white people I knew passed through the town going to or coming from Orlando. The native whites rode dusty horses, the Northern tourists chugged down the sandy village road in automobiles. The town knew the Southerners and never stopped cane chewing when they passed. But the Northerners were something else again. They were peered at cautiously from behind curtains by the timid. The more venturesome would come out on the porch to watch them go past and got just as much pleasure out of the tourists as the tourists got out of the village.

The front porch might seem a daring place for the rest of the town, but it was a gallery seat for me. My favorite place was atop the gate-post. Proscenium box for a born first-nighter. Not only did I enjoy the show, but I didn't mind the actors knowing that I liked it. I usually spoke to them in passing. I'd wave at them and when they returned my salute, I would say something like this: "Howdy-do-well-I-thank-you-where-you-goin'?" Usually automobile or the horse paused at this, and after a queer exchange of compliments, I would probably "go a piece of the way" with them, as we say in farthest Florida. If one of my family happened to come to the front in time to see me, of course negotiations would be rudely broken off. But even so, it is clear that I was the first "welcome-to-our-state" Floridian, and I hope the Miami Chamber of Commerce will please take notice.

During this period, white people differed from colored to me only in that they rode through town and never lived there. They liked to hear me "speak pieces" and sing and wanted to see me dance the parse-me-la, and gave me generously of their small silver for doing these things, which seemed strange to me for I wanted to do them so much that I needed bribing to stop. Only they didn't know it. The colored people gave no dimes. They deplored any joyful tendencies in me, but I was their Zora nevertheless. I belonged to them, to the nearby hotels, to the county—everybody's Zora.

But changes came in the family when I was thirteen, and I was sent to school in Jacksonville. I left Eatonville, the town of the oleanders, as Zora. When I disembarked from the river-boat at Jacksonville, she was no more. It seemed that I had suffered a sea change. I was not Zora of Orange County any more, I was now a little colored girl. I found it out in certain ways. In my heart as well as in the mirror, I became a fast brown—warranted not to rub nor run.

But I am not tragically colored. There is no great sorrow dammed up in my soul, nor lurking behind my eyes. I do not mind at all. I do not belong to the sobbing school of Negrohood who hold that nature somehow has given them a lowdown dirty deal and whose feelings are all hurt about it. Even in the helter-skelter skirmish that is my life, I have seen that the world is to the strong regardless of a little pigmentation more or less. No, I do not weep at the world—I am too busy sharpening my oyster knife.

Someone is always at my elbow reminding me that I am the granddaughter of slaves. It fails to register depression with me. Slavery is sixty years in the past. The operation was successful and the patient is doing well, thank you. The terrible struggle that made me an American out of a potential slave said "On the line!" The Reconstruction said "Get set!"; and the generation before said "Go!" I am off to a flying start and I must not halt in the stretch to look behind and weep. Slavery is the price I paid for civilization, and the choice was not with me. It is a bully adventure and worth all that I have paid through my ancestors for it. No one on earth ever had a greater chance for glory. The world to be won and nothing to be lost. It is thrilling to think—to know that for any act of mine, I shall get twice as much praise or twice as much blame. It is quite exciting to hold the center of the national stage, with the spectators not knowing whether to laugh or to weep.

The position of my white neighbor is much more difficult. No brown specter pulls up a chair beside me when I sit down to eat. No dark ghost thrusts its leg against mine in bed. The game of keeping what one has is never so exciting as the game of getting.

I do not always feel colored. Even now I often achieve the unconscious Zora of Eatonville before the Hegira. I feel most colored when I am thrown against a sharp white background.

For instance at Barnard. "Beside the waters of the Hudson" I feel my   10
race. Among the thousand white persons, I am a dark rock surged upon, and overswept, but through it all, I remain myself. When covered by the waters, I am; and the ebb but reveals me again.

Sometimes it is the other way around. A white person is set down in our midst, but the contrast is just as sharp for me. For instance, when I sit in the drafty basement that is The New World Cabaret with a white person, my color comes. We enter chatting about any little nothing that we have in common and are seated by the jazz waiters. In the abrupt way that jazz orchestras have, this one plunges into a number. It loses no time in circumlocutions, but gets right down to business. It constricts the thorax and splits the heart with its tempo and narcotic harmonies. This orchestra grows rambunctious, rears on its hind legs and attacks the tonal veil with primitive fury, rending it, clawing it until it breaks through to the jungle beyond. I follow those heathen—follow them exultingly. I dance wildly inside myself; I yell within, I whoop; I shake my assegai above my head, I hurl it true to the mark *yeeeeooww!* I am in the jungle and living in the jungle way. My face is painted red and yellow and my body is painted blue. My pulse is throbbing like a war drum. I want to slaughter something—give pain, give death to what, I do not know. But the piece ends. The men of the orchestra wipe their lips and rest their fingers. I creep back slowly to the veneer we call civilization with the last tone and find the white friend sitting motionless in his seat, smoking calmly.

"Good music they have here," he remarks, drumming the table with his fingertips.

Music. The great blobs of purple and red emotion have not touched him. He has only heard what I felt. He is far away and I see him but dimly across the ocean and the continent that have fallen between us. He is so pale with his whiteness then and I am *so* colored.

At certain times I have no race, I am *me*. When I set my hat at a certain angle and saunter down Seventh Avenue, Harlem City, feeling as snooty as the lions in front of the Forty-Second Street Library, for instance. So far as my feelings are concerned, Peggy Hopkins Joyce on the Boule Mich with her gorgeous raiment, stately carriage, knees knocking together in a most aristocratic manner, has nothing on me. The cosmic Zora emerges. I belong to no race nor time. I am the eternal feminine with its string of beads.

I have no separate feeling about being an American citizen and colored. I am merely a fragment of the Great Soul that surges within the boundaries. My country, right or wrong.

Sometimes, I feel discriminated against, but it does not make me angry. It merely astonishes me. How *can* any deny themselves the pleasure of my company? It's beyond me.

But in the main, I feel like a brown bag of miscellany propped against a wall. Against a wall in company with other bags, white, red and yellow. Pour out the contents, and there is discovered a jumble of small things priceless and worthless. A first-water diamond, an empty spool, bits of broken glass, lengths of string, a key to a door long since crumbled away, a rusty knife-blade, old shoes saved for a road that never was and never will be, a nail bent under the weight of things too heavy for any nail, a dried flower or two still a little fragrant. In your hand is the brown bag. On the ground before you is the jumble it held—so much like the jumble in the bags, could they be emptied, that all might be dumped in a single heap and the bags refilled without altering the content of any greatly. A bit of colored glass more or less would not matter. Perhaps that is how the Great Stuffer of Bags filled them in the first place—who knows?

Thinking about the Text

1. Zora Neale Hurston describes seeing herself differently depending upon the context. What factors shape how she sees herself?

2. Hurston often uses metaphors and similes to describe her feelings. For example, in paragraph 10 she writes, "I am a dark rock surged upon"; in paragraph 17, she explains, "I feel like a brown bag of miscellany." Choose a metaphor or simile that seems significant and explain why it is important to the essay and how it expresses the way Hurston sees herself and, perhaps, others.

3. Write an essay in which you reflect on how it feels to be you. Like Hurston does, use metaphors and similes to show some aspect of your identity.

GERTRUDE STEIN

Poetry and Grammar

1935

GERTRUDE STEIN (1874–1946) wrote plays, novels, poetry, and nonfiction on subjects ranging from art to relationships. A resident of France for most of her adult life, she was a patron of several artists, including Pablo Picasso and Henri Matisse. She is best known for *The Autobiography of Alice B. Toklas* (1933), an experimental memoir in which Stein takes on the voice of her partner to tell a first-person narrative and makes references to herself in the third person. "Poetry and Grammar" is drawn from Stein's essay by the same title, which was published in *Lectures in America* (1935), a collection of the major lectures she delivered.

WORDS HAVE TO DO EVERYTHING IN POETRY AND prose and some writers write more in articles and prepositions and some say you should write in nouns, and of course one has to think of everything.

A noun is a name of anything, why after a thing is named write about it. A name is adequate or it is not. If it is adequate then why go on calling it, if it is not then calling it by its name does no good.

People if you like to believe it can be made by their names. Call anybody Paul and they get to be a Paul call anybody Alice and they get to be an Alice perhaps yes perhaps no, there is something in that, but generally speaking, things once they are named the name does not go on doing anything to them and so why write in nouns. Nouns are the name of anything and just naming names is alright when you want to call a roll but is it any good for anything else. To be sure in many places in Europe as in America they do like to call rolls.

As I say a noun is a name of a thing and therefore slowly if you feel what is inside that thing you do not call it by the name by which it is known. Everybody knows that by the way they do when they are in love and a writer should always have that intensity of emotion about whatever is the object about which he writes. And therefore and I say it again more and more one does not use nouns.

Now what other things are there beside nouns, there are a lot of other things beside nouns.

When you are at school and learn grammar grammar is very exciting. I really do not know that anything has ever been more exciting than diagraming sentences. I suppose other things may be more exciting to others when they are at school but to me undoubtedly when I was at school the really completely exciting thing was diagraming sentences and that has been to me ever since the one thing that has been completely exciting and completely completing. I like the feeling the everlasting feeling of sentences as they diagram themselves.

In that way one is completely possessing something and incidentally one's self. Now in that diagraming of the sentences of course there are articles and prepositions and as I say there are nouns but nouns as I say even by definition are completely not interesting, the same thing is true of adjectives. Adjectives are not really and truly interesting. In a way anybody can know always has known that, because after all adjectives effect nouns and as nouns are not really interesting the thing that effects a not too interesting thing is of necessity not interesting. In a way as I say anybody knows that because of course the first thing that anybody takes out of anybody's writing are the adjectives. You see of yourself how true it is that which I have just said.

Beside the nouns and the adjectives there are verbs and adverbs. Verbs and adverbs are more interesting. In the first place they have one very nice quality and that is that they can be so mistaken. It is wonderful the number of mistakes a verb can make and that is equally true of its adverb. Nouns and adjectives never can make mistakes can never be mistaken but verbs can be so endlessly, both as to what they do and how they agree or disagree with whatever they do. The same is true of adverbs.

In that way any one can see that verbs and adverbs are more interesting than nouns and adjectives.

Beside being able to be mistaken and to make mistakes verbs can change to look like themselves or to look like something else, they are, so to speak on the move and adverbs move with them and each of them find themselves not at all annoying but very often very much mistaken. That is the reason any one can like what verbs can do. Then comes the thing that can of all things be most mistaken and they are prepositions. Prepositions can live one long life being really being nothing but absolutely nothing but mistaken and that makes them irritating if you feel that way about mistakes but certainly something that you can be continuously using and everlastingly enjoying. I like prepositions the best of all, and pretty soon we will go more completely into that.

Then there are articles. Articles are interesting just as nouns and adjectives are not. And why are they interesting just as nouns and adjectives are not. They are interesting because they do what a noun might

10

do if a noun was not so unfortunately so completely unfortunately the name of something. Articles please, a and an and the please as the name that follows cannot please. They the names that is the nouns cannot please, because after all you know well after all that is what Shakespeare meant when he talked about a rose by any other name.

I hope now no one can have any illusion about a noun or about the adjective that goes with the noun.

But an article an article remains as a delicate and a varied something and any one who wants to write with articles and knows how to use them will always have the pleasure that using something that is varied and alive can give. That is what articles are.

Beside that there are conjunctions, and a conjunction is not varied but it has a force that need not make any one feel that they are dull. Conjunctions have made themselves live by their work. They work and as they work they live and even when they do not work and in these days they do not always live by work still nevertheless they do live.

So you see why I like to write with prepositions and conjunctions and articles and verbs and adverbs but not with nouns and adjectives. If you read my writing you will you do see what I mean.   15

Of course then there are pronouns. Pronouns are not as bad as nouns because in the first place practically they cannot have adjectives go with them. That already makes them better than nouns.

Then beside not being able to have adjectives go with them, they of course are not really the name of anything. They represent some one but they are not its or his name. In not being his or its or her name they already have a greater possibility of being something than if they were as a noun is the name of anything. Now actual given names of people are more lively than nouns which are the name of anything and I suppose that this is because after all the name is only given to that person when they are born, there is at least the element of choice even the element of change and anybody can be pretty well able to do what they like, they may be born Walter and become Hub, in such a way they are not like a noun. A noun has been the name of something for such a very long time.

That is the reason that slang exists it is to change the nouns which have been names for so long. I say again. Verbs and adverbs and articles and conjunctions and prepositions are lively because they all do something and as long as anything does something it keeps alive.

Thinking about the Text

1. Gertrude Stein discusses various parts of speech, explaining which she finds most interesting. Which parts of speech does she favor? Why?

2. Stein's punctuation and sentence structure are not always conventional. For example, she often asks questions without including question marks, and she uses repetition in surprising ways. In paragraph 6, for instance, she describes diagramming sentences as "completely exciting and completely completing." Identify three sentences that are unusual in some way. What makes them unusual? How did these sentences affect the way you read and understood Stein's argument?

3. Choose one paragraph from Stein's essay and rewrite it using more conventional grammar, punctuation, and syntax. In what ways is your paragraph more effective? In what ways is Stein's more effective?

GEORGE ORWELL

Shooting an Elephant

1936

GEORGE ORWELL (1903–1950) wrote novels, essays, poetry, and criticism. He is known primarily for his fiction, especially *Animal Farm* (1945) and *Nineteen Eighty-Four* (1949), and his essays. "Shooting an Elephant" was first published in 1936 in the literary journal *New Writing* and later in Orwell's collection *Shooting an Elephant and Other Essays* (1950). Although Orwell's work has appeared in every edition of *The Norton Reader*, "Shooting an Elephant" did not appear until the fourth edition, when it was included in the chapter "On Politics and Government." Since then the essay has remained in all subsequent editions.

I N MOULMEIN, IN LOWER BURMA, I WAS HATED BY LARGE numbers of people—the only time in my life that I have been important enough for this to happen to me. I was sub-divisional police officer of the town, and in an aimless, petty kind of way anti-European feeling was very bitter. No one had the guts to raise a riot, but if a European woman went through the bazaars alone somebody would probably spit betel juice over her dress. As a police officer I was an obvious target and was baited whenever it seemed safe to do so. When a nimble Burman tripped me up on the football field and the referee (another Burman) looked the other way, the crowd yelled with hideous laughter. This happened more than once. In the end the sneering yellow faces of young men that met me everywhere, the insults hooted after me when I was at a safe distance, got badly on my nerves. The young Buddhist priests were the worst of all. There were several thousands of them in the town and none of them seemed to have anything to do except stand on street corners and jeer at Europeans.

All this was perplexing and upsetting. For at that time I had already made up my mind that imperialism was an evil thing and the sooner I chucked up my job and got out of it the better. Theoretically—and secretly, of course—I was all for the Burmese and all against their oppressors, the British. As for the job I was doing, I hated it more bitterly than I can perhaps make clear. In a job like that you see the dirty work of Empire at close quarters. The wretched prisoners huddling in the stinking cages of the lock-ups, the grey, cowed faces of the long-term convicts, the scarred buttocks of the men who had been flogged with bamboos—all these oppressed me with an intolerable sense of guilt. But I could get nothing into perspective. I was young and ill-educated and I had had to think out my problems in the utter silence that is imposed on every Englishman in the East. I did not even know that the British Empire is dying, still less did I know that it is a great deal better than the younger empires that are going to supplant it. All I knew was that I was stuck between my hatred of the empire I served and my rage against the evil-spirited little beasts who tried to make my job impossible. With one part of my mind I thought of the British Raj as an unbreakable tyranny, as something clamped down, in *saecula saeculorum,* upon the will of prostrate peoples; with another part I thought that the greatest joy in the world would be to drive a bayonet into a Buddhist priest's guts. Feelings like these are the normal by-products of imperialism; ask any Anglo-Indian official, if you can catch him off duty.

One day something happened which in a roundabout way was enlightening. It was a tiny incident in itself, but it gave me a better glimpse than I had had before of the real nature of imperialism—the real motives for which despotic governments act. Early one morning the sub-inspector at a police station the other end of the town rang me up on the 'phone and said that an elephant was ravaging the bazaar. Would I please come and do something about it? I did not know what I could do, but I wanted to see what was happening and I got on to a pony and started out. I took my rifle, an old .44 Winchester and much too small to kill an elephant, but I thought the noise might be useful *in terrorem.* Various Burmans stopped me on the way and told me about the elephant's doings. It was not, of course, a wild elephant, but a tame one which had gone "must." It had been chained up, as tame elephants always are when their attack of "must" is due, but on the previous night it had broken its chain and escaped. Its mahout, the only person who could manage it when it was in that state, had set out in pursuit, but had taken the wrong direction and was now twelve hours' journey away, and in the morning the elephant had suddenly reappeared in the town. The Burmese population had no weapons and were quite helpless against it. It had already destroyed somebody's bamboo hut, killed a cow and raided some fruit-stalls and devoured the stock; also it had met the municipal rubbish van and, when the driver jumped out and took to his heels, had turned the van over and inflicted violences upon it.

The Burmese sub-inspector and some Indian constables were waiting for me in the quarter where the elephant had been seen. It was a very poor quarter, a labyrinth of squalid bamboo huts, thatched with palm-leaf, winding all over a steep hillside. I remember that it was a cloudy, stuffy morning at the beginning of the rains. We began questioning the people as to where the elephant had gone and, as usual, failed to get any definite information. That is invariably the case in the East; a story always sounds clear enough at a distance, but the nearer you get to the scene of events the vaguer it becomes. Some of the people said that the elephant had gone in one direction, some said that he had gone in another, some professed not even to have heard of any elephant. I had almost made up my mind that the whole story was a pack of lies, when we heard yells a little distance away. There was a loud, scandalized cry of "Go away, child! Go away this instant!" and an old woman with a switch in her hand came round the corner of a hut, violently shooing away a crowd of naked children. Some more women followed, clicking their tongues and exclaiming; evidently there was something that the children ought not to have seen. I rounded the hut and saw a man's dead body sprawling in the mud. He was an Indian, a black Dravidian coolie, almost naked, and he could not have been dead many minutes. The people said that the elephant had come suddenly upon him round the corner of the hut, caught him with its trunk, put its foot on his back and ground him into the earth. This was the rainy season and the ground was soft, and his face had scored a trench a foot deep and a couple of yards long. He was lying on his belly with arms crucified and head sharply twisted to one side. His face was coated with mud, the eyes wide open, the teeth bared and grinning with an expression of unendurable agony. (Never tell me, by the way, that the dead look peaceful. Most of the corpses I have seen looked devilish.) The friction of the great beast's foot had stripped the skin from his back as neatly as one skins a rabbit. As soon as I saw the dead man I sent an orderly to a friend's house nearby to borrow an elephant rifle. I had already sent back the pony, not wanting it to go mad with fright and throw me if it smelt the elephant.

The orderly came back in a few minutes with a rifle and five cartridges, and meanwhile some Burmans had arrived and told us that the elephant was in the paddy fields below, only a few hundred yards away.

As I started forward practically the whole population of the quarter flocked out of the houses and followed me. They had seen the rifle and were all shouting excitedly that I was going to shoot the elephant. They had not shown much interest in the elephant when he was merely ravaging their homes, but it was different now that he was going to be shot. It was a bit of fun to them, as it would be to an English crowd; besides they wanted the meat. It made me vaguely uneasy. I had no intention of shooting the elephant—I had merely sent for the rifle to defend myself if necessary—and it is always unnerving to have a crowd following you. I marched down the hill, looking and feeling a fool, with the rifle over my shoulder and an ever-growing army of people jostling at my heels. At the bottom, when you got away from the huts, there was a metalled road and beyond that a miry waste of paddy fields a thousand yards across, not yet ploughed but soggy from the first rains and dotted with coarse grass. The elephant was standing eight yards from the road, his left side towards us. He took not the slightest notice of the crowd's approach. He was tearing up bunches of grass, beating them against his knees to clean them and stuffing them into his mouth.

I had halted on the road. As soon as I saw the elephant I knew with perfect certainty that I ought not to shoot him. It is a serious matter to shoot a working elephant—it is comparable to destroying a huge and costly piece of machinery—and obviously one ought not to do it if it can possibly be avoided. And at that distance, peacefully eating, the elephant looked no more dangerous than a cow. I thought then and I think now that his attack of "must" was already passing off; in which case he would merely wander harmlessly about until the mahout came back and caught him. Moreover, I did not in the least want to shoot him. I decided that I would watch him for a little while to make sure that he did not turn savage again, and then go home.

But at that moment I glanced round at the crowd that had followed me. It was an immense crowd, two thousand at the least and growing every minute. It blocked the road for a long distance on either side. I looked at the sea of yellow faces above the garish clothes—faces all happy and excited over this bit of fun, all certain that the elephant was going to be shot. They were watching me as they would watch a conjurer about to perform a trick. They did not like me, but with the magical rifle in my hands I was momentarily worth watching. And suddenly I realized that I should have to shoot the elephant after all. The people expected it of me and I had got to do it; I could feel their two thousand wills pressing me forward, irresistibly. And it was at this moment, as I stood there with the rifle in my hands, that I first grasped the hollowness, the futility of the white man's dominion in the East. Here was I, the white man with his gun, standing in front of the unarmed native crowd—seemingly the leading actor of the piece; but in reality I was only an absurd puppet pushed to and fro by the will of those yellow faces behind. I perceived in this moment that when the white man turns tyrant it is his own freedom that he destroys. He becomes a sort of hollow, posing dummy, the conventionalized figure of a sahib. For it is the condition of his rule that he shall spend his life in trying to impress the "natives," and so in every crisis he has got to do what the "natives" expect of him. He wears a mask, and his face grows to fit it. I had got to shoot the elephant. I had committed myself to doing it when I sent for the rifle. A sahib has got to act like a sahib; he has got to appear resolute, to know his own mind and do definite things. To come all that way, rifle in hand, with two thousand people marching at my heels, and then to trail feebly away, having done nothing—no, that was impossible. The crowd would laugh at me. And my whole life, every white man's life in the East, was one long struggle not to be laughed at.

But I did not want to shoot the elephant. I watched him beating his bunch of grass against his knees, with that preoccupied grandmotherly air that elephants have. It seemed to me that it would be murder to shoot him. At that age I was not squeamish about killing animals, but I had never shot an elephant and never wanted to. (Somehow it always seems worse to kill a *large* animal.) Besides, there was the beast's owner to be considered. Alive, the elephant was worth at least a hundred pounds; dead, he would only be worth the value of his tusks, five pounds, possibly. But I had got to act quickly. I turned to some experienced-looking Burmans who had been there when we arrived, and asked them how the elephant had been behaving. They all said the same thing: he took no notice of you if you left him alone, but he might charge if you went too close to him.

It was perfectly clear to me what I ought to do. I ought to walk up to within, say, twenty-five yards of the elephant and test his behavior. If he charged, I could shoot; if he took no notice of me, it would be safe to leave him until the mahout came back. But also I knew that I was going to do no such thing. I was a poor shot with a rifle and the ground was soft mud into which one would sink at every step. If the elephant charged and I missed him, I should have about as much chance as a toad under a steam-roller. But even then I was not thinking particularly of my own skin, only of the watchful yellow faces behind. For at that moment, with the crowd watching me, I was not afraid in the ordinary sense, as I would have been if I had been alone. A white man mustn't be frightened in front of "natives"; and so, in general, he isn't frightened. The sole thought in my mind was that if anything went wrong those two thousand Burmans would see me pursued, caught, trampled on and reduced to a grinning corpse like that Indian up the hill. And if that happened it was quite probable that some of them would laugh. That would never do. There was only one alternative. I shoved the cartridges into the magazine and lay down on the road to get a better aim.

The crowd grew very still, and a deep, low, happy sigh, as of people 10 who see the theatre curtain go up at last, breathed from innumerable throats. They were going to have their bit of fun after all. The rifle was a beautiful German thing with cross-hair sights. I did not then know that in shooting an elephant one would shoot to cut an imaginary bar running from ear-hole to ear-hole. I ought, therefore, as the elephant was sideways on, to have aimed straight at his ear-hole; actually I aimed several inches in front of this, thinking the brain would be further forward.

When I pulled the trigger I did not hear the bang or feel the kick—one never does when a shot goes home—but I heard the devilish roar of glee that went up from the crowd. In that instant, in too short a time, one would have thought, even for the bullet to get there, a mysterious, terrible change had come over the elephant. He neither stirred nor fell, but every line of his body had altered. He looked suddenly stricken, shrunken, immensely old, as though the frightful impact of the bullet had paralysed him without knocking him down. At last, after what seemed a long time—it might have been five seconds, I dare say—he sagged flabbily to his knees. His mouth slobbered. An enormous senility seemed to have settled upon him. One could have imagined him thousands of years old. I fired again into the same spot. At the second shot he did not collapse but climbed with desperate slowness to his feet and stood weakly upright, with legs sagging and head drooping. I fired a third time. That was the shot that did for him. You could see the agony of it jolt his whole body and knock the last remnant of strength from his legs. But in falling he seemed for a moment to rise, for as his hind legs collapsed beneath him he seemed to tower upward like a huge rock toppling, his trunk reaching skywards like a tree. He trumpeted, for the first and only time. And then down he came, his belly towards me, with a crash that seemed to shake the ground even where I lay.

I got up. The Burmans were already racing past me across the mud. It was obvious that the elephant would never rise again, but he was not dead. He was breathing very rhythmically with long rattling gasps, his great mound of a side painfully rising and falling. His mouth was wide open—I could see far down into caverns of pale pink throat. I waited a long time for him to die, but his breathing did not weaken. Finally I fired my two remaining shots into the spot where I thought his heart must be. The thick blood welled out of him like red velvet, but still he did not die. His body did not even jerk when the shots hit him, the tortured breathing continued without a pause. He was dying, very slowly and in great agony, but in some world remote from me where not even a bullet could damage him further. I felt that I had got to put an end to that dreadful noise. It seemed dreadful to see the great beast lying there, powerless to move and yet powerless to die, and not even to be able to finish him. I sent back for my small rifle and poured shot after shot into his heart and down his throat. They seemed to make no impression. The tortured gasps continued as steadily as the ticking of a clock.

In the end I could not stand it any longer and went away. I heard later that it took him half an hour to die. Burmans were bringing dahs and baskets even before I left, and I was told they had stripped his body almost to the bones by the afternoon.

Afterwards, of course, there were endless discussions about the shooting of the elephant. The owner was furious, but he was only an Indian and could do nothing. Besides, legally I had done the right thing, for a mad elephant has to be killed, like a mad dog, if its owner fails to control it. Among the Europeans opinion was divided. The older men said I was right, the younger men said it was a damn shame to shoot an elephant for killing a coolie, because an elephant was worth more than any damn Coringhee coolie. And afterwards I was very glad that the coolie had been killed; it put me legally in the right and it gave me a sufficient pretext for shooting the elephant. I often wondered whether any of the others grasped that I had done it solely to avoid looking a fool.

Thinking about the Text

1. What is George Orwell's main point or argument in this essay? Support your answer with evidence from the text.

2. Orwell writes that he did not want to shoot the elephant (paragraph 8). Why did he not want to shoot it? What reasons does he provide for shooting it? Does he regret his action? How can you tell? Support your answer with evidence from the text.

3. Orwell's essay shows the complexity of human motivations and feelings, how the choices we make are affected by forces as various as peer pressure, politics, ethics, and economics. Write an essay about a difficult decision you have had to make. Explain the situation and reflect on the factors that led to the decision you made and action you took.

LANGSTON HUGHES

Salvation

1940

LANGSTON HUGHES (1902–1967) wrote poetry, novels, plays, and nonfiction. Known primarily for his books of poetry— *The Weary Blues* (1926), *A New Song* (1938), *Montage of a Dream Deferred* (1951), and others—Hughes also wrote the autobiographies *The Big Sea* (1940) and *I Wonder as I Wander* (1956). "Salvation," which explores the intersection between religion and identity, is drawn from *The Big Sea*.

I WAS SAVED FROM SIN WHEN I WAS GOING ON THIRTEEN. BUT not really saved. It happened like this. There was a big revival at my Auntie Reed's church. Every night for weeks there had been much preaching, singing, praying, and shouting, and some very hardened sinners had been brought to Christ, and the membership of the church had grown by leaps and bounds. Then just before the revival ended, they held a special meeting for children, "to bring the young lambs to the fold." My aunt spoke of it for days ahead. That night I was escorted to the front row and placed on the mourners' bench with all the other young sinners, who had not yet been brought to Jesus.

My aunt told me that when you were saved you saw a light, and something happened to you inside! And Jesus came into your life! And God was with you from then on! She said you could see and hear and feel Jesus in your soul. I believed her. I had heard a great many old people say the same thing and it seemed to me they ought to know. So I sat there calmly in the hot, crowded church, waiting for Jesus to come to me.

The preacher preached a wonderful rhythmical sermon, all moans and shouts and lonely cries and dire pictures of hell, and then he sang a song about the ninety and nine safe in the fold, but one little lamb was left out in the cold. Then he said: "Won't you come? Won't you come to Jesus? Young lambs, won't you come?" And he held out his arms to all us young sinners there on the mourners' bench. And the little girls cried. And some of them jumped up and went to Jesus right away. But most of us just sat there.

A great many old people came and knelt around us and prayed, old women with jet-black faces and braided hair, old men with work-gnarled hands. And the church sang a song about the lower lights are burning, some poor sinners to be saved. And the whole building rocked with prayer and song.

Still I kept waiting to *see* Jesus.

Finally all the young people had gone to the altar and were saved, but one boy and me. He was a rounder's son named Westley. Westley and I were surrounded by sisters and deacons praying. It was very hot in the church, and getting late now. Finally Westley said to me in a whisper: "God damn! I'm tired o' sitting here. Let's get up and be saved." So he got up and was saved.

Then I was left all alone on the mourners' bench. My aunt came and knelt at my knees and cried, while prayers and songs swirled all around me in the little church. The whole congregation prayed for me alone, in a mighty wail of moans and voices. And I kept waiting serenely for Jesus, waiting, waiting—but he didn't come. I wanted to see him, but nothing happened to me. Nothing! I wanted something to happen to me, but nothing happened.

I heard the songs and the minister saying: "Why don't you come? My dear child, why don't you come to Jesus? Jesus is waiting for you. He wants you. Why don't you come? Sister Reed, what is this child's name?"

"Langston," my aunt sobbed.

"Langston, why don't you come? Why don't you come and be saved?   10
Oh, Lamb of God! Why don't you come?"

Now it was really getting late. I began to be ashamed of myself, holding everything up so long. I began to wonder what God thought about Westley, who certainly hadn't seen Jesus either, but who was now sitting proudly on the platform, swinging his knickerbockered legs and grinning down at me, surrounded by deacons and old women on their knees praying. God had not struck Westley dead for taking his name in vain or for lying in the temple. So I decided that maybe to save further trouble, I'd better lie, too, and say that Jesus had come, and get up and be saved.

So I got up.

Suddenly the whole room broke into a sea of shouting, as they saw me rise. Waves of rejoicing swept the place. Women leaped in the air. My aunt threw her arms around me. The minister took me by the hand and led me to the platform.

When things quieted down, in a hushed silence, punctuated by a few ecstatic "Amens," all the new young lambs were blessed in the name of God. Then joyous singing filled the room.

That night, for the last time in my life but one—for I was a big boy   15
twelve years old—I cried. I cried, in bed alone, and couldn't stop. I buried my head under the quilts, but my aunt heard me. She woke up and told my uncle I was crying because the Holy Ghost had come into my life, and because I had seen Jesus. But I was really crying because I couldn't bear to tell her that I had lied, that I had deceived everybody in the church, and I hadn't seen Jesus, and that now I didn't believe there was a Jesus any more, since he didn't come to help me.

Thinking about the Text

1. Langston Hughes contrasts his childhood perspective with the perspectives of older members of his church. What are some of the differences between Hughes as a child and the adults he characterizes?

2. Note the sensory details Hughes uses in this narrative—the sounds and sights he recalls. How do the actions of others affect the choice he made at the revival meeting?

3. Write about a significant event from your childhood. Use both reflection and sensory details to help reveal the significance of that event.

E. B. WHITE

Once More to the Lake

1941

E. B. WHITE (1899–1985) wrote essays as a staff member of the *New Yorker* and wrote a regular column for *Harper's Magazine*; he also wrote novels for children, including *Stuart Little* (1945), *Charlotte's Web* (1952), and *The Trumpet of the Swan* (1970). His essays have been collected in *One Man's Meat* (1942) and *Essays of E. B. White* (1977). "Once More to the Lake," which originally appeared in *Harper's Magazine* in 1941, is one of the few essays included in every edition of *The Norton Reader*.

ONE SUMMER, ALONG ABOUT 1904, MY FATHER RENTED A camp on a lake in Maine and took us all there for the month of August. We all got ringworm from some kittens and had to rub Pond's Extract on our arms and legs night and morning, and my father rolled over in a canoe with all his clothes on; but outside of that the vacation was a success and from then on none of us ever thought there was any place in the world like that lake in Maine. We returned summer after summer—always on August 1st for one month. I have since become a salt-water man, but sometimes in summer there are days when the restlessness of the tides and the fearful cold of the sea water and the incessant wind which blows across the afternoon and into the evening make me wish for the placidity of a lake in the woods. A few weeks ago this feeling got so strong I bought myself a couple of bass hooks and a spinner and returned to the lake where we used to go, for a week's fishing and to revisit old haunts.

I took along my son, who had never had any fresh water up his nose and who had seen lily pads only from train windows. On the journey over to the lake I began to wonder what it would be like. I wondered how time would have marred this unique, this holy spot—the coves and streams, the hills that the sun set behind, the camps and the paths behind the camps. I was sure the tarred road would have found it out and I wondered in what other ways it would be desolated. It is strange how much you can remember about places like that once you allow your mind to return into the grooves which lead back. You remember one thing, and that suddenly reminds you of another thing. I guess I remembered clearest of all the early mornings, when the lake was cool and motionless, remembered how the bedroom smelled of the lumber it was made of and of the wet woods whose scent entered through the screen. The partitions in the camp were thin and did not extend clear to the top of the rooms, and as I was always the first up I would dress softly so as not to wake the others, and sneak out into the sweet outdoors and start out in the canoe, keeping close along the shore in the long shadows of the pines. I remembered being very careful never to rub my paddle against the gunwale for fear of disturbing the stillness of the cathedral.

The lake had never been what you would call a wild lake. There were cottages sprinkled around the shores, and it was in farming country although the shores of the lake were quite heavily wooded. Some of the cottages were owned by nearby farmers, and you would live at the shore and eat your meals at the farmhouse. That's what our family did. But although it wasn't wild, it was a fairly large and undisturbed lake and there were places in it which, to a child at least, seemed infinitely remote and primeval.

I was right about the tar: it led to within half a mile of the shore. But when I got back there, with my boy, and we settled into a camp near a farmhouse and into the kind of summertime I had known, I could tell that it was going to be pretty much the same as it had been before—I knew it, lying in bed the first morning, smelling the bedroom, and hearing the boy sneak quietly out and go off along the shore in a boat. I began to sustain the illusion that he was I, and therefore, by simple transposition, that I was my father. This sensation persisted, kept cropping up all the time we were there. It was not an entirely new feeling, but in this setting it grew much stronger. I seemed to be living a dual existence. I would be in the middle of some simple act, I would be picking up a bait box or laying down a table fork, or I would be saying something, and suddenly it would be not I but my father who was saying the words or making the gesture. It gave me a creepy sensation.

We went fishing the first morning. I felt the same damp moss covering the worms in the bait can, and saw the dragonfly alight on the tip of my rod as it hovered a few inches from the surface of the water. It was the arrival of this fly that convinced me beyond any doubt that everything was as it always had been, that the years were a mirage and there had been no years. The small waves were the same, chucking the rowboat under the chin as we fished at anchor, and the boat was the same boat, the same color green and the ribs broken in the same places, and under the floor-boards the same fresh-water leavings and débris— the dead helgrammite, the wisps of moss, the rusty discarded fishhook, the dried blood from yesterday's catch. We stared silently at the tips of our rods, at the dragonflies that came and went. I lowered the tip of mine into the water, tentatively, pensively dislodging the fly, which darted two feet away, poised, darted two feet back, and came to rest again a little farther up the rod. There had been no years between the ducking of this dragonfly and the other one—the one that was part of memory. I looked at the boy, who was silently watching his fly, and it was my hands that held his rod, my eyes watching. I felt dizzy and didn't know which rod I was at the end of.

We caught two bass, hauling them in briskly as though they were mackerel, pulling them over the side of the boat in a businesslike manner without any landing net, and stunning them with a blow on the back of the head. When we got back for a swim before lunch, the lake was exactly where we had left it, the same number of inches from the dock, and there was only the merest suggestion of a breeze. This seemed an utterly enchanted sea, this lake you could leave to its own devices for a few hours and come back to, and find that it had not stirred, this constant and trustworthy body of water. In the shallows, the dark, water-soaked sticks and twigs, smooth and old, were undulating in clusters on the bottom against the clean ribbed sand, and the track of the mussel was plain. A school of minnows swam by, each minnow with its small individual shadow, doubling the attendance, so clear and sharp in the sunlight. Some of the other campers were in swimming, along the shore, one of them with a cake of soap, and the water felt thin and clear and unsubstantial. Over the years there had been this person with the cake of soap, this cultist, and here he was. There had been no years.

Up to the farmhouse to dinner through the teeming, dusty field, the road under our sneakers was only a two-track road. The middle track was missing, the one with the marks of the hooves and the splotches of dried, flaky manure. There had always been three tracks to choose from in choosing which track to walk in; now the choice was narrowed down to two. For a moment I missed terribly the middle alternative. But the way led past the tennis court, and something about the way it lay there in the sun reassured me; the tape had loosened along the backline, the alleys were green with plantains and other weeds, and the net (installed in June and removed in September) sagged in the dry noon, and the whole place steamed with midday heat and hunger and emptiness. There was a choice of pie for dessert, and one was blueberry and one was apple, and the waitresses were the same country girls, there having been no passage of time, only the illusion of it as in a dropped curtain—the waitresses were still fifteen; their hair had been washed, that was the only difference—they had been to the movies and seen the pretty girls with the clean hair.

Summertime, oh summertime, pattern of life indelible, the fade-proof lake, the woods unshatterable, the pasture with the sweetfern and the juniper forever and ever, summer without end; this was the background, and the life along the shore was the design, the cottages with their innocent and tranquil design, their tiny docks with the flagpole and the American flag floating against the white clouds in the blue sky, the little paths over the roots of the trees leading from camp to camp and the paths leading back to the outhouses and the can of lime for sprinkling, and at the souvenir counters at the store the miniature birch-bark canoes and the post cards that showed things looking a little better than they looked. This was the American family at play, escaping the city heat, wondering whether the newcomers in the camp at the head of the cove were "common" or "nice," wondering whether it was true that the people who drove up for Sunday dinner at the farmhouse were turned away because there wasn't enough chicken.

It seemed to me, as I kept remembering all this, that those times and those summers had been infinitely precious and worth saving. There had been jollity and peace and goodness. The arriving (at the beginning of August) had been so big a business in itself, at the railway station the farm wagon drawn up, the first smell of the pine-laden air, the first glimpse of the smiling farmer, and the great importance of the trunks and your father's enormous authority in such matters, and the feel of the wagon under you for the long ten-mile haul, and at the top of the last long hill catching the first view of the lake after eleven months of not seeing this cherished body of water. The shouts and cries of the other campers when they saw you, and the trunks to be unpacked, to give up their rich burden. (Arriving was less exciting nowadays, when you sneaked up in your car and parked it under a tree near the camp and took out the bags and in five minutes it was all over, no fuss, no loud wonderful fuss about trunks.)

Peace and goodness and jollity. The only thing that was wrong now,   10
really, was the sound of the place, an unfamiliar nervous sound of the outboard motors. This was the note that jarred, the one thing that would sometimes break the illusion and set the years moving. In those other summertimes all motors were inboard; and when they were at a little distance, the noise they made was a sedative, an ingredient of summer sleep. They were one-cylinder and two-cylinder engines, and some were make-and-break and some were jump-spark, but they all made a sleepy sound across the lake. The one-lungers throbbed and fluttered, and the twin-cylinder ones purred and purred, and that was a quiet sound too. But now the campers all had outboards. In the daytime, in the hot mornings, these motors made a petulant, irritable sound; at night, in the still evening when the afterglow lit the water, they whined about one's ears like mosquitoes. My boy loved our rented outboard, and his great desire was to achieve singlehanded mastery over it, and authority, and he soon learned the trick of choking it a little (but not too much), and the adjustment of the needle valve. Watching him I would remember the things you could do with the old one-cylinder engine with the heavy flywheel, how you could have it eating out of your hand if you got really close to it spiritually. Motor boats in those days didn't have clutches,

and you would make a landing by shutting off the motor at the proper time and coasting in with a dead rudder. But there was a way of reversing them, if you learned the trick, by cutting the switch and putting it on again exactly on the final dying revolution of the flywheel, so that it would kick back against compression and begin reversing. Approaching a dock in a strong following breeze, it was difficult to slow up sufficiently by the ordinary coasting method, and if a boy felt he had complete mastery over his motor, he was tempted to keep it running beyond its time and then reverse it a few feet from the dock. It took a cool nerve, because if you threw the switch a twentieth of a second too soon you would catch the flywheel when it still had speed enough to go up past center, and the boat would leap ahead, charging bull-fashion at the dock.

We had a good week at the camp. The bass were biting well and the sun shone endlessly, day after day. We would be tired at night and lie down in the accumulated heat of the little bedrooms after the long hot day and the breeze would stir almost imperceptibly outside and the smell of the swamp drift in through the rusty screens. Sleep would come easily and in the morning the red squirrel would be on the roof, tapping out his gay routine. I kept remembering everything, lying in bed in the mornings—the small steamboat that had a long rounded stern like the lip of a Ubangi, and how quietly she ran on the moonlight sails, when the older boys played their mandolins and the girls sang and we ate doughnuts dipped in sugar, and how sweet the music was on the water in the shining night, and what it had felt like to think about girls then. After breakfast we would go up to the store and the things were in the same place—the minnows in a bottle, the plugs and spinners disarranged and pawed over by the youngsters from the boys' camp, the fig newtons and the Beeman's gum. Outside, the road was tarred and cars stood in front of the store. Inside, all was just as it had always been, except there was more Coca-Cola and not so much Moxie and root beer and birch beer and sarsaparilla. We would walk out with a bottle of pop apiece and sometimes the pop would backfire up our noses and hurt.

We explored the streams, quietly, where the turtles slid off the sunny logs and dug their way into the soft bottom; and we lay on the town wharf and fed worms to the tame bass. Everywhere we went I had trouble making out which was I, the one walking at my side, the one walking in my pants.

One afternoon while we were there at that lake a thunderstorm came up. It was like the revival of an old melodrama that I had seen long ago with childish awe. The second-act climax of the drama of the electrical disturbance over a lake in America had not changed in any important respect. This was the big scene, still the big scene. The whole thing was so familiar, the first feeling of oppression and heat and a general air around camp of not wanting to go very far away. In midafternoon (it was all the same) a curious darkening of the sky, and a lull in everything that had made life tick; and then the way the boats suddenly swung the other way at their moorings with the coming of a breeze out of the new quarter, and the premonitory rumble. Then the kettle drum, then the snare, then the bass drum and cymbals, then crackling light against the dark, and the gods grinning and licking their chops in the hills. Afterward the calm, the rain steadily rustling in the calm lake, the return of light and hope and spirits, and the campers running out in joy and relief to go swimming in the rain, their bright cries perpetuating the deathless joke about how they were getting simply drenched, and the children screaming with delight at the new sensation of bathing in the rain, and the joke about getting drenched linking the generations in a strong indestructible chain. And the comedian who waded in carrying an umbrella.

When the others went swimming my son said he was going in too. He pulled his dripping trunks from the line where they had hung all through the shower, and wrung them out. Languidly, and with no thought of going in, I watched him, his hard little body, skinny and bare, saw him wince slightly as he pulled up around his vitals the small, soggy, icy garment. As he buckled the swollen belt suddenly my groin felt the chill of death.

Thinking about the Text

1. One of the themes of this essay is change and the passage of time. What had changed at the lake between the times E. B. White visited as a child and when he visited as an adult? What had not changed?

2. Personal essays and memoirs often include sensory language and images that invoke a sense of smell, taste, touch, sound, or sight. Identify several examples of sensory language in this essay that are especially effective. Explain why.

3. Write an essay describing a place you knew well in childhood, a place to which you returned years later. Use sensory language and details to show what had changed and what had remained the same.

VIRGINIA WOOLF

The Death of the Moth

1942

VIRGINIA WOOLF (1882–1941) wrote fiction and essays. In addition to the novels *Mrs. Dalloway* (1925), *To the Lighthouse* (1927), *Orlando* (1928), and others, Woolf is known for her books of essays: *A Room of One's Own* (1929), *The Moment and Other Essays* (1947), and *The Death of the Moth and Other Essays* (1942). With her husband, the writer Leonard Woolf, she was a member of the Bloomsbury Group, a collective of influential artists, writers, and philosophers. "The Death of the Moth" was the opening essay in the collection her husband compiled shortly after Woolf took her own life.

MOTHS THAT FLY BY DAY ARE NOT PROPERLY TO BE called moths; they do not excite that pleasant sense of dark autumn nights and ivy-blossom which the commonest yellow-underwing asleep in the shadow of the curtain never fails to rouse in us. They are hybrid creatures, neither gay like butterflies nor sombre like their own species. Nevertheless the present specimen, with his narrow hay-colored wings, fringed with a tassel of the same color, seemed to be content with life. It was a pleasant morning, mid-September, mild, benignant, yet with a keener breath than that of the summer months. The plough was already scoring the field opposite the window, and where the share had been, the earth was pressed flat and gleamed with moisture. Such vigor came rolling in from the fields and the down beyond that it was difficult to keep the eyes strictly turned upon the book. The rooks too were keeping one of their annual festivities; soaring round the tree tops until it looked as if a vast net with thousands of black knots in it had been cast up into the air; which, after a few moments sank slowly down upon the trees until every twig seemed to have a knot at the end of it. Then, suddenly, the net would be thrown into the air again in a wider circle this time, with the utmost clamor and vociferation, as though to be thrown into the air and settle slowly down upon the tree tops were a tremendously exciting experience.

The same energy which inspired the rooks, the ploughmen, the horses, and even, it seemed, the lean bare-backed downs, sent the moth fluttering from side to side of his square of the window-pane. One could not help watching him. One was, indeed, conscious of a queer feeling of pity for him. The possibilities of pleasure seemed that morning so enormous and so various that to have only a moth's part in life, and a day moth's at that, appeared a hard fate, and his zest in enjoying his meagre opportunities to the full, pathetic. He flew vigorously to one corner of his compartment, and, after waiting there a second, flew across to the other. What remained for him but to fly to a third corner and then to a fourth? That was all he could do, in spite of the size of the downs, the width of the sky, the far-off smoke of houses, and the romantic voice, now and then, of a steamer out at sea. What he could do he did. Watching him, it seemed as if a fiber, very thin but pure, of the enormous energy of the world had been thrust into his frail and diminutive body. As often as he crossed the pane, I could fancy that a thread of vital light became visible. He was little or nothing but life.

Yet, because he was so small, and so simple a form of the energy that was rolling in at the open window and driving its way through so many narrow and intricate corridors in my own brain and in those of other human beings, there was something marvellous as well as pathetic about him. It was as if someone had taken a tiny bead of pure life and decking it as lightly as possible with down and feathers, had set it dancing and zig-zagging to show us the true nature of life. Thus displayed one could not get over the strangeness of it. One is apt to forget all about life, seeing it humped and bossed and garnished and cumbered so that it has to move with the greatest circumspection and dignity. Again, the thought of all that life might have been had he been born in any other shape caused one to view his simple activities with a kind of pity.

After a time, tired by his dancing apparently, he settled on the window ledge in the sun, and, the queer spectacle being at an end, I forgot about him. Then, looking up, my eye was caught by him. He was trying to resume his dancing, but seemed either so stiff or so awkward that he could only flutter to the bottom of the window-pane; and when he tried to fly across it he failed. Being intent on other matters I watched these futile attempts for a time without thinking, unconsciously waiting for him to resume his flight, as one waits for a machine, that has stopped momentarily, to start again without considering the reason of its failure. After perhaps a seventh attempt he slipped from the wooden ledge and fell, fluttering his wings, on to his back on the window sill. The helplessness of his attitude roused me. It flashed upon me that he was in difficulties; he could no longer raise himself; his legs struggled vainly. But, as I stretched out a pencil, meaning to help him to right himself, it came over me that the failure and awkwardness were the approach of death. I laid the pencil down again.

The legs agitated themselves once more. I looked as if for the enemy   5
against which he struggled. I looked out of doors. What had happened there? Presumably it was midday, and work in the fields had stopped. Stillness and quiet had replaced the previous animation. The birds had taken themselves off to feed in the brooks. The horses stood still. Yet the power was there all the same, massed outside indifferent, impersonal, not attending to anything in particular. Somehow it was opposed to the little hay-colored moth. It was useless to try to do anything. One could only watch the extraordinary efforts made by those tiny legs against an oncoming doom which could, had it chosen, have submerged an entire city, not merely a city, but masses of human beings; nothing, I knew, had any chance against death. Nevertheless after a pause of exhaustion the legs fluttered again. It was superb this last protest, and so frantic that he succeeded at last in righting himself. One's sympathies, of course, were all on the side of life. Also, when there was nobody to care or to know, this gigantic effort on the part of an insignificant little moth, against a power of such magnitude, to retain what no one else valued or desired to keep, moved one strangely. Again, somehow, one saw life, a pure bead. I lifted the pencil again, useless though I knew it to be. But even as I did so, the unmistakable tokens of death showed themselves. The body relaxed, and instantly grew stiff. The struggle was over. The insignificant little creature now knew death. As I looked at the dead moth, this minute wayside triumph of so great a force over so mean an antagonist filled me with wonder. Just as life had been strange a few minutes before, so death was now as strange. The moth having righted himself now lay most decently and uncomplainingly composed. O yes, he seemed to say, death is stronger than I am.

Thinking about the Text

1. In this essay, Virginia Woolf mentions more than once that she feels pity for the moth. What is it about the moth that makes her feel pity?

2. Woolf uses several contrasts (for example, big and small, significant and insignificant) in this essay. What might be her purpose in doing so? Why do you think she chose to reflect on death by writing about a moth?

3. Write an essay in which you reflect on an abstraction (such as love, fear, joy, hatred, friendship, or loneliness) by describing a particular experience. As Woolf does, set the scene carefully by using specific details.

ALDO LEOPOLD

The Land Ethic

1949

ALDO LEOPOLD (1887–1948) was a wildlife manager, conservationist, and environmental writer. He is best known for his collection of journals and essays, *A Sand County Almanac* (1949), in which "The Land Ethic" appeared. In 1982, Leopold's five children established the Aldo Leopold Foundation, a nonprofit whose mission is environmental conservation. Leopold first delivered an earlier version of this essay at the American Association for the Advancement of Science meeting in May 1933. It was then published under the title "The Conservation Ethic" in the *Journal of Forestry* (1933).

WHEN GOD-LIKE ODYSSEUS RETURNED FROM THE wars in Troy, he hanged all on one rope a dozen slave-girls of his household whom he suspected of misbehavior during his absence.

This hanging involved no question of propriety. The girls were property. The disposal of property was then, as now, a matter of expediency, not of right and wrong.

Concepts of right and wrong were not lacking from Odysseus' Greece: witness the fidelity of his wife through the long years before at last his black-prowed galleys clove the wine-dark seas for home. The ethical structure of that day covered wives, but had not yet been extended to human chattels. During the three thousand years which have since elapsed, ethical criteria have been extended to many fields of conduct, with corresponding shrinkages in those judged by expediency only.

THE ETHICAL SEQUENCE

This extension of ethics, so far studied only by philosophers, is actually a process in ecological evolution. Its sequences may be described in ecological as well as in philosophical terms. An ethic, ecologically, is a limitation on freedom of action in the struggle for existence. An ethic, philosophically, is a differentiation of social from anti-social conduct. These are two definitions of one thing. The thing has its origin in the tendency of interdependent individuals or groups to evolve modes of co-operation. The ecologist calls these symbioses. Politics and economics are advanced symbioses in which the original free-for-all competition has been replaced, in part, by co-operative mechanisms with an ethical content.

The complexity of co-operative mechanisms has increased with population density, and with the efficiency of tools. It was simpler, for example, to define the anti-social uses of sticks and stones in the days of the mastodons than of bullets and billboards in the age of motors.

The first ethics dealt with the relation between individuals; the Mosaic Decalogue is an example. Later accretions dealt with the relation between the individual and society. The Golden Rule tries to integrate social organization to the individual.

There is as yet no ethic dealing with man's relation to land and to the animals and plants which grow upon it. Land, like Odysseus' slave-girls, is still property. The land-relation is still strictly economic, entailing privileges but not obligations.

The extension of ethics to this third element in human environment is, if I read the evidence correctly, an evolutionary possibility and an ecological necessity. It is the third step in a sequence. The first two have already been taken. Individual thinkers since the days of Ezekiel and Isaiah have asserted that the despoliation of land is not only inexpedient but wrong. Society, however, has not yet affirmed their belief. I regard the present conservation movement as the embryo of such an affirmation.

An ethic may be regarded as a mode of guidance for meeting ecological situations so new or intricate, or involving such deferred reactions, that the path of social expediency is not discernible to the average individual. Animal instincts are modes of guidance for the individual in meeting such situations. Ethics are possibly a kind of community instinct in-the-making.

THE COMMUNITY CONCEPT

All ethics so far evolved rest upon a single premise: that the individual   10
is a member of a community of interdependent parts. His instincts prompt him to compete for his place in that community, but his ethics prompt him also to cooperate (perhaps in order that there may be a place to compete for).

The land ethic simply enlarges the boundaries of the community to include soils, waters, plants, and animals, or collectively; the land.

This sounds simple: do we not already sing our love for and obligation to the land of the free and the home of the brave? Yes, but just what
and whom do we love? Certainly not the soil, which we are sending
helter-skelter downriver. Certainly not the waters, which we assume
have no function except to turn turbines, float barges, and carry off sew-
age. Certainly not the plants, of which we exterminate whole communities without batting an eye. Certainly not the animals, of which we
have already extirpated many of the largest and most beautiful species.
A land ethic of course cannot prevent the alteration, management, and
use of these "resources," but it does affirm their right to continued existence, and, at least in spots, their continued existence in a natural state.

In short, a land ethic changes the role of *Homo sapiens* from conqueror of the land-community to plain member and citizen of it. It
implies respect for his fellow-members, and also respect for the community as such.

In human history, we have learned (I hope) that the conqueror role is
eventually self-defeating. Why? Because it is implicit in such a role that
the conqueror knows, *ex cathedra*, just what makes the community clock
tick, and just what and who is valuable, and what and who is worthless,
in community life. It always turns out that he knows neither, and this is
why his conquests eventually defeat themselves.

In the biotic community, a parallel situation exists. Abraham knew   15
exactly what the land was for: it was to drip milk and honey into Abraham's mouth. At the present moment, the assurance with which we
regard this assumption is inverse to the degree of our education.

The ordinary citizen today assumes that science knows what makes
the community clock tick; the scientist is equally sure that he does not.
He knows that the biotic mechanism is so complex that its workings
may never be fully understood.

That man is, in fact, only a member of a biotic team is shown by
an ecological interpretation of history. Many historical events, hitherto
explained solely in terms of human enterprise, were actually biotic

interactions between people and land. The characteristics of the land determined the facts quite as potently as the characteristics of the men who lived on it.

Consider, for example, the settlement of the Mississippi valley. In the years following the Revolution, three groups were contending for its control: the native Indian, the French and English traders, and the American settlers. Historians wonder what would have happened if the English at Detroit had thrown a little more weight into the Indian side of those tipsy scales which decided the outcome of the colonial migration into the cane-lands of Kentucky. It is time now to ponder the fact that the cane-lands, when subjected to the particular mixture of forces represented by the cow, plow, fire, and axe of the pioneer, became bluegrass. What if the plant succession inherent in this dark and bloody ground had, under the impact of these forces, given us some worthless sedge, shrub, or weed? Would Boone and Kenton have held out? Would there have been any overflow into Ohio, Indiana, Illinois, and Missouri? Any Louisiana Purchase? Any transcontinental union of new states? Any Civil War?

Kentucky was one sentence in the drama of history. We are commonly told what the human actors in this drama tried to do, but we are seldom told that their success, or the lack of it, hung in large degree on the reaction of particular soils to the impact of the particular forces exerted by their occupancy. In the case of Kentucky, we do not even know where the bluegrass came from—whether it is a native species, or a stowaway from Europe.

Contrast the cane-lands with what hindsight tells us about the Southwest, where the pioneers were equally brave, resourceful, and persevering. The impact of occupancy here brought no bluegrass, or other plant fitted to withstand the bumps and buffetings of hard use. This region, when grazed by livestock, reverted through a series of more and more worthless grasses, shrubs, and weeds to a condition of unstable equilibrium. Each recession of plant types bred erosion; each increment to erosion bred a further recession of plants. The result today is a progressive and mutual deterioration, not only of plants and soils, but of the animal community subsisting thereon. The early settlers did not expect this: on the ciénegas of New Mexico some even cut ditches to hasten it. So subtle has been its progress that few residents of the region are aware of it. It is quite invisible to the tourist who finds this wrecked landscape colorful and charming (as indeed it is, but it bears scant resemblance to what it was in 1848).

This same landscape was "developed" once before, but with quite different results. The Pueblo Indians settled the Southwest in pre-Columbian times, but they happened *not* to be equipped with range livestock. Their civilization expired, but not because their land expired.

In India, regions devoid of any sod-forming grass have been settled, apparently without wrecking the land, by the simple expedient of carrying the grass to the cow, rather than vice versa. (Was this the result of some deep wisdom, or was it just good luck? I do not know.)

In short, the plant succession steered the course of history; the pioneer simply demonstrated, for good or ill, what successions inhered in the land. Is history taught in this spirit? It will be, once the concept of land as a community really penetrates our intellectual life.

THE ECOLOGICAL CONSCIENCE

Conservation is a state of harmony between men and land. Despite nearly a century of propaganda, conservation still proceeds at a snail's pace; progress still consists largely of letterhead pieties and convention oratory. On the back forty we still slip two steps backward for each forward stride.

The usual answer to this dilemma is "more conservation education." No one will debate this, but is it certain that only the *volume* of education needs stepping up? Is something lacking in the *content* as well?

It is difficult to give a fair summary of its content in brief form, but, as I understand it, the content is substantially this: obey the law, vote

right, join some organizations, and practice what conservation is profitable on your own land; the government will do the rest.

Is not this formula too easy to accomplish anything worth-while?
It defines no right or wrong, assigns no obligation, calls for no sacrifice, implies no change in the current philosophy of values. In respect
of land-use, it urges only enlightened self-interest. Just how far will
such education take us? An example will perhaps yield a partial answer.

By 1930 it had become clear to all except the ecologically blind that
southwestern Wisconsin's topsoil was slipping seaward. In 1933 the
farmers were told that if they would adopt certain remedial practices for
five years, the public would donate CCC labor to install them, plus the
necessary machinery and materials. The offer was widely accepted,
but the practices were widely forgotten when the five-year contract
period was up. The farmers continued only those practices that yielded
an immediate and visible economic gain for themselves.

This led to the idea that maybe farmers would learn more quickly
if they themselves wrote the rules. Accordingly the Wisconsin Legislature in 1937 passed the Soil Conservation District Law. This said to
farmers, in effect: *We, the public, will furnish you free technical service and
loan you specialized machinery, if you will write your own rules for land-
use. Each county may write its own rules, and these will have the force of
law.* Nearly all the counties promptly organized to accept the proffered
help, but after a decade of operation, *no county has yet written a single
rule.* There has been visible progress in such practices as strip-cropping,
pasture renovation, and soil liming, but none in fencing woodlots
against grazing, and none in excluding plow and cow from steep slopes.
The farmers, in short, have selected those remedial practices which
were profitable anyhow, and ignored those which were profitable to the
community, but not clearly profitable to themselves.

When one asks why no rules have been written, one is told that the   30
community is not yet ready to support them; education must precede

rules. But the education actually in progress makes no mention of obligations to land over and above those dictated by self-interest. The net result is that we have more education but less soil, fewer healthy woods, and as many floods as in 1937.

The puzzling aspect of such situations is that the existence of obligations over and above self-interest is taken for granted in such rural community enterprises as the betterment of roads, schools, churches, and baseball teams. Their existence is not taken for granted, nor as yet seriously discussed, in bettering the behavior of the water that falls on the land, or in the preserving of the beauty or diversity of the farm landscape. Land-use ethics are still governed wholly by economic self-interest, just as social ethics were a century ago.

To sum up: we asked the farmer to do what he conveniently could to save his soil, and he has done just that, and only that. The farmer who clears the woods off a 75 per cent slope, turns his cows into the clearing, and dumps its rainfall, rocks, and soil into the community creek, is still (if otherwise decent) a respected member of society. If he puts lime on his fields and plants his crops on contour, he is still entitled to all the privileges and emoluments of his Soil Conservation District. The District is a beautiful piece of social machinery, but it is coughing along on two cylinders because we have been too timid, and too anxious for quick success, to tell the farmer the true magnitude of his obligations. Obligations have no meaning without conscience, and the problem we face is the extension of the social conscience from people to land.

No important change in ethics was ever accomplished without an internal change in our intellectual emphasis, loyalties, affections, and convictions. The proof that conservation has not yet touched these foundations of conduct lies in the fact that philosophy and religion have not yet heard of it. In our attempt to make conservation easy, we have made it trivial.

THE OUTLOOK

It is inconceivable to me that an ethical relation to land can exist without love, respect, and admiration for land, and a high regard for its value. By value, I of course mean something far broader than mere economic value; I mean value in the philosophical sense.

Perhaps the most serious obstacle impeding the evolution of a land   35
ethic is the fact that our educational and economic system is headed away from, rather than toward, an intense consciousness of land. Your true modern is separated from the land by many middlemen, and by innumerable physical gadgets. He has no vital relation to it; to him it is the space between cities on which crops grow. Turn him loose for a day on the land, and if the spot does not happen to be a golf links or a "scenic" area, he is bored stiff. If crops could be raised by hydroponics instead of farming, it would suit him very well. Synthetic substitutes for wood, leather, wool, and other natural land products suit him better than the originals. In short, land is something he has "outgrown."

Almost equally serious as an obstacle to a land ethic is the attitude of the farmer for whom the land is still an adversary, or a taskmaster that keeps him in slavery. Theoretically, the mechanization of farming ought to cut the farmer's chains, but whether it really does is debatable.

One of the requisites for an ecological comprehension of land is an understanding of ecology, and this is by no means co-extensive with "education"; in fact, much higher education seems deliberately to avoid ecological concepts. An understanding of ecology does not necessarily originate in courses bearing ecological labels; it is quite as likely to be labeled geography, botany, agronomy, history, or economics. This is as it should be, but whatever the label, ecological training is scarce.

The case for a land ethic would appear hopeless but for the minority which is in obvious revolt against these "modern" trends.

The "key-log" which must be moved to release the evolutionary process for an ethic is simply this: quit thinking about decent land-use as solely an economic problem. Examine each question in terms of what is ethically and esthetically right, as well as what is economically expedient. A thing is right when it tends to preserve the integrity, stability, and beauty of the biotic community. It is wrong when it tends otherwise.

It of course goes without saying that economic feasibility limits   40
the tether of what can or cannot be done for land. It always has and it always will. The fallacy the economic determinists have tied around our collective neck, and which we now need to cast off, is the belief that economics determines *all* land-use. This is simply not true. An innumerable host of actions and attitudes, comprising perhaps the bulk of all land relations, is determined by the land-users' tastes and predilections, rather than by his purse. The bulk of all land relations hinges on investments of time, forethought, skill, and faith rather than on investments of cash. As a land-user thinketh, so is he.

I have purposely presented the land ethic as a product of social evolution because nothing so important as an ethic is ever "written." Only the most superficial student of history supposes that Moses "wrote" the Decalogue; it evolved in the minds of a thinking community, and Moses wrote a tentative summary of it for a "seminar." I say tentative because evolution never stops.

The evolution of a land ethic is an intellectual as well as emotional process. Conservation is paved with good intentions which prove to be futile, or even dangerous, because they are devoid of critical understanding either of the land, or of economic land-use. I think it is a truism that as the ethical frontier advances from the individual to the community, its intellectual content increases.

The mechanism of operation is the same for any ethic: social approbation for right actions: social disapproval for wrong actions.

By and large, our present problem is one of attitudes and implements. We are remodeling the Alhambra with a steam-shovel, and we are proud of our yardage. We shall hardly relinquish the shovel, which after all has many good points, but we are in need of gentler and more objective criteria for its successful use.

Thinking about the Text

1. According to Aldo Leopold, what is a "land ethic"? Point to the place in the essay where he defines this term, which is central to his argument.

2. "Despite nearly a century of propaganda," Leopold notes, "conservation still proceeds at a snail's pace" (paragraph 24). Why, according to Leopold, is that the case? More than a half-century later, is this still the case, or are conservation efforts now proceeding more quickly? Provide evidence to support your answer.

3. Leopold claims that a land ethic works the same way any other ethic does: "social approbation for right actions: social disapproval for wrong actions" (paragraph 43). Write an essay reporting on an environmental issue facing your home community, your school, your dorm, or some other community in which you see this kind of ethic at play.

DYLAN THOMAS

Memories of Christmas

1954

DYLAN THOMAS (1914–1953) was a Welsh poet known for poems such as "Do Not Go Gentle into That Good Night" and "Fern Hill," but he also wrote short stories and other prose works such as *Portrait of the Artist as a Young Dog* (1940) and *Under Milk Wood* (1954). "Memories of Christmas" began in 1945 as a talk written for the Welsh BBC program *Children's Hour*. Thomas recorded a longer version in 1952, which you can listen to on *YouTube*. It was later expanded into *A Child's Christmas in Wales* (1954).

ONE CHRISTMAS WAS SO MUCH LIKE ANOTHER, IN THOSE years, around the sea-town corner now, and out of all sound except the distant speaking of the voices I sometimes hear a moment before sleep, that I can never remember whether it snowed for six days and six nights when I was twelve or whether it snowed for twelve days and twelve nights when I was six; or whether the ice broke and the skating grocer vanished like a snowman through a white trap-door on that same Christmas Day that the mince-pies finished Uncle Arnold and we tobogganed down the seaward hill, all the afternoon, on the best tea-tray, and Mrs. Griffiths complained, and we threw a snowball at her niece, and my hands burned so, with the heat and the cold, when I held them in front of the fire, that I cried for twenty minutes and then had some jelly.

All the Christmases roll down the hill towards the Welsh-speaking sea, like a snowball growing whiter and bigger and rounder, like a cold and headlong moon bundling down the sky that was our street; and they stop at the rim of the ice-edged, fish-freezing waves, and I plunge my hands in the snow and bring out whatever I can find; holly or robins or pudding, squabbles and carols and oranges and tin whistles, and the fire in the front room, and bang go the crackers, and holy, holy, holy, ring the bells, and the glass bells shaking on the tree, and Mother Goose, and Struwelpeter—oh! the baby-burning flames and the clacking scissorman!—Billy Bunter and Black Beauty, Little Women and boys who have three helpings, Alice and Mrs. Potter's badgers, penknives, teddy-bears—named after a Mr. Theodore Bear, their inventor, or father who died recently in the United States—mouth-organs, tin soldiers, and blancmange, and Auntie Bessie playing "Pop Goes the Weasel" and "Nuts in May" and "Oranges and Lemons" on the untuned piano in the parlor all through the thimble-hiding musical-chairing blind-man's-buffing party at the end of the never-to-be-forgotten day at the end of the unremembered year.

In goes my hand into that wool-white bell-tongued ball of holidays resting at the margin of the carol-singing sea, and out come Mrs. Prothero and the firemen.

It was on the afternoon of the day of Christmas Eve, and I was in Mrs. Prothero's garden, waiting for cats, with her son Jim. It was snowing. It was always snowing at Christmas; December, in my memory, is white as Lapland, though there were no reindeers. But there were cats. Patient, cold, and callous, our hands wrapped in socks, we waited to snowball the cats. Sleek and long as jaguars and terrible-whiskered, spitting and snarling they would slink and sidle over the white back-garden walls, and the lynx-eyed hunters, Jim and I, fur-capped and moccasined trappers from Hudson's Bay off Eversley Road, would hurl our deadly snowballs at the green of their eyes. The wise cats never appeared. We were so still, Eskimo-footed arctic marksmen in the muffling silence of the eternal snows—eternal, ever since Wednesday— that we never heard Mrs. Prothero's first cry from her igloo at the bottom of the garden. Or, if we heard it at all, it was, to us, like the far-off challenge of our enemy and prey, the neighbor's Polar Cat. But soon the voice grew louder. "Fire!" cried Mrs. Prothero, and she beat the dinner-gong. And we ran down the garden, with the snowballs in our arms, towards the house, and smoke, indeed, was pouring out of the dining-room, and the gong was bombilating, and Mrs. Prothero was announcing ruin like a town-crier in Pompeii. This was better than all the cats in Wales standing on the wall in a row. We bounded into the house, laden with snowballs, and stopped at the open door of the smoke-filled room. Something was burning all right; perhaps it was Mr. Prothero, who always slept there after midday dinner with a newspaper over his face; but he was standing in the middle of the room, saying "A fine Christmas!" and smacking at the smoke with a slipper.

"Call the fire-brigade," cried Mrs. Prothero as she beat the gong. 5

"They won't be there," said Mr. Prothero, "it's Christmas."

There was no fire to be seen, only clouds of smoke and Mr. Prothero standing in the middle of them, waving his slipper as though he were conducting.

"Do something," he said.

And we threw all our snowballs into the smoke—I think we missed Mr. Prothero—and ran out of the house to the telephone-box.

"Let's call the police as well," Jim said.   10

"And the ambulance."

"And Ernie Jenkins, he likes fires."

But we only called the fire-brigade, and soon the fire-engine came and three tall men in helmets brought a hose into the house and Mr. Prothero got out just in time before they turned it on. Nobody could have had a noisier Christmas Eve. And when the firemen turned off the hose and were standing in the wet and smoky room, Jim's aunt, Miss Prothero, came downstairs and peered in at them. Jim and I waited, very quietly, to hear what she would say to them. She said the right thing, always. She looked at the three tall firemen in their shining helmets, standing among the smoke and cinders and dissolving snow-balls, and she said: "Would you like something to read?"

Now out of that bright white snowball of Christmas gone comes the stocking, the stocking of stockings, that hung at the foot of the bed with the arm of a golliwog dangling over the top and small bells ringing in the toes. There was a company, gallant and scarlet but never nice to taste though I always tried when very young, of belted and busbied and musketed lead soldiers so soon to lose their heads and legs in the wars on the kitchen table after the tea-things, the mince-pies, and the cakes that I helped to make by stoning the raisins and eating them, had been cleared away; and a bag of moist and many-colored jelly-babies and a folded flag and a false nose and a tram-conductor's cap and a machine that punched tickets and rang a bell; never a catapult; once, by a mistake that no one could explain, a little hatchet; and a rubber-buffalo, or it may have been a horse, with a yellow head and haphazard legs; and a celluloid duck that made, when you pressed it, a most unducklike noise, a mewing moo that an ambitious cat might make who wishes to be a cow; and a painting-book in which I could make the grass, the trees, the sea, and the animals any color I pleased: and still the dazzling sky-blue sheep are grazing in the red field under a flight of rainbow-beaked and pea-green birds.

Christmas morning was always over before you could say Jack Frost.   15
And look! suddenly the pudding was burning! Bang the gong and call the fire-brigade and the book-loving firemen! Someone found the silver three-penny-bit with a currant on it; and the someone was always Uncle Arnold. The motto in my cracker read:

Let's all have fun this Christmas Day,
Let's play and sing and shout hooray!

and the grown-ups turned their eyes towards the ceiling, and Auntie Bessie, who had already been frightened, twice, by a clock-work mouse, whimpered at the sideboard and had some elderberry wine. And someone put a glass bowl full of nuts on the littered table, and my uncle said, as he said once every year: "I've got a shoe-nut here. Fetch me a shoehorn to open it, boy."

And dinner was ended.

And I remember that on the afternoon of Christmas Day, when the others sat around the fire and told each other that this was nothing, no, nothing, to the great snowbound and turkey-proud Yule-log-crackling holly-berry-bedizined and kissing-under-the-mistletoe Christmas when *they* were children, I would go out, school-capped and gloved and muffered, with my bright new boots squeaking, into the white world on to the seaward hill, to call on Jim and Dan and Jack and to walk with them through the silent snowscape of our town.

We went padding through the streets, leaving huge deep footprints in the snow, on the hidden pavements.

"I bet people'll think there's been hippoes."

"What would you do if you saw a hippo coming down Terrace Road?"   20

"I'd go like this, bang! I'd throw him over the railings and roll him down the hill and then I'd tickle him under the ear and he'd wag his tail. . . ."

"What would you do if you saw *two* hippoes. . . . ?"

Iron-flanked and bellowing he-hippoes clanked and blundered and battered through the scudding snow towards us as we passed by Mr. Daniel's house.

"Let's post Mr. Daniel a snowball through his letter box."

"Let's write things in the snow."   25

"Let's write 'Mr. Daniel looks like a spaniel' all over his lawn."

"Look," Jack said, "I'm eating snow-pie."

"What's it taste like?"

"Like snow-pie," Jack said.

Or we walked on the white shore.   30

"Can the fishes see it's snowing?"

"They think it's the sky falling down."

The silent one-clouded heavens drifted on to the sea.

"All the old dogs have gone."

Dogs of a hundred mingled makes yapped in the summer at the sea-   35
rim and yelped at the trespassing mountains of the waves.

"I bet St. Bernards would like it now."

And we were snowblind travelers lost on the north hills, and the great dewlapped dogs, with brandy-flasks round their necks, ambled and shambled up to us, baying "Excelsior."

We returned home through the desolate poor sea-facing streets where only a few children fumbled with bare red fingers in the thick wheel-rutted snow and catcalled after us, their voices fading away, as we trudged uphill, into the cries of the dock-birds and the hooters of ships out in the white and whirling bay.

Bring out the tall tales now that we told by the fire as we roasted chestnuts and the gaslight bubbled low. Ghosts with their heads under their arms trailed their chains and said "whooo" like owls in the long nights when I dared not look over my shoulder; wild beasts lurked in the cubby-hole under the stairs where the gas-meter ticked. "Once upon a time," Jim said, "there were three boys, just like us, who got lost in the dark in the snow, near Bethesda Chapel, and this is what happened to them. . . ." It was the most dreadful happening I had ever heard.

And I remember that we went singing carols once, a night or two   40
before Christmas Eve, when there wasn't the shaving of a moon to light the secret, white-flying streets. At the end of a long road was a drive that led to a large house, and we stumbled up the darkness of the drive that night, each one of us afraid, each one holding a stone in his hand in case, and all of us too brave to say a word. The wind made through the drive-trees noises as of old and unpleasant and maybe web-footed men wheezing in caves. We reached the black bulk of the house.

"What shall we give them?" Dan whispered.

"'Hark the Herald'? 'Christmas comes but Once a Year'?"

"No," Jack said: "We'll sing 'Good King Wenceslas.' I'll count three."

One, two, three, and we began to sing, our voices high and seemingly distant in the snow-felted darkness round the house that was occupied by nobody we knew. We stood close together, near the dark door.

Good King Wenceslas looked out
On the Feast of Stephen.

And then a small, dry voice, like the voice of someone who has not   45
spoken for a long time, suddenly joined our singing: a small, dry voice from the other side of the door: a small, dry voice through the keyhole. And when we stopped running we were outside *our* house; the front room was lovely and bright; the gramophone was playing; we saw the red and white balloons hanging from the gas-bracket; uncles and aunts sat by the fire; I thought I smelt our supper being fried in the kitchen. Everything was good again, and Christmas shone through all the familiar town.

"Perhaps it was a ghost," Jim said.

"Perhaps it was trolls," Dan said, who was always reading.

"Let's go in and see if there's any jelly left," Jack said. And we did that.

Thinking about the Text

1. Dylan Thomas provides a mix of memories common to many Christmases of his childhood along with details about some specific events.
   What do you think his purpose was in mixing general recollections
   and specific events? Is there a particular message that comes across?

2. Thomas begins with two very long sentences, each comprising a
   paragraph. Why might he have made this stylistic choice? Identify
   other places in the text where he uses long sentences. What do those
   sections have in common with the two opening paragraphs?

3. Write about memories you have from childhood that revolve around
   a specific holiday. As Thomas does, include both details that recurred
   year after year and memories specific to one year.

JAMES BALDWIN

Stranger in the Village

1955

───────────────◦ᴗ◦───────────────

JAMES BALDWIN (1924–1987) wrote essays, novels, plays, and poems, often on race, religion, and sexuality. He is best known for the novels *Go Tell It on the Mountain* (1953) and *Giovanni's Room* (1956) and for his essay collection *Notes of a Native Son* (1955), which concludes with "Stranger in the Village." This essay has appeared in every edition of *The Norton Reader*, finding a home in several different chapters, including "On Civilization" in the first two editions, "On Politics and Government" in the third and fourth editions, and "Cultural Critique" in the ninth to the twelfth editions, among others. That it has fit in such an array of chapters over the last fifty years is a testament to its relevance across time and place.

───────────────◦ᴗ◦───────────────

FROM ALL AVAILABLE EVIDENCE NO BLACK MAN HAD EVER set foot in this tiny Swiss village before I came. I was told before arriving that I would probably be a "sight" for the village; I took this to mean that people of my complexion were rarely seen in Switzerland, and also that city people are always something of a "sight" outside of the city. It did not occur to me—possibly because I am an American—that there could be people anywhere who had never seen a Negro.

It is a fact that cannot be explained on the basis of the inaccessibility of the village. The village is very high, but it is only four hours from Milan and three hours from Lausanne. It is true that it is virtually unknown. Few people making plans for a holiday would elect to come here. On the other hand, the villagers are able, presumably, to come and go as they please—which they do: to another town at the foot of the mountain, with a population of approximately five thousand, the nearest place to see a movie or go to the bank. In the village there is no movie house, no bank, no library, no theater; very few radios, one jeep, one station wagon; and at the moment, one typewriter, mine, an invention which the woman next door to me here had never seen. There are about six hundred people living here, all Catholic—I conclude this from the fact that the Catholic church is open all year round, whereas the Protestant chapel, set off on a hill a little removed from the village, is open only in the summertime when the tourists arrive. There are four or five hotels, all closed now, and four or five *bistros*, of which, however, only two do any business during the winter. These two do not do a great deal, for life in the village seems to end around nine or ten o'clock. There are a few stores, butcher, baker, *épicerie*, a hardware store, and a money-changer—who cannot change travelers' checks, but must send them down to the bank, an operation which takes two or three days. There is something called the *Ballet Haus*, closed in the winter and used for God knows what, certainly not ballet, during the summer. There seems to be only one schoolhouse in the village, and this for the quite young children; I suppose this to mean that their older brothers and sisters at some point descend from these mountains in order to complete their education—possibly, again, to the town just below. The landscape is absolutely forbidding, mountains towering on all four sides, ice and snow as far as the eye can reach. In this white wilderness, men and women and children move all day, carrying washing, wood, buckets of milk or water, sometimes skiing on Sunday afternoons. All week long boys and young men are to be seen shoveling snow off the rooftops, or dragging wood down from the forest in sleds.

The village's only real attraction, which explains the tourist season, is the hot spring water. A disquietingly high proportion of these tourists are cripples, or semi-cripples, who come year after year—from other parts of Switzerland, usually—to take the waters. This lends the village, at the height of the season, a rather terrifying air of sanctity, as though it were a lesser Lourdes. There is often something beautiful, there is always something awful, in the spectacle of a person who has lost one of his faculties, a faculty he never questioned until it was gone, and who struggles to recover it. Yet people remain people, on crutches or indeed on deathbeds; and wherever I passed, the first summer I was here, among the native villagers or among the lame, a wind passed with me—of astonishment, curiosity, amusement, and outrage. That first summer I stayed two weeks and never intended to return. But I did return in the winter, to work; the village offers, obviously, no distractions whatever and has the further advantage of being extremely cheap. Now it is winter again, a year later, and I am here again. Everyone in the village knows my name, though they scarcely ever use it, knows that I come from America—though, this, apparently, they will never really believe: black men come from Africa—and everyone knows that I am the friend of the son of a woman who was born here, and that I am staying in their chalet. But I remain as much a stranger today as I was the first day I arrived, and the children shout *Neger! Neger!* as I walk along the streets.

It must be admitted that in the beginning I was far too shocked to have any real reaction. In so far as I reacted at all, I reacted by trying to be pleasant—it being a great part of the American Negro's education (long before he goes to school) that he must make people "like" him. This smile-and-the-world-smiles-with-you routine worked about as well in this situation as it had in the situation for which it was designed, which is to say that it did not work at all. No one, after all, can be liked whose human weight and complexity cannot be, or has not been, admitted. My smile was simply another unheard-of phenomenon which allowed them to see my teeth—they did not, really, see my smile and I began to think that, should I take to snarling, no one would notice any difference. All of the physical characteristics of the Negro which had caused me, in America, a very different and almost forgotten pain were nothing less than miraculous—or infernal—in the eyes of the village people. Some thought my hair was the color of tar, that it had the texture of wire, or the texture of cotton. It was jocularly suggested that I might let it all grow long and make myself a winter coat. If I sat in the sun for more than five minutes some daring creature was certain to come along and gingerly put his fingers on my hair, as though he were afraid of an electric shock, or put his hand on my hand, astonished that the color did not rub off. In all of this, in which it must be conceded there was the charm of genuine wonder and in which there were certainly no element of intentional unkindness, there was yet no suggestion that I was human: I was simply a living wonder.

I knew that they did not mean to be unkind, and I know it now; it is   5
necessary, nevertheless, for me to repeat this to myself each time that I walk out of the chalet. The children who shout *Neger!* have no way of knowing the echoes this sound raises in me. They are brimming with good humor and the more daring swell with pride when I stop to speak with them. Just the same, there are days when I cannot pause and smile, when I have no heart to play with them; when, indeed, I mutter sourly to myself, exactly as I muttered on the streets of a city these children

have never seen, when I was no bigger than these children are now: *Your* mother *was a nigger.* Joyce is right about history being a nightmare— but it may be the nightmare from which no one *can* awaken. People are trapped in history and history is trapped in them.

There is a custom in the village—I am told it is repeated in many villages—of "buying" African natives for the purpose of converting them to Christianity. There stands in the church all year round a small box with a slot for money, decorated with a black figurine, and into this box the villagers drop their francs. During the *carnaval* which precedes Lent, two village children have their faces blackened—out of which blood- less darkness their blue eyes shine like ice—and fantastic horsehair wigs are placed on their blond heads; thus disguised, they solicit among the villagers for money for the missionaries in Africa. Between the box in the church and the blackened children, the village "bought" last year six or eight African natives. This was reported to me with pride by the wife of one of the *bistro* owners and I was careful to express astonishment and pleasure at the solicitude shown by the village for the souls of black folks. The *bistro* owner's wife beamed with a pleasure far more genuine than my own and seemed to feel that I might now breathe more easily concerning the souls of at least six of my kinsmen.

I tried not to think of these so lately baptized kinsmen, of the price paid for them, or the peculiar price they themselves would pay, and said nothing about my father, who having taken his own conversion too literally never, at bottom, forgave the white world (which he described as heathen) for having saddled him with a Christ in whom, to judge at least from their treatment of him, they themselves no longer believed. I thought of white men arriving for the first time in an African vil- lage, strangers there, as I am a stranger here, and tried to imagine the astounded populace touching their hair and marveling at the color of their skin. But there is a great difference between being the first white man to be seen by Africans and being the first black man to be seen by whites. The white man takes the astonishment as tribute, for he arrives to conquer and to convert the natives, whose inferiority in relation to himself is not even to be questioned; whereas I, without a thought of conquest, find myself among a people whose culture controls me, has even, in a sense, created me, people who have cost me more in anguish and rage than they will ever know, who yet do not even know of my existence. The astonishment with which I might have greeted them, should they have stumbled into my African village a few hundred years ago, might have rejoiced their hearts. But the astonishment with which they greet me today can only poison mine.

And this is so despite everything I may do to feel differently, despite my friendly conversations with the *bistro* owner's wife, despite their three-year-old son who has at last become my friend, despite the *saluts* and *bonsoirs* which I exchange with people as I walk, despite the fact that I know that no individual can be taken to task for what history is doing, or has done. I say that the culture of these people controls me— but they can scarcely be held responsible for European culture. America comes out of Europe, but these people have never seen America, nor have most of them seen more of Europe than the hamlet at the foot of their mountain. Yet they move with an authority which I shall never have; and they regard me, quite rightly, not only as a stranger in their village but as a suspect latecomer, bearing no credentials, to everything they have—however unconsciously—inherited.

For this village, even were it incomparably more remote and incredibly more primitive, is the West, the West onto which I have been so strangely grafted. These people cannot be, from the point of view of power, strangers anywhere in the world; they have made the modern world, in effect, even if they do not know it. The most illiterate among them is related, in a way that I am not, to Dante, Shakespeare, Michelangelo, Aeschylus, Da Vinci, Rembrandt, and Racine; the cathedral at Chartres says something to them which it cannot say to me, as indeed would New York's Empire State Building, should anyone here ever see it. Out of their hymns and dances come Beethoven and Bach. Go back a few centuries and they are in their full glory—but I am in Africa, watching the conquerors arrive.

The rage of the disesteemed is personally fruitless, but it is also abso- 10 lutely inevitable; this rage, so generally discounted, so little understood even among the people whose daily bread it is, is one of the things that makes history. Rage can only with difficulty, and never entirely, be brought under the domination of the intelligence and is therefore not susceptible to any arguments whatever. This is a fact which ordinary representatives of the *Herrenvolk,* having never felt this rage and being unable to imagine, quite fail to understand. Also, rage cannot be hidden, it can only be dissembled. This dissembling deludes the thoughtless, and strengthens rage and adds, to rage, contempt. There are, no doubt, as many ways of coping with the resulting complex of tensions as there are black men in the world, but no black man can hope ever to be entirely liberated from this internal warfare—rage, dissembling, and contempt having inevitably accompanied his first realization of the power of white men. What is crucial here is that, since white men represent in the black man's world so heavy a weight, white men have for black men a reality which is far from being reciprocal; and hence all black men have toward all white men an attitude which is designed, really, either to rob the white man of the jewel of his naïveté, or else to make it cost him dear.

The black man insists, by whatever means he finds at his disposal, that the white man cease to regard him as an exotic rarity and recognize him as a human being. This is a very charged and difficult moment, for there is a great deal of will power involved in the white man's naïveté. Most people are not naturally reflective any more than they are naturally malicious, and the white man prefers to keep the black man at a certain human remove because it is easier for him thus to preserve his simplicity and avoid being called to account for crimes committed by his forefathers, or his neighbors. He is inescapably aware, nevertheless, that he is in a better position in the world than black men are, nor can he quite put to death the suspicion that he is hated by black men therefore.

He does not wish to be hated, neither does he wish to change places, and at this point in his uneasiness he can scarcely avoid having recourse to those legends which white men have created about black men, the most usual effect of which is that the white man finds himself enmeshed, so to speak, in his own language which describes hell, as well as the attributes which lead one to hell, as being as black as night.

Every legend, moreover, contains its residuum of truth, and the root function of language is to control the universe by describing it. It is of quite considerable significance that black men remain, in the imagination, and in overwhelming numbers in fact, beyond the disciplines of salvation; and this despite the fact that the West has been "buying" African natives for centuries. There is, I should hazard, an instantaneous necessity to be divorced from this so visibly unsaved stranger, in whose heart, moreover, one cannot guess what dreams of vengeance are being nourished; and, at the same time, there are few things on earth more attractive than the idea of the unspeakable liberty which is allowed the unredeemed. When, beneath the black mask, a human being begins to make himself felt one cannot escape a certain awful wonder as to what kind of human being it is. What one's imagination makes of other people is dictated, of course, by the laws of one's own personality and it is one of the ironies of black-white relations that, by means of what the white man imagines the black man to be, the black man is enabled to know who the white man is.

I have said, for example, that I am as much a stranger in this village today as I was the first summer I arrived, but this is not quite true. The villagers wonder less about the texture of my hair than they did then, and wonder rather more about me. And the fact that their wonder now exists on another level is reflected in their attitudes and in their eyes. There are the children who make those delightful, hilarious, sometimes astonishingly grave overtures of friendship in the unpredictable fashion of children; other children, having been taught that the devil is a black man, scream in genuine anguish as I approach. Some of the older women never pass without a friendly greeting, never pass, indeed, if it seems that they will be able to engage me in conversation; other women look down or look away or rather contemptuously smirk. Some of the men drink with me and suggest that I learn how to ski—partly, I gather, because they cannot imagine what I would look like on skis—and want to know if I am married, and ask questions about my *métier.* But some of the men have accused *le sale nègre*—behind my back—of stealing wood and there is already in the eyes of some of them that peculiar, intent, paranoiac malevolence which one sometimes surprises in the eyes of American white men when, out walking with their Sunday girl, they see a Negro male approach.

There is a dreadful abyss between the streets of this village and the streets of the city in which I was born, between the children who shout *Neger!* today and those who shouted *Nigger!* yesterday—the abyss is experience, the American experience. The syllable hurled behind me today expresses, above all, wonder: I am a stranger here. But I am not a stranger in America and the same syllable riding on the American air expresses the war my presence has occasioned in the American soul.

For this village brings home to me this fact: that there was a day, 15 and not really a very distant day, when Americans were scarcely Americans at all but discontented Europeans, facing a great unconquered continent and strolling, say, into a marketplace and seeing black men for the first time. The shock this spectacle afforded is suggested, surely, by the promptness with which they decided that these black men were not really men but cattle. It is true that the necessity on the part of the settlers of the New World of reconciling their moral assumptions with the fact—and the necessity—of slavery enhanced immensely the charm of this idea, and it is also true that this idea expresses, with a truly American bluntness, the attitude which to varying extents all masters have had toward all slaves.

But between all former slaves and slave-owners and the drama which begins for Americans over three hundred years ago at Jamestown, there are at least two differences to be observed. The American Negro slave could not suppose, for one thing, as slaves in past epochs had supposed and often done, that he would ever be able to wrest the power from his master's hands. This was a supposition which the modern era, which was to bring about such vast changes in the aims and dimensions of power, put to death; it only begins, in unprecedented fashion, and with dreadful implications, to be resurrected today. But even had this supposition persisted with undiminished force, the American Negro slave could not have used it to lend his condition dignity, for the reason that this supposition rests on another: that the slave in exile yet remains related to his past, has some means—if only in memory—of revering and sustaining the forms of his former life, is able, in short, to maintain his identity.

This was not the case with the American Negro slave. He is unique among the black men of the world in that his past was taken from him, almost literally, at one blow. One wonders what on earth the first slave found to say to the first dark child he bore. I am told that there are Haitians able to trace their ancestry back to African kings, but any American Negro wishing to go back so far will find his journey through time abruptly arrested by the signature on the bill of sale which served as the entrance paper for his ancestor. At the time—to say nothing of the circumstances—of the enslavement of the captive black man who was to become the American Negro, there was not the remotest possibility that he would ever take power from his master's hands. There was no reason to suppose that his situation would ever change, nor was there, shortly, anything to indicate that his situation had ever been different. It was his necessity, in the words of E. Franklin Frazier, to find a "motive for living under American culture or die." The identity of the American Negro comes out of this extreme situation, and the evolution of this identity was a source of the most intolerable anxiety in the minds and the lives of his masters.

For the history of the American Negro is unique also in this: that the question of his humanity, and of his rights therefore as a human being, became a burning one for several generations of Americans, so burning a question that it ultimately became one of those used to divide the nation. It is out of this argument that the venom of the epithet *Nigger!* is derived. It is an argument which Europe has never had, and hence Europe quite sincerely fails to understand how or why the argument arose in the first place, why its effects are frequently disastrous and always so unpredictable, why it refuses until today to be entirely settled. Europe's black possessions remained—and do remain—in Europe's colonies, at which remove they represented no threat whatever to European identity. If they posed any problem at all for the European conscience it was a problem which remained comfortingly abstract: in effect, the black man, as a *man* did not exist for Europe. But in America, even as a slave, he was an inescapable part of the general social fabric and no American could escape having an attitude toward him. Americans attempt until today to make an abstraction of the Negro, but the very nature of these abstractions reveals the tremendous effects the presence of the Negro has had on the American character.

When one considers the history of the Negro in America it is of the greatest importance to recognize that the moral beliefs of a person, or a people, are never really as tenuous as life—which is not moral—very often causes them to appear; these create for them a frame of reference and a necessary hope, the hope being that when life has done its worst they will be enabled to rise above themselves and to triumph over life. Life would scarcely be bearable if this hope did not exist. Again, even when the worst has been said, to betray a belief is not by any means to have put oneself beyond its power; the betrayal of a belief is not the same thing as ceasing to believe. If this were not so there would be no moral standards in the world at all. Yet one must also recognize that morality is based on ideas and that all ideas are dangerous—dangerous because ideas can only lead to action and where the action leads no man can say. And dangerous in this respect: that confronted with the impossibility of remaining faithful to one's beliefs, and the equal impossibility of becoming free of them, one can be driven to the most inhuman excesses. The ideas on which American beliefs are based are not, though Americans often seem to think so, ideas which originated in America. They came out of Europe. And the establishment of democracy on the American continent was scarcely as radical a break with the past as was the necessity, which Americans faced, of broadening this concept to include black men.

This was, literally, a hard necessity. It was impossible, for one thing,   20
for Americans to abandon their beliefs, not only because these beliefs alone seemed able to justify the sacrifices they had endured and the blood that they had spilled, but also because these beliefs afforded them their only bulwark against a moral chaos as absolute as the physical chaos of the continent it was their destiny to conquer. But in the situation in which Americans found themselves, these beliefs threatened an idea which, whether or not one likes to think so, is the very warp and woof of the heritage of the West, the idea of white supremacy.

Americans have made themselves notorious by the shrillness and the brutality with which they have insisted on this idea, but they did not invent it; and it has escaped the world's notice that those very excesses of which Americans have been guilty imply a certain, unprecedented uneasiness over the idea's life and power, if not, indeed, the idea's validity. The idea of white supremacy rests simply on the fact that white men are the creators of civilization (the present civilization, which is the only one that matters; all previous civilizations are simply "contributions" to our own) and are therefore civilization's guardians and defenders. Thus it was impossible for Americans to accept the black man as one of themselves, for to do so was to jeopardize their status as white men. But not so to accept him was to deny his human reality, his human weight and complexity, and the strain of denying the overwhelmingly undeniable forced Americans into rationalizations so fantastic that they approached the pathological.

At the root of the American Negro problem is the necessity of the American white man to find a way of living with the Negro in order to be able to live with himself. And the history of this problem can be reduced to the means used by Americans—lynch law and law, segregation and legal acceptance, terrorization and concession—either to come to terms with this necessity, or to find a way around it, or (most usually) to find a way of doing both these things at once. The resulting spectacle, at once foolish and dreadful, led someone to make the quite accurate observation that "the Negro-in-America is a form of insanity which overtakes white men."

In this long battle, a battle by no means finished, the unforeseeable effects of which will be felt by many future generations, the white man's motive was the protection of his identity; the black man was motivated by the need to establish an identity. And despite the terrorization which the Negro in America endured and endures sporadically until today, despite the cruel and totally inescapable ambivalence of his status in his country, the battle for his identity has long ago been won. He is not a visitor to the West, but a citizen there, an American; as American as the Americans who despise him, the Americans who fear him, the Americans who love him—the Americans who became less than themselves, or rose to be greater than themselves by virtue of the fact that the challenge he represented was inescapable. He is perhaps the only black man in the world whose relationship to white men is more terrible, more subtle, and more meaningful than the relationship of bitter possessed to uncertain possessors. His survival depended, and his development depends, on his ability to turn his peculiar status in the Western world to his own advantage and, it may be, to the very great advantage of that world. It remains for him to fashion out of his experience that which will give him sustenance, and a voice.

The cathedral at Chartres, I have said, says something to the people of this village which it cannot say to me; but it is important to understand that this cathedral says something to me which it cannot say to them. Perhaps they are struck by the power of the spires, the glory of the windows; but they have known God, after all, longer than I have known him, and in a different way, and I am terrified by the slippery bottomless well to be found in the crypt, down which heretics were hurled to death, and by the obscene, inescapable gargoyles jutting out of the stone and seeming to say that God and the devil can never be divorced. I doubt that the villagers think of the devil when they face a cathedral because they have never been identified with the devil. But I must accept the status which myth, if nothing else, gives me in the West before I can hope to change the myth.

Yet, if the American Negro has arrived at his identity by virtue of   25
the absoluteness of his estrangement from his past, American white men still nourish the illusion that there is some means of recovering the European innocence, of returning to a state in which black men do not exist. This is one of the greatest errors Americans can make. The identity they fought so hard to protect has, by virtue of that battle, undergone a change: Americans are as unlike any other white people in the world as it is possible to be. I do not think, for example, that it is too much to suggest that the American vision of the world—which allows so little reality, generally speaking, for any of the darker forces in human life, which tends until today to paint moral issues in glaring black and white—owes a great deal to the battle waged by Americans to maintain between themselves and black men a human separation which could not be bridged. It is only now beginning to be borne in on us—very faintly, it must be admitted, very slowly, and very much against our will—that this vision of the world is dangerously inaccurate, and perfectly useless. For it protects our moral high-mindedness at the terrible expense of weakening our grasp of reality. People who shut their eyes to reality simply invite their own destruction, and anyone who insists on remaining in a state of innocence long after that innocence is dead turns himself into a monster.

The time has come to realize that the interracial drama acted out on the American continent has not only created a new black man, it has created a new white man, too. No road whatever will lead Americans back to the simplicity of this European village where white men still have the luxury of looking on me as a stranger. I am not, really, a stranger any longer for any American alive. One of the things that distinguishes Americans from other people is that no other people has ever been so deeply involved in the lives of black men, and vice versa. This fact faced, with all its implications, it can be seen that the history of the American Negro problem is not merely shameful, it is also something of an achievement. For even when the worst has been said, it must also be added that the perpetual challenge posed by this problem was always, somehow, perpetually met. It is precisely this black-white experience which may prove of indispensable value to us in the world we face today. This world is white no longer, and it will never be white again.

Thinking about the Text

1. James Baldwin spends roughly half of the essay recounting his experience in a small Swiss village and the rest of the essay reflecting on the roots and effects of "the interracial drama acted out on the American continent" (paragraph 26). How does Baldwin's reception in the Swiss village help him frame a larger cultural critique?

2. Like Baldwin, Zora Neale Hurston in "How It Feels to Be Colored Me" (pp. 11–16) describes her feelings and sense of identity in various situations and communities—and as an American. In what ways do their experiences and how they write about them differ? What might account for such differences?

3. Traveling to an unfamiliar place can often help us reflect on our own identity and place in a community, perhaps even allowing us to see our own family, home community, or country with more clarity. Write about an experience you have had as a stranger in a new place or unfamiliar circumstance. How were you received by others? How did you see them? Did this experience make you see your home community or country in a new way?

MARTIN LUTHER KING JR.

Letter from Birmingham Jail

1963

MARTIN LUTHER KING JR. (1929–1968), a minister and civil rights activist, wrote primarily speeches and sermons, which he published in books such as *Strength to Love* (1963) and *Why We Can't Wait* (1964). "Letter from Birmingham Jail" was written in April 1963 at the height of the civil rights movement when King was arrested for civil disobedience after participating in a peaceful protest. It was a response to an open letter addressed to King by eight, moderate clergymen who encouraged the black community to stop demonstrating. King's letter appeared in a range of political and religious publications—*Liberation*, the *Christian Century*, and the *New Leader*—in June of that year and was later included in King's book *Why We Can't Wait*. This letter has been published in every edition of *The Norton Reader* since the second edition.

MY DEAR FELLOW CLERGYMEN:[1]

While confined here in the Birmingham city jail, I came across your recent statement calling my present activities "unwise and untimely." Seldom do I pause to answer criticism of my work and ideas. If I sought to answer all the criticisms that cross my desk, my secretaries would have little time for anything other than such correspondence in the course of the day, and I would have no time for constructive work. But since I feel that you are men of genuine good will and that your criticisms are sincerely set forth, I want to try to answer your statement in what I hope will be patient and reasonable terms.

I think I should indicate why I am here in Birmingham, since you have been influenced by the view which argues against "outsiders coming in." I have the honor of serving as president of the Southern Christian Leadership Conference, an organization operating in every southern state, with headquarters in Atlanta, Georgia. We have some eighty-five affiliated organizations across the South, and one of them is the Alabama Christian Movement for Human Rights. Frequently we share staff, educational, and financial resources with our affiliates. Several months ago the affiliate here in Birmingham asked us to be on call to engage in a nonviolent direct-action program if such were deemed necessary. We readily consented, and when the hour came we lived up to our promise. So I, along with several members of my staff, am here because I was invited here. I am here because I have organizational ties here.

1. This response to a published statement by eight fellow clergymen from Alabama (Bishop C. C. J. Carpenter, Bishop Joseph A. Durick, Rabbi Milton L. Grafman, Bishop Paul Hardin, Bishop Nolan B. Harmon, the Reverend George M. Murray, the Reverend Edward V. Ramage and the Reverend Earl Stallings) was composed under somewhat constricting circumstances. Begun on the margins of the newspaper in which the statement appeared while I was in jail, the letter was continued on scraps of writing paper supplied by a friendly Negro trusty, and concluded on a pad my attorneys were eventually permitted to leave me. Although the text remains in substance unaltered, I have indulged in the author's prerogative of polishing it for publication [King's note].

But more basically, I am in Birmingham because injustice is here. Just as the prophets of the eighth century B.C. left their villages and carried their "thus saith the Lord" far beyond the boundaries of their home towns, and just as the Apostle Paul left his village of Tarsus and carried the gospel of Jesus Christ to the far corners of the Greco-Roman world, so am I compelled to carry the gospel of freedom beyond my own home town. Like Paul, I must constantly respond to the Macedonian call for aid.

Moreover, I am cognizant of the interrelatedness of all communities and states. I cannot sit idly by in Atlanta and not be concerned about what happens in Birmingham. Injustice anywhere is a threat to justice everywhere. We are caught in an inescapable network of mutuality, tied in a single garment of destiny. Whatever affects one directly, affects all indirectly. Never again can we afford to live with the narrow, provincial "outside agitator" idea. Anyone who lives inside the United States can never be considered an outsider anywhere within its bounds.

You deplore the demonstrations taking place in Birmingham. But   5 your statement, I am sorry to say, fails to express a similar concern for the conditions that brought about the demonstrations. I am sure that none of you would want to rest content with the superficial kind of social analysis that deals merely with effects and does not grapple with underlying causes. It is unfortunate that demonstrations are taking place in Birmingham, but it is even more unfortunate that the city's white power structure left the Negro community with no alternative.

In any nonviolent campaign there are four basic steps: collection of the facts to determine whether injustices exist; negotiation; self-purification; and direct action. We have gone through all these steps in Birmingham. There can be no gainsaying the fact that racial injustice engulfs this community. Birmingham is probably the most thoroughly segregated city in the United States. Its ugly record of brutality is widely known. Negroes have experienced grossly unjust treatment in the courts.

There have been more unsolved bombings of Negro homes and churches in Birmingham than in any other city in the nation. These are the hard, brutal facts of the case. On the basis of these conditions, Negro leaders sought to negotiate with the city fathers. But the latter consistently refused to engage in good-faith negotiation.

Then, last September, came the opportunity to talk with leaders of Birmingham's economic community. In the course of the negotiations, certain promises were made by the merchants—for example, to remove the stores' humiliating racial signs. On the basis of these promises, the Reverend Fred Shuttlesworth and the leaders of the Alabama Christian Movement for Human Rights agreed to a moratorium on all demonstrations. As the weeks and months went by, we realized that we were the victims of a broken promise. A few signs, briefly removed, returned; the others remained.

As in so many past experiences, our hopes had been blasted, and the shadow of deep disappointment settled upon us. We had no alternative except to prepare for direct action, whereby we would present our very bodies as a means of laying our case before the conscience of the local and the national community. Mindful of the difficulties involved, we decided to undertake a process of self-purification. We began a series of workshops on nonviolence, and we repeatedly asked ourselves: "Are you able to accept blows without retaliating?" "Are you able to endure the ordeal of jail?" We decided to schedule our direct-action program for the Easter season, realizing that except for Christmas, this is the main shopping period of the year. Knowing that a strong economic-withdrawal program would be the by-product of direct action, we felt that this would be the best time to bring pressure to bear on the merchants for the needed change.

Then it occurred to us that Birmingham's mayoral election was coming up in March, and we speedily decided to postpone action until after election day. When we discovered that the Commissioner of Public Safety, Eugene "Bull" Connor, had piled up enough votes to be in the run-off, we decided again to postpone action until the day after the run-off so that the demonstrations could not be used to cloud the issues. Like many others, we wanted to see Mr. Connor defeated, and to this end we endured postponement after postponement. Having aided in this community need, we felt that our direct-action program could be delayed no longer.

You may well ask, "Why direct action? Why sit-ins, marches, and so 10 forth? Isn't negotiation a better path?" You are quite right in calling for negotiation. Indeed, this is the very purpose of direct action. Nonviolent direct action seeks to create such a crisis and foster such a tension that a community which has constantly refused to negotiate is forced to confront the issue. It seeks so to dramatize the issue that it can no longer be ignored. My citing the creation of tension as part of the work of the nonviolent-resister may sound rather shocking. But I must confess that I am not afraid of the word "tension." I have earnestly opposed violent tension, but there is a type of constructive, nonviolent tension which is necessary for growth. Just as Socrates felt that it was necessary to create a tension in the mind so that individuals could rise from the bondage of myths and half-truths to the unfettered realm of creative analysis and objective appraisal, so must we see the need for nonviolent gadflies to create the kind of tension in society that will help men rise from the dark depths of prejudice and racism to the majestic heights of understanding and brotherhood.

The purpose of our direct-action program is to create a situation so crisis-packed that it will inevitably open the door to negotiation. I therefore concur with you in your call for negotiation. Too long has our beloved Southland been bogged down in a tragic effort to live in monologue rather than dialogue.

One of the basic points in your statement is that the action that I and my associates have taken in Birmingham is untimely. Some have asked: "Why didn't you give the new city administration time to act?" The only answer that I can give to this query is that the new Birmingham administration must be prodded about as much as the outgoing one, before it will act. We are sadly mistaken if we feel that the election of Albert Boutwell as mayor will bring the millennium to Birmingham. While Mr. Boutwell is a much more gentle person than Mr. Connor, they are both segregationists, dedicated to maintenance of the status quo. I have hoped that Mr. Boutwell will be reasonable enough to see the futility of massive resistance to desegregation. But he will not see this without pressure from devotees of civil rights. My friends, I must say to you that we have not made a single gain in civil rights without determined legal and nonviolent pressure. Lamentably, it is an historical fact that privileged groups seldom give up their privileges voluntarily. Individuals may see the moral light and voluntarily give up their unjust posture; but, as Reinhold Niebuhr has reminded us, groups tend to be more immoral than individuals.

We know through painful experience that freedom is never voluntarily given by the oppressor; it must be demanded by the oppressed. Frankly, I have yet to engage in a direct-action campaign that was "well timed" in the view of those who have not suffered unduly from the disease of segregation. For years now I have heard the word "Wait!" It rings in the ear of every Negro with piercing familiarity. This "Wait" has almost always meant "Never." We must come to see, with one of our distinguished jurists, that "justice too long delayed is justice denied."

We have waited for more than 340 years for our constitutional and God-given rights. The nations of Asia and Africa are moving with jet-like speed toward gaining political independence, but we still creep at horse-and-buggy pace toward gaining a cup of coffee at a lunch counter. Perhaps it is easy for those who have never felt the stinging darts of segregation to say, "Wait." But when you have seen vicious mobs lynch your mothers and fathers at will and drown your sisters and brothers at whim; when you have seen hate-filled policemen curse, kick, and even kill your black brothers and sisters; when you see the vast majority of your twenty million Negro brothers smothering in an airtight cage of poverty in the midst of an affluent society; when you suddenly find your tongue twisted and your speech stammering as you seek to explain to your six-year-old daughter why she can't go to the public amusement park that has just been advertised on television, and see tears welling up in her eyes when she is told that Funtown is closed to colored children, and see ominous clouds of inferiority beginning to form in her little mental sky, and see her beginning to distort her personality by developing an unconscious bitterness toward white people; when you have to concoct an answer for a five-year-old son who is asking, "Daddy, why do white people treat colored people so mean?"; when you take a cross-country drive and find it necessary to sleep night after night in the uncomfortable corners of your automobile because no motel will accept you; when you are humiliated day in and day out by nagging signs reading "white" and "colored"; when your first name becomes "nigger," your middle name becomes "boy" (however old you are) and your last name becomes "John," and your wife and mother are never given the respected title "Mrs."; when you are harried by day and haunted by night by the fact that you are a Negro, living constantly at tiptoe stance, never quite knowing what to expect next, and are plagued with inner fears and outer resentments; when you are forever fighting a degenerating sense of "nobodiness"—then you will understand why we find it difficult to wait. There comes a time when the cup of endurance runs over, and men are no longer willing to be plunged into the abyss of despair. I hope, sirs, you can understand our legitimate and unavoidable impatience.

You express a great deal of anxiety over our willingness to break   15
laws. This is certainly a legitimate concern. Since we so diligently urge people to obey the Supreme Court's decision of 1954 outlawing segregation in the public schools, at first glance it may seem rather paradoxical for us consciously to break laws. One may well ask: "How can you advocate breaking some laws and obeying others?" The answer lies in the fact that there are two types of laws: just and unjust. I would be the first to advocate obeying just laws. One has not only a legal but a

moral responsibility to obey just laws. Conversely, one has a moral responsibility to disobey unjust laws. I would agree with St. Augustine that "an unjust law is no law at all."

Now, what is the difference between the two? How does one determine whether a law is just or unjust? A just law is a man-made code that squares with the moral law or the law of God. An unjust law is a code that is out of harmony with the moral law. To put it in the terms of St. Thomas Aquinas: An unjust law is a human law that is not rooted in eternal law and natural law. Any law that uplifts human personality is just. Any law that degrades human personality is unjust. All segregation statutes are unjust because segregation distorts the soul and damages the personality. It gives the segregator a false sense of superiority and the segregated a false sense of inferiority. Segregation, to use the terminology of the Jewish philosopher Martin Buber, substitutes an "I-it" relationship for an "I-thou" relationship and ends up relegating persons to the status of things. Hence segregation is not only politically, economically, and sociologically unsound, it is morally wrong and sinful. Paul Tillich has said that sin is separation. Is not segregation an existential expression of man's tragic separation, his awful estrangement, his terrible sinfulness? Thus it is that I can urge men to obey the 1954 decision of the Supreme Court, for it is morally right; and I can urge them to disobey segregation ordinances, for they are morally wrong.

Let us consider a more concrete example of just and unjust laws. An unjust law is a code that a numerical or power majority group compels a minority group to obey but does not make binding on itself. This is *difference* made legal. By the same token, a just law is a code that a majority compels a minority to follow and that it is willing to follow itself. This is *sameness* made legal.

Let me give another explanation. A law is unjust if it is inflicted on a minority that, as a result of being denied the right to vote, had no part in enacting or devising the law. Who can say that the legislature of Alabama which set up that state's segregation laws was democratically elected? Throughout Alabama all sorts of devious methods are used to prevent Negroes from becoming registered voters, and there are some counties in which, even though Negroes constitute a majority of the population, not a single Negro is registered. Can any law enacted under such circumstances be considered democratically structured?

Sometimes a law is just on its face and unjust in its application. For instance, I have been arrested on a charge of parading without a permit. Now, there is nothing wrong in having an ordinance which requires a permit for a parade. But such an ordinance becomes unjust when it is used to maintain segregation and to deny citizens the First-Amendment privilege of peaceful assembly and protest.

I hope you are able to see the distinction I am trying to point out. In no sense do I advocate evading or defying the law, as would the rabid segregationist. That would lead to anarchy. One who breaks an unjust law must do so openly, lovingly, and with a willingness to accept the penalty. I submit that an individual who breaks a law that conscience tells him is unjust, and who willingly accepts the penalty of imprisonment in order to arouse the conscience of the community over its injustice, is in reality expressing the highest respect for law.

Of course, there is nothing new about this kind of civil disobedience. It was evidenced sublimely in the refusal of Shadrach, Meshach, and Abednego to obey the laws of Nebuchadnezzar, on the ground that a higher moral law was at stake. It was practiced superbly by the early Christians, who were willing to face hungry lions and the excruciating pain of chopping blocks rather than submit to certain unjust laws of the Roman Empire. To a degree, academic freedom is a reality today because Socrates practiced civil disobedience. In our own nation, the Boston Tea Party represented a massive act of civil disobedience.

We should never forget that everything Adolf Hitler did in Germany was "legal" and everything the Hungarian freedom fighters did in Hungary was "illegal." It was "illegal" to aid and comfort a Jew in Hitler's Germany. Even so, I am sure that, had I lived in Germany at the time, I would have aided and comforted my Jewish brothers. If today I lived in a Communist country where certain principles dear to the Christian faith are suppressed, I would openly advocate disobeying that country's anti-religious laws.

I must make two honest confessions to you, my Christian and Jewish brothers. First, I must confess that over the past few years I have been gravely disappointed with the white moderate. I have almost reached the regrettable conclusion that the Negro's great stumbling block in his stride toward freedom is not the White Citizen's Counciler or the Ku Klux Klanner, but the white moderate, who is more devoted to "order" than to justice; who prefers a negative peace which is the absence of tension to a positive peace which is the presence of justice; who constantly says, "I agree with you in the goal you seek, but I cannot agree with your methods of direct action"; who paternalistically believes he can set the timetable for another man's freedom; who lives by a mythical concept of time and who constantly advises the Negro to wait for a "more convenient season." Shallow understanding from people of good will is more frustrating than absolute misunderstanding from people of ill will. Lukewarm acceptance is much more bewildering than outright rejection.

I had hoped that the white moderate would understand that law and order exist for the purpose of establishing justice and that when they fail in this purpose they become the dangerously structured dams that block the flow of social progress. I had hoped that the white moderate would understand that the present tension in the South is a necessary phase of the transition from an obnoxious negative peace, in which the Negro passively accepted his unjust plight, to a substantive and positive peace, in which all men will respect the dignity and worth of human personality. Actually, we who engage in nonviolent direct action are not the creators of tension. We merely bring to the surface the hidden tension that is already alive. We bring it out in the open, where it can be seen and dealt with. Like a boil that can never be cured so long as it is covered up but must be opened with all its ugliness to the natural medicines of air and light, injustice must be exposed, with all the tension its exposure creates, to the light of human conscience and the air of national opinion, before it can be cured.

In your statement you assert that our actions, even though peaceful, must be condemned because they precipitate violence. But is this a logical assertion? Isn't this like condemning a robbed man because his possession of money precipitated the evil act of robbery? Isn't this like condemning Socrates because his unswerving commitment to truth and his philosophical inquiries precipitated the act by the misguided populace in which they made him drink hemlock? Isn't this like condemning Jesus because his unique God-consciousness and never-ceasing devotion to God's will precipitated the evil act of crucifixion? We must come to see that, as the federal courts have consistently affirmed, it is wrong to urge an individual to cease his efforts to gain his basic constitutional rights because the quest may precipitate violence. Society must protect the robbed and punish the robber.

I had also hoped that the white moderate would reject the myth concerning time in relation to the struggle for freedom. I have just received a letter from a white brother in Texas. He writes: "All Christians know that the colored people will receive equal rights eventually, but it is possible that you are in too great a religious hurry. It has taken Christianity almost two thousand years to accomplish what it has. The teachings of Christ take time to come to earth." Such an attitude stems from a tragic misconception of time, from the strangely irrational notion that there is something in the very flow of time that will inevitably cure all ills. Actually, time itself is neutral; it can be used either destructively or constructively. More and more I feel that the people of ill will have used time much more effectively than have the people of good will. We will have to repent in this generation not merely for the hateful words and actions of the bad people, but for the appalling silence of the good people. Human progress never rolls in on wheels of inevitability; it comes through the tireless efforts of men willing to be co-workers with God, and without this hard work, time itself becomes an ally of the forces of social stagnation. We must use time creatively, in the knowledge that the time is always ripe to do right. Now is the time to make real the promise of democracy and transform our pending national elegy into a creative psalm of brotherhood. Now is the time to lift our national policy from the quicksand of racial injustice to the solid rock of human dignity.

You speak of our activity in Birmingham as extreme. At first I was rather disappointed that fellow clergymen would see my nonviolent efforts as those of an extremist. I began thinking about the fact that I stand in the middle of two opposing forces in the Negro community. One is a force of complacency, made up in part of Negroes who, as a result of long years of oppression, are so drained of self-respect and a sense of "somebodiness" that they have adjusted to segregation; and in part of a few middle-class Negroes who, because of a degree of academic and economic security and because in some ways they profit by segregation, have become insensitive to the problems of the masses. The other force is one of bitterness and hatred, and it comes perilously close to advocating violence. It is expressed in the various black nationalist groups that are springing up across the nation, the largest and best-known being Elijah Muhammad's Muslim movement. Nourished by the Negro's frustration over the continued existence of racial discrimination, this movement is made up of people who have lost faith in America, who have absolutely repudiated Christianity, and who have concluded that the white man is an incorrigible "devil."

I have tried to stand between these two forces, saying that we need emulate neither the "do-nothingism" of the complacent nor the hatred and despair of the black nationalist. For there is the more excellent way of love and non-violent protest. I am grateful to God that, through the influence of the Negro church, the way of nonviolence became an integral part of our struggle.

If this philosophy had not emerged, by now many streets of the South would, I am convinced, be flowing with blood. And I am further convinced that if our white brothers dismiss as "rabblerousers" and "outside agitators" those of us who employ nonviolent direct action, and if they refuse to support our nonviolent efforts, millions of Negroes will, out of frustration and despair, seek solace and security in black-nationalist ideologies—a development that would inevitably lead to a frightening racial nightmare.

Oppressed people cannot remain oppressed forever. The yearning   30 for freedom eventually manifests itself, and that is what has happened to the American Negro. Something within has reminded him of his birthright of freedom, and something without has reminded him that it can be gained. Consciously or unconsciously, he has been caught up by the *Zeitgeist,* and with his black brothers of Africa and his brown and yellow brothers of Asia, South America, and the Caribbean, the United States Negro is moving with a sense of great urgency toward the promised land of racial justice. If one recognizes this vital urge that has engulfed the Negro community, one should readily understand why public demonstrations are taking place. The Negro has many pent-up resentments and latent frustrations, and he must release them. So let him march; let him make prayer pilgrimages to the city hall; let him go on freedom rides—and try to understand why he must do so. If his repressed emotions are not released in nonviolent ways, they will seek expression through violence; this is not a threat but a fact of history. So I have not said to my people, "Get rid of your discontent." Rather, I have tried to say that this normal and healthy discontent can be channeled into the creative outlet of nonviolent direct action. And now this approach is being termed extremist.

But though I was initially disappointed at being categorized as an extremist, as I continued to think about the matter I gradually gained a measure of satisfaction from the label. Was not Jesus an extremist for love: "Love your enemies, bless them that curse you, do good to them that hate you, and pray for them which despitefully use you, and perse-cute you." Was not Amos an extremist for justice: "Let justice roll down like waters and righteousness like an ever-flowing stream." Was not Paul an extremist for the Christian gospel: "I bear in my body the marks of the Lord Jesus." Was not Martin Luther an extremist: "Here I stand; I cannot do otherwise, so help me God." And John Bunyan: "I will stay in jail to the end of my days before I make a butchery of my conscience." And Abraham Lincoln: "This nation cannot survive half slave and half free." And Thomas Jefferson: "We hold these truths to be self-evident, that all men are created equal. . . ." So the question is not whether we will be extremists, but what kind of extremists we will be. Will we be extremists for hate or for love? Will we be extremists for the preserva-tion of injustice or for the extension of justice? In that dramatic scene on Calvary's hill three men were crucified. We must never forget that all three were crucified for the same crime—the crime of extremism. Two were extremists for immorality, and thus fell below their environ-ment. The other, Jesus Christ, was an extremist for love, truth, and goodness, and thereby rose above his environment. Perhaps the South, the nation, and the world are in dire need of creative extremists.

I had hoped that the white moderate would see this need. Perhaps I was too optimistic; perhaps I expected too much. I suppose I should have realized that few members of the oppressor race can understand the deep groans and passionate yearnings of the oppressed race, and still fewer have the vision to see that injustice must be rooted out by strong, persistent, and determined action. I am thankful, however, that some of our white brothers in the South have grasped the meaning of this social revolution and committed themselves to it. They are still all too few in quantity, but they are big in quality. Some—such as Ralph McGill, Lillian Smith, Harry Golden, James McBridge Dabbs, Ann Braden, and Sarah Patton Boyle—have written about our struggle in eloquent and prophetic terms. Others have marched with us down nameless streets of the South. They have languished in filthy, roach-infested jails, suffering the abuse and brutality of policemen who view them as "dirty nigger-lovers." Unlike so many of their moderate brothers and sisters, they have recognized the urgency of the moment and sensed the need for powerful "action" antidotes to combat the disease of segregation.

Let me take note of my other major disappointment. I have been so greatly disappointed with the white church and its leadership. Of course, there are some notable exceptions. I am not unmindful of the fact that each of you has taken some significant stands on this issue. I commend you, Reverend Stallings, for your Christian stand on this past Sunday, in welcoming Negroes to your worship service on a nonsegregated basis. I commend the Catholic leaders of this state for integrating Spring Hill College several years ago.

But despite these notable exceptions, I must honestly reiterate that I have been disappointed with the church. I do not say this as one of those negative critics who can always find something wrong with the church. I say this as a minister of the gospel, who loves the church; who was nurtured in its bosom; who has been sustained by its spiritual blessings and who will remain true to it as long as the cord of life shall lengthen.

When I was suddenly catapulted into the leadership of the bus pro-   35
test in Montgomery, Alabama, a few years ago, I felt we would be supported by the white church. I felt that the white ministers, priests, and rabbis of the South would be among our strongest allies. Instead, some have been outright opponents, refusing to understand the freedom movement and misrepresenting its leaders; all too many others have been more cautious than courageous and have remained silent behind the anesthetizing security of stained-glass windows.

In spite of my shattered dreams, I came to Birmingham with the hope that the white religious leadership of this community would see the justice of our cause and, with deep moral concern, would serve as the channel through which our just grievances could reach the power structure. I had hoped that each of you would understand. But again I have been disappointed.

I have heard numerous southern religious leaders admonish their worshipers to comply with a desegregation decision because it is the law, but I have longed to hear white ministers declare: "Follow this decree because integration is morally right and because the Negro is your brother." In the midst of blatant injustices inflicted upon the Negro, I have watched white churchmen stand on the sideline and mouth pious irrelevancies and sanctimonious trivialities. In the midst of a mighty struggle to rid our nation of racial and economic injustice, I have heard many ministers say: "Those are social issues, with which the gospel has no real concern." And I have watched many churches commit themselves to a completely otherworldly religion which makes a strange, un-Biblical distinction between body and soul, between the sacred and the secular.

I have traveled the length and breadth of Alabama, Mississippi, and all the other southern states. On sweltering summer days and crisp autumn mornings I have looked at the South's beautiful churches with their lofty spires pointing heavenward. I have beheld the impressive outlines of her massive religious-education buildings. Over and over I have found myself asking: "What kind of people worship here? Who is their God? Where were their voices when the lips of Governor Barnett dripped with words of interposition and nullification? Where were they when Governor Wallace gave a clarion call for defiance and hatred? Where were their voices of support when bruised and weary Negro men and women decided to rise from the dark dungeons of complacency to the bright hills of creative protest?"

Yes, these questions are still in my mind. In deep disappointment I have wept over the laxity of the church. But be assured that my tears have been tears of love. There can be no deep disappointment where there is not deep love. Yes, I love the church. How could I do otherwise? I am in the rather unique position of being the son, the grandson, and the great-grandson of preachers. Yes, I see the church as the body of Christ. But, oh! How we have blemished and scarred that body through social neglect and through fear of being nonconformists.

There was a time when the church was very powerful—in the time   40
when the early Christians rejoiced at being deemed worthy to suffer for what they believed. In those days the church was not merely a thermometer that recorded the ideas and principles of popular opinion; it was a thermostat that transformed the mores of society. Whenever the early Christians entered a town, the people in power became disturbed and immediately sought to convict the Christians for being "disturbers of the peace" and "outside agitators." But the Christians pressed on, in the conviction that they were "a colony of heaven," called to obey God rather than man. Small in number, they were big in commitment. They were too God-intoxicated to be "astronomically intimidated." By their effort and example they brought an end to such ancient evils as infanticide and gladiatorial contests.

Things are different now. So often the contemporary church is a weak, ineffectual voice with an uncertain sound. So often it is an archdefender of the status quo. Far from being disturbed by the presence of the church, the power structure of the average community is consoled by the church's silent—and often even vocal—sanction of things as they are.

But the judgment of God is upon the church as never before. If today's church does not recapture the sacrificial spirit of the early church, it will lose its authenticity, forfeit the loyalty of millions, and be dismissed as an irrelevant social club with no meaning for the twentieth century. Every day I meet young people whose disappointment with the church has turned into outright disgust.

Perhaps I have once again been too optimistic. Is organized religion too inextricably bound to the status quo to save our nation and the world? Perhaps I must turn my faith to the inner spiritual church, the church within the church, as the true *ekklesia* and the hope of the world. But again I am thankful to God that some noble souls from the ranks of organized religion have broken loose from the paralyzing chains of conformity and joined us as active partners in the struggle for freedom. They have left their secure congregations and walked the streets of Albany, Georgia, with us. They have gone down the highways of the South on tortuous rides for freedom. Yes, they have gone to jail with us. Some have been dismissed from their churches, have lost the support of their bishops and fellow ministers. But they have acted in the faith that right defeated is stronger than evil triumphant. Their witness has been the spiritual salt that has preserved the true meaning of the gospel in these troubled times. They have carved a tunnel of hope through the dark mountain of disappointment.

I hope the church as a whole will meet the challenge of this decisive hour. But even if the church does not come to the aid of justice, I have no despair about the future. I have no fear about the outcome of our struggle in Birmingham, even if our motives are at present misunderstood. We will reach the goal of freedom in Birmingham and all over the nation, because the goal of America is freedom. Abused and scorned though we may be, our destiny is tied up with America's destiny. Before the pilgrims landed at Plymouth, we were here. Before the pen of Jefferson etched the majestic words of the Declaration of Independence across the pages of history, we were here. For more than two centuries our forebears labored in this country without wages; they made cotton king; they built the homes of their masters while suffering gross injustice and shameful humiliation—and yet out of a bottomless vitality they continued to thrive and develop. If the inexpressible cruelties of slavery could not stop us, the opposition we now face will surely fail. We will win our freedom because the sacred heritage of our nation and the eternal will of God are embodied in our echoing demands.

Before closing I feel impelled to mention one other point in your 45 statement that has troubled me profoundly. You warmly commended the Birmingham police force for keeping "order" and "preventing

violence." I doubt that you would have so warmly commended the
police force if you had seen its dogs sinking their teeth into unarmed,
nonviolent Negroes. I doubt that you would so quickly commend the
policemen if you were to observe their ugly and inhumane treatment of
Negroes here in the city jail; if you were to watch them push and curse
old Negro women and young Negro girls; if you were to see them slap
and kick old Negro men and young boys; if you were to observe them, as
they did on two occasions, refuse to give us food because we wanted
to sing our grace together. I cannot join you in your praise of the Birmingham police department.

It is true that the police have exercised a degree of discipline in handling the demonstrators. In this sense they have conducted themselves
rather "non-violently" in public. But for what purpose? To preserve the
evil system of segregation. Over the past few years I have consistently
preached that nonviolence demands that the means we use must be as
pure as the ends we seek. I have tried to make clear that it is wrong to
use immoral means to attain moral ends. But now I must affirm that it is
just as wrong, or perhaps even more so, to use moral means to preserve
immoral ends. Perhaps Mr. Connor and his policemen have been rather
nonviolent in public, as was Chief Pritchett in Albany, Georgia, but they
have used the moral means of nonviolence to maintain the immoral end
of racial injustice. As T. S. Eliot has said, "The last temptation is the
greatest treason: To do the right deed for the wrong reason."

I wish you had commended the Negro sit-inners and demonstrators
of Birmingham for their sublime courage, their willingness to suffer,
and their amazing discipline in the midst of great provocation. One day
the South will recognize its real heroes. They will be the James Mere-
diths, with the noble sense of purpose that enables them to face jeering
and hostile mobs, and with the agonizing loneliness that characterizes
the life of the pioneer. They will be old, oppressed, battered Negro
women, symbolized in a seventy-two-year-old woman in Montgomery,
Alabama, who rose up with a sense of dignity and with her people

decided not to ride segregated buses, and who responded with ungrammatical profundity to one who inquired about her weariness: "My feets is tired, but my soul is at rest." They will be the young high school and college students, the young ministers of the gospel and a host of their elders, courageously and nonviolently sitting in at lunch counters and willingly going to jail for conscience' sake. One day the South will know that when these disinherited children of God sat down at lunch counters, they were in reality standing up for what is best in the American dream and for the most sacred values in our Judaeo-Christian heritage, thereby bringing our nation back to those great wells of democracy which were dug deep by the founding fathers in their formulation of the Constitution and the Declaration of Independence.

Never before have I written so long a letter. I'm afraid it is much too long to take your precious time. I can assure you that it would have been much shorter if I had been writing from a comfortable desk, but what else can one do when he is alone in a narrow jail cell, other than write long letters, think long thoughts, and pray long prayers?

If I have said anything in this letter that overstates the truth and indicates an unreasonable impatience, I beg you to forgive me. If I have said anything that understates the truth and indicates my having a patience that allows me to settle for anything less than brotherhood, I beg God to forgive me.

I hope this letter finds you strong in the faith. I also hope that circumstances will soon make it possible for me to meet each of you, not as an integrationist or a civil-rights leader but as a fellow clergyman and a Christian brother. Let us all hope that the dark clouds of racial prejudice will soon pass away and the deep fog of misunderstanding will be lifted from our fear-drenched communities, and in some not too distant tomorrow the radiant stars of love and brotherhood will shine over our great nation with all their scintillating beauty.

Yours for the cause of Peace and Brotherhood,

MARTIN LUTHER KING JR.

Thinking about the Text

1. One way of persuading others to trust our arguments is to establish our ethos, showing that we know what we're talking about and demonstrating goodwill. How does Martin Luther King Jr. establish his ethos in this letter?

2. King is writing to an audience of other ministers. What sources does he cite in order to persuade this audience to accept his argument?

3. Reread the long sentence that comprises much of paragraph 14. Why might King have chosen to write such a long sentence to convey the information it provides? What is the effect?

4. Write a letter to someone with whom you disagree about a significant issue. Be sure to establish your knowledge and goodwill and use sources that will be persuasive to your audience.

JOAN DIDION

On Keeping a Notebook

1966

JOAN DIDION (b. 1934) writes novels, memoirs, and essays. She is best known for her books *Slouching Towards Bethlehem* (1968) and the *The White Album* (1979), which capture the spirit of California in the 1960s and 1970s, respectively, and *The Year of Magical Thinking* (2005), a memoir about the sudden death of her husband, John Gregory Dunne. "On Keeping a Notebook" was first published in *Holiday*, a travel magazine, in 1966 and later included in *Slouching Towards Bethlehem*.

"**T**HAT WOMAN ESTELLE,'" THE NOTE READS, "'IS partly the reason why George Sharp and I are separated today.' *Dirty crepe-de-Chine wrapper, hotel bar, Wilmington RR, 9:45 a.m. August Monday morning.*"

Since the note is in my notebook, it presumably has some meaning to me. I study it for a long while. At first I have only the most general notion of what I was doing on an August Monday morning in the bar of the hotel across from the Pennsylvania Railroad station in Wilmington, Delaware (waiting for a train? missing one? 1960? 1961? why Wilmington?), but I do remember being there. The woman in the dirty crepe-de-Chine wrapper had come down from her room for a beer, and the bartender had heard before the reason why George Sharp and she were separated today. "Sure," he said, and went on mopping the floor. "You told me." At the other end of the bar is a girl. She is talking, pointedly, not to the man beside her but to a cat lying in the triangle of sunlight cast through the open door. She is wearing a plaid silk dress from Peck & Peck, and the hem is coming down.

Here is what it is: the girl has been on the Eastern Shore, and now she is going back to the city, leaving the man beside her, and all she can see ahead are the viscous summer sidewalks and the 3 a.m. long-distance calls that will make her lie awake and then sleep drugged through all the steaming mornings left in August (1960? 1961?). Because she must go directly from the train to lunch in New York, she wishes that she had a safety pin for the hem of the plaid silk dress, and she also wishes that she could forget about the hem and the lunch and stay in the cool bar that smells of disinfectant and malt and make friends with the woman in the crepe-de-Chine wrapper. She is afflicted by a little self-pity, and she wants to compare Estelles. That is what that was all about.

Why did I write it down? In order to remember, of course, but exactly what was it I wanted to remember? How much of it actually happened? Did any of it? Why do I keep a notebook at all? It is easy to deceive oneself on all those scores. The impulse to write things down is a peculiarly compulsive one, inexplicable to those who do not share it, useful only accidentally, only secondarily, in the way that any compulsion tries to justify itself. I suppose that it begins or does not begin in the cradle. Although I have felt compelled to write things down since I was five years old, I doubt that my daughter ever will, for she is a singularly blessed and accepting child, delighted with life exactly as life presents itself to her, unafraid to go to sleep and unafraid to wake up. Keepers of private notebooks are a different breed altogether, lonely and resistant rearrangers of things, anxious malcontents, children afflicted apparently at birth with some presentiment of loss.

My first notebook was a Big Five tablet, given to me by my mother   5 with the sensible suggestion that I stop whining and learn to amuse myself by writing down my thoughts. She returned the tablet to me a few years ago; the first entry is an account of a woman who believed herself to be freezing to death in the Arctic night, only to find, when day broke, that she had stumbled onto the Sahara Desert, where she would die of the heat before lunch. I have no idea what turn of a five-year-old's mind could have prompted so insistently "ironic" and exotic a story, but it does reveal a certain predilection for the extreme which has dogged me into adult life; perhaps if I were analytically inclined I would find it a truer story than any I might have told about Donald Johnson's birthday party or the day my cousin Brenda put Kitty Litter in the aquarium.

So the point of my keeping a notebook has never been, nor is it now, to have an accurate factual record of what I have been doing or thinking. That would be a different impulse entirely, an instinct for reality which I sometimes envy but do not possess. At no point have I ever been able successfully to keep a diary; my approach to daily life ranges from the grossly negligent to the merely absent, and on those few occasions when I have tried dutifully to record a day's events, boredom has so overcome me that the results are mysterious at best. What is this business about "shopping, typing piece, dinner with E, depressed"? Shopping for what?

Typing what piece? Who is É? Was this "E" depressed, or was I depressed? Who cares?

In fact I have abandoned altogether that kind of pointless entry; instead I tell what some would call lies. "That's simply not true," the members of my family frequently tell me when they come up against my memory of a shared event. "The party was *not* for you, the spider was *not* a black widow, *it wasn't that way at all*." Very likely they are right, for not only have I always had trouble distinguishing between what happened and what merely might have happened, but I remain unconvinced that the distinction, for my purposes, matters. The cracked crab that I recall having for lunch the day my father came home from Detroit in 1945 must certainly be embroidery, worked into the day's pattern to lend verisimilitude; I was ten years old and would not now remember the cracked crab. The day's events did not turn on cracked crab. And yet it is precisely that fictitious crab that makes me see the afternoon all over again, a home movie run all too often, the father bearing gifts, the child weeping, an exercise in family love and guilt. Or that is what it was to me. Similarly, perhaps it never did snow that August in Vermont; perhaps there never were flurries in the night wind, and maybe no one else felt the ground hardening and summer already dead even as we pretended to bask in it, but that was how it felt to me, and it might as well have snowed, could have snowed, did snow.

How it felt to me: that is getting closer to the truth about a notebook. I sometimes delude myself about why I keep a notebook, imagine that some thrifty virtue derives from preserving everything observed. See enough and write it down, I tell myself, and then some morning when the world seems drained of wonder, some day when I am only going through the motions of doing what I am supposed to do, which is write— on that bankrupt morning I will simply open my notebook and there it will all be, a forgotten account with accumulated interest, paid passage back to the world out there: dialogue overheard in hotels and elevators and at the hat-check counter in Pavillon (one middle-aged man shows

his hat check to another and says, "That's my old football number");
impressions of Bettina Aptheker and Benjamin Sonnenberg and Teddy
("Mr. Acapulco") Stauffer; careful *aperçus* about tennis bums and failed
fashion models and Greek shipping heiresses, one of whom taught me a
significant lesson (a lesson I could have learned from F. Scott Fitzgerald,
but perhaps we all must meet the very rich for ourselves) by asking, when
I arrived to interview her in her orchid-filled sitting room on the second
day of a paralyzing New York blizzard, whether it was snowing outside.

I imagine, in other words, that the notebook is about other people.
But of course it is not. I have no real business with what one stranger
said to another at the hat-check counter in Pavillon; in fact I suspect that
the line "That's my old football number" touched not my own imagination
at all, but merely some memory of something once read, probably "The
Eighty-Yard Run." Nor is my concern with a woman in a dirty crepe-de-
Chine wrapper in a Wilmington bar. My stake is always, of course, in
the unmentioned girl in the plaid silk dress. *Remember what it was to be
me:* that is always the point.

It is a difficult point to admit. We are brought up in the ethic that others, any others, all others, are by definition more interesting than ourselves; taught to be diffident, just this side of self-effacing. ("You're the
least important person in the room and don't forget it," Jessica Mitford's
governess would hiss in her ear on the advent of any social occasion; I
copied that into my notebook because it is only recently that I have been
able to enter a room without hearing some such phrase in my inner ear.)
Only the very young and the very old may recount their dreams at breakfast, dwell upon self, interrupt with memories of beach picnics and
favorite Liberty lawn dresses and the rainbow trout in a creek near Colorado Springs. The rest of us are expected, rightly, to affect absorption in
other people's favorite dresses, other people's trout.

And so we do. But our notebooks give us away, for however dutifully
we record what we see around us, the common denominator of all we

see is always, transparently, shamelessly, the implacable "I." We are not talking here about the kind of notebook that is patently for public consumption, a structural conceit for binding together a series of graceful *pensées;* we are talking about something private, about bits of the mind's string too short to use, an indiscriminate and erratic assemblage with meaning only for its maker.

And sometimes even the maker has difficulty with the meaning. There does not seem to be, for example, any point in my knowing for the rest of my life that, during 1964, 720 tons of soot fell on every square mile of New York City, yet there it is in my notebook, labeled "FACT." Nor do I really need to remember that Ambrose Bierce liked to spell Leland Stanford's name "£eland $tanford" or that "smart women almost always wear black in Cuba," a fashion hint without much potential for practical application. And does not the relevance of these notes seem marginal at best?:

> In the basement museum of the Inyo County Courthouse in Independence, California, sign pinned to a mandarin coat: "This MANDARIN COAT was often worn by Mrs. Minnie S. Brooks when giving lectures on her TEAPOT COLLECTION."
> Redhead getting out of car in front of Beverly Wilshire Hotel, chinchilla stole, Vuitton bags with tags reading:
>
> MRS LOU FOX
>
> HOTEL SAHARA
>
> VEGAS

Well, perhaps not entirely marginal. As a matter of fact, Mrs. Minnie S. Brooks and her MANDARIN COAT pull me back into my own childhood, for although I never knew Mrs. Brooks and did not visit Inyo County until I was thirty, I grew up in just such a world, in houses cluttered with Indian relics and bits of gold ore and ambergris and the souvenirs my Aunt Mercy Farnsworth brought back from the Orient. It is a long way from that world to Mrs. Lou Fox's world, where we all live now, and is it not just as well to remember that? Might not Mrs. Minnie S. Brooks help me to remember what I am? Might not Mrs. Lou Fox help me to remember what I am not?

But sometimes the point is harder to discern. What exactly did I have in mind when I noted down that it cost the father of someone I know $650 a month to light the place on the Hudson in which he lived before the Crash? What use was I planning to make of this line by Jimmy Hoffa: "I may have my faults, but being wrong ain't one of them"? And although I think it interesting to know where the girls who travel with the Syndicate have their hair done when they find themselves on the West Coast, will I ever make suitable use of it? Might I not be better off just passing it on to John O'Hara? What is a recipe for sauerkraut doing in my notebook? What kind of magpie keeps this notebook? *"He was born the night the Titanic went down."* That seems a nice enough line, and I even recall who said it, but is it not really a better line in life than it could ever be in fiction?

But of course that is exactly it: not that I should ever use the line,   15
but that I should remember the woman who said it and the afternoon I heard it. We were on her terrace by the sea, and we were finishing the wine left from lunch, trying to get what sun there was, a California winter sun. The woman whose husband was born the night the *Titanic* went down wanted to rent her house, wanted to go back to her children in Paris. I remember wishing that I could afford the house, which cost $1,000 a month. "Someday you will," she said lazily. "Someday it all comes." There in the sun on her terrace it seemed easy to believe in someday, but later I had a low-grade afternoon hangover and ran over a black snake on the way to the supermarket and was flooded with inexplicable fear when I heard the checkout clerk explaining to the man ahead of me why she was finally divorcing her husband. "He left me no choice," she said over and over as she punched the register. "He has a

little seven-month-old baby by her, he left me no choice." I would like to believe that my dread then was for the human condition, but of course it was for me, because I wanted a baby and did not then have one and because I wanted to own the house that cost $1,000 a month to rent and because I had a hangover.

It all comes back. Perhaps it is difficult to see the value in having one's self back in that kind of mood, but I do see it; I think we are well advised to keep on nodding terms with the people we used to be whether we find them attractive company or not. Otherwise they turn up unannounced and surprise us, come hammering on the mind's door at 4 a.m. of a bad night and demand to know who deserted them, who betrayed them, who is going to make amends. We forget all too soon the things we thought we could never forget. We forget the loves and the betrayals alike, forget what we whispered and what we screamed, forget who we were. I have already lost touch with a couple of people I used to be; one of them, a seventeen-year-old, presents little threat, although it would be of some interest to me to know again what it feels like to sit on a river levee drinking vodka-and-orange-juice and listening to Les Paul and Mary Ford and their echoes sing "How High the Moon" on the car radio. (You see I still have the scenes, but I no longer perceive myself among those present, no longer could even improvise the dialogue.) The other one, a twenty-three-year-old, bothers me more. She was always a good deal of trouble, and I suspect she will reappear when I least want to see her, skirts too long, shy to the point of aggravation, always the injured party, full of recriminations and little hurts and stories I do not want to hear again, at once saddening me and angering me with her vulnerability and ignorance, an apparition all the more insistent for being so long banished.

It is a good idea, then, to keep in touch, and I suppose that keeping in touch is what notebooks are all about. And we are all on our own when it comes to keeping those lines open to ourselves: your notebook will never help me, nor mine you. *"So what's new in the whiskey business?"*

What could that possibly mean to you? To me it means a blonde in a Pucci bathing suit sitting with a couple of fat men by the pool at the Beverly Hills Hotel. Another man approaches, and they all regard one another in silence for a while. "So what's new in the whiskey business?" one of the fat men finally says by way of welcome, and the blonde stands up, arches one foot and dips it in the pool, looking all the while at the cabaña where Baby Pignatari is talking on the telephone. That is all there is to that, except that several years later I saw the blonde coming out of Saks Fifth Avenue in New York with her California complexion and a voluminous mink coat. In the harsh wind that day she looked old and irrevocably tired to me, and even the skins in the mink coat were not worked the way they were doing them that year, not the way she would have wanted them done, and there is the point of the story. For a while after that I did not like to look in the mirror, and my eyes would skim the newspapers and pick out only the deaths, the cancer victims, the premature coronaries, the suicides, and I stopped riding the Lexington Avenue IRT because I noticed for the first time that all the strangers I had seen for years—the man with the seeing-eye dog, the spinster who read the classified pages every day, the fat girl who always got off with me at Grand Central—looked older than they once had.

It all comes back. Even that recipe for sauerkraut: even that brings it back. I was on Fire Island when I first made that sauerkraut, and it was raining, and we drank a lot of bourbon and ate the sauerkraut and went to bed at ten, and I listened to the rain and the Atlantic and felt safe. I made the sauerkraut again last night and it did not make me feel any safer, but that is, as they say, another story.

Thinking about the Text

1. List several reasons for keeping a notebook. What is Joan Didion's reason for doing so? How might it differ from your own or someone else's?

2. Didion claims that her notebook will never help you, just as yours will never help her (paragraph 17). Why is that? How does her characterization of her own notebook support that claim?

3. Have you ever kept a journal (the kind of notebook Didion describes, a diary, or a journal devoted to a specific aspect of your life)? Why? Write an essay in which you reflect on your own reasons for either keeping or not keeping a journal.

MAYA ANGELOU

Champion of the World

1969

MAYA ANGELOU (1928–2014) wrote essays, memoirs, and poetry. She is best known for her first memoir, *I Know Why the Caged Bird Sings* (1969), and for her poem "On the Pulse of Morning" (1993), which she read at President William Clinton's inauguration. Angelou published her seventh and final volume of autobiography, *Mom & Me & Mom*, in 2013. In this selection from *I Know Why the Caged Bird Sings*, Angelou recalls listening to the 1935 boxing match between Joe Louis and Primo Carnera.

THE LAST INCH OF SPACE WAS FILLED, YET PEOPLE CONTIN-
ued to wedge themselves along the walls of the Store. Uncle
Willie had turned the radio up to its last notch so that
youngsters on the porch wouldn't miss a word. Women sat
on kitchen chairs, dining-room chairs, stools, and upturned wooden
boxes. Small children and babies perched on every lap available and
men leaned on the shelves or on each other.

The apprehensive mood was shot through with shafts of gaiety, as a
black sky is streaked with lightning.

"I ain't worried 'bout this fight. Joe's gonna whip that cracker like it's
open season."

"He gone whip him till that white boy call him Momma."

At last the talking finished and the string-along songs about razor   5
blades were over and the fight began.

"A quick jab to the head." In the Store the crowd grunted. "A left to
the head and a right and another left." One of the listeners cackled like
a hen and was quieted.

"They're in a clinch, Louis is trying to fight his way out."

Some bitter comedian on the porch said, "That white man don't
mind hugging that niggah now, I betcha."

"The referee is moving in to break them up, but Louis finally pushed
the contender away and it's an uppercut to the chin. The contender is
hanging on, now he's backing away. Louis catches him with a short
left to the jaw."

A tide of murmuring assent poured out the door and into the yard.   10

"Another left and another left. Louis is saving that mighty right. . . ."
The mutter in the store had grown into a baby roar and it was pierced by
the clang of a bell and the announcer's "That's the bell for round three,
ladies and gentlemen."

As I pushed my way into the Store I wondered if the announcer gave
any thought to the fact that he was addressing as "ladies and gentle-

men" all the Negroes around the world who sat sweating and praying, glued to their "Master's voice."

There were only a few calls for RC Colas, Dr Peppers, and Hires root beer. The real festivities would begin after the fight. Then even the old Christian ladies who taught their children and tried themselves to practice turning the other cheek would buy soft drinks, and if the Brown Bomber's victory was a particularly bloody one they would order peanut patties and Baby Ruths also.

Bailey and I laid the coins on top of the cash register. Uncle Willie didn't allow us to ring up sales during a fight. It was too noisy and might shake up the atmosphere. When the gong rang for the next round we pushed through the near-sacred quiet to the herd of children outside.

"He's got Louis against the ropes and now it's a left to the body and   15 a right to the ribs. Another right to the body, it looks like it was low. . . . Yes, ladies and gentlemen, the referee is signaling but the contender keeps raining the blows on Louis. It's another to the body, and it looks like Louis is going down."

My race groaned. It was our people falling. It was another lynching, yet another Black man hanging on a tree. One more woman ambushed and raped. A Black boy whipped and maimed. It was hounds on the trail of a man running through slimy swamps. It was a white woman slapping her maid for being forgetful.

The men in the Store stood away from the walls and at attention. Women greedily clutched the babes on their laps while on the porch the shufflings and smiles, flirting and pinchings of a few minutes before were gone. This might be the end of the world. If Joe lost we were back in slavery and beyond help. It would all be true; the accusations that we were lower types of human beings. Only a little higher than apes. True that we were stupid and ugly and lazy and dirty and unlucky and worst of all, that God himself hated us and ordained us to be hewers of wood and drawers of water, forever and ever, world without end.

We didn't breathe. We didn't hope. We waited.

"He's off the ropes, ladies and gentlemen. He's moving towards the corner of the ring." There was no time to be relieved. The worst might still happen.

"And now it looks like Joe is mad. He's caught Carnera with a left hook   20 to the head and a right to the head. It's a left jab to the body and another left to the head. There's a left cross and a right to the head. The contender's right eye is bleeding and he can't seem to keep his block up. Louis is penetrating every block. The referee is moving in, but Louis sends a left to the body and it's an uppercut to the chin and the contender is dropping. He's on the canvas, ladies and gentlemen."

Babies slid to the floor as women stood up and men leaned toward the radio.

"Here's the referee. He's counting. One, two, three, four, five, six, seven. . . . Is the contender trying to get up again?"

All the men in the store shouted, "NO."

"—eight, nine, ten." There were a few sounds from the audience, but they seemed to be holding themselves in against tremendous pressure.

"The fight is all over, ladies and gentlemen. Let's get the microphone   25 over to the referee. . . . Here he is. He's got the Brown Bomber's hand, he's holding it up. . . . Here he is. . . ."

Then the voice, husky and familiar, came to wash over us—"The winnah, and still heavyweight champeen of the world . . . Joe Louis."

Champion of the world. A Black boy. Some Black mother's son. He was the strongest man in the world. People drank Coca-Colas like ambrosia and ate candy bars like Christmas. Some of the men went behind the Store and poured white lightning in their soft-drink bottles, and a few of the bigger boys followed them. Those who were not chased away came back blowing their breath in front of themselves like proud smokers.

It would take an hour or more before the people would leave the Store and head for home. Those who lived too far had made arrangements to stay in town. It wouldn't be fit for a Black man and his family to be caught on a lonely country road on a night when Joe Louis had proved that we were the strongest people in the world.

Thinking about the Text

1. In Maya Angelou's depiction, Joe Louis's success in this match was enormously important to her community. Where in her essay does she highlight this significance? Why was it so important?

2. Angelou and others at the store listened to the fight on the radio. How might that fact have influenced the way she wrote about the fight? What does she see? What does she hear?

3. Write a narrative about an event you've attended. It might be a sports event, a wedding, a concert, a political rally, or something else. In describing the event, pay attention to the crowd or audience as well as to the event they were watching. Who was present? What were they wearing? What, if anything, were they eating? What did they say and do? Try to show why the event was significant to those in attendance.

VERTAMAE SMART-GROSVENOR

The Kitchen Crisis

1970

VERTAMAE SMART-GROSVENOR (b. 1938) writes about food and has appeared regularly on National Public Radio. She hosted her own radio program *Seasonings*, a show about holiday cooking and food culture. She is best known for her cookbook-memoir *Vibration Cooking: or, the Travel Notes of a Geechee Girl* (1970). "The Kitchen Crisis" was first published in Toni Cade's edited collection *The Black Woman: An Anthology* (1970).

i do not consider myself a writer, i am a rapper. therefore do not read
this piece silently . . . rap it aloud.

THERE IS CONFUSION IN THE KITCHEN!
we've got to develop kitchen consciousness or we may very
well see the end of kitchens as we now know them. kitchens
are getting smaller. in some apts the closet is bigger than the
kitchen. something that i saw the other day leads me to believe that
there may well be a subversive plot to take kitchens out of the home and
put them in the street. i was sitting in the park knitting my old man a
pair of socks for next winter when a tall well dressed man in his mid
thirties sat next to me.

i didn't pay him no mind until he went into his act.

he pulled his irish linen hankie from his lapel, spread it on his lap,
opened his attache case, took out a box, popped a pill, drank from his
thermos jug, and turned and offered the box to me. thank you no said i.
"i never eat with strangers."

that would have been all except that i am curious black and i looked at   5
the label on the box, then i screamed. the box said INSTANT LUNCH PILL:
(imitation ham and cheese on rye, with diet cola, and apple pie flavor).
i sat frozen while he did his next act. he folded his hankie, put it back in
his lapel, packed his thermos jug away, and took out a piece of yellow
plastic and blew into it, in less than 3 minutes it had turned into a yellow plastic castro convertible couch.

enough is enough i thought to myself. so i dropped the knitting and ran
like hell. last i saw of that dude he was stretched out on the couch reading portnoys complaint.

the kitchens that are still left in the home are so instant they might as
well be out to lunch.

instant milk, instant coffee, instant tea, instant potatoes, instant old
fashioned oatmeal, everything is preprepared for the unprepared woman
in the kitchen. the chicken is pre cut. the flour is pre measured, the rice

is minute, the salt is pre seasoned, and the peas are pre buttered. just goes to show you white folks will do anything for their women. they had to invent instant food because the servant problem got so bad that their women had to get in the kitchen herself with her own two little lily white hands. it is no accident that in the old old south where they had slaves that they was eating fried chicken, coated with batter, biscuits so light they could have flown across the mason dixon line if they had wanted to. they was eating pound cake that had to be beat 800 strokes. who do you think was doing this beating?

it sure wasnt missy. missy was beating the upstairs house nigger for not bringing her mint julep quick enough.

massa was out beating the field niggers for not hoeing the cotton fast enough. meanwhile up in the north country where they didnt have no slaves to speak of they was eating baked beans and so called new england boiled dinner.

it aint no big thing to put everything in one pot and let it cook. missy wasnt about to go through changes and whup no pound cake for 800 strokes. black men and black women have been whipping up fine food for centuries and outside of black bottom pie and nigger toes there is no reference to our contribution and participation in and to the culinary arts. when they do mention our food they act like it is some obscure thing that niggers down south made up and dont nobody else in the world eat it.

food aint nothing but food.

food is universal.

everybody eats.

a potato is a patata and not irish as white folks would have you believe.

watermelons is prehistoric and eaten all ober de world.

the russians make a watermelon beer. in the orient they dry and roast and salt the seeds. when old chris got here the indians was eating hominy grits. and before he "discovered" this country the greeks and romans were smacking on collard greens. blackeyed peas aint nothing but dried cow peas whose name in sanskrit traces its lineage back to the days before history was recorded. uh ah excuse me boss, means befo you-all was recording history. uh ah i know this is hard for you to believe suh but i got it from one of yo history books and i know you-all wouldnt talk with no forked tongue about history.

the cooking of food is one of the highest of all the human arts. we need to develop food consciousness.
so called enlightened people will rap for hours about jean paul sartre,   20
campus unrest, the feminine mystique, black power,' and tania, but mention food and they say, rather proudly too, "i'm a bad cook." some go so far as to boast "i cant even boil water without burning it."
that is a damn shame.
bad cooks got a bad life style.
food is life.
food changes up into blood, blood into cells, cells into energy, energy changes up into the forces which make up your life style.
so if one takes a creative, imaginative, loving, serious attitude toward   25
life everything one does will reflect one attitude hence when one cooks this attitude will be served at the table. and it will be good.
so bad cooks got a bad life style and i dont mean bad like we (blacks) mean bad i mean bad bad.
come on give a damn. anybody can get it together for vacation. change up and daily walk through kitchen life like you was on an endless holi-day. aint no use to save yourself for vacation. it's here now.
make every and each moment count like time was running out. that will cool out that matter of guess who is coming to dinner and make it a fact that DINNER IS SERVED.

one of the best meals i was ever served was at my friend bella's. bella served an elegant meal in her two room cold water tub in kitchen six story walk up flat. she had a round oak table with carved legs, covered with a floor length off white shaker lace tablecloth. in the center was a carved african gourd filled with peanuts, persimmons, lemons and limes. to start off we had fresh squeezed tangerine juice in chilled champagne glasses. then scrambled eggs, sliced red onions marinated in lemon juice and pickapeppa sauce, fried green tomatoes, on cobalt blue china plates. hot buttermilk biscuits with homemade apple jelly on limoges saucers (bella got them from goodwill for 10 cent a piece) and fresh ground bustelo coffee served in mugs that bella made in pottery class at the neighborhood anti poverty pro community cultural workshop for people in low socio economic ethnic groups.

you are what you eat.   30
i was saying that a long time before the movie came out but it doesnt bother me that they stole my line. white folks are always stealing and borrowing and discovering and making myths. you take terrapins. diamondback terrapins. the so called goremays squeal with epicurean delight at the very mention of the word. there is a mystique surrounding the word. diamondback terrapins.
are you ready for the demystification of diamondback terrapins????????
they ain't nothing but salt water turtles.
slaves on the eastern shores used to eat them all the time. the slaves was eating so many that a law was passed to making it a crime to feed slaves terrapins more than 3 times a week.
white folks discovered terrapins, ate them all up and now they are all but extinct (terrapins).
oh there are a few left on terrapin reservations but the chances of see-   35
ing one in your neighborhood is not likely.

in my old neighborhood (fairfax s.c.) we always talk about how folks in new york will give you something to drink but nothing to eat. after having lived for several years in fun city i understand how the natives got into this.

with the cost of living as high as it is here i understand how you can
become paranoid and weird about your food. i understand where they
are coming from but i thank the creator that there is still a cultural gap
between me and the natives. on the other hand you cant be no fool
about it. it dont make sense to take food out your childrens mouths to
give to the last lower east side poet who knocks on your door but you
can give up a margarine sandwich and a glass of water. cant you? eating
is a very personal thing.

some people will sit down and eat with anybody.

that is very uncool. you cant eat with everybody.

you got to have the right vibrations.   40

if you dont get good vibrations from someone, cancel them out for eating. (other things too.)

that is the only way to keep bad kitchen vibes at a minimum. tell those
kind of folks that you will meet them in a luncheonette or a bar.

even at the risk of static from family and friends PRO TECT YO KITCH'N. it's
hard though. sometimes look like in spite of all you do and as careful as
you try to be a rapscallion will slip right in your kitchen. i cant stand
rapscallions. among other things they are insensitive. you ask them
"may i offer you something" "some coffee tea juice water milk juice or
maybe an alcoholic beverage."

they always answer "nah nutin for me" or else they say "i'll have tea if
you got tea bags" or "coffee if it is instant i dont want to put you through
no trouble." check that out! talking about not going to any trouble. hell
they already in your house and that is trouble and personal. what the
rapscallions are really saying is dont go to any trouble for me cause i
wouldnt go to none for you. rapscallions dont mind taking the alcoholic
drink because it is impersonal. nothing of you is in that. all you got to
do is pour from a bottle. they dont feel that you have extended yourself
for them so they wont have to do no trouble for you in return. in most
other cultures when you enter a persons home you and the host share a
moment together by partaking of something. rapscallions love to talk

about culture but their actions prove they aint got none. they dont understand that it is about more than the coffee tea or drink of water.
it's about extending yourself.   45
so watch out for rapscallions. they'll mess up your kitchen vibes.
PROTECT YOUR KITCHEN

Thinking about the Text

1. In her author's note at the beginning of the essay, Vertamae Smart-
   Grosvenor asks her audience not to read silently but to rap her essay
   aloud. Read a section of this essay silently and then perform it
   orally. Certain features—for instance, the lack of capitalization and
   conventional paragraph indents, the colloquial language, and the
   repetition—might affect the way you read the essay. How did your
   two reading experiences differ? Which did you prefer? Why?

2. Smart-Grosvenor uses humor and sarcasm to make serious points.
   Locate the places in the essay in which she uses humor. What point
   is she making?

3. Do you agree that there is a "kitchen crisis"? If so, what is the nature
   of the crisis? If not, why is the state of the kitchen fine as is? Write an
   essay responding to Smart-Grosvenor. Try to use humor to make a
   claim about whether there is, indeed, a kitchen crisis.

ANNIE DILLARD

Sight into Insight

1974

ANNIE DILLARD (b. 1945) writes nonfiction, fiction, and poetry. She is best known for a book of philosophical nature writing—*Pilgrim at Tinker Creek* (1974), for which she won a Pulitzer Prize in 1975—and her essay collection *Teaching a Stone to Talk*, which includes the widely anthologized "Living Like Weasels" (1982). Dillard's latest book, *The Abundance* (2015), is her collection of new and previously published essays. "Sight into Insight" was published in 1974, both in *Harper's Magazine* and *Pilgrim at Tinker Creek*.

WHEN I WAS SIX OR SEVEN YEARS OLD, GROWING UP IN Pittsburgh, I used to take a penny of my own and hide it for someone else to find. It was a curious compulsion; sadly, I've never been seized by it since. For some reason I always "hid" the penny along the same stretch of sidewalk up the street. I'd cradle it at the roots of a maple, say, or in a hole left by a chipped-off piece of sidewalk. Then I'd take a piece of chalk and, starting at either end of the block, draw huge arrows leading up to the penny from both directions. After I learned to write I labeled the arrows "SURPRISE AHEAD" or "MONEY THIS WAY." I was greatly excited, during all this arrowdrawing, at the thought of the first lucky passerby who would receive in this way, regardless of merit, a free gift from the universe. But I never lurked about. I'd go straight home and not give the matter another thought, until, some months later, I would be gripped by the impulse to hide another penny.

There are lots of things to see, unwrapped gifts and free surprises. The world is fairly studded and strewn with pennies cast broadside from a generous hand. But—and this is the point—who gets excited by a mere penny? If you follow one arrow, if you crouch motionless on a bank to watch a tremulous ripple thrill on the water, and are rewarded by the sight of a muskrat kit paddling from its den, will you count that sight a chip of copper only, and go your rueful way? It is very dire poverty indeed for a man to be so malnourished and fatigued that he won't stoop to pick up a penny. But if you cultivate a healthy poverty and simplicity, so that finding a penny will make your day, then, since the world is in fact planted in pennies, you have with your poverty bought a lifetime of days. What you see is what you get.

Unfortunately, nature is very much a now-you-see-it, now-you-don't affair. A fish flashes, then dissolves in the water before my eyes like so much salt. Deer apparently ascend bodily into heaven; the brightest oriole fades into leaves. These disappearances stun me into stillness and concentration; they say of nature that it conceals with a grand nonchalance, and they say of vision that it is a deliberate gift, the revelation of a dancer who for my eyes only flings away her seven veils.

For nature does reveal as well as conceal: now-you-don't-see-it, now-you-do. For a week this September migrating red-winged blackbirds were feeding heavily down by Tinker Creek at the back of the house. One day I went out to investigate the racket; I walked up to a tree, an Osage orange, and a hundred birds flew away. They simply materialized out of the tree. I saw a tree, then a whisk of color, then a tree again. I walked closer and another hundred blackbirds took flight. Not a branch, not a twig budged: the birds were apparently weightless as well as invisible. Or, it was as if the leaves of the Osage orange had been freed from a spell in the form of redwinged blackbirds; they flew from the tree, caught my eye in the sky, and vanished. When I looked again at the tree, the leaves had reassembled as if nothing had happened. Finally I walked directly to the trunk of the tree and a final hundred, the real diehards, appeared, spread, and vanished. How could so many hide in the tree without my seeing them? The Osage orange, unruffled, looked just as it had looked from the house, when three hundred red-winged blackbirds cried from its crown. I looked upstream where they flew, and they were gone. Searching, I couldn't spot one. I wandered upstream to force them to play their hand, but they'd crossed the creek and scattered. One show to a customer. These appearances catch at my throat; they are the free gifts, the bright coppers at the roots of trees.

It's all a matter of keeping my eyes open. Nature is like one of those line 5 drawings that are puzzles for children: Can you find hidden in the tree a duck, a house, a boy, a bucket, a giraffe, and a boot? Specialists can find the most incredibly hidden things. A book I read when I was young recommended an easy way to find caterpillars: you simply find some fresh caterpillar droppings, look up, and there's your caterpillar. More recently an author advised me to set my mind at ease about those piles of cut stems on the ground in grassy fields. Field mice make them; they cut the grass down by degrees to reach the seeds at the head. It seems that when the grass is tightly packed, as in a field of ripe grain, the blade won't topple at a single cut through the stem; instead, the cut stem simply drops vertically, held in the crush of grain. The mouse severs the bottom again and again, the stem keeps dropping an inch at a time, and finally the head is low enough for the mouse to reach the seeds. Meanwhile the mouse is positively littering the field with its little piles of cut stems into which, presumably, the author is constantly stumbling.

If I can't see these minutiae, I still try to keep my eyes open. I'm always on the lookout for ant lion traps in sandy soil, monarch pupae near milkweed, skipper larvae in locust leaves. These things are utterly common, and I've not seen one. I bang on hollow trees near water, but so far no flying squirrels have appeared. In flat country I watch every sunset in hopes of seeing the green ray. The green ray is a seldom-seen streak of light that rises from the sun like a spurting fountain at the moment of sunset; it throbs into the sky for two seconds and disappears. One more reason to keep my eyes open. A photography professor at the University of Florida just happened to see a bird die in midflight; it jerked, died, dropped, and smashed on the ground.

I squint at the wind because I read Stewart Edward White: "I have always maintained that if you looked closely enough you could *see* the wind—the dim, hardly-made-out, fine débris fleeing high in the air." White was an excellent observer, and devoted an entire chapter of *The Mountains* to the subject of seeing deer: "As soon as you can forget the naturally obvious and construct an artificial obvious, then you too will see deer."

But the artificial obvious is hard to see. My eyes account for less than 1 percent of the weight of my head; I'm bony and dense; I see what I expect. I once spent a full three minutes looking at a bullfrog that was so unexpectedly large I couldn't see it even though a dozen enthusiastic campers were shouting directions. Finally I asked, "What color am I looking for?" and a fellow said, "Green." When at last I picked out the frog, I saw what painters are up against: the thing wasn't green at all, but the color of wet hickory bark.

The lover can see, and the knowledgeable. I visited an aunt and uncle at a quarter-horse ranch in Cody, Wyoming. I couldn't do much of anything useful, but I could, I thought, draw. So, as we all sat around the kitchen table after supper, I produced a sheet of paper and drew a horse. "That's one lame horse," my aunt volunteered. The rest of the family joined in: "Only place to saddle that one is his neck"; "Looks like we better shoot the poor thing, on account of those terrible growths." Meekly, I slid the pencil and paper down the table. Everyone in that family, including my three young cousins, could draw a horse. Beautifully. When the paper came back it looked as though five shining, real quarter horses had been corraled by mistake with a papier-mâché moose; the real horses seemed to gaze at the monster with a steady, puzzled air. I stay away from horses now, but I can do a creditable goldfish. The point is that I just don't know what the lover knows; I just can't see the artificial obvious that those in the know construct. The herpetologist asks the native, "Are there snakes in that ravine?" "Nosir." And the herpetologist comes home with, yessir, three bags full. Are there butterflies on that mountain? Are the bluets in bloom, are there arrowheads here, or fossil shells in the shale?

Peeping through my keyhole I see within the range of only about 30 percent of the light that comes from the sun; the rest is infrared and some little ultraviolet, perfectly apparent to many animals, but invisible to me. A nightmare network of ganglia, charged and firing without my knowledge, cuts and splices what I do see, editing it for my brain. Donald E. Carr points out that the sense impressions of one-celled animals are *not* edited for the brain: "This is philosophically interesting in a rather mournful way, since it means that only the simplest animals perceive the universe as it is."

A fog that won't burn away drifts and flows across my field of vision. When you see fog move against a backdrop of deep pines, you don't see the fog itself, but streaks of clearness floating across the air in dark shreds. So I see only tatters of clearness through a pervading obscurity. I can't distinguish the fog from the overcast sky; I can't be sure if the light is direct or reflected. Everywhere darkness and the presence of the unseen appalls. We estimate now that only one atom dances alone in every cubic meter of intergalactic space. I blink and squint. What planet or power yanks Halley's Comet out of orbit? We haven't seen it yet; it's a question of distance, density, and the pallor of reflected light. We rock, cradled in the swaddling band of darkness. Even the simple darkness of night whispers suggestions to the mind. This summer, in August, I stayed at the creek too late.

Where Tinker Creek flows under the sycamore log bridge to the tear-shaped island, it is slow and shallow, fringed thinly in cattail marsh. At this spot an astonishing bloom of life supports vast breeding popula-tions of insects, fish, reptiles, birds, and mammals. On windless sum-mer evenings I stalk along the creek bank or straddle the sycamore log in absolute stillness, watching for muskrats. The night I stayed too late I was hunched on the log staring spellbound at spreading, reflected stains of lilac on the water. A cloud in the sky suddenly lighted as if turned on by a switch; its reflection just as suddenly materialized on the water upstream, flat and floating, so that I couldn't see the creek bottom, or life in the water under the cloud. Downstream, away from the cloud on the water, water turtles smooth as beans were gliding down with the current in a series of easy, weightless push-offs, as men bound on the moon. I didn't know whether to trace the progress of one turtle I was sure of, risking sticking my face in one of the bridge's spider webs made invisible by the gathering dark, or take a chance on seeing the carp, or scan the mudbank in hope of seeing a muskrat, or follow the last of the swallows who caught at my heart and trailed it after them like stream-ers as they appeared from directly below, under the log, flying upstream with their tails forked, so fast.

But shadows spread and deepened and stayed. After thousands of years we're still strangers to darkness, fearful aliens in an enemy camp with our arms crossed over our chests. I stirred. A land turtle on the bank, startled, hissed the air from its lungs and withdrew to its shell. An uneasy pink here, an unfathomable blue there, gave great suggestion of lurking beings. Things were going on. I couldn't see whether that rustle I heard was a distant rattlesnake, slit-eyed, or a nearby sparrow kicking in the dry flood debris slung at the foot of a willow. Tremendous action roiled the water everywhere I looked, big action, inexplicable. A tremor welled up beside a gaping muskrat burrow in the bank and I caught my breath, but no muskrat appeared. The ripples continued to fan upstream with a steady, powerful thrust. Night was knitting an eyeless mask over my face, and I still sat transfixed. A distant airplane, a delta wing out of nightmare, made a gliding shadow on the creek's bottom that looked like a stingray cruising upstream. At once a black fin slit the pink cloud on the water, shearing it in two. The two halves merged together and seemed to dissolve before my eyes. Darkness pooled in the cleft of the creek and rose, as water collects in a well. Untamed, dreaming lights flickered over the sky. I saw hints of hulking underwater shadows, two pale splashes out of the water, and round ripples rolling close together from a blackened center.

At last I stared upstream where only the deepest violet remained of the cloud, a cloud so high its underbelly still glowed, its feeble color reflected from a hidden sky lighted in turn by a sun halfway to China. And out of that violet, a sudden enormous black body arced over the water. Head and tail, if there was a head and tail, were both submerged in cloud. I saw only one ebony fling, a headlong dive to darkness; then the waters closed, and the lights went out.

I walked home in a shivering daze, up hill and down. Later I lay open-mouthed in bed, my arms flung wide at my sides to steady the whirling darkness. At this latitude I'm spinning 836 miles an hour round the earth's axis; I feel my sweeping fall as a breakneck arc like the dive of dolphins, and the hollow rushing of wind raises the hairs on my neck and the side of my face. In orbit around the sun I'm moving 64,800 miles an hour. The solar system as a whole, like a merry-go-round unhinged, 15

spins, bobs, and blinks at the speed of 43,200 miles an hour along a
course set east of Hercules. Someone has piped, and we are dancing a
tarantella until the sweat pours. I open my eyes and I see dark, muscled
forms curl out of water, with flapping gills and flattened eyes. I close
my eyes and I see stars, deep stars giving way to deeper stars, deeper
stars bowing to deepest stars at the crown of an infinite cone.

"Still," wrote Van Gogh in a letter, "a great deal of light falls on everything." If we are blinded by darkness, we are also blinded by light. Sometimes here in Virginia at sunset low clouds on the southern or northern
horizon are completely invisible in the lighted sky. I only know one is
there because I can see its reflection in still water. The first time I discovered this mystery I looked from cloud to no-cloud in bewilderment,
checking my bearings over and over, thinking maybe the ark of the cov-
enant was just passing by south of Dead Man Mountain. Only much
later did I learn the explanation: polarized light from the sky is very
much weakened by reflection, but the light in clouds isn't polarized. So
invisible clouds pass among visible clouds, till all slide over the mountains; so a greater light extinguishes a lesser as though it didn't exist.

   In the great meteor shower of August, the Perseid, I wail all day for
the shooting stars I miss. They're out there showering down committing
hara-kiri in a flame of fatal attraction, and hissing perhaps at last into
the ocean. But at dawn what looks like a blue dome clamps down over
me like a lid on a pot. The stars and planets could smash and I'd never
know. Only a piece of ashen moon occasionally climbs up or down the
inside of the dome, and our local star without surcease explodes on our
heads. We have really only that one light, one source for all power, and
yet we must turn away from it by universal decree. Nobody here on the
planet seems aware of this strange, powerful taboo, that we all walk
about carefully averting our faces, this way and that, lest our eyes be
blasted forever.

   Darkness appalls and light dazzles; the scrap of visible light that
doesn't hurt my eyes hurts my brain. What I see sets me swaying. Size

and distance and the sudden swelling of meanings confuse me, bowl me over. I straddle the sycamore log bridge over Tinker Creek in the summer. I look at the lighted creek bottom: snail tracks tunnel the mud in quavering curves. A crayfish jerks, but by the time I absorb what has happened, he's gone in a billowing smoke screen of silt. I look at the water; minnows and shiners. If I'm thinking minnows, a carp will fill my brain till I scream. I look at the water's surface: skaters, bubbles, and leaves sliding down. Suddenly, my own face, reflected, startles me witless. Those snails have been tracking my face! Finally, with a shuddering wrench of the will, I see clouds, cirrus clouds. I'm dizzy, I fall in.

This looking business is risky. Once I stood on a humped rock on nearby Purgatory Mountain, watching through binoculars the great autumn hawk migration below, until I discovered that I was in danger of joining the hawks on a vertical migration of my own. I was used to binoculars, but not, apparently, to balancing on humped rocks while looking through them. I reeled. Everything advanced and receded by turns; the world was full of unexplained foreshortenings and depths. A distant huge object, a hawk the size of an elephant, turned out to be the browned bough of a nearby loblolly pine. I followed a sharp-shinned hawk against a featureless sky, rotating my head unawares as it flew, and when I lowered the glass a glimpse of my own looming shoulder sent me staggering. What prevents the men at Palomar from falling, voiceless and blinded, from their tiny, vaulted chairs?

I reel in confusion: I don't understand what I see. With the naked   20 eye I can see two million light-years to the Andromeda galaxy. Often I slop some creek water in a jar, and when I get home I dump it in a white china bowl. After the silt settles I return and see tracings of minute snails on the bottom, a planarian or two winding round the rim of water, roundworms shimmying, frantically, and finally, when my eyes have adjusted to these dimensions, amoebae. At first the amoebae look like *muscae volitantes*, those curled moving spots you seem to see in your eyes when you stare at a distant wall. Then I see the amoebae as drops of water congealed, bluish, translucent, like chips of sky in the bowl. At length I choose one individual and give myself over to its idea of an evening. I see it dribble a grainy foot before it on its wet, unfathomable way. Do its unedited sense impressions include the fierce focus of my eyes? Shall I take it outside and show it Andromeda, and blow its little endoplasm? I stir the water with a finger, in case it's running out of oxygen. Maybe I should get a tropical aquarium with motorized bubblers and lights, and keep this one for a pet. Yes, it would tell its fissioned descendants, the universe is two feet by five, and if you listen closely you can hear the buzzing music of the spheres.

Oh, it's mysterious, lamplit evenings here in the galaxy, one after the other. It's one of those nights when I wander from window to window, looking for a sign. But I can't see. Terror and a beauty insoluble are a riband of blue woven into the fringe of garments of things both great and small. No culture explains, no bivouac offers real haven or rest. But it could be that we are not seeing something. Galileo thought comets were an optical illusion. This is fertile ground: since we are certain that they're not, we can look at what our scientists have been saying with fresh hope. What if there are *really* gleaming, castellated cities hung upside-down over the desert sand? What limpid lakes and cool date palms have our caravans always passed untried? Until, one by one, by the blindest of leaps, we light on the road to these places, we must stumble in darkness and hunger. I turn from the window. I'm blind as a bat, sensing only from every direction the echo of my own thin cries.

I chanced on a wonderful book called *Space and Sight*, by Marius Von Senden. When Western surgeons discovered how to perform safe cataract operations, they ranged across Europe and America operating on dozens of men and women of all ages who had been blinded by cataracts since birth. Von Senden collected accounts of such cases; the histories are fascinating. Many doctors had tested their patients' sense perceptions and ideas of space both before and after the operations. The vast majority of patients, of both sexes and all ages, had, in Von Senden's opinion, no idea of space whatsoever. Form, distance, and size were so many meaningless syllables. A patient "had no idea of depth, confusing it with roundness." Before the operation a doctor would give a blind patient a cube and a sphere; the patient would tongue it or feel it with his hands, and name it correctly. After the operation the doctor would show the same objects to the patient without letting him touch them; now he had no clue whatsoever to what he was seeing. One patient called lemonade "square" because it pricked on his tongue as a square shape pricked on the touch of his hands. Of another post-operative patient the doctor writes, "I have found in her no notion of size, for example, not even within the narrow limits which she might have encompassed with the aid of touch. Thus when I asked her to show me how big her mother was, she did not stretch out her hands, but set her two index fingers a few inches apart."

For the newly sighted, vision is pure sensation unencumbered by meaning. When a newly sighted girl saw photographs and paintings, she asked, " 'Why do they put those dark marks all over them?' 'Those aren't dark marks,' her mother explained, 'those are shadows. That is one of the ways the eye knows that things have shape. If it were not for shadows, many things would look flat.' 'Well, that's how things do look,' Joan answered. 'Everything looks flat with dark patches.' "

In general the newly sighted see the world as a dazzle of "color-patches." They are pleased by the sensation of color, and learn quickly to name the colors, but the rest of seeing is tormentingly difficult. Soon after his operation a patient "generally bumps into one of these color-patches and observes them to be substantial, since they resist him as tactual objects do. In walking about it also strikes him—or can if he pays attention—that he is continually passing in between the colors he sees, that he can go past a visual object, that a part of it then steadily disappears from view; and that in spite of this, however he twists and turns—whether entering the room from the door, for example, or return-ing back to it—he always has a visual space in front of him. Thus he gradually comes to realize that there is also a space behind him, which he does not see."

The mental effort involved in these reasonings proves overwhelming   25 for many patients. It oppresses them to realize that they have been visible to people all along, perhaps unattractively so, without their knowledge or consent. A disheartening number of them refuse to use their new vision, continuing to go over objects with their tongues, and lapsing into apathy and despair.

On the other hand, many newly sighted people speak well of the world, and teach us how dull our own vision is. To one patient, a human hand, unrecognized, is "something bright and then holes." Shown a bunch of grapes, a boy calls out, "It is dark, blue and shiny. . . . It isn't smooth, it has bumps and hollows." A little girl visits a garden. "She is greatly astonished, and can scarcely be persuaded to answer, stands speechless in front of the tree, which she only names on taking hold of it, and then as 'the tree with the lights in it.' " Another patient, a twenty-two-year-old girl, was dazzled by the world's brightness and kept her eyes shut for two weeks. When at the end of that time she opened her eyes again, she did not recognize any objects, but "the more she now directed her gaze upon everything about her, the more it could be seen how an expression of gratification and astonishment overspread her features; she repeatedly exclaimed: 'Oh God! How beautiful!' "

I saw color-patches for weeks after I read this wonderful book. It was summer; the peaches were ripe in the valley orchards. When I woke in the morning, color-patches wrapped round my eyes, intricately, leaving not one unfilled spot. All day long I walked among shifting color-patches that parted before me like the Red Sea and closed again in silence, transfigured, wherever I looked back. Some patches swelled and loomed, while others vanished utterly, and dark marks flitted at random over the whole dazzling sweep. But I couldn't sustain the illusion of flatness. I've been around for too long. Form is condemned to an eternal danse macabre with meaning: I couldn't unpeach the peaches. Nor can I remember ever having seen without understanding; the color-patches of infancy are lost. My brain then must have been smooth as any balloon. I'm told I reached for the moon; many babies do. But the color-patches of infancy swelled as meaning filled them; they arrayed themselves in solemn ranks down distance which unrolled and stretched before me like a plain. The moon rocketed away. I live now in a world of shadows that shape and distance color, a world where space makes a kind of terrible sense. What Gnosticism is this, and what physics? The fluttering patch I saw in my nursery window—silver and green and shape-shifting blue—is gone; a row of Lombardy poplars takes its place, mute, across the distant lawn. That humming oblong creature pale as light that stole along the walls of my room at night, stretching exhila-ratingly around the corners, is gone, too, gone the night I ate of the bittersweet fruit, put two and two together and puckered forever my brain. Martin Buber tells this tale: "Rabbi Mendel once boasted to his teacher Rabbi Elimelekh that evenings he saw the angel who rolls away the light before the darkness, and mornings the angel who rolls away the darkness before the light. 'Yes,' said Rabbi Elimelekh, 'in my youth I saw that too. Later on you don't see these things anymore.'"

Why didn't someone hand those newly sighted people paints and brushes from the start, when they still didn't know what anything was? Then maybe we all could see color-patches too, the world unraveled from reason, Eden before Adam gave names. The scales would drop from my eyes; I'd see trees like men walking; I'd run down the road against all orders, hallooing and leaping.

Seeing is of course very much a matter of verbalization. Unless I call my attention to what passes before my eyes, I simply won't see it. If Tinker Mountain erupted, I'd be likely to notice. But if I want to notice the lesser cataclysms of valley life, I have to maintain in my head a running

description of the present. It's not that I'm observant; it's just that I talk
too much. Otherwise, especially in a strange place, I'll never know
what's happening. Like a blind man at the ball game, I need a radio.

When I see this way I analyze and pry. I hurl over logs and roll away   30
stones; I study the bank a square foot at a time, probing and tilting my
head. Some days when a mist covers the mountains, when the muskrats
won't show and the microscope's mirror shatters, I want to climb up the
blank blue dome as a man would storm the inside of a circus tent, wildly,
dangling, and with a steel knife claw a rent in the top, peep, and, if I
must, fall.

But there is another kind of seeing that involves a letting go. When I
see this way I sway transfixed and emptied. The difference between the
two ways of seeing is the difference between walking with and without
a camera. When I walk with a camera I walk from shot to shot, reading
the light on a calibrated meter. When I walk without a camera, my own
shutter opens, and the moment's light prints on my own silver gut.
When I see this second way I am above all an unscrupulous observer.

It was sunny one evening last summer at Tinker Creek; the sun was
low in the sky, upstream. I was sitting on the sycamore log bridge with
the sunset at my back, watching the shiners the size of minnows who
were feeding over the muddy sand in skittery schools. Again and again,
one fish, then another, turned for a split second across the current and
flash! the sun shot out from its silver side. I couldn't watch for it. It was
always just happening somewhere else, and it drew my vision just as it
disappeared: flash! like a sudden dazzle of the thinnest blade, a sparking
over a dun and olive ground at chance intervals from every direction.
Then I noticed white specks, some sort of pale petals, small, floating
from under my feet on the creek's surface, very slow and steady. So I
blurred my eyes and gazed toward the brim of my hat and saw a new
world. I saw the pale white circles roll up, roll up, like the world's turning, mute and perfect, and I saw the linear flashes, gleaming silver, like
stars being born at random down a rolling scroll of time. Something

broke and something opened. I filled up like a new wineskin. I breathed an air like light; I saw a light like water. I was the lip of a fountain the creek filled forever; I was ether, the leaf in the zephyr; I was flesh-flake, feather, bone.

When I see this way I see truly. As Thoreau says, I return to my senses. I am the man who watches the baseball game in silence in an empty stadium. I see the game purely; I'm abstracted and dazed. When it's all over and the white-suited players lope off the green field to their shadowed dugouts, I leap to my feet, I cheer and cheer.

But I can't go out and try to see this way. I'll fail, I'll go mad. All I can do is try to gag the commentator, to hush the noise of useless interior babble that keeps me from seeing just as surely as a newspaper dangled before my eyes. The effort is really a discipline requiring a lifetime of dedicated struggle; it marks the literature of saints and monks of every order east and west, under every rule and no rule, discalced and shod. The world's spiritual geniuses seem to discover universally that the mind's muddy river, this ceaseless flow of trivia and trash, cannot be dammed, and that trying to dam it is a waste of effort that might lead to madness. Instead you must allow the muddy river to flow unheeded in the dim channels of consciousness; you raise your sights; you look along it, mildly, acknowledging its presence without interest and gazing beyond it into the realm of the real where subjects and objects act and rest purely, without utterance. "Launch into the deep," says Jacques Ellul, "and you shall see."

The secret of seeing, then, is the pearl of great price. If I thought he 35 could teach me to find it and keep it forever I would stagger barefoot across a hundred deserts after any lunatic at all. But although the pearl may be found, it may not be sought. The literature of illumination reveals this above all: although it comes to those who wait for it, it is always, even to the most practiced and adept, a gift and a total surprise. I return from one walk knowing where the killdeer nests in the field by the creek and the hour the laurel blooms. I return from the same walk a day later scarcely knowing my own name. Litanies hum in my ears; my tongue flaps in my mouth, *Alim non*, alleluia! I cannot cause light; the most I can do is try to put myself in the path of its beam. It is possible, in deep space, to sail on solar wind. Light, be it particle or wave, has force: you rig a giant sail and go. The secret of seeing is to sail on solar wind. Hone and spread your spirit till you yourself are a sail, whetted, translucent, broadside to the merest puff.

When her doctor took her bandages off and led her into the garden, the girl who was no longer blind saw "the tree with the lights in it." It was for this tree I searched through the peach orchards of summer, in the forests of fall and down winter and spring for years. Then one day I was walking along Tinker Creek thinking of nothing at all and I saw the tree with the lights in it. I saw the backyard cedar where the mourning doves roost charged and transfigured, each cell buzzing with flame. I stood on the grass with the lights in it, grass that was wholly fire, utterly focused and utterly dreamed. It was less like seeing than like being for the first time seen, knocked breathless by a powerful glance. The flood of fire abated, but I'm still spending the power. Gradually the lights went out in the cedar, the colors died, the cells unflamed and disappeared. I was still ringing. I had been my whole life a bell, and never knew it until at that moment I was lifted and struck. I have since only very rarely seen the tree with the lights in it. The vision comes and goes, mostly goes, but I live for it, for the moment when the mountains open and a new light roars in spate through the crack, and the mountains slam.

Thinking about the Text

1. According to Annie Dillard, what are some of the factors that affect how and what a person sees?

2. Compare Henry David Thoreau's journal entry, "Observation" (pp. 3–5), to Dillard's essay on seeing. Do any of Dillard's examples illustrate Thoreau's more general claims about observation? Are there any ways in which their views on observation differ? Cite specific passages to support your response.

3. Spend at least fifteen minutes observing something—you might watch people or, like Dillard, you could observe some aspect of the natural world. In an essay, describe *what* you saw and reflect on *how* you see. As you develop your essay, consider researching some other sources on observation and, as Dillard does in her writing, weave quotations from those sources into your essay.

A. BARTLETT GIAMATTI

The Green Fields of the Mind

1977

A. BARTLETT GIAMATTI (1938–1989) wrote essays about literature, higher education, and baseball. He was a professor at and then president of Yale University before becoming Commissioner of Major League Baseball. "The Green Fields of the Mind" was first published in the *Yale Alumni Magazine* in 1977 and was later included in *A Great and Glorious Game: Baseball Writings of A. Bartlett Giamatti* (1998).

IT BREAKS YOUR HEART. IT IS DESIGNED TO BREAK YOUR HEART. The game begins in the spring, when everything else begins again, and it blossoms in the summer, filling the afternoons and evenings, and then as soon as the chill rains come, it stops and leaves you to face the fall alone. You count on it, rely on it to buffer the passage of time, to keep the memory of sunshine and high skies alive, and then just when the days are all twilight, when you need it most, it stops. Today, October 2, a Sunday of rain and broken branches and leaf-clogged drains and slick streets, it stopped, and summer was gone.

Somehow, the summer seemed to slip by faster this time. Maybe it wasn't this summer, but all the summers that, in this my 40th summer, slipped by so fast. There comes a time when every summer will have something of autumn about it. Whatever the reason, it seemed to me that I was investing more and more in baseball, making the game do more of the work that keeps time fat and slow and lazy. I was counting on the game's deep patterns, three strikes, three outs, three times three innings, and its deepest impulse, to go out and back, to leave and to return home, to set the order of the day and to organize the daylight. I wrote a few things this last summer, this summer that did not last, noth-ing grand but some things, and yet that work was just camouflage. The real activity was done with the radio—not the all-seeing, all-falsifying television—and was the playing of the game in the only place it will last, the enclosed green field of the mind. There, in that warm, bright place, what the old poet called Mutability does not so quickly come.

But out here, on Sunday, October 2, where it rains all day, Dame Mutability never loses. She was in the crowd at Fenway yesterday, a grey day full of bluster and contradiction, when the Red Sox came up in the last of the ninth trailing Baltimore 8–5, while the Yankees, rain-delayed against Detroit, only needing to win one or have Boston lose one to win it all, sat in New York washing down cold cuts with beer and watching the Boston game. Boston had won two, the Yankees had lost two, and suddenly it seemed as if the whole season might go to the last day, or beyond, except here was Boston losing 8–5, while New York sat in its family room and put its feet up. Lynn, both ankles hurting now as they had in July, hits a single down the right-field line. The crowd stirs. It is on its feet. Hobson, third baseman, former Bear Bryant quarterback, strong, quiet, over 100 RBIs, goes for three breaking balls and is out. The goddess smiles and encourages her agent, a canny journeyman named Nelson Briles.

Now comes a pinch hitter, Bernie Carbo, onetime Rookie of the Year, erratic, quick, a shade too handsome, so laid-back he is always, in his soul, stretched out in the tall grass, one arm under his head, watching the clouds and laughing; now he looks over some low stuff unworthy of him and then, uncoiling, sends one out, straight on a rising line, over the center-field wall, no cheap Fenway shot, but all of it, the physics as elegant as the arc the ball describes.

New England is on its feet, roaring. The summer will not pass. Roaring, they recall the evening, late and cold, in 1975, the sixth game of the World Series, perhaps the greatest baseball game played in the last fifty years, when Carbo, loose and easy, had uncoiled to tie the game that Fisk would win. It is 8–7, one out, and school will never start, rain will never come, sun will warm the back of your neck forever. Now Bailey, picked up from the National League recently, big arms, heavy gut, experienced, new to the league and the club; he fouls off two and then, checking, tentative, a big man off balance, he pops a soft liner to the first baseman. It is suddenly darker and later, and the announcer doing the game coast to coast, a New Yorker who works for a New York television station, sounds relieved. His little world, well-lit, hot-combed, split-second-timed, had no capacity to absorb this much gritty, grainy, contrary reality.

Cox swings a bat, stretches his long arms, bends his back, the rookie from Pawtucket who broke in two weeks earlier with a record six straight hits, the kid drafted ahead of Fred Lynn, rangy, smooth, cool. The count runs two and two, Briles is cagey, nothing too good, and Cox swings,

5

the ball beginning toward the mound and then, in a jaunty, wayward dance, skipping past Briles, feinting to the right, skimming the last of the grass, finding the dirt, moving now like some small, purposeful marine creature negotiating the green deep, easily avoiding the jagged rock of second base, traveling steady and straight now out into the dark, silent recesses of center field.

The aisles are jammed, the place is on its feet, the wrappers, the programs, the Coke cups and peanut shells, the detritus of an afternoon; the anxieties, the things that have to be done tomorrow, the regrets about yesterday, the accumulation of a summer: all forgotten, while hope, the anchor, bites and takes hold where a moment before it seemed we would be swept out with the tide. Rice is up. Rice whom Aaron had said was the only one he'd seen with the ability to break his records. Rice the best clutch hitter on the club, with the best slugging percentage in the league. Rice, so quick and strong he once checked his swing halfway through and snapped the bat in two. Rice the Hammer of God sent to scourge the Yankees, the sound was overwhelming, fathers pounded their sons on the back, cars pulled off the road, households froze, New England exulted in its blessedness, and roared its thanks for all good things, for Rice and for a summer stretching halfway through October. Briles threw, Rice swung, and it was over. One pitch, a fly to center, and it stopped. Summer died in New England and like rain sliding off a roof, the crowd slipped out of Fenway, quickly, with only a steady murmur of concern for the drive ahead remaining of the roar. Mutability had turned the seasons and translated hope to memory once again. And, once again, she had used baseball, our best invention to stay change, to bring change on. That is why it breaks my heart, that game—not because in New York they could win because Boston lost; in that, there is a rough justice, and a reminder to the Yankees of how slight and fragile are the circumstances that exalt one group of human beings over another. It breaks my heart because it was meant to, because it was meant to foster in me again the illusion that there was something abiding, some pattern and some impulse that could come together to make a reality that would resist the corrosion; and because, after it had fostered again that most hungered-for illusion, the game was meant to stop, and betray precisely what it promised.

Of course, there are those who learn after the first few times. They grow out of sports. And there are others who were born with the wisdom to know that nothing lasts. These are the truly tough among us, the ones who can live without illusion, or without even the hope of illusion. I am not that grown-up or up-to-date. I am a simpler creature, tied to more primitive patterns and cycles. I need to think something lasts forever, and it might as well be that state of being that is a game; it might as well be that, in a green field, in the sun.

Thinking about the Text

1. A. Bartlett Giamatti focuses on a paradox in his essay, writing that baseball is both "our best invention to stay change" and one that "bring[s] change on" (paragraph 7). What does he mean by this? How does his essay demonstrate this paradox?

2. Giamatti seems to suggest that listening to a game on the radio is better than watching it on "the all-seeing, all-falsifying television" (paragraph 2). Why? Which medium do you prefer—and why?

3. Write an essay reflecting on something that occurs annually that has special meaning to you—a sport, a holiday, a music festival, or some other event. Like Giamatti does in writing about baseball, show why you consider that annual event significant.

WILLIAM ZINSSER

College Pressures

1979

WILLIAM ZINSSER (1922–2015) wrote journalism and other nonfiction, often on the craft of writing. He is best known for his book *On Writing Well* (1976). From 2010 to 2011 he wrote for *Zinsser on Friday*, his blog for the *American Scholar* that covered topics such as writing, the arts, and pop culture. He wrote "College Pressures" when he was the head of Branford College, a residential college at Yale University. It was first published in *Blair and Ketchum's Country Journal* (1979), a small circulation bimonthly magazine about rural life, which has since ceased publication.

Dear Carlos: I desperately need a dean's excuse for my chem mid-term which will begin in about 1 hour. All I can say is that I totally blew it this week. I've fallen incredibly, inconceivably behind.

Carlos: Help! I'm anxious to hear from you. I'll be in my room and won't leave it until I hear from you. Tomorrow is the last day for . . .

Carlos: I left town because I started bugging out again. I stayed up all night to finish a take-home make-up exam & am typing it to hand in on the 10th. It was due on the 5th. P.S. I'm going to the dentist. Pain is pretty bad.

Carlos: Probably by Friday I'll be able to get back to my studies. Right now I'm going to take a long walk. This whole thing has taken a lot out of me.

Carlos: I'm really up the proverbial creek. The problem is I really *bombed* the history final. Since I need that course for my major I . . .

Carlos: Here follows a tale of woe. I went home this weekend, had to help my Mom, & caught a fever so didn't have much time to study. My professor . . .

Carlos: Aargh! Trouble. Nothing original but everything's piling up at once. To be brief, my job interview . . .

Hey Carlos, good news! I've got mononucleosis.

Who are these wretched supplicants, scribbling notes so laden with anxiety, seeking such miracles of postponement and balm? They are men and women who belong to Branford College, one of the twelve residential colleges at Yale University, and the messages are just a few of the hundreds that they left for their dean, Carlos Hortas—often slipped under his door at 4 A.M.—last year.

But students like the ones who wrote those notes can also be found on campuses from coast to coast—especially in New England and at many other private colleges across the country that have high academic standards and highly motivated students. Nobody could doubt that the notes are real. In their urgency and their gallows humor they are authentic voices of a generation that is panicky to succeed.

My own connection with the message writers is that I am master of Branford College. I live in its Gothic quadrangle and know the students well. (We have 485 of them.) I am privy to their hopes and fears—and also to their stereo music and their piercing cries in the dead of night ("Does anybody *ca-a-are?*"). If they went to Carlos to ask how to get through tomorrow, they come to me to ask how to get through the rest of their lives.

Mainly I try to remind them that the road ahead is a long one and that it will have more unexpected turns than they think. There will be plenty of time to change jobs, change careers, change whole attitudes and approaches. They don't want to hear such liberating news. They want a map—right now—that they can follow unswervingly to career security, financial security, Social Security and, presumably, a prepaid grave.

What I wish for all students is some release from the clammy grip of 5 the future. I wish them a chance to savor each segment of their education as an experience in itself and not as a grim preparation for the next step. I wish them the right to experiment, to trip and fall, to learn that defeat is as instructive as victory and is not the end of the world.

My wish, of course, is naive. One of the few rights that America does not proclaim is the right to fail. Achievement is the national god, venerated in our media—the million-dollar athlete, the wealthy executive—and glorified in our praise of possessions. In the presence of such a potent state religion, the young are growing up old.

I see four kinds of pressure working on college students today: economic pressure, parental pressure, peer pressure, and self-induced pressure. It is easy to look around for villains—to blame the colleges for charging too much money, the professors for assigning too much work, the parents for pushing their children too far, the students for driving themselves too hard. But there are no villains; only victims.

"In the late 1960s," one dean told me, "the typical question that I got from students was 'Why is there so much suffering in the world?' or 'How can I make a contribution?' Today it's 'Do you think it would look better for getting into law school if I did a double major in history and political science, or just majored in one of them?'" Many other deans confirmed this pattern. One said: "They're trying to find an edge—the intangible something that will look better on paper if two students are about equal."

Note the emphasis on looking better. The transcript has become a sacred document, the passport to security. How one appears on paper is more important than how one appears in person. *A* is for Admirable and *B* is for Borderline, even though, in Yale's official system of grading, *A* means "excellent" and *B* means "very good." Today, looking very good is no longer good enough, especially for students who hope to go on to law school or medical school. They know that entrance into the better schools will be an entrance into the better law firms and better medical practices where they will make a lot of money. They also know that the odds are harsh. Yale Law School, for instance, matriculates 170 students from an applicant pool of 3,700; Harvard enrolls 550 from a pool of 7,000.

It's all very well for those of us who write letters of recommendation   10 for our students to stress the qualities of humanity that will make them good lawyers or doctors. And it's nice to think that admission officers are really reading our letters and looking for the extra dimension of commitment or concern. Still, it would be hard for a student not to visualize these officers shuffling so many transcripts studded with *A*s that they regard a *B* as positively shameful.

The pressure is almost as heavy on students who just want to gradu-ate and get a job. Long gone are the days of the "gentleman's C," when students journeyed through college with a certain relaxation, sampling a wide variety of courses—music, art, philosophy, classics, anthropology, poetry, religion—that would send them out as liberally educated men and women. If I were an employer I would rather employ graduates who have this range and curiosity than those who narrowly pursued safe sub-jects and high grades. I know countless students whose inquiring minds exhilarate me. I like to hear the play of their ideas. I don't know if they are getting As or Cs, and I don't care. I also like them as people. The country needs them, and they will find satisfying jobs. I tell them to relax. They can't.

Nor can I blame them. They live in a brutal economy. Tuition, room, and board at most private colleges now comes to at least $7,000, not counting books and fees. This might seem to suggest that the colleges are getting rich. But they are equally battered by inflation. Tuition cov-ers only 60 percent of what it costs to educate a student, and ordinarily the remainder comes from what colleges receive in endowments, grants, and gifts. Now the remainder keeps being swallowed by the cruel costs—higher every year—of just opening the doors. Heating oil is up. Insurance is up. Postage is up. Health-premium costs are up. Everything is up. Deficits are up. We are witnessing in America the creation of a brotherhood of paupers—colleges, parents, and students, joined by the common bond of debt.

Today it is not unusual for a student, even if he works part time at college and full time during the summer, to accrue $5,000 in loans after four years—loans that he must start to repay within one year after graduation. Exhorted at commencement to go forth into the world, he is already behind as he goes forth. How could he not feel under pres-sure throughout college to prepare for this day of reckoning? I have used "he," incidentally, only for brevity. Women at Yale are under no less pressure to justify their expensive education to themselves, their parents, and society. In fact, they are probably under more pressure. For although they leave college superbly equipped to bring fresh leadership to traditionally male jobs, society hasn't yet caught up with this fact.

Along with economic pressure goes parental pressure. Inevitably, the two are deeply intertwined.

I see many students taking pre-medical courses with joyless tenac- 15 ity. They go off to their labs as if they were going to the dentist. It saddens me because I know them in other corners of their life as cheerful people.

"Do you want to go to medical school?" I ask them.

"I guess so," they say, without conviction, or "Not really."

"Then why are you going?"

"Well, my parents want me to be a doctor. They're paying all this money and . . ."

Poor students, poor parents. They are caught in one of the oldest 20 webs of love and duty and guilt. The parents mean well; they are trying to steer their sons and daughters toward a secure future. But the sons and daughters want to major in history or classics or philosophy— subjects with no "practical" value. Where's the payoff on the humanities? It's not easy to persuade such loving parents that the humanities do indeed pay off. The intellectual faculties developed by studying subjects like history and classics—an ability to synthesize and relate, to weigh cause and effect, to see events in perspective—are just the faculties that make creative leaders in business or almost any general field. Still, many fathers would rather put their money on courses that point toward a specific profession—courses that are pre-law, pre-medical, pre-business, or, as I sometimes heard it put, "pre-rich."

But the pressure on students is severe. They are truly torn. One part of them feels obligated to fulfill their parents' expectations; after all, their parents are older and presumably wiser. Another part tells them that the expectations that are right for their parents are not right for them.

I know a student who wants to be an artist. She is very obviously an artist and will be a good one—she has already had several modest local exhibits. Meanwhile she is growing as a well-rounded person and taking humanistic subjects that will enrich the inner resources out of which her art will grow. But her father is strongly opposed. He thinks that an artist is a "dumb" thing to be. The student vacillates and tries to please everybody. She keeps up with her art somewhat furtively and takes some of the "dumb" courses her father wants her to take—at least they are dumb courses for her. She is a free spirit on a campus of tense students—no small achievement in itself—and she deserves to follow her muse.

Peer pressure and self-induced pressure are also intertwined, and they begin almost at the beginning of freshman year.

"I had a freshman student I'll call Linda," one dean told me, "who came in and said she was under terrible pressure because her roommate, Barbara, was much brighter and studied all the time. I couldn't tell her that Barbara had come in two hours earlier to say the same thing about Linda."

The story is almost funny—except that it's not. It's symptomatic of 25 all the pressures put together. When every student thinks every other student is working harder and doing better, the only solution is to study harder still. I see students going off to the library every night after dinner and coming back when it closes at midnight. I wish they would sometimes forget about their peers and go to a movie. I hear the clacking of typewriters in the hours before dawn. I see the tension in their eyes when exams are approaching and papers are due: *Will I get everything done?*

Probably they won't. They will get sick. They will get "blocked." They will sleep. They will oversleep. They will bug out. *Hey Carlos, help!*

Part of the problem is that they do more than they are expected to do. A professor will assign five-page papers. Several students will start

writing ten-page papers to impress him. Then more students will write
ten-page papers, and a few will raise the ante to fifteen. Pity the poor
student who is still just doing the assignment.

"Once you have twenty or thirty percent of the student population
deliberately overexerting," one dean points out, "it's bad for everybody.
When a teacher gets more and more effort from his class, the student
who is doing normal work can be perceived as not doing well. The tactic
works, psychologically."

Why can't the professor just cut back and not accept longer papers?
He can, and he probably will. But by then the term will be half over and
the damage done. Grade fever is highly contagious and not easily
reversed. Besides, the professor's main concern is with his course. He
knows his students only in relation to the course and doesn't know that
they are also overexerting in their other courses. Nor is it really his
business. He didn't sign up for dealing with the student as a whole
person and with all the emotional baggage the student brought along
from home. That's what deans, masters, chaplains, and psychiatrists
are for.

To some extent this is nothing new: a certain number of professors   30
have always been self-contained islands of scholarship and shyness,
more comfortable with books than with people. But the new pauperism
has widened the gap still further, for professors who actually like to
spend time with students don't have as much time to spend. They also
are overexerting. If they are young, they are busy trying to publish in
order not to perish, hanging by their finger nails onto a shrinking profession. If they are old and tenured, they are buried under the duties of
administering departments—as departmental chairmen or members of
committees—that have been thinned out by the budgetary axe.

Ultimately it will be the students' own business to break the circles in
which they are trapped. They are too young to be prisoners of their parents' dreams and their classmates' fears. They must be jolted into believing in themselves as unique men and women who have the power to
shape their own future.

"Violence is being done to the undergraduate experience," says Carlos Hortas. "College should be open-ended: at the end it should open many, many roads. Instead, students are choosing their goal in advance, and their choices narrow as they go along. It's almost as if they think that the country has been codified in the type of jobs that exist—that they've got to fit into certain slots. Therefore, fit into the best-paying slot.

"They ought to take chances. Not taking chances will lead to a life of colorless mediocrity. They'll be comfortable. But something in the spirit will be missing."

I have painted too drab a portrait of today's students, making them seem a solemn lot. That is only half of their story; if they were so dreary I wouldn't so thoroughly enjoy their company. The other half is that they are easy to like. They are quick to laugh and to offer friendship. They are not introverts. They are unusually kind and are more considerate of one another than any student generation I have known.

Nor are they so obsessed with their studies that they avoid sports   35
and extracurricular activities. On the contrary, they juggle their crowded hours to play on a variety of teams, perform with musical and dramatic groups, and write for campus publications. But this in turn is one more cause of anxiety. There are too many choices. Academically, they have 1,300 courses to select from; outside class they have to decide how much spare time they can spare and how to spend it.

This means that they engage in fewer extracurricular pursuits than their predecessors did. If they want to row on the crew and play in the symphony they will eliminate one; in the '60s they would have done both. They also tend to choose activities that are self-limiting. Drama, for instance, is flourishing in all twelve of Yale's residential colleges as it never has before. Students hurl themselves into these productions— as actors, directors, carpenters, and technicians—with a dedication to create the best possible play, knowing that the day will come when the run will end and they can get back to their studies.

They also can't afford to be the willing slave of organizations like the *Yale Daily News.* Last spring at the one-hundredth anniversary banquet of that paper—whose past chairmen include such once and future kings as Potter Stewart, Kingman Brewster, and William F. Buckley, Jr.— much was made of the fact that the editorial staff used to be small and totally committed and that "newsies" routinely worked fifty hours a week. In effect they belonged to a club; Newsies is how they defined themselves at Yale. Today's student will write one or two articles a week, when he can, and he defines himself as a student. I've never heard the word Newsie except at the banquet.

If I have described the modern undergraduate primarily as a driven creature who is largely ignoring the blithe spirit inside who keeps trying to come out and play, it's because that's where the crunch is, not only at Yale but throughout American education. It's why I think we should all be worried about the values that are nurturing a generation so fearful of risk and so goal-obsessed at such an early age.

I tell students that there is no one "right" way to get ahead—that each of them is a different person, starting from a different point and bound for a different destination. I tell them that change is a tonic and that all the slots are not codified nor the frontiers closed. One of my ways of telling them is to invite men and women who have achieved success outside the academic world to come and talk informally with my students during the year. They are heads of companies or ad agencies, editors of magazines, politicians, public officials, television magnates, labor leaders, business executives, Broadway producers, artists, writers, economists, photographers, scientists, historians—a mixed bag of achievers.

I ask them to say a few words about how they got started. The stu- 40 dents assume that they started in their present profession and knew all along that it was what they wanted to do. Luckily for me, most of them got into their field by a circuitous route, to their surprise, after many detours. The students are startled. They can hardly conceive of a career that was not pre-planned. They can hardly imagine allowing the hand of God or chance to nudge them down some unforeseen trail.

Thinking about the Text

1. What college pressures does William Zinsser identify? How are they intertwined? Are there any pressures you would add to those he lists and describes?

2. Zinsser's essay was published in 1979. Which parts of his essay still seem relevant? Which parts seem less relevant? In what ways have specific pressures changed, intensified, or lessened?

3. Zinsser claims that one source of pressure for college students is that they are too focused on specific goals and future employment. He suggests listening to the stories of those who have become successful in a particular field—often "by a circuitous route" (paragraph 40). Interview and then write a profile of someone who has a career in a field that interests you.

LEWIS THOMAS

Notes on Punctuation

1979

LEWIS THOMAS (1913–1993) was a scientist, physician, and writer of poetry and essays. He regularly wrote essays for the *New England Journal of Medicine*, many of which he published in books such as *The Lives of a Cell: Notes of a Biology Watcher* (1974). "Notes on Punctuation" was published in *The Medusa and the Snail: More Notes of a Biology Watcher* (1979).

THERE ARE NO PRECISE RULES ABOUT PUNCTUATION (Fowler lays out some general advice (as best he can under the complex circumstances of English prose (he points out, for example, that we possess only four stops (the comma, the semicolon, the colon and the period (the question mark and exclamation point are not, strictly speaking, stops; they are indicators of tone (oddly enough, the Greeks employed the semicolon for their question mark (it produces a strange sensation to read a Greek sentence which is a straightforward question: Why weepest thou; (instead of Why weepest thou? (and, of course, there are parentheses (which are surely a kind of punctuation making this whole much more complicated by having to count up the left-handed parentheses in order to be sure of closing with the right number (but if the parentheses were left out, with nothing to work with but the stops, we would have considerably more flexibility in the deploying of layers of meaning than if we tried to separate all the clauses by physical barriers (and in the latter case, while we might have more precision and exactitude for our meaning, we would lose the essential flavor of language, which is its wonderful ambiguity)))))))))))).

The commas are the most useful and usable of all the stops. It is highly important to put them in place as you go along. If you try to come back after doing a paragraph and stick them in the various spots that tempt you you will discover that they tend to swarm like minnows into all sorts of crevices whose existence you hadn't realized and before you know it the whole long sentence becomes immobilized and lashed up squirming in commas. Better to use them sparingly, and with affection, precisely when the need for each one arises, nicely, by itself.

I have grown fond of semicolons in recent years. The semicolon tells you that there is still some question about the preceding full sentence; something needs to be added; it reminds you sometimes of the Greek usage. It is almost always a greater pleasure to come across a semicolon than a period. The period tells you that that is that; if you didn't get all the meaning you wanted or expected, anyway you got all the writer intended to parcel out and now you have to move along. But with a semi-colon there you get a pleasant little feeling of expectancy; there is more to come; read on; it will get clearer.

Colons are a lot less attractive, for several reasons: firstly, they give you the feeling of being rather ordered around, or at least having your nose pointed in a direction you might not be inclined to take if left to yourself, and, secondly, you suspect you're in for one of those sentences that will be labeling the points to be made: firstly, secondly and so forth, with the implication that you haven't sense enough to keep track of a sequence of notions without having them numbered. Also, many writers use this system loosely and incompletely, starting out with number one and number two as though counting off on their fingers but then going on and on without the succession of labels you've been led to expect, leaving you floundering about searching for the ninthly or seventeenthly that ought to be there but isn't.

Exclamation points are the most irritating of all. Look! they say, look at what I just said! How amazing is my thought! It is like being forced to watch someone else's small child jumping up and down crazily in the center of the living room shouting to attract attention. If a sentence really has something of importance to say, something quite remarkable, it doesn't need a mark to point it out. And if it is really, after all, a banal sentence needing more zing, the exclamation point simply emphasizes its banality!

Quotation marks should be used honestly and sparingly, when there is a genuine quotation at hand, and it is necessary to be very rigorous about the words enclosed by the marks. If something is to be quoted, the *exact* words must be used. If part of it must be left out because of space limitations, it is good manners to insert three dots to indicate the omis-sion, but it is unethical to do this if it means connecting two thoughts which the original author did not intend to have tied together. Above all, quotation marks should not be used for ideas that you'd like to disown, things in the air so to speak. Nor should they be put in place around clichés; if you want to use a cliché you must take full responsibility for it yourself and not try to job it off on anon., or on society. The most objectionable misuse of quotation marks, but one which illustrates the dangers of misuse in ordinary prose, is seen in advertising, especially in advertisements for small restaurants, for example "just around the corner," or "a good place to eat." No single, identifiable, citable person ever really said, for the record, "just around the corner," much less "a good place to eat," least likely of all for restaurants of the type that use this type of prose.

The dash is a handy device, informal and essentially playful, telling you that you're about to take off on a different tack but still in some way connected with the present course—only you have to remember that the dash is there, and either put a second dash at the end of the notion to let the reader know that he's back on course, or else end the sentence, as here, with a period.

The greatest danger in punctuation is for poetry. Here it is necessary to be as economical and parsimonious with commas and periods as with the words themselves, and any marks that seem to carry their own subtle meanings, like dashes and little rows of periods, even semicolons and question marks, should be left out altogether rather than inserted to clog up the thing with ambiguity. A single exclamation point in a poem, no matter what else the poem has to say, is enough to destroy the whole work.

The things I like best in T. S. Eliot's poetry, especially in the *Four Quartets,* are the semicolons. You cannot hear them, but they are there, laying out the connections between the images and the ideas. Sometimes you get a glimpse of a semicolon coming, a few lines farther on, and it is like climbing a steep path through woods and seeing a wooden bench just at a bend in the road ahead, a place where you can expect to sit for a moment, catching your breath.

Commas can't do this sort of thing; they can only tell you how the different parts of a complicated thought are to be fitted together, but you can't sit, not even take a breath, just because of a comma,   10

Thinking about the Text

1. Read the topic sentence of each paragraph in Lewis Thomas's essay. Which ones provide the clearest guidance? Which ones are most confusing? Why might Thomas have made some of his topic sentences direct and clear and others less so?

2. Like Ellen Lupton and J. Abbott Miller in "Period Styles: A Punctuated History" (pp. 315–22), Thomas illustrates his claims about punctuation by using the marks he discusses, often in surprising ways. Compare these two essays. Which one illustrates its points more effectively? Why? Provide examples to support your answer.

3. Thomas points to objectionable uses of quotation marks, especially in advertising (see paragraph 6). He also finds exclamation points irritating (paragraph 5). Find one or more examples of a use of punctuation that you find objectionable (for example, from a printed or online text, an advertisement, a bathroom wall, a sign, a menu). In a short essay, make a case for why that punctuation should be changed or deleted. If possible, include an image (a photo or screen shot) to show the examples you discuss.

D. KEITH MANO

How to Keep from Getting Mugged

1982

D. KEITH MANO (b. 1942) is a novelist and nonfiction writer.
His work has appeared in magazines such as *Esquire*, *Sports
Illustrated*, and *People*. His novels include *Take Five* (1998), a
story about a man who loses each of his senses one by one,
and *Topless* (1991), a crime thriller. He was also a longtime
columnist for *National Review*. "How to Keep from Getting
Mugged" was first published in *Playboy* in 1982.

L EARN TO WALK GAS-FAST. BOOK IT, BABY: LAY A BIG BATCH behind. Not in panic, mind you: never run. A power-purposeful, elbow-out, crazy kind of stride. The way people moved in old silent films—you know, right before they fell into an open manhole. Wave one hand now and then, as if you'd just seen three armed friends and were about to hail a cab. Your attitude should be: "Busy signal, dit-dit-dit. Can't fit you in today, fellas. Catch me tomorrow." In a real halfway-house neighborhood, walk dead street center: follow that white line; avoid ambush cover. Who's gonna mug you when he might get hit by a truck while doing it? Oh, you should see me squeeze out sneaker juice: I am Rapid City: I have no staying power, g'bye. A thug will get depressed by energy. He'd rather come down on someone wearing orthopedic pants. Also, if you can manage it, be tall.

Sing aloud. Mutter a lot. Preach Jesus. Interrogate yourself. Say things like: "Oh, the onion bagel won't come off. Oh, it hurts. Mmmm-mmhuh. Mmmmm. Please, Ma, don't send me back to the nutria farm again. No. Oh, no. That three-foot roach is still swimming in my water bed. Ah. Oh. Ech." Muggers are superstitious. They don't like to attack loony people: Might be a cousin on the paternal side. Make sure your accent is very New York (or L. A. or Chicago or wherever). Tourists are considered table-grade meat: heck, who'd miss his super-saver flight to attend a three-month trial? Most of all, eschew eye contact. If your vision says, "Uh-oh, this creep is after my wallet," this creep may feel a *responsibility* to yank you off. Keep both pupils straight ahead, in close-order drill. Do not flash a bank-and-turn indicator. Sure, you may walk past the place you're headed for, but, *shees*, no system is perfect.

Dress way down. Mom-and-pop candy-store owners take their cash to deposit in an old brown Bohack bag. Me, I *wear* the bag. I own two basic outfits: One has the *haute couture* of some fourth-hand algebra-textbook cover; my second best was cut using three dish drainers as a pattern. If stagflation were human, it'd look like me. No one messes with D.K.M., they figure I'm messed up enough now. But when you gotta go in finery, turn your tux jacket inside out and put a basketball kneepad around one trouser leg. Peg your collar. Stitch a white shoelace through your patent-leather pump. Recall what Jesus said about excessive glad-ragging (*Matthew*, chapter six): "Consider the lilies of the field. . . . *even* Solomon in all his glory was not arrayed as one of these—so, *nu*, what happens? They get picked, *Dummkopf*."

Thinking about the Text

1. D. Keith Mano's essay is a "how to" essay. What advice does he give? Who was the original audience? How is his advice geared to that audience?

2. This essay is humorous, not only because of the advice Mano offers but because of his use of style. Describe some prominent feature of Mano's essay—perhaps the author's use of sound (alliteration, slant rhyme), his tone, or his use of colloquial language—and explain how it adds to the humor.

3. What would change in this essay if it were written for a different audience (women, the elderly, some other group)? Rewrite one paragraph of Mano's essay with a different audience in mind. Give the advice and use the language and style that would appeal to your chosen audience.

ALICE WALKER

Beauty: When the Other Dancer Is the Self

1983

ALICE WALKER (b. 1944) writes fiction, poetry, and essays. She is best known for her novel *The Color Purple* (1982), which made Walker the first African American woman to win the Pulitzer Prize for fiction. It has since been adapted into a successful movie and Broadway musical. She has published several collections of essays, including *Living by the Word* (1988) and *In Search of Our Mothers' Gardens* (1983), in which "Beauty: When the Other Dancer Is the Self" appeared.

I T IS A BRIGHT SUMMER DAY IN 1947. MY FATHER, A FAT, FUNNY man with beautiful eyes and a subversive wit, is trying to decide which of his eight children he will take with him to the county fair. My mother, of course, will not go. She is knocked out from getting most of us ready: I hold my neck stiff against the pressure of her knuckles as she hastily completes the braiding and then beribboning of my hair.

My father is the driver for the rich old white lady up the road. Her name is Miss Mey. She owns all the land for miles around, as well as the house in which we live. All I remember about her is that she once offered to pay my mother thirty-five cents for cleaning her house, raking up piles of her magnolia leaves, and washing her family's clothes, and that my mother—she of no money, eight children, and a chronic earache—refused it. But I do not think of this in 1947. I am two and a half years old. I want to go everywhere my daddy goes. I am excited at the prospect of riding in a car. Someone has told me fairs are fun. That there is room in the car for only three of us doesn't faze me at all. Whirling happily in my starchy frock, showing off my biscuit-polished patent-leather shoes and lavender socks, tossing my head in a way that makes my ribbons bounce, I stand, hands on hips, before my father. "Take me, Daddy," I say with assurance; "I'm the prettiest!"

Later, it does not surprise me to find myself in Miss Mey's shiny black car, sharing the back seat with the other lucky ones. Does not surprise me that I thoroughly enjoy the fair. At home that night I tell the unlucky ones all I can remember about the merry-go-round, the man who eats live chickens, and the teddy bears, until they say: that's enough, baby Alice. Shut up now, and go to sleep.

It is Easter Sunday, 1950. I am dressed in a green, flocked, scalloped-hem dress (handmade by my adoring sister, Ruth) that has its own smooth satin petticoat and tiny hot-pink roses tucked into each scallop. My shoes, new T-strap patent leather, again highly biscuit-polished. I am six years old and have learned one of the longest Easter speeches to be heard that day, totally unlike the speech I said when I was two: "Easter lilies/pure and white/blossom in/the morning light." When I rise to give my speech I do so on a great wave of love and pride and expectation. People in the church stop rustling their new crinolines. They seem to hold their breath. I can tell they admire my dress, but it is my spirit, bordering on sassiness (womanishness), they secretly applaud.

"That girl's a little *mess*," they whisper to each other, pleased.   5

Naturally I say my speech without stammer or pause, unlike those who stutter, stammer, or, worst of all, forget. This is before the word "beautiful" exists in people's vocabulary, but "Oh, isn't she the *cutest* thing!" frequently floats my way. "And got so much sense!" they gratefully add. . . . for which thoughtful addition I thank them to this day.

It was great fun being cute. But then, one day, it ended.

I am eight years old and a tomboy. I have a cowboy hat, cowboy boots, checkered shirt and pants, all red. My playmates are my brothers, two and four years older than I. Their colors are black and green, the only difference in the way we are dressed. On Saturday nights we all go to the picture show, even my mother; Westerns are her favorite kind of movie. Back home, "on the ranch," we pretend we are Tom Mix, Hopalong Cassidy, Lash LaRue (we've even named one of our dogs Lash LaRue); we chase each other for hours rustling cattle, being outlaws, delivering damsels from distress. Then my parents decide to buy my brothers guns. These are not "real" guns. They shoot "BBs," copper pellets my brothers say will kill birds. Because I am a girl, I do not get a gun. Instantly I am relegated to the position of Indian. Now there appears a great distance between us. They shoot and shoot at everything with their new guns. I try to keep up with my bow and arrows.

One day while I am standing on top of our makeshift "garage"— pieces of tin nailed across some poles—holding my bow and arrow and looking out toward the fields, I feel an incredible blow in my right eye. I look down just in time to see my brother lower his gun.

Both brothers rush to my side. My eye stings, and I cover it with my   10 hand. "If you tell," they say, "we will get a whipping. You don't want that to happen, do you?" I do not. "Here is a piece of wire," says the older brother, picking it up from the roof; "say you stepped on one end of it and the other flew up and hit you." The pain is beginning to start. "Yes," I say, "Yes, I will say that is what happened." If I do not say this is what happened, I know my brothers will find ways to make me wish I had. But now I will say anything that gets me to my mother.

Confronted by our parents we stick to the lie agreed upon. They place me on a bench on the porch and I close my left eye while they examine the right. There is a tree growing from underneath the porch that climbs past the railing to the roof. It is the last thing my right eye sees. I watch as its trunk, its branches, and then its leaves are blotted out by the rising blood.

I am in shock. First there is intense fever, which my father tries to break using lily leaves bound around my head. Then there are chills: my mother tries to get me to eat soup. Eventually, I do not know how, my parents learn what has happened. A week after the "accident" they take me to see a doctor. "Why did you wait so long to come?" he asks, looking into my eye and shaking his head. "Eyes are sympathetic," he says. "If one is blind, the other will likely become blind too."

This comment of the doctor's terrifies me. But it is really how I look that bothers me most. Where the BB pellet struck there is a glob of whitish scar tissue, a hideous cataract, on my eye. Now when I stare at people—a favorite pastime, up to now—they will stare back. Not at the "cute" little girl, but at her scar. For six years I do not stare at anyone, because I do not raise my head.

Years later, in the throes of a mid-life crisis, I ask my mother and sister whether I changed after the "accident." "No," they say, puzzled. "What do you mean?"

What do I mean?   15

I am eight, and, for the first time, doing poorly in school, where I have been something of a whiz since I was four. We have just moved to the place where the "accident" occurred. We do not know any of the

people around us because this is a different county. The only time I see
the friends I knew is when we go back to our old church. The new school
is the former state penitentiary. It is a large stone building, cold and
drafty, crammed to overflowing with boisterous, ill-disciplined children.
On the third floor there is a huge circular imprint of some partition that
has been torn out.

"What used to be here?" I ask a sullen girl next to me on our way
past it to lunch.

"The electric chair," says she.

At night I have nightmares about the electric chair, and about all
the people reputedly "fried" in it. I am afraid of the school, where all the
students seem to be budding criminals.

"What's the matter with your eye?" they ask, critically.   20

When I don't answer (I cannot decide whether it was an "accident"
or not), they shove me, insist on a fight.

My brother, the one who created the story about the wire, comes to
my rescue. But then brags so much about "protecting" me, I become sick.

After months of torture at the school, my parents decide to send me
back to our old community, to my old school. I live with my grandparents
and the teacher they board. But there is no room for Phoebe, my cat. By
the time my grandparents decide there is room, and I ask for my cat, she
cannot be found. Miss Yarborough, the boarding teacher, takes me under
her wing, and begins to teach me to play the piano. But soon she marries
an African—a "prince," she says—and is whisked away to his continent.

At my old school there is at least one teacher who loves me. She is
the teacher who "knew me before I was born" and bought my first baby
clothes. It is she who makes life bearable. It is her presence that finally
helps me turn on the one child at the school who continually calls me
"one-eyed bitch." One day I simply grab him by his coat and beat him
until I am satisfied. It is my teacher who tells me my mother is ill.

My mother is lying in bed in the middle of the day, something I have   25
never seen. She is in too much pain to speak. She has an abscess in her

ear. I stand looking down on her, knowing that if she dies, I cannot live. She is being treated with warm oils and hot bricks held against her cheek. Finally a doctor comes. But I must go back to my grandparents' house. The weeks pass but I am hardly aware of it. All I know is that my mother might die, my father is not so jolly, my brothers still have their guns, and I am the one sent away from home.

"You did not change," they say.

Did I imagine the anguish of never looking up?

I am twelve. When relatives come to visit I hide in my room. My cousin Brenda, just my age, whose father works in the post office and whose mother is a nurse, comes to find me. "Hello," she says. And then she asks, looking at my recent school picture, which I did not want taken, and on which the "glob," as I think of it, is clearly visible, "You still can't see out of that eye?"

"No," I say, and flop back on the bed over my book.

That night, as I do almost every night, I abuse my eye. I rant and rave   30
at it, in front of the mirror. I plead with it to clear up before morning. I tell it I hate and despise it. I do not pray for sight. I pray for beauty.

"You did not change," they say.

I am fourteen and baby-sitting for my brother Bill, who lives in Boston. He is my favorite brother and there is a strong bond between us. Understanding my feelings of shame and ugliness he and his wife take me to a local hospital, where the "glob" is removed by a doctor named O. Henry. There is still a small bluish crater where the scar tissue was, but the ugly white stuff is gone. Almost immediately I become a different person from the girl who does not raise her head. Or so I think. Now that I've raised my head I win the boyfriend of my dreams. Now that I've raised my head I have plenty of friends. Now that I've raised my head class-work comes from my lips as faultlessly as Easter speeches did, and I leave high school as valedictorian, most popular student, and *queen,* hardly believing my luck. Ironically, the girl who was voted most beautiful in our class (and was) was later shot twice through the chest by a male companion, using a "real" gun, while she was pregnant. But that's another story in itself. Or is it?

"You did not change," they say.

It is now thirty years since the "accident." A beautiful journalist comes to visit and to interview me. She is going to write a cover story for her magazine that focuses on my latest book. "Decide how you want to look on the cover," she says. "Glamorous, or whatever."

Never mind "glamorous," it is the "whatever" that I hear. Suddenly   35
all I can think of is whether I will get enough sleep the night before the photography session: if I don't, my eye will be tired and wander, as blind eyes will.

At night in bed with my lover I think up reasons why I should not appear on the cover of a magazine. "My meanest critics will say I've sold out," I say. "My family will now realize I write scandalous books."

"But what's the real reason you don't want to do this?" he asks.

"Because in all probability," I say in a rush, "my eye won't be straight."

"It will be straight enough," he says. Then, "Besides, I thought you'd made your peace with that."

And I suddenly remember that I have.   40

I remember:

I am talking to my brother Jimmy, asking if he remembers anything unusual about the day I was shot. He does not know I consider that day the last time my father, with his sweet home remedy of cool lily leaves, chose me, and that I suffered and raged inside because of this. "Well," he says, "all I remember is standing by the side of the highway with Daddy, trying to flag down a car. A white man stopped, but when Daddy said he needed somebody to take his little girl to the doctor, he drove off."

I remember:

I am in the desert for the first time. I fall totally in love with it. I am so overwhelmed by its beauty, I confront for the first time, consciously, the meaning of the doctor's words years ago: "Eyes are sympathetic. If one is blind, the other will likely become blind too." I realize I have dashed about the world madly, looking at this, looking at that, storing up images against the fading of the light. *But I might have missed seeing the desert!* The shock of that possibility—and gratitude for over twenty-five years of sight—sends me literally to my knees. Poem after poem comes—which is perhaps how poets pray.

On Sight

I am so thankful I have seen
The Desert
And the creatures in the desert
And the desert Itself.

The desert has its own moon
Which I have seen
With my own eye.
There is no flag on it.

Trees of the desert have arms
All of which are always up
That is because the moon is up
The sun is up

Also the sky
The stars
Clouds
None with flags.

If there were flags, I doubt
the trees would point.
Would you?

But mostly, I remember this: 45
I am twenty-seven, and my baby daughter is almost three. Since her birth I have worried about her discovery that her mother's eyes are

different from other people's. Will she be embarrassed? I think. What will she say? Every day she watches a television program called "Big Blue Marble." It begins with a picture of the earth as it appears from the moon. It is bluish, a little battered-looking, but full of light, with whitish clouds swirling around it. Every time I see it I weep with love, as if it is a picture of Grandma's house. One day when I am putting Rebecca down for her nap, she suddenly focuses on my eye. Something inside me cringes, gets ready to try to protect myself. All children are cruel about physical differences, I know from experience, and that they don't always mean to be is another matter. I assume Rebecca will be the same.

But no-o-o-o. She studies my face intently as we stand, her inside and me outside her crib. She even holds my face maternally between her dimpled little hands. Then, looking every bit as serious and lawyerlike as her father, she says, as if it may just possibly have slipped my attention: "Mommy, there's a *world* in your eye." (As in, "Don't be alarmed, or do anything crazy.") And then, gently, but with great interest: "Mommy, where did you *get* that world in your eye?"

For the most part, the pain left then. (So what, if my brothers grew up to buy even more powerful pellet guns for their sons and to carry real guns themselves. So what, if a young "Morehouse man" once nearly fell off the steps of Trevor Arnett Library because he thought my eyes were blue.) Crying and laughing I ran to the bathroom, while Rebecca mumbled and sang herself off to sleep. Yes indeed, I realized, looking into the mirror. There *was* a world in my eye. And I saw that it was possible to love it: that in fact, for all it had taught me of shame and anger and inner vision, I *did* love it. Even to see it drifting out of orbit in boredom, or rolling up out of fatigue, not to mention floating back at attention in excitement (bearing witness, a friend has called it), deeply suitable to my personality, and even characteristic of me.

That night I dream I am dancing to Stevie Wonder's song "Always" (the name of the song is really "As," but I hear it as "Always"). As I dance, whirling and joyous, happier than I've ever been in my life, another bright-faced dancer joins me. We dance and kiss each other and hold each other through the night. The other dancer has obviously come through all right, as I have done. She is beautiful, whole and free. And she is also me.

Thinking about the Text

1. What helps Alice Walker come to accept a part of her appearance that once made her feel ashamed? Is it one experience or a series of experiences? Cite passages from her text as support for your answer.

2. Walker structures her essay by writing a series of vignettes in the present tense, shifting to the past tense in just a couple of paragraphs, most notably paragraph 48. Look carefully at her use of present and past tense. Why do you think she chose to write most of the essay in the present, and why do you think she chose to use the past tense in paragraph 48?

3. Write an essay that explores some aspect of your identity or experience. As Walker does, try using a series of vignettes written in the present tense.

BRENT STAPLES

Black Men and Public Space

1986

BRENT STAPLES (b. 1951) is an editorial writer for the *New York Times* and author of the memoir *Parallel Time: Growing Up in Black and White* (1994). "Black Men and Public Space" first appeared in *Ms. Magazine* in 1986 under the title "Just Walk on By." He often writes about the role of race in American culture. A revised version was published later that year under its current title in *Harper's Magazine*.

MY FIRST VICTIM WAS A WOMAN—WHITE, WELL DRESSED, probably in her early twenties. I came upon her late one evening on a deserted street in Hyde Park, a relatively affluent neighborhood in an otherwise mean, impoverished section of Chicago. As I swung onto the avenue behind her, there seemed to be a discreet, uninflammatory distance between us. Not so. She cast back a worried glance. To her, the youngish black man—a broad six feet two inches with a beard and billowing hair, both hands shoved into the pockets of a bulky military jacket—seemed menacingly close. After a few more quick glimpses, she picked up her pace and was soon running in earnest. Within seconds she disappeared into a cross street.

That was more than a decade ago, I was twenty-two years old, a graduate student newly arrived at the University of Chicago. It was in the echo of that terrified woman's footfalls that I first began to know the unwieldy inheritance I'd come into—the ability to alter public space in ugly ways. It was clear that she thought herself the quarry of a mugger, a rapist, or worse. Suffering a bout of insomnia, however, I was stalking sleep, not defenseless wayfarers. As a softy who is scarcely able to take a knife to a raw chicken—let alone hold one to a person's throat—I was surprised, embarrassed, and dismayed all at once. Her flight made me feel like an accomplice in tyranny. It also made it clear that I was indistinguishable from the muggers who occasionally seeped into the area from the surrounding ghetto. That first encounter, and those that followed, signified that a vast, unnerving gulf lay between nighttime pedestrians—particularly women—and me. And I soon gathered that being perceived as dangerous is a hazard in itself. I only needed to turn a corner into a dicey situation, or crowd some frightened, armed person in a foyer somewhere, or make an errant move after being pulled over by a policeman. Where fear and weapons meet—and they often do in urban America—there is always the possibility of death.

In that first year, my first away from my hometown, I was to become thoroughly familiar with the language of fear. At dark, shadowy intersections, I could cross in front of a car stopped at a traffic light and elicit the *thunk, thunk, thunk, thunk* of the driver—black, white, male, or female—hammering down the door locks. On less traveled streets after dark, I grew accustomed to but never comfortable with people crossing to the other side of the street rather than pass me. Then there were the standard unpleasantries with policemen, doormen, bouncers, cabdrivers, and others whose business it is to screen out troublesome individuals *before* there is any nastiness.

I moved to New York nearly two years ago and I have remained an avid night walker. In central Manhattan, the near-constant crowd cover minimizes tense one-on-one street encounters. Elsewhere—in SoHo, for example, where sidewalks are narrow and tightly spaced buildings shut out the sky—things can get very taut indeed.

After dark, on the warrenlike streets of Brooklyn where I live, I   5
often see women who fear the worst from me. They seem to have set their faces on neutral, and with their purse straps strung across their chests bandolier-style, they forge ahead as though bracing themselves against being tackled. I understand, of course, that the danger they perceive is not a hallucination. Women are particularly vulnerable to street violence, and young black males are drastically overrepresented among the perpetrators of that violence. Yet these truths are no solace against the kind of alienation that comes of being ever the suspect, a fearsome entity with whom pedestrians avoid making eye contact.

It is not altogether clear to me how I reached the ripe old age of twenty-two without being conscious of the lethality nighttime pedestrians attributed to me. Perhaps it was because in Chester, Pennsylvania, the small, angry industrial town where I came of age in the 1960s, I was scarcely noticeable against a backdrop of gang warfare, street knifings, and murders. I grew up one of the good boys, had perhaps a half-dozen fistfights. In retrospect, my shyness of combat has clear sources.

As a boy, I saw countless tough guys locked away; I have since buried several, too. They were babies, really—a teenage cousin, a brother of twenty-two, a childhood friend in his mid-twenties—all gone down in episodes of bravado played out in the streets. I came to doubt the virtues of intimidation early on. I chose, perhaps unconsciously, to remain a shadow—timid, but a survivor.

The fearsomeness mistakenly attributed to me in public places often has a perilous flavor. The most frightening of these confusions occurred in the late 1970s and early 1980s, when I worked as a journalist in Chicago. One day, rushing into the office of a magazine I was writing for with a deadline story in hand, I was mistaken for a burglar. The office manager called security and, with an ad hoc posse, pursued me through the labyrinthine halls, nearly to my editor's door. I had no way of proving who I was. I could only move briskly toward the company of someone who knew me.

Another time I was on assignment for a local paper and killing time before an interview. I entered a jewelry store on the city's affluent Near North Side. The proprietor excused herself and returned with an enormous red Doberman pinscher straining at the end of a leash. She stood, the dog extended toward me, silent to my questions, her eyes bulging nearly out of her head. I took a cursory look around, nodded, and bade her good night.

Relatively speaking, however, I never fared as badly as another black 10 male journalist. He went to nearby Waukegan, Illinois, a couple of summers ago to work on a story about a murderer who was born there. Mistaking the reporter for the killer, police officers hauled him from his car at gunpoint and but for his press credentials would probably have tried to book him. Such episodes are not uncommon. Black men trade tales like this all the time.

Over the years, I learned to smother the rage I felt at so often being taken for a criminal. Not to do so would surely have led to madness. I now take precautions to make myself less threatening. I move about with care, particularly late in the evening. I give a wide berth to nervous people on subway platforms during the wee hours, particularly when I have exchanged business clothes for jeans. If I happen to be entering a building behind some people who appear skittish, I may walk by, letting them clear the lobby before I return, so as not to seem to be following them. I have been calm and extremely congenial on those rare occasions when I've been pulled over by the police.

And on late-evening constitutionals I employ what has proved to be an excellent tension-reducing measure: I whistle melodies from Beethoven and Vivaldi and the more popular classical composers. Even steely New Yorkers hunching toward nighttime destinations seem to relax, and occasionally they even join in the tune. Virtually everybody seems to sense that a mugger wouldn't be warbling bright, sunny selections from Vivaldi's *Four Seasons*. It is my equivalent of the cowbell that hikers wear when they know they are in bear country.

Thinking about the Text

1. How does Brent Staples describe himself in this essay? How does he say he's perceived by others? What strategies does he use to change other people's perceptions?

2. D. Keith Mano (see "How to Keep from Getting Mugged" on pp. 165–67) deals with a similar topic from a different perspective. How might he respond to Staples? And how do you think Staples might respond to Mano?

3. Staples writes about "the language of fear" (paragraph 3)—both what it feels like to be seen as threatening and how those who feel afraid behave. There are times when everyone feels afraid. Write a letter to the author; explain the circumstances of a time when you felt afraid (or caused someone else to be nervous) and reflect on ways of communicating when fear is involved.

NANCY MAIRS

On Being a Cripple

1986

NANCY MAIRS (b. 1943) writes essays on topics as diverse as spirituality, gender, and disability. Her books include *Plaintext: Deciphering a Woman's Life* (1986), *Carnal Acts* (1990), *Ordinary Time* (1993), *Waist-High in the World: A Life Among the Nondisabled* (1996), and *A Dynamic God: Living an Unconventional Catholic Faith* (2007). "On Being a Cripple" was first published in *Plaintext*, Mairs's book of personal essays about life with multiple sclerosis.

> To escape is nothing. Not to escape is nothing.
> —LOUISE BOGAN

THE OTHER DAY I WAS THINKING OF WRITING AN ESSAY ON being a cripple. I was thinking hard in one of the stalls of the women's room in my office building, as I was shoving my shirt into my jeans and tugging up my zipper. Preoccupied, I flushed, picked up my book bag, took my cane down from the hook, and unlatched the door. So many movements unbalanced me, and as I pulled the door open I fell over backward, landing fully clothed on the toilet seat with my legs splayed in front of me: the old beetle-on-its-back routine. Saturday afternoon, the building deserted, I was free to laugh aloud as I wriggled back to my feet, my voice bouncing off the yellowish tiles from all directions. Had anyone been there with me, I'd have been still and faint and hot with chagrin. I decided that it was high time to write the essay.

First, the matter of semantics. I am a cripple. I choose this word to name me. I choose from among several possibilities, the most common of which are "handicapped" and "disabled." I made the choice a number of years ago, without thinking, unaware of my motives for doing so. Even now, I'm not sure what those motives are, but I recognize that they are complex and not entirely flattering. People—crippled or not—wince at the word "cripple," as they do not at "handicapped" or "disabled." Perhaps I want them to wince. I want them to see me as a tough customer, one to whom the fates/gods/viruses have not been kind, but who can face the brutal truth of her existence squarely. As a cripple, I swagger.

But, to be fair to myself, a certain amount of honesty underlies my choice. "Cripple" seems to me a clean word, straightforward and precise. It has an honorable history, having made its first appearance in the Lindisfarne Gospel in the tenth century. As a lover of words, I like the accuracy with which it describes my condition: I have lost the full use of my limbs. "Disabled," by contrast, suggests any incapacity, physical or mental. And I certainly don't like "handicapped," which implies that I have deliberately been put at a disadvantage, by whom I can't imagine (my God is not a Handicapper General), in order to equalize chances in the great race of life. These words seem to me to be moving away from my condition, to be widening the gap between word and reality. Most remote is the recently coined euphemism "differently abled," which partakes of the same semantic hopefulness that transformed countries from "undeveloped" to "underdeveloped," then to "less developed," and finally to "developing" nations. People have continued to starve in those countries during the shift. Some realities do not obey the dictates of language.

Mine is one of them. Whatever you call me, I remain crippled. But I don't care what you call me, so long as it isn't "differently abled," which strikes me as pure verbal garbage designed, by its ability to describe anyone, to describe no one. I subscribe to George Orwell's thesis that "the slovenliness of our language makes it easier for us to have foolish thoughts." And I refuse to participate in the degeneration of the language to the extent that I deny that I have lost anything in the course of this calamitous disease; I refuse to pretend that the only differences between you and me are the various ordinary ones that distinguish any one person from another. But call me "disabled" or "handicapped" if you like. I have long since grown accustomed to them; and if they are vague, at least they hint at the truth. Moreover, I use them myself. Society is no readier to accept crippledness than to accept death, war, sex, sweat, or wrinkles. I would never refer to another person as a cripple. It is the word I use to name only myself.

I haven't always been crippled, a fact for which I am soundly grate- 5
ful. To be whole of limb is, I know from experience, infinitely more pleasant and useful than to be crippled; and if that knowledge leaves one open to bitterness at my loss, the physical soundness I once enjoyed (though I did not enjoy it half enough) is well worth the occasional stab of regret. Though never any good at sports, I was a normally active

child and young adult. I climbed trees, played hopscotch, jumped rope, skated, swam, rode my bicycle, sailed. I despised team sports, spending some of the wretchedest afternoons of my life, sweaty and humiliated, behind a field-hockey stick and under a basketball hoop. I tramped alone for miles along the bridle paths that webbed the woods behind the house I grew up in. I swayed through countless dim hours in the arms of one man or another under the scattered shot of light from mirrored balls, and gyrated through countless more as Tab Hunter and Johnny Mathis gave way to the Rolling Stones, Creedence Clearwater Revival, Cream. I walked down the aisle. I pushed baby carriages, changed tires in the rain, marched for peace.

When I was twenty-eight I started to trip and drop things. What at first seemed my natural clumsiness soon became too pronounced to shrug off. I consulted a neurologist, who told me that I had a brain tumor. A battery of tests, increasingly disagreeable, revealed no tumor. About a year and a half later I developed a blurred spot in one eye. I had, at last, the episodes "disseminated in space and time" requisite for a diagnosis: multiple sclerosis. I have never been sorry for the doctor's initial misdiagnosis, however. For almost a week, until the negative results of the tests were in, I thought that I was going to die right away. Every day for the past nearly ten years, then, has been a kind of gift. I accept all gifts.

Multiple sclerosis is a chronic degenerative disease of the central nervous system, in which the myelin that sheathes the nerves is somehow eaten away and scar tissue forms in its place, interrupting the nerves' signals. During its course, which is unpredictable and uncontrollable, one may lose vision, hearing, speech, the ability to walk, control of bladder and/or bowels, strength in any or all extremities, sensitivity to touch, vibration, and/or pain, potency, coordination of movements—the list of possibilities is lengthy and, yes, horrifying. One may also lose one's sense of humor. That's the easiest to lose and the hardest to survive without.

In the past ten years, I have sustained some of these losses. Characteristic of MS are sudden attacks, called exacerbations, followed by remissions, and these I have not had. Instead, my disease has been slowly progressive. My left leg is now so weak that I walk with the aid of a brace and a cane; and for distances I use an Amigo, a variation on the electric wheelchair that looks rather like an electrified kiddie car. I no longer have much use of my left hand. Now my right side is weakening as well. I still have the blurred spot in my right eye. Overall, though, I've been lucky so far. My world has, of necessity, been circumscribed by my losses, but the terrain left me has been ample enough for me to continue many of the activities that absorb me: writing, teaching, raising children and cats and plants and snakes, reading, speaking publicly about MS and depression, even playing bridge with people patient and honorable enough to let me scatter cards every which way without sneaking a peek.

Lest I begin to sound like Pollyanna, however, let me say that I don't like having MS. I hate it. My life holds realities—harsh ones, some of them—that no right-minded human being ought to accept without grumbling. One of them is fatigue. I know of no one with MS who does not complain of bone-weariness; in a disease that presents an astonishing variety of symptoms, fatigue seems to be a common factor. I wake up in the morning feeling the way most people do at the end of a bad day, and I take it from there. As a result, I spend a lot of time *in extremis* and, impatient with limitation, I tend to ignore my fatigue until my body breaks down in some way and forces rest. Then I miss picnics, dinner parties, poetry readings, the brief visits of old friends from out of town. The offspring of a puritanical tradition of exceptional venerability, I cannot view these lapses without shame. My life often seems a series of small failures to do as I ought.

I lead, on the whole, an ordinary life, probably rather like the one I 10 would have led had I not had MS. I am lucky that my predilections were already solitary, sedentary, and bookish—unlike the world-famous French cellist I have read about, or the young woman I talked with one long afternoon who wanted only to be a jockey. I had just begun graduate school when I found out something was wrong with me, and I have remained, interminably, a graduate student. Perhaps I would not have if I'd thought I had the stamina to return to a full-time job as a technical editor; but I've enjoyed my studies.

In addition to studying, I teach writing courses. I also teach medical students how to give neurological examinations. I pick up freelance editing jobs here and there. I have raised a foster son and sent him into the world, where he has made me two grandbabies, and I am still escorting my daughter and son through adolescence. I go to Mass every Saturday. I am a superb, if messy, cook. I am also an enthusiastic laundress, capable of sorting a hamper full of clothes into five subtly differentiated piles, but a terrible housekeeper. I can do italic writing and, in an emergency, bathe an oil-soaked cat. I play a fiendish game of Scrabble. When I have the time and the money, I like to sit on my front steps with my husband, drinking Amaretto and smoking a cigar, as we imagine our counterparts in Leningrad and make sure that the sun gets down once more behind the sharp childish scrawl of the Tucson Mountains.

This lively plenty has its bleak complement, of course, in all the things I can no longer do. I will never run again, except in dreams, and one day I may have to write that I will never walk again. I like to go camping, but I can't follow George and the children along the trails that wander out of a campsite through the desert or into the mountains. In fact, even on the level I've learned never to check the weather or try to hold a coherent conversation: I need all my attention for my wayward feet. Of late, I have begun to catch myself wondering how people can propel themselves without canes. With only one usable hand, I have to select my clothing with care not so much for style as for ease of ingress and egress, and even so, dressing can be laborious. I can no longer do fine stitchery, pick up babies, play the piano, braid my hair. I am immobilized by acute attacks of depression, which may or may not be physiologically related to MS but are certainly its logical concomitant.

These two elements, the plenty and the privation, are never pure, nor are the delight and wretchedness that accompany them. Almost every pickle that I get into as a result of my weakness and clumsiness—and I get into plenty—is funny as well as maddening and sometimes painful. I recall one May afternoon when a friend and I were going out for a drink after finishing up at school. As we were climbing into opposite sides of my car, chatting, I tripped and fell, flat and hard, onto the asphalt parking lot, my abrupt departure interrupting him in mid-sentence. "Where'd you go?" he called as he came around the back of the car to find me hauling myself up by the door frame. "Are you all right?" Yes, I told him, I was fine, just a bit rattly, and we drove off to find a shady patio and some beer. When I got home an hour or so later, my daughter greeted me with "What have you done to yourself?" I looked down. One elbow of my white turtleneck with the green froggies, one knee of my white trousers, one white kneesock were blood-soaked. We peeled off the clothes and inspected the damage, which was nasty enough but not alarming. That part wasn't funny: The abrasions took a long time to heal, and one got a little infected. Even so, when I think of my friend talking earnestly, suddenly, to the hot thin air while I dropped from his view as though through a trap door, I find the image as silly as something from a Marx Brothers movie.

I may find it easier than other cripples to amuse myself because I live propped by the acceptance and the assistance and, sometimes, the amusement of those around me. Grocery clerks tear my checks out of my checkbook for me, and sales clerks find chairs to put into dressing rooms when I want to try on clothes. The people I work with make sure I teach at times when I am least likely to be fatigued, in places I can get to, with the materials I need. My students, with one anonymous exception (in an end-of-the-semester evaluation), have been unperturbed by my disability. Some even like it. One was immensely cheered by the information that I paint my own fingernails; she decided, she told me, that if I could go to such trouble over fine details, she could keep on writing essays. I suppose I became some sort of bright-fingered muse. She wrote good essays, too.

The most important struts in the framework of my existence, of   15
course, are my husband and children. Dismayingly few marriages survive the MS test, and why should they? Most twenty-two- and nineteen-
year-olds, like George and me, can vow in clear conscience, after a
childhood of chicken pox and summer colds, to keep one another in
sickness and in health so long as they both shall live. Not many are
equipped for catastrophe: the dismay, the depression, the extra work,
the boredom that a degenerative disease can insinuate into a relationship.
And our society, with its emphasis on fun and its association of fun
with physical performance, offers little encouragement for a whole spouse
to stay with a crippled partner. Children experience similar stresses
when faced with a crippled parent, and they are more helpless, since
parents and children can't usually get divorced. They hate, of course,
to be different from their peers, and the child whose mother is tacking
down the aisle of a school auditorium packed with proud parents like
a Cape Cod dinghy in a stiff breeze jolly well stands out in a crowd.
Deprived of legal divorce, the child can at least deny the mother's disability, even her existence, forgetting to tell her about recitals and PTA
meetings, refusing to accompany her to stores or church or the movies,
never inviting friends to the house. Many do.

But I've been limping along for ten years now, and so far George and
the children are still at my left elbow, holding tight. Anne and Matthew
vacuum floors and dust furniture and haul trash and rake up dog droppings and button my cuffs and bake lasagna and Toll House cookies with
just enough grumbling so I know that they don't have brain fever. And
far from hiding me, they're forever dragging me by racks of fancy clothes
or through teeming school corridors, or welcoming gaggles of friends
while I'm wandering through the house in Anne's filmy pink babydoll
pajamas. George generally calls before he brings someone home, but he
does just as many dumb thankless chores as the children. And they all
yell at me, laugh at some of my jokes, write me funny letters when we're

apart—in short, treat me as an ordinary human being for whom they have some use. I think they like me. Unless they're faking. . . .

Faking. There's the rub. Tugging at the fringes of my consciousness always is the terror that people are kind to me only because I'm a cripple. My mother almost shattered me once, with that instinct mothers have—blind, I think, in this case, but unerring nonetheless—for striking blows along the fault-lines of their children's hearts, by telling me, in an attack on my selfishness, "We all have to make allowances for you, of course, because of the way you are." From the distance of a couple of years, I have to admit that I haven't any idea just what she meant, and I'm not sure that she knew either. She was awfully angry. But at the time, as the words thudded home, I felt my worst fear, suddenly realized. I could bear being called selfish: I am. But I couldn't bear the corroboration that those around me were doing in fact what I'd always suspected them of doing, professing fondness while silently putting up with me because of the way I am. A cripple. I've been a little cracked ever since.

Along with this fear that people are secretly accepting shoddy goods comes a relentless pressure to please—to prove myself worth the burdens I impose, I guess, or to build a substantial account of goodwill against which I may write drafts in times of need. Part of the pressure arises from social expectations. In our society, anyone who deviates from the norm had better find some way to compensate. Like fat people, who are expected to be jolly, cripples must bear their lot meekly and cheerfully. A grumpy cripple isn't playing by the rules. And much of the pressure is self-generated. Early on I vowed that, if I had to have MS, by God I was going to do it well. This is a class act, ladies and gentlemen. No tears, no recriminations, no faintheartedness.

One way and another, then, I wind up feeling like Tiny Tim, peering over the edge of the table at the Christmas goose, waving my crutch, piping down God's blessing on us all. Only sometimes I don't want to play

Tiny Tim. I'd rather be Caliban, a most scurvy monster. Fortunately, at home no one much cares whether I'm a good cripple or a bad cripple as long as I make vichyssoise with fair regularity. One evening several years ago, Anne was reading at the dining-room table while I cooked dinner. As I opened a can of tomatoes, the can slipped in my left hand and juice spattered me and the counter with bloody spots. Fatigued and infuriated, I bellowed, "I'm so sick of being crippled!" Anne glanced at me over the top of her book. "There now," she said, "do you feel better?" "Yes," I said, "yes, I do." She went back to her reading. I felt better. That's about all the attention my scurviness ever gets.

Because I hate being crippled, I sometimes hate myself for being a cripple. Over the years I have come to expect—even accept—attacks of violent self-loathing. Luckily, in general our society no longer connects deformity and disease directly with evil (though a charismatic once told me that I have MS because a devil is in me) and so I'm allowed to move largely at will, even among small children. But I'm not sure that this revision of attitude has been particularly helpful. Physical imperfection, even freed of moral disapprobation, still defies and violates the ideal, especially for women, whose confinement in their bodies as objects of desire is far from over. Each age, of course, has its ideal, and I doubt that ours is any better or worse than any other. Today's ideal woman, who lives on the glossy pages of dozens of magazines, seems to be between the ages of eighteen and twenty-five; her hair has body, her teeth flash white, her breath smells minty, her underarms are dry; she has a career but is still a fabulous cook, especially of meals that take less than twenty minutes to prepare; she does not ordinarily appear to have a husband or children; she is trim and deeply tanned; she jogs, swims, plays tennis, rides a bicycle, sails, but does not bowl; she travels widely, even to out-of-the-way places like Finland and Samoa, always in the company of the ideal man, who possesses a nearly identical set of characteristics. There are a few exceptions. Though usually white and often blonde, she may be black, Hispanic, Asian, or Native American, so long as she is unusu-

20

ally sleek. She may be old, provided she is selling a laxative or is Lauren Bacall. If she is selling a detergent, she may be married and have a flock of strikingly messy children. But she is never a cripple.

Like many women I know, I have always had an uneasy relationship with my body. I was not a popular child, largely, I think now, because I was peculiar: intelligent, intense, moody, shy, given to unexpected actions and inexplicable notions and emotions. But as I entered adolescence, I believed myself unpopular because I was homely: my breasts too flat, my mouth too wide, my hips too narrow, my clothing never quite right in fit or style. I was not, in fact, particularly ugly, old photographs inform me, though I was well off the ideal; but I carried this sense of self-alienation with me into adulthood, where it regenerated in response to the depredations of MS. Even with my brace I walk with a limp so pronounced that, seeing myself on the videotape of a television program on the disabled, I couldn't believe that anything but an inchworm could make progress humping along like that. My shoulders droop and my pelvis thrusts forward as I try to balance myself upright, throwing my frame into a bony S. As a result of contractures, one shoulder is higher than the other and I carry one arm bent in front of me, the fingers curled into a claw. My left arm and leg have wasted into pipe-stems, and I try always to keep them covered. When I think about how my body must look to others, especially to men, to whom I have been trained to display myself, I feel ludicrous, even loathsome.

At my age, however, I don't spend much time thinking about my appearance. The burning egocentricity of adolescence, which assures one that all the world is looking all the time, has passed, thank God, and I'm generally too caught up in what I'm doing to step back, as I used to, and watch myself as though upon a stage. I'm also too old to believe in the accuracy of self-image. I know that I'm not a hideous crone, that in fact, when I'm rested, well dressed, and well made up, I look fine. The self-loathing I feel is neither physically nor intellectually substantial. What I hate is not me but a disease.

I am not a disease.

And a disease is not—at least not singlehandedly—going to determine who I am, though at first it seemed to be going to. Adjusting to a
chronic incurable illness, I have moved through a process similar to that
outlined by Elisabeth Kübler-Ross in *On Death and Dying*. The major
difference—and it is far more significant than most people recognize—
is that I can't be sure of the outcome, as the terminally ill cancer patient
can. Research studies indicate that, with proper medical care, I may
achieve a "normal" life span. And in our society, with its vision of death
as the ultimate evil, worse even than decrepitude, the response to such
news is, "Oh well, at least you're not going to *die*." Are there worse
things than dying? I think that there may be.

I think of two women I know, both with MS, both enough older than   25
I to have served me as models. One took to her bed several years ago and
has been there ever since. Although she can sit in a high-backed wheelchair, because she is incontinent she refuses to go out at all, even though
incontinence pants, which are readily available at any pharmacy, could
protect her from embarrassment. Instead, she stays at home and insists
that her husband, a small quiet man, a retired civil servant, stay there
with her except for a quick weekly foray to the supermarket. The other
woman, whose illness was diagnosed when she was eighteen, a nursing
student engaged to a young doctor, finished her training, married her
doctor, accompanied him to Germany when he was in the service, bore
three sons and a daughter, now grown and gone. When she can, she travels with her husband; she plays bridge, embroiders, swims regularly; she
works, like me, as a symptomatic-patient instructor of medical students
in neurology. Guess which woman I hope to be.

At the beginning, I thought about having MS almost incessantly.
And because of the unpredictable course of the disease, my thoughts
were always terrified. Each night I'd get into bed wondering whether I'd
get out again the next morning, whether I'd be able to see, to speak, to
hold a pen between my fingers. Knowing that the day might come when

I'd be physically incapable of killing myself, I thought perhaps I ought to do so right away, while I still had the strength. Gradually I came to understand that the Nancy who might one day lie inert under a bedsheet, arms and legs paralyzed, unable to feed or bathe herself, unable to reach out for a gun, a bottle of pills, was not the Nancy I was at present, and that I could not presume to make decisions for that future Nancy, who might well not want in the least to die. Now the only provision I've made for the future Nancy is that when the time comes—and it is likely to come in the form of pneumonia, friend to the weak and the old—I am not to be treated with machines and medications. If she is unable to communicate by then, I hope she will be satisfied with these terms.

Thinking all the time about having MS grew tiresome and intrusive, especially in the large and tragic mode in which I was accustomed to considering my plight. Months and even years went by without catastrophe (at least without one related to MS), and really I was awfully busy, what with George and children and snakes and students and poems, and I hadn't the time, let alone the inclination, to devote myself to being a disease. Too, the richer my life became, the funnier it seemed, as though there were some connection between largesse and laughter, and so my tragic stance began to waver until, even with the aid of a brace and a cane, I couldn't hold it for very long at a time.

After several years I was satisfied with my adjustment. I had suffered my grief and fury and terror, I thought, but now I was at ease with my lot. Then one summer day I set out with George and the children across the desert for a vacation in California. Part way to Yuma I became aware that my right leg felt funny. "I think I've had an exacerbation," I told George. "What shall we do?" he asked. "I think we'd better get the hell to California," I said, "because I don't know whether I'll ever make it again." So we went on to San Diego and then to Orange, up the Pacific Coast Highway to Santa Cruz, across to Yosemite, down to Sequoia and Joshua Tree, and so back over the desert to home. It was a fine two-week trip, filled with friends and fair weather, and I wouldn't have missed it for the world, though I did in fact make it back to California two years later. Nor would there have been any point in missing it, since in MS, once the symptoms have appeared, the neurological damage has been done, and there's no way to predict or prevent that damage.

The incident spoiled my self-satisfaction, however. It renewed my grief and fury and terror, and I learned that one never finishes adjusting to MS. I don't know now why I thought one would. One does not, after all, finish adjusting to life, and MS is simply a fact of my life—not my favorite fact, of course—but as ordinary as my nose and my tropical fish and my yellow Mazda station wagon. It may at any time get worse, but no amount of worry or anticipation can prepare me for a new loss. My life is a lesson in losses. I learn one at a time.

And I had best be patient in the learning, since I'll have to do it like   30
it or not. As any rock fan knows, you can't always get what you want. Particularly when you have MS. You can't, for example, get cured. In recent years researchers and the organizations that fund research have started to pay MS some attention even though it isn't fatal; perhaps they have begun to see that life is something other than a quantitative phenomenon, that one may be very much alive for a very long time in a life that isn't worth living. The researchers have made some progress toward understanding the mechanism of the disease: It may well be an autoimmune reaction triggered by a slowacting virus. But they are nowhere near its prevention, control, or cure. And most of us want to be cured. Some, unable to accept incurability, grasp at one treatment after another, no matter how bizarre: megavitamin therapy, gluten-free diet, injections of cobra venom, hypothermal suits, lymphocytopharesis, hyperbaric chambers. Many treatments are probably harmless enough, but none are curative.

The absence of a cure often makes MS patients bitter toward their doctors. Doctors are, after all, the priests of modern society, the new shamans, whose business is to heal, and many an MS patient roves from one to another, searching for the "good" doctor who will make him well. Doctors too think of themselves as healers, and for this reason many have trouble dealing with MS patients, whose disease in its intransigence defeats their aims and mocks their skills. Too few doctors, it is true, treat their patients as whole human beings, but the reverse is also true. I have always tried to be gentle with my doctors, who often have more at stake in terms of ego than I do. I may be frustrated, maddened, depressed by the incurability of my disease, but I am not diminished by it, and they are. When I push myself up from my seat in the waiting room and stumble toward them, I incarnate the limitation of their powers. The least I can do is refuse to press on their tenderest spots.

This gentleness is part of the reason that I'm not sorry to be a cripple. I didn't have it before. Perhaps I'd have developed it anyway—how could I know such a thing?—and I wish I had more of it, but I'm glad of what I have. It has opened and enriched my life enormously, this sense that my frailty and need must be mirrored in others, that in searching for and shaping a stable core in a life wrenched by change and loss, change and loss, I must recognize the same process, under individual conditions, in the lives around me. I do not deprecate such knowledge, however I've come by it.

All the same, if a cure were found, would I take it? In a minute. I may be a cripple, but I'm only occasionally a loony and never a saint. Anyway, in my brand of theology God doesn't give bonus points for a limp. I'd take a cure; I just don't need one. A friend who also has MS startled me once by asking, "Do you ever say to yourself, 'Why me, Lord?'" "No, Michael, I don't," I told him, "because whenever I try, the only response I can think of is 'Why not?'" If I could make a cosmic deal, who would I put in my place? What in my life would I give up in exchange for sound limbs and a thrilling rush of energy? No one. Nothing. I might as well do the job myself. Now that I'm getting the hang of it.

Thinking about the Text

1. How would you describe Nancy Mairs's tone in this essay? Cite specific passages to support your answer.

2. Mairs writes that she is "not a disease" (paragraph 23). How do the lists and anecdotes she includes illustrate this claim?

3. Is there a word that you'd choose to describe yourself (or someone else—a close friend, perhaps, or a famous athlete, or your grandma)? Write an essay in which you analyze the meaning and connotations of the word and explain your reasoning for thinking the word describes yourself or that person.

GLORIA ANZALDÚA

How to Tame a Wild Tongue

1987

GLORIA ANZALDÚA (1942–2004) wrote essays, criticism, poems, and children's books. She is best known for her co-edited collection (with Cherríe Moraga) *This Bridge Called My Back: Writings by Radical Women of Color* (1981) and for her essay and poetry collection *Borderlands/La Frontera: The New Mestiza* (1987), a collection of experimental essays that combine English, Spanish, and Chicano Spanish, and in which "How to Tame a Wild Tongue" first appeared. All notes are the author's. It was her request that no translations of Spanish or Chicano Spanish be included.

"W E'RE GOING TO HAVE TO CONTROL YOUR tongue," the dentist says, pulling out all the metal from my mouth. Silver bits plop and tinkle into the basin. My mouth is a motherlode.

The dentist is cleaning out my roots. I get a whiff of the stench when I gasp. "I can't cap that tooth yet, you're still draining," he says.

"We're going to have to do something about your tongue," I hear the anger rising in his voice. My tongue keeps pushing out the wads of cotton, pushing back the drills, the long thin needles. "I've never seen anything as strong or as stubborn," he says. And I think, how do you tame a wild tongue, train it to be quiet, how do you bridle and saddle it? How do you make it lie down?

> "Who is to say that robbing a people of its language is less
> violent than war?"
>   —RAY GWYN SMITH[1]

I remember being caught speaking Spanish at recess—that was good for three licks on the knuckles with a sharp ruler. I remember being sent to the corner of the classroom for "talking back" to the Anglo teacher when all I was trying to do was tell her how to pronounce my name. "If you want to be American, speak 'American.' If you don't like it, go back to Mexico where you belong."

"I want you to speak English. *Pa'hallar buen trabajo tienes que saber hablar el inglés bien. Qué vale toda tu educación si todavía hablas inglés con un* 'accent,'" my mother would say, mortified that I spoke English like a Mexican. At Pan American University, I, and all Chicano students were required to take two speech classes. Their purpose: to get rid of our accents.

Attacks on one's form of expression with the intent to censor are a violation of the First Amendment. *El Anglo con cara de inocente*

---

1. Ray Gwyn Smith, *Moorland Is Cold Country*, unpublished book.

nos arrancó la lengua. Wild tongues can't be tamed, they can only be cut out.

OVERCOMING THE TRADITION OF SILENCE

Ahogadas, escupimos el oscuro.
Peleando con nuestra propia sombra
el silencio nos sepulta.

En boca cerrada no entran moscas. "Flies don't enter a closed mouth" is a saying I kept hearing when I was a child. *Ser habladora* was to be a gossip and a liar, to talk too much. *Muchachitas bien criadas,* well-bred girls don't answer back. *Es una falta de respeto* to talk back to one's mother or father. I remember one of the sins I'd recite to the priest in the confession box the few times I went to confession: talking back to my mother, *hablar pa' 'trás, repelar. Hocicona, repelona, chismosa,* having a big mouth, questioning, carrying tales are all signs of being *mal criada.* In my culture they are all words that are derogatory if applied to women—I've never heard them applied to men.

The first time I heard two women, a Puerto Rican and a Cuban, say the word "*nosotras,*" I was shocked. I had not known the word existed. Chicanas use *nosotros* whether we're male or female. We are robbed of our female being by the masculine plural. Language is a male discourse.

And our tongues have become
dry the wilderness has
dried out our tongues and
we have forgotten speech. —IRENA KLEPFISZ[2]

2. Irena Klepfisz, "*Di rayze aheym*/The Journey Home," in *The Tribe of Dina: A Jewish Women's Anthology,* Melanie Kaye/Kantrowitz and Irena Klepfisz, eds. (Montpelier, VT: Sinister Wisdom Books, 1986), 49.

Even our own people, other Spanish speakers *nos quieren poner candados en la boca*. They would hold us back with their bag of *reglas de academia*.

Oyé como ladra: el lenguaje de la frontera

Quien tiene boca se equivoca.   —MEXICAN SAYING

"*Pocho*, cultural traitor, you're speaking the oppressor's language   10
by speaking English, you're ruining the Spanish language," I have been
accused by various Latinos and Latinas. Chicano Spanish is considered
by the purist and by most Latinos deficient, a mutilation of Spanish.

But Chicano Spanish is a border tongue which developed naturally.
Change, *evolución, enriquecimiento de palabras nuevas por invención o
adopción* have created variants of Chicano Spanish, *un nuevo lenguaje.
Un lenguaje que corresponde a un modo de vivir.* Chicano Spanish is not
incorrect, it is a living language.

For a people who are neither Spanish nor live in a country in which
Spanish is the first language; for a people who live in a country in
which English is the reigning tongue but who are not Anglo; for a people
who cannot entirely identify with either standard (formal, Castilian)
Spanish nor standard English, what recourse is left to them but to
create their own language? A language which they can connect their
identity to, one capable of communicating the realities and values
true to themselves—a language with terms that are neither *español ni
inglés,* but both. We speak a patois, a forked tongue, a variation of two
languages.

Chicano Spanish sprang out of the Chicanos' need to identify ourselves as a distinct people. We needed a language with which we could
communicate with ourselves, a secret language. For some of us, language is a homeland closer than the Southwest—for many Chicanos
today live in the Midwest and the East. And because we are a complex,

heterogeneous people, we speak many languages. Some of the languages we speak are:

1. Standard English
2. Working class and slang English
3. Standard Spanish
4. Standard Mexican Spanish
5. North Mexican Spanish dialect
6. Chicano Spanish (Texas, New Mexico, Arizona and California have regional variations)
7. Tex-Mex
8. *Pachuco* (called *caló*)

My "home" tongues are the languages I speak with my sister and brothers, with my friends. They are the last five listed, with 6 and 7 being closest to my heart. From school, the media and job situations, I've picked up standard and working class English. From Mamagrande Locha and from reading Spanish and Mexican literature, I've picked up Standard Spanish and Standard Mexican Spanish. From *los recién llegados,* Mexican immigrants, and *braceros,* I learned the North Mexican dialect. With Mexicans I'll try to speak either Standard Mexican Spanish or the North Mexican dialect. From my parents and Chicanos living in the Valley, I picked up Chicano Texas Spanish, and I speak it with my mom, younger brother (who married a Mexican and who rarely mixes Spanish with English), aunts and older relatives.

With Chicanas from *Nuevo México* or *Arizona* I will speak Chicano   15
Spanish a little, but often they don't understand what I'm saying. With most California Chicanas I speak entirely in English (unless I forget). When I first moved to San Francisco, I'd rattle off something in Spanish, unintentionally embarrassing them. Often it is only with another Chicana *tejana* that I can talk freely.

Words distorted by English are known as anglicisms or *pochismos*. The *pocho* is an anglicized Mexican or American of Mexican origin who speaks Spanish with an accent characteristic of North Americans and who distorts and reconstructs the language according to the influence of English.[3] Tex-Mex, or Spanglish, comes most naturally to me. I may switch back and forth from English to Spanish in the same sentence or in the same word. With my sister and my brother Nune and with Chicano *tejano* contemporaries I speak in Tex-Mex.

From kids and people my own age I picked up *Pachuco*. *Pachuco* (the language of the zoot suiters) is a language of rebellion, both against Standard Spanish and Standard English. It is a secret language. Adults of the culture and outsiders cannot understand it. It is made up of slang words from both English and Spanish. *Ruca* means girl or woman, *vato* means guy or dude, *chale* means no, *simón* means yes, *churo* is sure, talk is *periquiar, pigionear* means petting, *que gacho* means how nerdy, *ponte águila* means watch out, death is called *la pelona*. Through lack of practice and not having others who can speak it, I've lost most of the *Pachuco* tongue.

CHICANO SPANISH

Chicanos, after 250 years of Spanish/Anglo colonization, have developed significant differences in the Spanish we speak. We collapse two adjacent vowels into a single syllable and sometimes shift the stress in certain words such as *maíz/maiz, cohete/cuete*. We leave out certain consonants when they appear between vowels: *lado/lao, mojado/mojao*. Chicanos from South Texas pronounced *f* as *j* as in *jue (fue)*. Chicanos use "archaisms," words that are no longer in the Spanish language, words that have been evolved out. We say *semos, truje, haiga, ansina,* and *naiden*. We retain the "archaic" *j*, as in *jalar*, that derives from an earlier *h* (the

---

3. R. C. Ortega, *Dialectología Del Barrio*, trans. Hortencia S. Alwan (Los Angeles, CA: R. C. Ortega Publisher & Bookseller, 1977), 132.

French *halar* or the Germanic *halon* which was lost to standard Spanish in the 16th century), but which is still found in several regional dialects such as the one spoken in South Texas. (Due to geography, Chicanos from the Valley of South Texas were cut off linguistically from other Spanish speakers. We tend to use words that the Spaniards brought over from Medieval Spain. The majority of the Spanish colonizers in Mexico and the Southwest came from Extremadura—Hernán Cortés was one of them—and Andalucía. Andalucians pronounce *ll* like a *y*, and their *d*'s tend to be absorbed by adjacent vowels: *tirado* becomes *tirao*. They brought *el lenguaje popular, dialectos y regionalismos.*[4])

Chicanos and other Spanish speakers also shift *ll* to *y* and *z* to *s*.[5] We leave out initial syllables, saying *tar* for *estar, toy* for *estoy, hora* for *ahora* (*cubanos* and *puertorriqueños* also leave out initial letters of some words). We also leave out the final syllable such as *pa* for *para*. The intervocalic *y*, the *ll* as in *tortilla, ella, botella*, gets replaced by *tortia* or *tortiya, ea, botea*. We add an additional syllable at the beginning of certain words: *atocar* for *tocar, agastar* for *gastar*. Sometimes we'll say *lavaste las vacijas*, other times *lavates* (substituting the *ates* verb endings for the *aste*).

We use anglicisms, words borrowed from English: *bola* from ball, 20 *carpeta* from carpet, *máchina de lavar* (instead of *lavadora*) from washing machine. Tex-Mex argot, created by adding a Spanish sound at the beginning or end of an English word such as *cookiar* for cook, *watchar* for watch, *parkiar* for park, and *rapiar* for rape, is the result of the pressures on Spanish speakers to adapt to English.

We don't use the word *vosotros/as* or its accompanying verb form. We don't say *claro* (to mean yes), *imagínate*, or *me emociona*, unless we picked up Spanish from Latinas, out of a book, or in a classroom. Other Spanish-speaking groups are going through the same, or similar, development in their Spanish.

---

4. Eduardo Hernandéz-Chávez, Andrew D. Cohen, and Anthony F. Beltramo, *El Lenguaje de los Chicanos: Regional and Social Characteristics of Language Used by Mexican Americans* (Arlington, VA: Center for Applied Linguistics, 1975), 39.

5. Hernandéz-Chávez, xvii.

LINGUISTIC TERRORISM

Deslenguadas. Somos los del español deficiente. We are your linguistic nightmare, your linguistic aberration, your linguistic *mestisaje*,
the subject of your *burla*. Because we speak with tongues of fire
we are culturally crucified. Racially, culturally and linguistically
somos huérfanos—we speak an orphan tongue.

Chicanas who grew up speaking Chicano Spanish have internalized the
belief that we speak poor Spanish. It is illegitimate, a bastard language.
And because we internalize how our language has been used against us by
the dominant culture, we use our language differences against each other.

Chicana feminists often skirt around each other with suspicion and
hesitation. For the longest time I couldn't figure it out. Then it dawned
on me. To be close to another Chicana is like looking into the mirror. We
are afraid of what we'll see there. *Pena.* Shame. Low estimation of self.
In childhood we are told that our language is wrong. Repeated attacks
on our native tongue diminish our sense of self. The attacks continue
throughout our lives.

Chicanas feel uncomfortable talking in Spanish to Latinas, afraid
of their censure. Their language was not outlawed in their countries.
They had a whole lifetime of being immersed in their native tongue;
generations, centuries in which Spanish was a first language, taught in
school, heard on radio and TV, and read in the newspaper.

If a person, Chicana or Latina, has a low estimation of my native   25
tongue, she also has a low estimation of me. Often with *mexicanas y
latinas* we'll speak English as a neutral language. Even among Chicanas
we tend to speak English at parties or conferences. Yet, at the same time,
we're afraid the other will think we're *agringadas* because we don't speak
Chicano Spanish. We oppress each other trying to out-Chicano each
other, vying to be the "real" Chicanas, to speak like Chicanos. There is
no one Chicano language just as there is no one Chicano experience. A
monolingual Chicana whose first language is English or Spanish is just

as much a Chicana as one who speaks several variants of Spanish. A Chicana from Michigan or Chicago or Detroit is just as much a Chicana as one from the Southwest. Chicano Spanish is as diverse linguistically as it is regionally.

By the end of this century, Spanish speakers will comprise the biggest minority group in the U.S., a country where students in high schools and colleges are encouraged to take French classes because French is considered more "cultured." But for a language to remain alive it must be used.[6] By the end of this century English, and not Spanish, will be the mother tongue of most Chicanos and Latinos.

So, if you want to really hurt me, talk badly about my language. Ethnic identity is twin skin to linguistic identity—I am my language. Until I can take pride in my language, I cannot take pride in myself. Until I can accept as legitimate Chicano Texas Spanish, Tex-Mex and all the other languages I speak, I cannot accept the legitimacy of myself. Until I am free to write bilingually and to switch codes without having always to translate, while I still have to speak English or Spanish when I would rather speak Spanglish, and as long as I have to accommodate the English speakers rather than having them accommodate me, my tongue will be illegitimate.

I will no longer be made to feel ashamed of existing. I will have my voice: Indian, Spanish, white. I will have my serpent's tongue—my woman's voice, my sexual voice, my poet's voice. I will overcome the tradition of silence.

My fingers
move sly against your palm
Like women everywhere, we speak in code. . . .

—MELANIE KAYE/KANTROWITZ[7]

---

6. Irena Klepfisz, "Secular Jewish Identity: Yidishkayt in America," in *The Tribe of Dina*, Kaye/Kantrowitz and Klepfisz, eds., 43.

7. Melanie Kaye/Kantrowitz, "Sign," in *We Speak in Code: Poems and Other Writings* (Pittsburgh, PA: Motheroot Publications, Inc., 1980), 85.

"Vistas," corridos, y comida: My Native Tongue

In the 1960s, I read my first Chicano novel. It was *City of Night* by John
Rechy, a gay Texan, son of a Scottish father and a Mexican mother. For
days I walked around in stunned amazement that a Chicano could write
and could get published. When I read *I Am Joaquín*[8] I was surprised to
see a bilingual book by a Chicano in print. When I saw poetry written in
Tex-Mex for the first time, a feeling of pure joy flashed through me. I felt
like we really existed as a people. In 1971, when I started teaching High
School English to Chicano students, I tried to supplement the required
texts with works by Chicanos, only to be reprimanded and forbidden to
do so by the principal. He claimed that I was supposed to teach "American" and English literature. At the risk of being fired, I swore my students
to secrecy and slipped in Chicano short stories, poems, a play. In graduate school, while working toward a Ph.D., I had to "argue" with one advisor after the other, semester after semester, before I was allowed to make
Chicano literature an area of focus.

Even before I read books by Chicanos or Mexicans, it was the Mexi-   30
can movies I saw at the drive-in—the Thursday night special of $1.00 a
carload—that gave me a sense of belonging. *"Vámonos a las vistas,"* my
mother would call out and we'd all—grandmother, brothers, sister and
cousins—squeeze into the car. We'd wolf down cheese and bologna
white bread sandwiches while watching Pedro Infante in melodramatic
tear-jerkers like *Nosotros los pobres,* the first "real" Mexican movie (that
was not an imitation of European movies). I remember seeing *Cuando
los hijos se van* and surmising that all Mexican movies played up the love
a mother has for her children and what ungrateful sons and daughters
suffer when they are not devoted to their mothers. I remember the
singing-type "westerns" of Jorge Negrete and Miguel Aceves Mejía.

---

8. Rodolfo Gonzales, *I Am Joaquín/Yo Soy Joaquín* (New York, NY: Bantam Books,
1972). It was first published in 1967.

When watching Mexican movies, I felt a sense of homecoming as well as alienation. People who were to amount to something didn't go to Mexican movies, or *bailes* or tune their radios to *bolero, rancherita,* and *corrido* music.

The whole time I was growing up, there was *norteño* music sometimes called North Mexican border music, or Tex-Mex music, or Chicano music, or *cantina* (bar) music. I grew up listening to *conjuntos,* three- or four-piece bands made up of folk musicians playing guitar, *bajo sexto,* drums and button accordion, which Chicanos had borrowed from the German immigrants who had come to Central Texas and Mexico to farm and build breweries. In the Rio Grande Valley, Steve Jordan and Little Joe Hernández were popular, and Flaco Jiménez was the accordion king. The rhythms of Tex-Mex music are those of the polka, also adapted from the Germans, who in turn had borrowed the polka from the Czechs and Bohemians.

I remember the hot, sultry evenings when *corridos*—songs of love and death on the Texas-Mexican borderlands—reverberated out of cheap amplifiers from the local *cantinas* and wafted in through my bedroom window.

Corridos first became widely used along the South Texas/Mexican border during the early conflict between Chicanos and Anglos. The *corridos* are usually about Mexican heroes who do valiant deeds against the Anglo oppressors. Pancho Villa's song, "*La cucaracha,*" is the most famous one. *Corridos* of John F. Kennedy and his death are still very popular in the Valley. Older Chicanos remember Lydia Mendoza, one of the great border *corrido* singers who was called *la Gloria de Tejas.* Her "*El tango negro,*" sung during the Great Depression, made her a singer of the people. The everpresent *corridos* narrated one hundred years of border history, bringing news of events as well as entertaining. These folk musicians and folk songs are our chief cultural mythmakers, and they made our hard lives seem bearable.

I grew up feeling ambivalent about our music. Country-western and rock-and-roll had more status. In the 50s and 60s, for the slightly educated and *agringado* Chicanos, there existed a sense of shame at being caught listening to our music. Yet I couldn't stop my feet from thumping to the music, could not stop humming the words, nor hide from myself the exhilaration I felt when I heard it.

There are more subtle ways that we internalize identification, especially in the forms of images and emotions. For me food and certain smells are tied to my identity, to my homeland. Woodsmoke curling up to an immense blue sky; woodsmoke perfuming my grandmother's clothes, her skin. The stench of cow manure and the yellow patches on the ground; the crack of a .22 rifle and the reek of cordite. Homemade white cheese sizzling in a pan, melting inside a folded *tortilla*. My sister Hilda's hot, spicy *menudo, chile colorado* making it deep red, pieces of *panza* and hominy floating on top. My brother Carito barbecuing *fajitas* in the backyard. Even now and 3,000 miles away, I can see my mother spicing the ground beef, pork and venison with *chile*. My mouth salivates at the thought of the hot steaming *tamales* I would be eating if I were home.

Si le preguntas a mi mamá, "¿Qué eres?"

"Identity is the essential core of who
we are as individuals, the conscious
experience of the self inside."   —KAUFMAN[9]

Nosotros los Chicanos straddle the borderlands. On one side of us, we are constantly exposed to the Spanish of the Mexicans, on the other side we hear the Anglos' incessant clamoring so that we forget our language. Among ourselves we don't say *nosotros los americanos, o nosotros los españoles, o nosotros los hispanos.* We say *nosotros los mexicanos* (by

9. Gershen Kaufman, *Shame: The Power of Caring* (Cambridge, MA: Shenkman Books, 1980), 68.

mexicanos we do not mean citizens of Mexico; we do not mean a national identity, but a racial one). We distinguish between *mexicanos del otro lado* and *mexicanos de este lado*. Deep in our hearts we believe that being Mexican has nothing to do with which country one lives in. Being Mexican is a state of soul—not one of mind, not one of citizenship. Neither eagle nor serpent, but both. And like the ocean, neither animal respects borders.

> *Dime con quien andas y te diré quien eres.*
> (Tell me who your friends are and I'll tell you who you are.)
> —MEXICAN SAYING

Si le preguntas a mi mamá, "¿Qué eres?" te dirá, "Soy mexicana." My brothers and sister say the same. I sometimes will answer *"soy mexicana"* and at others will say *"soy Chicana" o "soy tejana."* But I identified as *"Raza"* before I ever identified as *"mexicana"* or "Chicana."

As a culture, we call ourselves Spanish when referring to ourselves as a linguistic group and when copping out. It is then that we forget our predominant Indian genes. We are 70 to 80% Indian.[10] We call ourselves Hispanic[11] or Spanish-American or Latin American or Latin when linking ourselves to other Spanish-speaking peoples of the Western hemisphere and when copping out. We call ourselves Mexican-American[12] to signify we are neither Mexican nor American, but more the noun "American" than the adjective "Mexican" (and when copping out).

Chicanos and other people of color suffer economically for not acculturating. This voluntary (yet forced) alienation makes for psychological conflict, a kind of dual identity—we don't identify with the Anglo-American cultural values and we don't totally identify with the

10. John R. Chávez, *The Lost Land: The Chicano Image of the Southwest* (Albuquerque: U of New Mexico P, 1984), 88–90.

11. "Hispanic" is derived from *Hispanis (España,* a name given to the Iberian Peninsula in ancient times when it was a part of the Roman Empire) and is a term designated by the U.S. government to make it easier to handle us on paper.

12. In 1848 the Treaty of Guadalupe Hidalgo created the Mexican-American.

Mexican cultural values. We are a synergy of two cultures with various
degrees of Mexicanness or Angloness. I have so internalized the bor-
derland conflict that sometimes I feel like one cancels out the other and
we are zero, nothing, no one. *A veces no soy nada ni nadie. Pero hasta
cuando no lo soy, lo soy.*

When not copping out, when we know we are more than nothing,   40
we call ourselves Mexican, referring to race and ancestry; *mestizo* when
affirming both our Indian and Spanish (but we hardly ever own our
Black ancestry); Chicano when referring to a politically aware people
born and/or raised in the U.S.; *Raza* when referring to Chicanos; *teja-
nos* when we are Chicanos from Texas.

Chicanos did not know we were a people until 1965 when Cesar
Chavez and the farmworkers united and *I Am Joaquín* was published
and *la Raza Unida* party was formed in Texas. With that recognition, we
became a distinct people. Something momentous happened to the Chicano soul—we became aware of our reality and acquired a name and a
language (Chicano Spanish) that reflected that reality. Now that we had
a name, some of the fragmented pieces began to fall together—who we
were, what we were, how we had evolved. We began to get glimpses of
what we might eventually become.

Yet the struggle of identities continues, the struggle of borders is our
reality still. One day the inner struggle will cease and a true integration
take place. In the meantime, *tenémos que hacer la lucha. ¿Quién está prot-
egiendo los ranchos de mi gente? ¿Quién está tratando de cerrar la fisura entre
la india y el blanco en nuestra sangre? El Chicano, si, el Chicano que anda
como un ladrón en su propia casa.*

Los Chicanos, how patient we seem, how very patient. There is the quiet of
the Indian about us.[13] We know how to survive. When other races have

13. Anglos, in order to alleviate their guilt for dispossessing the Chicano, stressed the
Spanish part of us and perpetrated the myth of the Spanish Southwest. We have accepted
the fiction that we are Hispanic, that is Spanish, in order to accommodate ourselves to
the dominant culture and its abhorrence of Indians. Chávez, 88–91.

given up their tongue, we've kept ours. We know what it is to live under the hammer blow of the dominant *norteamericano* culture. But more than we count the blows, we count the days the weeks the years the centuries the eons until the white laws and commerce and customs will rot in the deserts they've created, lie bleached. *Humildes* yet proud, *quietos* yet wild, *nosotros los mexicanos-Chicanos* will walk by the crumbling ashes as we go about our business. Stubborn, persevering, impenetrable as stone, yet possessing a malleability that renders us unbreakable, we, the *mestizas* and *mestizos*, will remain.

Thinking about the Text

1. In paragraph 27, Gloria Anzaldúa links her ethnic and linguistic identity, stating, "I am my language." Later in the essay, she writes about other elements of her life and culture that have shaped her identity. What are some of those elements? How did they shape Anzaldúa?

2. Anzaldúa includes many Spanish words and phrases in her writing without providing translation. How does that stylistic feature of her prose support her argument? How did that choice affect the way you read her essay?

3. Write an essay in which you reflect on your own identity. What factors have shaped you?

SCOTT RUSSELL SANDERS

Under the Influence

1989

—◊—

SCOTT RUSSELL SANDERS (b. 1945) writes fiction, nonfiction, and books for children. He is especially known for his
essay collections, including *The Paradise of Bombs* (1987),
Writing from the Center (1995), and *The Force of Spirit* (2000).
Many of his most popular essays have been collected in *Earth
Works: Selected Essays* (2012). He is also a professor emeritus
at Indiana University in Bloomington. "Under the Influence"
was first published in *Harper's Magazine* (1989).

—◊—

MY FATHER DRANK. HE DRANK AS A GUT-PUNCHED boxer gasps for breath, as a starving dog gobbles food—compulsively, secretly, in pain and trembling. I use the past tense not because he ever quit drinking but because he quit living. That is how the story ends for my father, age sixty-four, heart bursting, body cooling and forsaken on the linoleum of my brother's trailer. The story continues for my brother, my sister, my mother, and me, and will continue so long as memory holds.

In the perennial present of memory, I slip into the garage or barn to see my father tipping back the flat green bottles of wine, the brown cylinders of whiskey, the cans of beer disguised in paper bags. His Adam's apple bobs, the liquid gurgles, he wipes the sandy-haired back of a hand over his lips, and then, his bloodshot gaze bumping into me, he stashes the bottle or can inside his jacket, under the workbench, between two bales of hay, and we both pretend the moment has not occurred.

"What's up, buddy?" he says, thick-tongued and edgy.

"Sky's up," I answer, playing along.

"And don't forget prices," he grumbles. "Prices are always up. And taxes."

In memory, his white 1951 Pontiac with the stripes down the hood and the Indian head on the snout jounces to a stop in the driveway; or it is the 1956 Ford station wagon, or the 1963 Rambler shaped like a toad, or the sleek 1969 Bonneville that will do 120 miles per hour on straight-aways; or it is the robin's-egg blue pickup, new in 1980, battered in 1981, the year of his death. He climbs out, grinning dangerously, unsteady on his legs, and we children interrupt our game of catch, our building of snow forts, our picking of plums, to watch in silence as he weaves past into the house, where he slumps into his overstuffed chair and falls asleep. Shaking her head, our mother stubs out the cigarette he has left smoldering in the ashtray. All evening, until our bedtimes, we tiptoe past him, as past a snoring dragon. Then we curl in our fearful sheets, listening. Eventually he wakes with a grunt, Mother slings accusations at him, he snarls back, she yells, he growls, their voices clashing. Before long, she retreats to their bedroom, sobbing—not from the blows of fists, for he never strikes her, but from the force of words.

Left alone, our father prowls the house, thumping into furniture, rummaging in the kitchen, slamming doors, turning the pages of the newspaper with a savage crackle, muttering back at the late-night drivel from television. The roof might fly off, the walls might buckle from the pressure of his rage. Whatever my brother and sister and mother may be thinking on their own rumpled pillows, I lie there hating him, loving him, fearing him, knowing I have failed him. I tell myself he drinks to ease an ache that gnaws at his belly, an ache I must have caused by disappointing him somehow, a murderous ache I should be able to relieve by doing all my chores, earning A's in school, winning baseball games, fixing the broken washer and the burst pipes, bringing in money to fill his empty wallet. He would not hide the green bottles in his tool box, would not sneak off to the barn with a lump under his coat, would not fall asleep in the daylight, would not roar and fume, would not drink himself to death, if only I were perfect.

I am forty-two as I write these words, and I know full well now that my father was an alcoholic, a man consumed by disease rather than by disappointment. What had seemed to me a private grief is in fact a public scourge. In the United States alone some ten or fifteen million people share his ailment, and behind the doors they slam in fury or disgrace, countless other children tremble. I comfort myself with such knowledge, holding it against the throb of memory like an ice pack against a bruise. There are keener sources of grief: poverty, racism, rape, war. I do not wish to compete for a trophy in suffering. I am only trying to understand the corrosive mixture of helplessness, responsibility, and shame that I learned to feel as the son of an alcoholic. I realize now that I did not cause my father's illness, nor could I have cured it. Yet for all this grown-up knowledge, I am still ten years old, my own son's age, and as that boy I struggle in guilt and confusion to save my father from pain.

Consider a few of our synonyms for *drunk*: tipsy, tight, pickled, soused, and plowed; stoned and stewed, lubricated and inebriated, juiced and sluiced; three sheets to the wind, in your cups, out of your mind, under the table; lit up, tanked up, wiped out; besotted, blotto, bombed, and buzzed; plastered, polluted, putrified; loaded or looped, boozy, woozy, fuddled, or smashed; crocked and shit-faced, corked and pissed, snockered and sloshed.

It is a mostly humorous lexicon, as the lore that deals with drunks— in jokes and cartoons, in plays, films, and television skits—is largely comic. Aunt Matilda nips elderberry wine from the sideboard and burps politely during supper. Uncle Fred slouches to the table glassy-eyed, wearing a lamp shade for a hat and murmuring, "Candy is dandy but liquor is quicker." Inspired by cocktails, Mrs. Somebody recounts the events of her day in a fuzzy dialect, while Mr. Somebody nibbles her ear and croons a bawdy song. On the sofa with Boyfriend, Daughter giggles, licking gin from her lips, and loosens the bows in her hair. Junior knocks back some brews with his chums at the Leopard Lounge and stumbles home to the wrong house, wonders foggily why he cannot locate his pajamas, and crawls naked into bed with the ugliest girl in school. The family dog slurps from a neglected martini and wobbles to the nursery, where he vomits in Baby's shoe.

It is all great fun. But if in the audience you notice a few laughing faces turn grim when the drunk lurches on stage, don't be surprised, for these are the children of alcoholics. Over the grinning mask of Dionysus, the leering mask of Bacchus, these children cannot help seeing the bloated features of their own parents. Instead of laughing, they wince, they mourn. Instead of celebrating the drunk as one freed from constraints, they pity him as one enslaved. They refuse to believe *in vino veritas*, having seen their befuddled parents skid away from truth toward folly and oblivion. And so these children bite their lips until the lush staggers into the wings.

My father, when drunk, was neither funny nor honest; he was pathetic, frightening, deceitful. There seemed to be a leak in him somewhere, and he poured in booze to keep from draining dry. Like a torture victim who refuses to squeal, he would never admit that he had touched a drop, not even in his last year, when he seemed to be dissolving in alcohol before our very eyes. I never knew him to lie about anything, ever, except about this one ruinous fact. Drowsy, clumsy, unable to fix a bicycle tire, throw a baseball, balance a grocery sack, or walk across the room, he was stripped of his true self by drink. In a matter of minutes, the contents of a bottle could transform a brave man into a coward, a buddy into a bully, a gifted athlete and skilled carpenter and shrewd businessman into a bumbler. No dictionary of synonyms for *drunk* would soften the anguish of watching our prince turn into a frog.

Father's drinking became the family secret. While growing up, we children never breathed a word of it beyond the four walls of our house. To this day, my brother and sister rarely mention it, and then only when I press them. I did not confess the ugly, bewildering fact to my wife until his wavering walk and slurred speech forced me to. Recently, on the seventh anniversary of my father's death, I asked my mother if she ever spoke of his drinking to friends. "No, no, never," she replied hastily. "I couldn't bear for anyone to know."

The secret bores under the skin, gets in the blood, into the bone, and stays there. Long after you have supposedly been cured of malaria, the fever can flare up, the tremors can shake you. So it is with the fevers of shame. You swallow the bitter quinine of knowledge, and you learn to feel pity and compassion toward the drinker. Yet the shame lingers in your marrow, and, because of the shame, anger.

For a long stretch of my childhood we lived on a military reservation 15 in Ohio, an arsenal where bombs were stored underground in bunkers, vintage airplanes burst into flames, and unstable artillery shells boomed nightly at the dump. We had the feeling, as children, that we played in a mine field, where a heedless footfall could trigger an explosion. When Father was drinking, the house, too, became a mine field. The least bump could set off either parent.

The more he drank, the more obsessed Mother became with stopping him. She hunted for bottles, counted the cash in his wallet, sniffed at his breath. Without meaning to snoop, we children blundered left and right into damning evidence. On afternoons when he came home from work sober, we flung ourselves at him for hugs, and felt against our ribs the telltale lump in his coat. In the barn we tumbled on the hay and heard beneath our sneakers the crunch of buried glass. We tugged open a drawer in his workbench, looking for screwdrivers or crescent wrenches, and spied a gleaming six-pack among the tools. Playing tag, we darted around the house just in time to see him sway on the rear stoop and heave a finished bottle into the woods. In his good night kiss we smelled the cloying sweetness of Clorets, the mints he chewed to camouflage his dragon's breath.

I can summon up that kiss right now by recalling Theodore Roethke's lines about his own father in "My Papa's Waltz":

> The whiskey on your breath
> Could make a small boy dizzy;
> But I hung on like death:
> Such waltzing was not easy.

Such waltzing was hard, terribly hard, for with a boy's scrawny arms I was trying to hold my tipsy father upright.

For years, the chief source of those incriminating bottles and cans was a grimy store a mile from us, a cinder block place called Sly's, with two gas pumps outside and a moth-eaten dog asleep in the window. A strip of flypaper, speckled the year round with black bodies, coiled in the doorway. Inside, on rusty metal shelves or in wheezing coolers, you could find pop and Popsicles, cigarettes, potato chips, canned soup, raunchy postcards, fishing gear, Twinkies, wine, and beer. When Father drove anywhere on errands, Mother would send us kids along as guards, warning us not to let him out of our sight. And so with one or more of us on board, Father would cruise up to Sly's, pump a dollar's worth of gas or plump the tires with air, and then, telling us to wait in the car, he would head for that fly-spangled doorway.

Dutiful and panicky, we cried, "Let us go in with you!"

"No," he answered. "I'll be back in two shakes." 20

"Please!"

"No!" he roared. "Don't you budge, or I'll jerk a knot in your tails!"

So we stayed put, kicking the seats, while he ducked inside. Often, when he had parked the car at a careless angle, we gazed in through the window and saw Mr. Sly fetching down from a shelf behind the cash register two green pints of Gallo wine. Father swigged one of them right there at the counter, stuffed the other in his pocket, and then out he came, a bulge in his coat, a flustered look on his red face.

Because the Mom and Pop who ran the dump were neighbors of ours, living just down the tar-blistered road, I hated them all the more for poisoning my father. I wanted to sneak in their store and smash the bottles and set fire to the place. I also hated the Gallo brothers, Ernest and Julio, whose jovial faces shone from the labels of their wine, labels I would find, torn and curled, when I burned the trash. I noted the Gallo brothers' address, in California, and I studied the road atlas to see how far that was from Ohio, because I meant to go out there and tell Ernest and Julio what they were doing to my father, and then, if they showed no mercy, I would kill them.

While growing up on the back roads and in the country schools and 25 cramped Methodist churches of Ohio and Tennessee, I never heard the word *alcoholism,* never happened across it in books or magazines. In the nearby towns, there were no addiction treatment programs, no community mental health centers, no Alcoholics Anonymous chapters, no therapists. Left alone with our grievous secret, we had no way of understanding Father's drinking except as an act of will, a deliberate folly or cruelty, a moral weakness, a sin. He drank because he chose to, pure and simple. Why our father, so playful and competent and kind when sober, would choose to ruin himself and punish his family, we could not fathom.

Our neighborhood was high on the Bible, and the Bible was hard on drunkards. "Woe to those who are heroes at drinking wine, and valiant men in mixing strong drink," wrote Isaiah. "The priest and the prophet reel with strong drink, they are confused with wine, they err in vision, they stumble in giving judgment. For all tables are full of vomit, no place is without filthiness." We children had seen those fouled tables at the local truck stop where the notorious boozers hung out, our father occasionally among them. "Wine and new wine take away the understanding," declared the prophet Hosea. We had also seen evidence of that in our father, who could multiply seven-digit numbers in his head when sober, but when drunk could not help us with fourth-grade math. Proverbs warned: "Do not look at wine when it is red, when it sparkles in the cup and goes down smoothly. At the last it bites like a serpent, and stings like an adder. Your eyes will see strange things, and your mind utter perverse things." Woe, woe.

Dismayingly often, these biblical drunkards stirred up trouble for their own kids. Noah made fresh wine after the flood, drank too much of it, fell asleep without any clothes on, and was glimpsed in the buff by his son Ham, whom Noah promptly cursed. In one passage—it was so shocking we had to read it under our blankets with flashlights—the patriarch Lot fell down drunk and slept with his daughters. The sins of the fathers set their children's teeth on edge.

Our ministers were fond of quoting St. Paul's pronouncement that drunkards would not inherit the kingdom of God. These grave preachers assured us that the wine referred to during the Last Supper was in fact grape juice. Bible and sermons and hymns combined to give us the impression that Moses should have brought down from the mountain another stone tablet, bearing the Eleventh Commandment: Thou shalt not drink.

The scariest and most illuminating Bible story apropos of drunkards was the one about the lunatic and the swine. Matthew, Mark, and Luke each told a version of the tale. We knew it by heart: When Jesus climbed out of his boat one day, this lunatic came charging up from the graveyard, stark naked and filthy, frothing at the mouth, so violent that he broke the strongest chains. Nobody would go near him. Night and day for years this madman had been wailing among the tombs and bruising himself with stones. Jesus took one look at him and said, "Come out of the man, you unclean spirits!" for he could see that the lunatic was possessed by demons. Meanwhile, some hogs were conveniently rooting nearby. "If we have to come out," begged the demons, "at least let us go into those swine." Jesus agreed. The unclean spirits entered the hogs, and the hogs rushed straight off a cliff and plunged into a lake. Hearing the story in Sunday school, my friends thought mainly of the pigs. (How big a splash did they make? Who paid for the lost pork?) But I thought of the redeemed lunatic, who bathed himself and put on clothes and calmly sat at the feet of Jesus, restored—so the Bible said—to "his right mind."

When drunk, our father was clearly in his wrong mind. He became   30 a stranger, as fearful to us as any graveyard lunatic, not quite frothing at the mouth but fierce enough, quick-tempered, explosive; or else he grew maudlin and weepy, which frightened us nearly as much. In my boyhood despair, I reasoned that maybe he wasn't to blame for turning into an ogre. Maybe, like the lunatic, he was possessed by demons. I found support for my theory when I heard liquor referred to as "spirits," when the newspapers reported that somebody had been arrested for "driving under the influence," and when church ladies railed against that "demon drink."

If my father was indeed possessed, who would exorcise him? If he was a sinner, who would save him? If he was ill, who would cure him? If he suffered, who would ease his pain? Not ministers or doctors, for we could not bring ourselves to confide in them; not the neighbors, for we pretended they had never seen him drunk; not Mother, who fussed and pleaded but could not budge him; not my brother and sister, who were only kids. That left me. It did not matter that I, too, was only a child, and a bewildered one at that. I could not excuse myself.

On first reading a description of delirium tremens—in a book on alcoholism I smuggled from the library—I thought immediately of the frothing lunatic and the frenzied swine. When I read stories or watched films about grisly metamorphoses—Dr. Jekyll becoming Mr. Hyde, the mild husband changing into a werewolf, the kindly neighbor taken over by a brutal alien—I could not help seeing my own father's mutation from sober to drunk. Even today, knowing better, I am attracted by the demonic theory of drink, for when I recall my father's transformation, the emergence of his ugly second self, I find it easy to believe in possession by unclean spirits. We never knew which version of Father would come home from work, the true or the tainted, nor could we guess how far down the slope toward cruelty he would slide.

How far a man *could* slide we gauged by observing our back-road neighbors—the out-of-work miners who had dragged their families to our corner of Ohio from the desolate hollows of Appalachia, the tightfisted farmers, the surly mechanics, the balked and broken men. There was, for example, whiskey-soaked Mr. Jenkins, who beat his wife and kids so hard we could hear their screams from the road. There was Mr. Lavo the wino, who fell asleep smoking time and again, until one night his disgusted wife bundled up the children and went outside and left him in his easy chair to burn; he awoke on his own, staggered out coughing into the yard, and pounded her flat while the children looked on and the shack turned to ash. There was the truck driver, Mr. Sampson, who tripped over his son's tricycle one night while drunk and got so mad that he jumped into his semi and drove away, shifting through the dozen gears, and never came back. We saw the bruised children of these fathers clump onto our school bus, we saw the abandoned children huddle in the pews at church, we saw the stunned and battered mothers begging for help at our doors.

Our own father never beat us, and I don't think he ever beat Mother, but he threatened often. The Old Testament Yahweh was not more terrible in his wrath. Eyes blazing, voice booming, Father would pull out his belt and swear to give us a whipping, but he never followed through, never needed to, because we could imagine it so vividly. He shoved us, pawed us with the back of his hand, as an irked bear might smack a cub, not to injure, just to clear a space. I can see him grabbing Mother by the hair as she cowers on a chair during a nightly quarrel. He twists her neck back until she gapes up at him, and then he lifts over her skull a glass quart bottle of milk, the milk running down his forearm; and he yells at her, "Say just one more word, one goddamn word, and I'll shut you up!" I fear she will prick him with her sharp tongue, but she is terrified into silence, and so am I, and the leaking bottle quivers in the air, and milk slithers through the red hair of my father's uplifted arm, and the entire scene is there to this moment, the head jerked back, the club raised.

When the drink made him weepy, Father would pack a bag and kiss   35
each of us children on the head, and announce from the front door that he was moving out. "Where to?" we demanded, fearful each time that he would leave for good, as Mr. Sampson had roared away for good in his diesel truck. "Someplace where I won't get hounded every minute," Father would answer, his jaw quivering. He stabbed a look at Mother, who might say, "Don't run into the ditch before you get there," or, "Good riddance," and then he would slink away. Mother watched him go with arms crossed over her chest, her face closed like the lid on a box of

snakes. We children bawled. Where could he go? To the truck stop, that den of iniquity? To one of those dark, ratty flophouses in town? Would he wind up sleeping under a railroad bridge or on a park bench or in a cardboard box, mummied in rags, like the bums we had seen on our trips to Cleveland and Chicago? We bawled and bawled, wondering if he would ever come back.

He always did come back, a day or a week later, but each time there was a sliver less of him.

In Kafka's *The Metamorphosis*, which opens famously with Gregor Samsa waking up from uneasy dreams to find himself transformed into an insect, Gregor's family keep reassuring themselves that things will be just fine again, "When he comes back to us." Each time alcohol transformed our father, we held out the same hope, that he would really and truly come back to us, our authentic father, the tender and playful and competent man, and then all things would be fine. We had grounds for such hope. After his weepy departures and chapfallen returns, he would sometimes go weeks, even months without drinking. Those were glad times. Joy banged inside my ribs. Every day without the furtive glint of bottles, every meal without a fight, every bedtime without sobs encouraged us to believe that such bliss might go on forever.

Mother was fooled by just such a hope all during the forty-odd years she knew this Greeley Ray Sanders. Soon after she met him in a Chicago delicatessen on the eve of World War II and fell for his butter-melting Mississippi drawl and his wavy red hair, she learned that he drank heavily. But then so did a lot of men. She would soon coax or scold him into breaking the nasty habit. She would point out to him how ugly and foolish it was, this bleary drinking, and then he would quit. He refused to quit during their engagement, however, still refused during the first years of marriage, refused until my sister came along. The shock of fatherhood sobered him, and he remained sober through my birth at the end of the war and right on through until we moved in 1951 to the

Ohio arsenal, that paradise of bombs. Like all places that make a business of death, the arsenal had more than its share of alcoholics and drug
addicts and other varieties of escape artists. There I turned six and
started school and woke into a child's flickering awareness, just in time
to see my father begin sneaking swigs in the garage.

He sobered up again for most of a year at the height of the Korean
War, to celebrate the birth of my brother. But aside from that dry spell,
his only breaks from drinking before I graduated from high school were
just long enough to raise and then dash our hopes. Then during the
fall of my senior year—the time of the Cuban missile crisis, when it
seemed that the nightly explosions at the munitions dump and the nightly
rages in our household might spread to engulf the globe—Father collapsed. His liver, kidneys, and heart all conked out. The doctors saved
him, but only by a hair. He stayed in the hospital for weeks, going through
a withdrawal so terrible that Mother would not let us visit him. If he
wanted to kill himself, the doctors solemnly warned him, all he had to
do was hit the bottle again. One binge would finish him.

Father must have believed them, for he stayed dry the next fifteen   40
years. It was an answer to prayer, Mother said, it was a miracle. I believe
it was a reflex of fear, which he sustained over the years through courage
and pride. He knew a man could die from drink, for his brother Roscoe had. We children never laid eyes on doomed Uncle Roscoe, but in
the stories Mother told us he became a fairy-tale figure, like a boy who
took the wrong turning in the woods and was gobbled up by the wolf.

The fifteen-year dry spell came to an end with Father's retirement in
the spring of 1978. Like many men, he gave up his identity along with
his job. One day he was a boss at the factory, with a brass plate on his
door and a reputation to uphold; the next day he was a nobody at home.
He and Mother were leaving Ontario, the last of the many places to
which his job had carried them, and they were moving to a new house
in Mississippi, his childhood stomping grounds. As a boy in Mississippi,
Father sold Coca-Cola during dances while the moonshiners peddled

their brew in the parking lot; as a young blade, he fought in bars and in the ring, seeking a state Golden Gloves championship; he gambled at poker, hunted pheasants, raced motorcycles and cars, played semi-professional baseball, and, along with all his buddies—in the Black Cat Saloon, behind the cotton gin, in the woods—he drank. It was a perilous youth to dream of recovering.

After his final day of work, Mother drove on ahead with a car full of begonias and violets, while Father stayed behind to oversee the packing. When the van was loaded, the sweaty movers broke open a six-pack and offered him a beer.

"Let's drink to retirement!" they crowed. "Let's drink to freedom! to fishing! hunting! loafing! Let's drink to a guy who's going home!"

At least I imagine some such words, for that is all I can do, imagine, and I see Father's hand trembling in midair as he thinks about the fifteen sober years and about the doctors' warning, and he tells himself *God damnit, I am a free man,* and *Why can't a free man drink one beer after a lifetime of hard work?* and I see his arm reaching, his fingers closing, the can tilting to his lips. I even supply a label for the beer, a swaggering brand that promises on television to deliver the essence of life. I watch the amber liquid pour down his throat, the alcohol steal into his blood, the key turn in his brain.

Soon after my parents moved back to Father's treacherous stomping   45
ground, my wife and I visited them in Mississippi with our five-year-old daughter. Mother had been too distraught to warn me about the return of the demons. So when I climbed out of the car that bright July morning and saw my father napping in the hammock, I felt uneasy, for in all his sober years I had never known him to sleep in daylight. Then he lurched upright, blinked his bloodshot eyes, and greeted us in a syrupy voice. I was hurled back helpless into childhood.

"What's the matter with Papaw?" our daughter asked.

"Nothing," I said. "Nothing!"

Like a child again, I pretended not to see him in his stupor, and behind my phony smile I grieved. On that visit and on the few that remained before his death, once again I found bottles in the workbench, bottles in the woods. Again his hands shook too much for him to run a saw, to make his precious miniature furniture, to drive straight down back roads. Again he wound up in the ditch, in the hospital, in jail, in treatment centers. Again he shouted and wept. Again he lied. "I never touched a drop," he swore. "Your mother's making it up."

I no longer fancied I could reason with the men whose names I found on the bottles—Jim Beam, Jack Daniels—nor did I hope to save my father by burning down a store. I was able now to press the cold statistics about alcoholism against the ache of memory: ten million victims, fifteen million, twenty. And yet, in spite of my age, I reacted in the same blind way as I had in childhood, ignoring biology, forgetting numbers, vainly seeking to erase through my efforts whatever drove him to drink. I worked on their place twelve and sixteen hours a day, in the swelter of Mississippi summers, digging ditches, running electrical wires, planting trees, mowing grass, building sheds, as though what nagged at him was some list of chores, as though by taking his worries on my shoulders I could redeem him. I was flung back into boyhood, acting as though my father would not drink himself to death if only I were perfect.

I failed of perfection; he succeeded in dying. To the end, he considered himself not sick but sinful. "Do you want to kill yourself?" I asked him. "Why not?" he answered. "Why the hell not? What's there to save?" To the end, he would not speak about his feelings, would not or could not give a name to the beast that was devouring him.   50

In silence, he went rushing off the cliff. Unlike the biblical swine, however, he left behind a few of the demons to haunt his children. Life with him and the loss of him twisted us into shapes that will be familiar to other sons and daughters of alcoholics. My brother became a rebel, my sister retreated into shyness, I played the stalwart and dutiful son who would hold the family together. If my father was unstable, I would be a rock. If he squandered money on drink, I would pinch every penny.

If he wept when drunk—and only when drunk—I would not let myself weep at all. If he roared at the Little League umpire for calling my pitches balls, I would throw nothing but strikes. Watching him flounder and rage, I came to dread the loss of control. I would go through life without making anyone mad. I vowed never to put in my mouth or veins any chemical that would banish my everyday self. I would never make a scene, never lash out at the ones I loved, never hurt a soul. Through hard work, relentless work, I would achieve something dazzling—in the classroom, on the basketball floor, in the science lab, in the pages of books—and my achievement would distract the world's eyes from his humiliation. I would become a worthy sacrifice, and the smoke of my burning would please God.

It is far easier to recognize these twists in my character than to undo them. Work has become an addiction for me, as drink was an addiction for my father. Knowing this, my daughter gave me a placard for the wall: WORKAHOLIC. The labor is endless and futile, for I can no more redeem myself through work than I could redeem my father. I still panic in the face of other people's anger, because his drunken temper was so terrible. I shrink from causing sadness or disappointment even to strangers, as though I were still concealing the family shame. I still notice every twitch of emotion in the faces around me, having learned as a child to read the weather in faces, and I blame myself for their least pang of unhappiness or anger. In certain moods I blame myself for everything. Guilt burns like acid in my veins.

I am moved to write these pages now because my own son, at the age of ten, is taking on himself the griefs of the world, and in particular the griefs of his father. He tells me that when I am gripped by sadness he feels responsible; he feels there must be something he can do to spring me from depression, to fix my life. And that crushing sense of responsibility is exactly what I felt at the age of ten in the face of my father's drinking. My son wonders if I, too, am possessed. I write, therefore, to drag into the light what eats at me—the fear, the guilt, the shame—so that my own children may be spared.

I still shy away from nightclubs, from bars, from parties where the solvent is alcohol. My friends puzzle over this, but it is no more peculiar than for a man to shy away from the lions' den after seeing his father torn apart. I took my own first drink at the age of twenty-one, half a glass of burgundy. I knew the odds of my becoming an alcoholic were four times higher than for the sons of nonalcoholic fathers. So I sipped warily.

I still do—once a week, perhaps, a glass of wine, a can of beer, noth- 55
ing stronger, nothing more. I listen for the turning of a key in my brain.

Thinking about the Text

1. In what ways did the culture in which Scott Russell Sanders was reared shape his understanding of his father's alcoholism? Cite passages from the essay to support your answer.

2. Sanders quotes and makes allusions to popular culture, Greek mythology, and other sources, comparing and contrasting his own experience of living with an alcoholic to other representations of drunkenness. In what ways were his experiences similar to and different from those he found in other texts?

3. Write about some aspect of your childhood that helped shape who you are today. As Sanders does, show with quotations and allusions how your own experience has been similar to and different from the experiences represented in books, on television, or in films.

TERRY TEMPEST WILLIAMS

The Clan of One-Breasted Women

1989

———————————————✧———————————————

TERRY TEMPEST WILLIAMS (b. 1955) writes memoirs and essays on the environment, family, art, and spirituality. She is known primarily for her memoir *Refuge: An Unnatural History of Family and Place* (1991). Her essay collections include *An Unspoken Hunger: Stories from the Field* (1994), *Desert Quartet: An Erotic Landscape* (1995), and *Red: Passion and Patience in the Desert* (2001). "The Clan of One-Breasted Women" first appeared in the journal *Witness* (1989) and was then included as the epilogue to *Refuge*. All notes are the author's.

———————————————✧———————————————

I BELONG TO A CLAN OF ONE-BREASTED WOMEN. MY MOTHER, MY grandmothers, and six aunts have all had mastectomies. Seven are dead. The two who survive have just completed rounds of chemotherapy and radiation.

I've had my own problems: two biopsies for breast cancer and a small tumor between my ribs diagnosed as "a border-line malignancy."

This is my family history.

Most statistics tell us breast cancer is genetic, hereditary, with rising percentages attached to fatty diets, childlessness, or becoming pregnant after thirty. What they don't say is living in Utah may be the greatest hazard of all.

We are a Mormon family with roots in Utah since 1847. The word-of-wisdom, a religious doctrine of health, kept the women in my family aligned with good foods: no coffee, no tea, tobacco, or alcohol. For the most part, these women were finished having their babies by the time they were thirty. And only one faced breast cancer prior to 1960. Traditionally, as a group of people, Mormons have a low rate of cancer.

Is our family a cultural anomaly? The truth is we didn't think about it. Those who did, usually the men, simply said, "bad genes." The women's attitude was stoic. Cancer was part of life. On February 16, 1971, the eve before my mother's surgery, I accidently picked up the telephone and overheard her ask my grandmother what she could expect.

"Diane, it is one of the most spiritual experiences you will ever encounter."

I quietly put down the receiver.

Two days later, my father took my three brothers and me to the hospital to visit her. She met us in the lobby in a wheelchair. No bandages were visible. I'll never forget her radiance, the way she held herself in a purple velour robe and how she gathered us around her.

"Children, I am fine. I want you to know I felt the arms of God   10
around me."

We believed her. My father cried. Our mother, his wife, was thirty-eight years old.

Two years ago, after my mother's death from cancer, my father and I were having dinner together. He had just returned from St. George where his construction company was putting in natural gas lines for towns in southern Utah. He spoke of his love for the country: the sandstoned landscape, bare-boned and beautiful. He had just finished hiking the Kolob trail in Zion National Park. We got caught up in reminiscing, recalling with fondness our walk up Angel's Landing on his fiftieth birthday and the years our family had vacationed there. This was a remembered landscape where we had been raised.

Over dessert, I shared a recurring dream of mine. I told my father that for years, as long as I could remember, I saw this flash of light in the night in the desert. That this image had so permeated my being, I could not venture south without seeing it again, on the horizon, illuminating buttes and mesas.

"You did see it," he said.

"Saw what?" I asked, a bit tentative.   15

"The bomb. The cloud. We were driving home from Riverside, California. You were sitting on your mother's lap. She was pregnant. In fact, I remember the date, September 7, 1957. We had just gotten out of the Service. We were driving north, past Las Vegas. It was an hour or so before dawn, when this explosion went off. We not only heard it, but felt it. I thought the oil tanker in front of us had blown up. We pulled over and suddenly, rising from the desert floor, we saw it, clearly, this golden-stemmed cloud, the mushroom. The sky seemed to vibrate with an eerie pink glow. Within a few minutes, a light ash was raining on the car."

I stared at my father. This was new information to me.

"I thought you knew that," my father said. "It was a common occurrence in the fifties."

It was at this moment I realized the deceit I had been living under. Children growing up in the American Southwest, drinking contaminated milk from contaminated cows, even from the contaminated breasts of their mother, my mother—members, years later, of the Clan of One-Breasted Women.

It is a well-known story in the Desert West, "The Day We Bombed Utah,"   20
or perhaps, "The Years We Bombed Utah."[1] Above ground atomic testing in Nevada took place from January 27, 1951, through July 11, 1962. Not only were the winds blowing north, covering "low use segments of the population" with fallout and leaving sheep dead in their tracks, but the climate was right.[2] The United States of the 1950s was red, white, and blue. The Korean War was raging. McCarthyism was rampant. Ike was it and the Cold War was hot. If you were against nuclear testing, you were for a Communist regime.

Much has been written about this "American nuclear tragedy." Public health was secondary to national security. The Atomic Energy Commissioner, Thomas Murray, said, "Gentlemen, we must not let anything interfere with this series of tests, nothing."[3]

Again and again, the American public was told by its government, in spite of burns, blisters, and nausea, "It has been found that the tests may be conducted with adequate assurance of safety under conditions prevailing at the bombing reservations."[4] Assuaging public fears was simply a matter of public relations. "Your best action," an Atomic Energy Commission booklet read, "is not to be worried about fallout." A news

1. Fuller, John G., *The Day We Bombed Utah* (New York: New American Library, 1984).
2. Discussion on March 14, 1988, with Carole Gallagher, photographer and author, *American Ground Zero: The Secret Nuclear War*, published by Random House, 1994.
3. Szasz, Ferenc M., "Downwind From the Bomb," *Nevada Historical Society Quarterly*, Fall 1987. Vol. XXX, No. 3, p. 185.
4. Fradkin, Philip L., *Fallout* (Tucson: University of Arizona Press, 1989), 98.

release typical of the times stated, "We find no basis for concluding that harm to any individual has resulted from radioactive fallout."[5]

On August 30, 1979, during Jimmy Carter's presidency, a suit was filed entitled "Irene Allen vs. the United States of America." Mrs. Allen was the first to be alphabetically listed with twenty-four test cases, representative of nearly 1200 plaintiffs seeking compensation from the United States government for cancers caused from nuclear testing in Nevada.

Irene Allen lived in Hurricane, Utah. She was the mother of five children and had been widowed twice. Her first husband with their two oldest boys had watched the tests from the roof of the local high school. He died of leukemia in 1956. Her second husband died of pancreatic cancer in 1978.

In a town meeting conducted by Utah Senator Orrin Hatch, shortly   25
before the suit was filed, Mrs. Allen said, "I am not blaming the government, I want you to know that, Senator Hatch. But I thought if my testimony could help in any way so this wouldn't happen again to any of the generations coming up after us . . . I am really happy to be here this day to bear testimony of this."[6]

God-fearing people. This is just one story in an anthology of thousands.

On May 10, 1984, Judge Bruce S. Jenkins handed down his opinion. Ten of the plaintiffs were awarded damages. It was the first time a federal court had determined that nuclear tests had been the cause of cancers. For the remaining fourteen test cases, the proof of causation was not sufficient. In spite of the split decision, it was considered a landmark ruling.[7] It was not to remain so for long.

In April, 1987, the 10th Circuit Court of Appeals overturned Judge Jenkins' ruling on the basis that the United States was protected from

5. Ibid., 109.

6. Town meeting held by Senator Orrin Hatch in St. George, Utah, April 17, 1979, transcript, 26–28.

7. Fradkin, *Fallout*, 228.

suit by the legal doctrine of sovereign immunity, the centuries-old idea from England in the days of absolute monarchs.[8]

In January, 1988, the Supreme Court refused to review the Appeals Court decision. To our court system, it does not matter whether the United States Government was irresponsible, whether it lied to its citizens or even that citizens died from the fallout of nuclear testing. What matters is that our government is immune. "The King can do no wrong."

In Mormon culture, authority is respected, obedience is revered, and   30 independent thinking is not. I was taught as a young girl not to "make waves" or "rock the boat."

"Just let it go—" my mother would say. "You know how you feel, that's what counts."

For many years, I did just that—listened, observed, and quietly formed my own opinions within a culture that rarely asked questions because they had all the answers. But one by one, I watched the women in my family die common, heroic deaths. We sat in waiting rooms hoping for good news, always receiving the bad. I cared for them, bathed their scarred bodies and kept their secrets. I watched beautiful women become bald as cytoxan, cisplatin and adriamycin were injected into their veins. I held their foreheads as they vomited green-black bile and I shot them with morphine when the pain became inhuman. In the end, I witnessed their last peaceful breaths, becoming a midwife to the rebirth of their souls. But the price of obedience became too high.

The fear and inability to question authority that ultimately killed rural communities in Utah during atmospheric testing of atomic weapons was the same fear I saw being held in my mother's body. Sheep. Dead sheep. The evidence is buried.

8. U.S. vs. Allen, 816 Federal Reporter, 2d/1417 (10th Circuit Court 1987), cert. denied, 108 S. CT. 694 (1988).

I cannot prove that my mother, Diane Dixon Tempest, or my grand-mothers, Lettie Romney Dixon and Kathryn Blackett Tempest, along with my aunts contracted cancer from nuclear fallout in Utah. But I can't prove they didn't.

My father's memory was correct, the September blast we drove 35 through in 1957 was part of Operation Plumbbob, one of the most intensive series of bomb tests to be initiated. The flash of light in the night in the desert I had always thought was a dream developed into a family nightmare. It took fourteen years, from 1957 to 1971, for can-cer to show up in my mother—the same time, Howard L. Andrews, an authority on radioactive fallout at the National Institutes of Health, says radiation cancer requires to become evident.[9] The more I learn about what it means to be a "downwinder," the more questions I drown in.

What I do know, however, is that as a Mormon woman of the fifth generation of "Latter-Day-Saints," I must question everything, even if it means losing my faith, even if it means becoming a member of a border tribe among my own people. Tolerating blind obedience in the name of patriotism or religion ultimately takes our lives.

When the Atomic Energy Commission described the country north of the Nevada Test Site as "virtually uninhabited desert terrain," my family members were some of the "virtual uninhabitants."

One night, I dreamed women from all over the world circling a blazing fire in the desert. They spoke of change, of how they hold the moon in their bellies and wax and wane with its phases. They mocked at the presumption of even-tempered beings and made promises that they would never fear the witch inside themselves. The women danced wildly as sparks broke away from the flames and entered the night sky as stars.

9. Fradkin, Op. cit., 116.

And they sang a song given to them by Shoshoni grandmothers:

Ah ne nah, nah
nin nah nah—
Ah ne nah, nah
nin nah nah—
Nyaga mutzi
oh ne nay—
Nyaga mutzi
oh ne nay—[10]

The women danced and drummed and sang for weeks, preparing   40
themselves for what was to come. They would reclaim the desert for the
sake of their children, for the sake of the land.

A few miles downwind from the fire circle, bombs were being tested.
Rabbits felt the tremors. Their soft leather pads on paws and feet recognized the shaking sands while the roots of mesquite and sage were
smoldering. Rocks were hot from the inside out and dust devils hummed
unnaturally. And each time there was another nuclear test, ravens watched
the desert heave. Stretch marks appeared. The land was losing its muscle.

The women couldn't bear it any longer. They were mothers. They
had suffered labor pains but always under the promise of birth. The red
hot pains beneath the desert promised death only as each bomb became
a stillborn. A contract had been broken between human beings and the
land. A new contract was being drawn by the women who understood
the fate of the earth as their own.

Under the cover of darkness, ten women slipped under the barbed
wire fence and entered the contaminated country. They were trespass-

10. This song was sung by the Western Shoshone women as they crossed the line at the
Nevada Test Site on March 18, 1988, as part of their "Reclaim the Land" action. The translation they gave was: "Consider the rabbits how gently they walk on the earth. Consider
the rabbits how gently they walk on the earth. We remember them. We can walk gently
also. We remember them. We can walk gently also."

ing. They walked toward the town of Mercury in moonlight, taking their cues from coyote, kit fox, antelope squirrel, and quail. They moved quietly and deliberately through the maze of Joshua trees. When a hint of daylight appeared they rested, drinking tea and sharing their rations of food. The women closed their eyes. The time had come to protest with the heart, that to deny one's genealogy with the earth was to commit treason against one's soul.

At dawn, the women draped themselves in mylar, wrapping long streamers of silver plastic around their arms to blow in the breeze. They wore clear masks that became the faces of humanity. And when they arrived on the edge of Mercury, they carried all the butterflies of a summer day in their wombs. They paused to allow their courage to settle.

The town which forbids pregnant women and children to enter because of radiation risks to their health was asleep. The women moved through the streets as winged messengers, twirling around each other in slow motion, peeking inside homes and watching the easy sleep of men and women. They were astonished by such stillness and periodically would utter a shrill note or low cry just to verify life.

The residents finally awoke to what appeared as strange apparitions. Some simply stared. Others called authorities, and in time, the women were apprehended by wary soldiers dressed in desert fatigues. They were taken to a white, square building on the other edge of Mercury. When asked who they were and why they were there, the women replied, "We are mothers and we have come to reclaim the desert for our children."

The soldiers arrested them. As the ten women were blindfolded and handcuffed, they began singing:

You can't forbid us everything
You can't forbid us to think—
You can't forbid our tears to flow
And you can't stop the songs that we sing.

The women continued to sing louder and louder, until they heard the voices of their sisters moving across the mesa.

Ah ne nah, nah
nin nah nah—
Ah ne nah, nah
nin nah nah—
Nyaga mutzi
oh ne nay—
Nyaga mutzi
oh ne nay—

"Call for re-enforcement," one soldier said.

"We have," interrupted one woman. "We have—and you have no   50 idea of our numbers."

On March 18, 1988, I crossed the line at the Nevada Test Site and was arrested with nine other Utahns for trespassing on military lands. They are still conducting nuclear tests in the desert. Ours was an act of civil disobedience. But as I walked toward the town of Mercury, it was more than a gesture of peace. It was a gesture on behalf of the Clan of One-Breasted Women.

As one officer cinched the handcuffs around my wrists, another frisked my body. She found a pen and a pad of paper tucked inside my left boot.

"And these?" she asked sternly.

"Weapons," I replied.

Our eyes met. I smiled. She pulled the leg of my trousers back over   55 my boot.

"Step forward, please," she said as she took my arm.

We were booked under an afternoon sun and bussed to Tonapah, Nevada. It was a two-hour ride. This was familiar country to me. The

Joshua trees standing their ground had been named by my ancestors who believed they looked like prophets pointing west to the promised land. These were the same trees that bloomed each spring, flowers appearing like white flames in the Mojave. And I recalled a full moon in May when my mother and I had walked among them, flushing out mourning doves and owls.

The bus stopped short of town. We were released. The officials thought it was a cruel joke to leave us stranded in the desert with no way to get home. What they didn't realize is that we were home, soul-centered and strong, women who recognized the sweet smell of sage as fuel for our spirits.

Thinking about the Text

1. Several times in this essay, Terry Tempest Williams mentions that she comes from a Mormon family. Explain the ways in which this information is important to the story she tells.

2. What is Williams's argument? What kinds of evidence does she use to support her argument? Has she convinced you—and if not, why not? (For an example of a student essay that analyzes Williams's argument, see Elizabeth Krotulis's "A Passion for Justice: The Use of Persuasion in 'The Clan of One-Breasted Women'" on pp. 467–72.)

3. Write an argument about an issue that is important to you. As Williams does, use both personal narrative and data and information from other sources to convince your readers that the issue matters and that your argument is one they should take seriously.

MAGGIE HELWIG

Hunger

1989

MAGGIE HELWIG (b. 1961) is a Canadian author of poetry, fiction, and essays. Her books of essays include *Apocalypse Jazz* (1993) and *Real Bodies* (1999). She is also an Anglican priest and social justice activist. "Hunger" was first published in the Canadian journal *This Magazine* (1989).

CONSIDER THAT IT IS NOW NORMAL FOR NORTH AMERICAN women to have eating disorders. Consider that anorexia—deliberate starvation—and bulimia—self-induced vomiting—and obsessive patterns for weight-controlling exercise are now the ordinary thing for young women, and are spreading at a frightening rate to older women, to men, to ethnic groups and social classes that were once "immune." Consider that some surveys suggest that 80 per cent of the women on an average university campus have borderline-to-severe eating disorders; that it is almost impossible to get treatment unless the problem is life threatening; that, in fact, if it is not life-threatening it is not considered a problem at all. I once sat in a seminar on nutritional aspects of anorexia, and ended up listening to people tell me how to keep my weight down. All this is happening in one of the richest countries in the world, a society devoted to consumption. Amazing as it may seem, we have normalized anorexia and bulimia, even turned them into an industry.

We've also trivialized them: made them into nothing more than an exaggerated conformity with basically acceptable standards of behavior. Everyone wants to be thin and pretty, after all. Some people take it a little too far; you have to get them back on the right track, but it's all a question of knowing just how far is proper.

The consumer society has gone so far we can even buy into hunger.

But that is not what it's about. You do not stuff yourself with food and force yourself to vomit just because of fashion magazines. You do not reduce yourself to the condition of a skeleton in order to be attractive. This is not just a problem of proportion. This is the nightmare of consumerism acted out in women's bodies.

This is what we are saying as we starve: it is not all right. It is not all right. It is not all right.

There've always been strange or disordered patterns of eating, associated mainly with religious extremism or psychological problems (which some, not myself, would say were the same thing). But the complex of

ideas, fears, angers and actions that make up contemporary anorexia
and bulimia seems to be of fairly recent origin. Anorexia did not exist as
a recognized pattern until the 1960s, and bulimia not until later than
that—and at first they were deeply shocking. The idea that privileged
young women (the first group to be affected) were voluntarily starving
themselves, sometimes to death, or regularly sticking their fingers down
their throats to make themselves throw up, shook the culture badly. It
was a fad, in a sense, the illness of the month, but it was also a scandal,
and a source of something like horror.

Before this, though, before anorexia had a widely recognized name,
one of the first women to succumb to it had made her own scandalous
stand, and left a body of writing that still has a lot to say about the real
meaning of voluntary hunger.

Simone Weil was a brilliant, disturbed, wildly wrong-headed and
astonishingly perceptive young French woman who died from the com-
plications of self-starvation in America during World War II, at the age
of 34. She never, of course, wrote directly about her refusal to eat—
typically for any anorexic, she insisted she ate perfectly adequate
amounts. But throughout her philosophical and theological writing
(almost all of it fragments and essays collected after her death), she
examines and uses the symbolism of hunger, eating and food.

Food occupied, in fact, a rather important and valued position in her
philosophy—she once referred to food as "the irrefutable proof of the
reality of the universe," and at another time said that the foods served
at Easter and Christmas, the turkey and *marron glacés*, were "the true
meaning of the feast"; although she could also take the more conventional puritan position that desire for food is a "base motive." She spoke
often of eating God (acceptable enough in a Christian context) and of
being eaten by God (considerably less so). The great tragedy of our lives,
she said, is that we cannot really eat God; and also "it may be that vice,
depravity and crime are almost always . . . attempts to eat beauty."

But it is her use of the symbolism of hunger that explains her death. 10
"We have to go down into ourselves to the abode of the desire which is
not imaginary. Hunger: we imagine kinds of food, but the hunger itself
is real: we have to fasten onto the hunger."

Hunger, then, was a search for reality, for the irreducible need that
lies beyond all imaginary satisfactions. Weil was deeply perturbed by
the "materialism" of her culture; though she probably could not have
begun to imagine the number of imaginary and illusory "satisfactions"
now available. Simply, she wanted truth. She wanted to reduce herself
to the point where she would *know* what needs, and what foods, were
real and true.

Similarly, though deeply drawn to the Catholic faith, she refused to
be baptized and to take Communion (to, in fact, eat God). "I cannot
help wondering whether in these days when so large a proportion of
humanity is sunk in materialism, God does not want there to be some
men and women who have given themselves to him and to Christ and
who yet remain outside the Church." For the sake of honesty, of truth,
she maintained her hunger.

Weil, a mystic and a political activist simultaneously until the end of
her short life—she was one of the first French intellectuals to join the
Communist party and one of the first to leave, fought in the Spanish
civil war and worked in auto factories—could not bear to have life be
less than a total spiritual and political statement. And her statement of
protest, of dissatisfaction, her statement of hunger, finally destroyed her.

The term anorexia nervosa was coined in the 19th century, but it
was not until sometime in the 1960s that significant—and constantly
increasing—numbers of well-off young women began dying of starvation, and not until the early 1970s that it became public knowledge.

It is the nature of our times that the explanations proffered were psy- 15
chological and individualistic; yet, even so, it was understood as being,
on some level, an act of protest. And of course symbolically, it could

hardly be other—it was, simply, a hunger strike. The most common interpretation, at that point, was that it was a sort of adolescent rebellion against parental control, an attempt, particularly, to escape from an overcontrolling mother. It was a fairly acceptable paradigm for the period, although many mothers were justifiably disturbed; sometimes deeply and unnecessarily hurt. The theory still has some currency, and is not entirely devoid of truth.

But can it be an accident that this happened almost precisely to coincide with the growth of the consumer society, a world based on a level of material consumption that, by the end of the 1960s, had become very nearly uncontrollable? Or with the strange, underground guilt that has made "conspicuous consumption" a matter of consuming vast amounts and *hiding it*, of million-dollar minimalism? With the development of what is possibly the most emotionally depleted society in history, where the only "satisfactions" seem to be the imaginary ones, the material buy-offs?

To be skeletally, horribly thin makes one strong statement. It says, I am hungry. What I have been given is not sufficient, not real, not true, not acceptable. I am starving. To reject food, whether by refusing it or by vomiting it back, says simply, I will not consume. I will not participate. This is not real.

Hunger is the central nightmare image of our society. Of all the icons of horror the last few generations have offered us, we have chosen, above all, pictures of hunger—the emaciated prisoners of Auschwitz and Belsen, Ethiopian children with bloated bellies and stick-figure limbs. We carry in our heads these nightmares of the extreme edge of hunger.

And while we may not admit to guilt about our level of consumption in general, we admit freely to guilt about eating, easily equate food with "sin." We cannot accept hunger of our own, cannot afford to consider it.

It is, traditionally, women who carry our nightmares. It was women   20
who became possessed by the Devil, women who suffered from "hys-

terical disorders," women who, in all popular culture, are the targets of the "monster." One of the roles women are cast in is that of those who act out the subconscious fears of their society. And it is women above all, in this time, who carry our hunger.

It is the starving women who embody the extremity of hunger that terrifies and fascinates us, and who insist that they are not hungry. It is the women sticking their fingers down their throats who act out the equation of food and sin, who deny hunger and yet embody endless, unfulfilled appetite. It is these women who live through every implication of our consumption and our hunger, our guilt and ambiguity and our awful need for something real to fill us.

We have too much; and it is poison.

*   *   *

As eating disorders became increasingly widespread, they also became increasingly trivialized, incorporated into a framework already "understood" all too well. Feminist writers had, early on, noted that anorexia had to be linked with the increasing thinness of models and other glamor icons, as part of a larger cultural trend. This is true enough as a starting point, for the symbolic struggle being waged in women's bodies happens on many levels, and is not limited to pathology cases. Unfortunately, this single starting point was seized on by "women's magazines" and popularizing accounts in general. Anorexia was now understandable, almost safe really, it was just fashion gone out of control. Why, these women were *accepting* the culture, they just needed a sense of proportion. What a relief.

Now it could be condoned. Now it could, in fact, become the basis for an industry; could be incorporated neatly into consumer society. According to Jane Fonda the solution to bulimia is to remain equally unhealthily thin by buying the 20-minute workout and becoming an obsessive fitness follower (at least for those who can afford it). The diet clinic industry, the Nutrisystem package, the aerobics boom. An advertising industry that plays equally off desire and guilt, for they now reinforce each other. Thousands upon thousands of starving, tormented women, not "sick" enough to be taken seriously, not really troubled at all.

One does not reduce oneself to the condition of a skeleton in order   25
to be fashionable. One does not binge and vomit daily as an acceptable means of weight control. One does not even approach or imagine or dream of these things if one is not in some sort of trouble. If it were as simple as fashion, surely we would not be so ashamed to speak of these things, we would not feel that either way, whether we eat or do not eat, we are doing something wrong.

I was anorexic for eight years. I nearly died. It was certainly no help to me to be told I was taking fashion too far—I knew perfectly well that had nothing to do with it. It did not help much to be told I was trying to escape from my mother, since I lived away from home and was in only occasional contact with my family; it did not help much to be approached on an individualistic, psychological level. In fact, the first person I was able to go to for help was a charismatic Catholic, who at least understood that I was speaking in symbols of spiritual hunger.

I knew that I had something to say, that things were not all right, that I had to make that concretely, physically obvious. I did not hate or look down on my body—I spoke through it and with it.

Women are taught to take guilt, concern, problems, onto themselves personally; and especially onto their bodies. But we are trying to talk about something that is only partly personal. Until we find new ways of saying it and find the courage to talk to the world about the world, we will speak destruction to ourselves. We must come to know what we are saying—and say it.

Thinking about the Text

1. Explain the connections Maggie Helwig makes among women, eating disorders, spiritual hunger, and consumerism. How does Helwig's explanation of eating disorders differ from other explanations you have encountered?

2. Both Helwig and Terry Tempest Williams (see "The Clan of One-Breasted Women" on pp. 231–41) write about women's bodies. What are some of the different ways women use their bodies to make a statement in each of these essays?

3. Write an essay reflecting on another way people make some kind of statement with their bodies—tattoos, piercings, cosmetic surgery, manner of dress, and so on. As Helwig does, provide statistics and at least one specific example to illuminate your reflection.

GARRISON KEILLOR

How to Write a Letter
Postcards

1989

GARRISON KEILLOR (b. 1942) writes stories and essays, which
have been published in magazines such as the *New Yorker*
and the *Atlantic*. He is known primarily for his radio program *A Prairie Home Companion* and for his stories about a
fictional Midwestern town, Lake Wobegon. The two selections here were first published in his book of stories and
letters, *We Are Still Married* (1989).

How to Write a Letter

W E SHY PERSONS NEED TO WRITE A LETTER NOW AND then, or else we'll dry up and blow away. It's true. And I speak as one who loves to reach for the phone, dial the number, and talk. I say, "Big Bopper here—what's shakin', babes?" The telephone is to shyness what Hawaii is to February, it's a way out of the woods, *and yet*: a letter is better.

Such a sweet gift—a piece of handmade writing, in an envelope that is not a bill, sitting in our friend's path when she trudges home from a long day spent among wahoos and savages, a day our words will help repair. They don't need to be immortal, just sincere. She can read them twice and again tomorrow: *You're someone I care about, Corinne, and think of often and every time I do you make me smile.*

We need to write, otherwise nobody will know who we are. They will have only a vague impression of us as A Nice Person, because, frankly, we don't shine at conversation, we lack the confidence to thrust our faces forward and say, "Hi, I'm Heather Hooten; let me tell you about my week." Mostly we say "Uh-huh" and "Oh, really." People smile and look over our shoulder, looking for someone else to meet.

So a shy person sits down and writes a letter. To be known by another person—to meet and talk freely on the page—to be close despite distance. To escape from anonymity and be our own sweet selves and express the music of our souls.

Same thing that moves a giant rock star to sing his heart out in front of 123,000 people moves us to take ballpoint in hand and write a few lines to our dear Aunt Eleanor. *We want to be known.* We want her to

5

know that we have fallen in love, that we quit our job, that we're moving to New York, and we want to say a few things that might not get said in casual conversation: *Thank you for what you've meant to me, I am very happy right now.*

The first step in writing letters is to get over the guilt of *not* writing. You don't "owe" anybody a letter. Letters are a gift. The burning shame you feel when you see unanswered mail makes it harder to pick up a pen and makes for a cheerless letter when you finally do. *I feel bad about not writing, but I've been so busy,* etc. Skip this. Few letters are obligatory, and they are *Thanks for the wonderful gift* and *I am terribly sorry to hear about George's death* and *Yes, you're welcome to stay with us next month*, and not many more than that. Write those promptly if you want to keep your friends. Don't worry about the others, except love letters, of course. When your true love writes, *Dear Light of My Life, Joy of My Heart, O Lovely Pulsating Core of My Sensate Life*, some response is called for.

Some of the best letters are tossed off in a burst of inspiration, so keep your writing stuff in one place where you can sit down for a few minutes and (*Dear Roy, I am in the middle of a book entitled* We Are Still Married *but thought I'd drop you a line. Hi to your sweetie, too*) dash off a note to a pal. Envelopes, stamps, address book, everything in a drawer so you can write fast when the pen is hot.

A blank white eight-by-eleven sheet can look as big as Montana if the pen's not so hot—try a smaller page and write boldly. Or use a note card with a piece of fine art on the front; if your letter ain't good, at least they get the Matisse. Get a pen that makes a sensuous line, get a comfortable typewriter, a friendly word processor—which feels easy to the hand.

Sit for a few minutes with the blank sheet in front of you, and meditate on the person you will write to, let your friend come to mind until you can almost see her or him in the room with you. Remember the last time you saw each other and how your friend looked and what you said and what perhaps was unsaid between you, and when your friend becomes real to you, start to write.

Write the salutation—*Dear* You—and take a deep breath and plunge   10
in. A simple declarative sentence will do, followed by another and another and another. Tell us what you're doing and tell it like you were talking to us. Don't think about grammar, don't think about lit'ry style, don't try to write dramatically, just give us your news. Where did you go, who did you see, what did they say, what do you think?

If you don't know where to begin, start with the present moment: *I'm sitting at the kitchen table on a rainy Saturday morning. Everyone is gone and the house is quiet.* Let your simple description of the present moment lead to something else, let the letter drift gently along.

The toughest letter to crank out is one that is meant to impress, as we all know from writing job applications; if it's hard work to slip off a letter to a friend, maybe you're trying too hard to be terrific. A letter is only a report to someone who already likes you for reasons other than your brilliance. Take it easy.

Don't worry about form. It's not a term paper. When you come to the end of one episode, just start a new paragraph. You can go from a few lines about the sad state of pro football to the fight with your mother to your fond memories of Mexico to your cat's urinary-tract infection to a few thoughts on personal indebtedness and on to the kitchen sink and what's in it. The more you write, the easier it gets, and when you have a True True Friend to write to, a *compadre*, a soul sibling, then it's like driving a car down a country road, you just get behind the keyboard and press on the gas.

Don't tear up the page and start over when you write a bad line—try to write your way out of it. Make mistakes and plunge on. Let the letter cook along and let yourself be bold. Outrage, confusion, love—whatever is in your mind, let it find a way to the page. Writing is a means of discovery, always, and when you come to the end and write

Yours ever or *Hugs and kisses*, you'll know something you didn't when you wrote *Dear Pal*.

Probably your friend will put your letter away, and it'll be read again   15
a few years from now—and it will improve with age. And forty years
from now, your friend's grandkids will dig it out of the attic and read it,
a sweet and precious relic of the ancient eighties that gives them a
sudden clear glimpse of you and her and the world we old-timers knew.
You will then have created an object of art. Your simple lines about
where you went, who you saw, what they said, will speak to those children and they will feel in their hearts the humanity of our times.

You can't pick up a phone and call the future and tell them about our
times. You have to pick up a piece of paper.

Postcards

A POSTCARD TAKES ABOUT FIFTY WORDS GRACEFULLY, which is how to write one. A few sweet strokes in a flowing hand—pink roses, black-face sheep in a wet meadow, the sea, the Swedish coast—your friend in Washington gets the idea. She doesn't need your itinerary to know that you remember her.

Fifty words is a strict form but if you write tiny and sneak over into the address side to squeeze in a hundred, the grace is gone and the result is not a poem but notes for a letter you don't have time to write, which will make her feel cheated.

So many persons traveling to a strange land are inclined to see its life so clearly, its essential national character, they could write a book about it as other foreign correspondents have done ("highly humorous . . . definitely a must"), but fifty words is a better length for what you really know.

Fifty words and a picture. Say you are in Scotland, the picture is of your hotel, a stone pile looking across the woods of Druimindarroch to Loch Nan Uamh near the village of Arisaig. You've never seen this country. For the past year you've worked like a prisoner in the mines. Write.

Scotland is the most beautiful country in the world and I am drinking coffee in the library of what once was the manor of people who inherited everything and eventually lost it. Thus it became a hotel. I'm with

English people whose correctness is overpowering. What wild good luck to be here. And to be an American! I'm so happy, bubba.

In the Highlands, many one-lane roads which widen at curves and hills—a driving thrill, especially when following a native who drives like hell—you stick close to him, like the second car of the roller-coaster, but lose your nerve. Sixty mph down a one-lane winding road. I prefer a career.

The arrogance of Americans who, without so much as a *"mi scusi"* or *"bitte"* or *"s'il vous plaît,"* words that a child could learn easily, walk up to a stranger and say, "Say, where's the museum?" as if English and rudeness rule the world, never ceases to amaze. You hear the accent and sink under the table.

Woke up at six, dark. Switzerland. Alps. Raining. Lights of villages high in the sky. Too dark to see much so snoozed awhile. Woke up in sunny Italy. Field after field of corn, like Iowa in August. Mamas, papas, grammas, grampas, little babies. Skinny trees above the whitewashed houses.

Arrived in Venice. A pipe had burst at the hotel and we were sent to another not as good. Should you spend time arguing for a refund? Went to San Marco, on which the doges overspent. A cash register in the sanctuary: five hundred lire to see the gold altar. Now we understand the Reformation.

On the train to Vienna, she, having composed the sentences carefully from old memory of intermediate German, asked the old couple if the train went to Vienna. *"Ja, ja!"* Did we need to change trains? *"Nein."*

Later she successfully ordered dinner and registered at the hotel. *Mein wundercompanion.*

People take me for an American tourist and stare at me, maybe because I walk slow and stare at them, so today I walked like a bat out of hell along the Ringstrasse, past the Hofburg Palace to Stephans Platz and back, and if anyone stared, I didn't notice. Didn't see much of Vienna but felt much better.

One week in a steady drizzle of German and now I am starting to lose my grip on English, I think. Don't know what to write. How are you? Are the Twins going to be in the World Series?

You get to Mozart's apartment through the back door of a restaurant. Kitchen smells, yelling, like at Burger King. The room where he wrote *Figaro* is bare, as if he moved out this morning. It's a nice apartment. His grave at the cemetery is now marked, its whereabouts being unknown. Mozart our brother.

Copenhagen is raining and all the Danes seem unperturbed. A calm humorous people. Kids are the same as anywhere, wild, and nobody hits them. Men wear pastels, especially turquoise. Narrow streets, no cars, little shops, and in the old square a fruit stand and an old woman with flowers yelling, "wōsa for tew-va!"

Sunbathing yesterday. A fine woman took off her shirt, jeans, pants, nearby, and lay on her belly, then turned over. Often she sat up to apply oil. Today my back is burned bright red (as St. Paul warns) from my lying and looking at her so long but who could ignore such beauty and *so generous*.

Thinking about the Text

1. Garrison Keillor claims that "shy persons need to write a letter now and then" (paragraph 1). List the ways he notes that friends communicate with one another. What kinds of writing are best suited to different personalities? Why?

2. Compare the strategies that Keillor suggests for writing letters and postcards. Which ones do you find most useful? Why?

3. Think about some of the kinds of communication that have largely replaced letters and postcards: email, texts, social media status updates, tweets, *Instagram* posts, and so on. Choose one, and use it to write instructions explaining "how to" communicate using that medium.

JUDITH ORTIZ COFER

More Room

1990

JUDITH ORTIZ COFER (b. 1952) writes poetry, fiction, and
nonfiction, including both memoirs and essays. Her most
recent memoir, *The Cruel Country* (2015), is about her return
to Puerto Rico when her mother was diagnosed with cancer.
Cofer is best known for her memoir *Silent Dancing: A Partial
Remembrance of a Puerto Rican Childhood* (1990), in which
"More Room" first appeared.

MY GRANDMOTHER'S HOUSE IS LIKE A CHAMBERED nautilus; it has many rooms, yet it is not a mansion. Its proportions are small and its design simple. It is a house that has grown organically, according to the needs of its inhabitants. To all of us in the family it is known as *la casa de Mamá*. It is the place of our origin; the stage for our memories and dreams of Island life.

I remember how in my childhood it sat on stilts; this was before it had a downstairs. It rested on its perch like a great blue bird, not a flying sort of bird, more like a nesting hen, but with spread wings. Grandfather had built it soon after their marriage. He was a painter and housebuilder by trade, a poet and meditative man by nature. As each of their eight children were born, new rooms were added. After a few years, the paint did not exactly match, nor the materials, so that there was a chronology to it, like the rings of a tree, and Mamá could tell you the history of each room in her *casa*, and thus the genealogy of the family along with it.

Her room is the heart of the house. Though I have seen it recently, and both woman and room have diminished in size, changed by the new perspective of my eyes, now capable of looking over countertops and tall beds, it is not this picture I carry in my memory of Mamá's *casa*. Instead, I see her room as a queen's chamber where a small woman loomed large, a throne-room with a massive four-poster bed in its center which stood taller than a child's head. It was on this bed where her own children had been born that the smallest grandchildren were allowed to take naps in the afternoons; here too was where Mamá secluded herself to dispense private advice to her daughters, sitting on the edge of the bed, looking down at whoever sat on the rocker where generations of babies had been sung to sleep. To me she looked like a wise empress right out of the fairy tales I was addicted to reading.

Though the room was dominated by the mahogany four-posters, it also contained all of Mamá's symbols of power. On her dresser instead of cosmetics there were jars filled with herbs: *yerba buena, yerba mala,* the making of purgatives and teas to which we were all subjected during childhood crises. She had a steaming cup for anyone who could not, or would not, get up to face life on any given day. If the acrid aftertaste of her cures for malingering did not get you out of bed, then it was time to call *el doctor.*

And there was the monstrous chifforobe she kept locked with a little   5 golden key she did not hide. This was a test of her dominion over us; though my cousins and I wanted a look inside that massive wardrobe more than anything, we never reached for that little key lying on top of her Bible on the dresser. This was also where she placed her earrings and rosary at night. God's word was her security system. This chifforobe was the place where I imagined she kept jewels, satin slippers, and elegant sequined, silk gowns of heart-breaking fineness. I lusted after those imaginary costumes. I had heard that Mamá had been a great beauty in her youth, and the belle of many balls. My cousins had other ideas as to what she kept in that wooden vault: its secret could be money (Mamá did not hand cash to strangers, banks were out of the question, so there were stories that her mattress was stuffed with dollar bills, and that she buried coins in jars in her garden under rosebushes, or kept them in her inviolate chifforobe); there might be that legendary gun salvaged from the Spanish-American conflict over the Island. We went wild over suspected treasures that we made up simply because children have to fill locked trunks with something wonderful.

On the wall above the bed hung a heavy silver crucifix. Christ's agonized head hung directly over Mamá's pillow. I avoided looking at this weapon suspended over where her head would lay; and on the rare occasions when I was allowed to sleep on that bed, I scooted down to the safe middle of the mattress, where her body's impression took me in like a mother's lap. Having taken care of the obligatory religious decoration with a crucifix, Mamá covered the other walls with objects sent to her over the years by her children in the States. *Los Nueva Yores* were represented by, among other things, a postcard of Niagara Falls from her son Hernán, postmarked, Buffalo, N.Y. In a conspicuous gold frame hung a large color photograph of her daughter Nena, her husband and their five children at the entrance to Disneyland in California. From us she had gotten a black lace fan. Father had brought it to her from a tour of duty with the Navy in Europe (on Sundays she would remove it from its hook on the wall to fan herself at Sunday mass). Each year more items were added as the family grew and dispersed, and every object in the room had a story attached to it, a *cuento* which Mamá would bestow on anyone who received the privilege of a day alone with her. It was almost worth pretending to be sick, though the bitter herb purgatives of the body were a big price to pay for the spirit revivals of her story-telling.

Mamá slept alone on her large bed, except for the times when a sick grandchild warranted the privilege, or when a heartbroken daughter came home in need of more than herbal teas. In the family there is a story about how this came to be.

When one of the daughters, my mother or one of her sisters, tells the *cuento* of how Mamá came to own her nights, it is usually preceded by the qualifications that Papá's exile from his wife's room was not a result of animosity between the couple, but that the act had been Mamá's famous bloodless coup for her personal freedom. Papá was the benevolent dictator of her body and her life who had had to be banished from her bed so that Mamá could better serve her family. Before the telling, we had to agree that the old man was not to blame. We all recognized that in the family Papá was as an *alma de Dios*, a saintly, soft-spoken presence whose main pleasures in life, such as writing poetry and reading the Spanish large-type editions of *Reader's Digest*, always took place outside the vortex of Mamá's crowded realm. It was not his fault, after all, that every year or so he planted a babyseed in Mamá's fertile body, keeping her from leading the active life she needed and desired. He loved her and the babies. Papá composed odes and lyrics to celebrate births and anniversaries and hired musicians to accompany him in singing them to his family and friends at extravagant pig-roasts he threw yearly. Mamá and the oldest girls worked for days preparing the food. Papá sat for hours in his painter's shed, also his study and library, composing the songs. At these celebrations he was also known to give long speeches in praise of God, his fecund wife, and his beloved island. As a middle child, my mother remembers these occasions as a time when the women sat in the kitchen and lamented their burdens, while the men feasted out in the patio, their rum-thickened voice rising in song and praise for each other, *compañeros* all.

It was after the birth of her eighth child, after she had lost three at birth or in infancy, that Mamá made her decision. They say that Mamá had had a special way of letting her husband know that they were expecting, one that had begun when, at the beginning of their marriage, he had built her a house too confining for her taste. So, when she discovered her first pregnancy, she supposedly drew plans for another room, which he dutifully executed. Every time a child was due, she would demand, *more space, more space.* Papá acceded to her wishes, child after child, since he had learned early that Mamá's renowned temper was a thing that grew like a monster along with a new belly. In this way Mamá got the house that she wanted, but with each child she lost in heart and energy. She had knowledge of her body and perceived that if she had any more children, her dreams and her plans would have to be permanently forgotten, because she would be a chronically ill woman, like Flora with her twelve children: asthma, no teeth, in bed more than on her feet.

And so, after my youngest uncle was born, she asked Papá to build a   10 large room at the back of the house. He did so in joyful anticipation. Mamá had asked him special things this time: shelves on the walls, a private entrance. He thought that she meant this room to be a nursery where several children could sleep. He thought it was a wonderful idea. He painted it his favorite color, sky blue, and made large windows looking out over a green hill and the church spires beyond. But nothing happened. Mamá's belly did not grow, yet she seemed in a frenzy of activity over

the house. Finally, an anxious Papá approached his wife to tell her that
the new room was finished and ready to be occupied. And Mamá, they
say, replied: "Good, it's for *you*."

And so it was that Mamá discovered the only means of birth control
available to a Catholic woman of her time: sacrifice. She gave up the
comfort of Papá's sexual love for something she deemed greater:
the right to own and control her body, so that she might live to meet her
grandchildren—me among them—so that she could give more of herself
to the ones already there, so that she could be more than a channel for
other lives, so that even now that time has robbed her of the elasticity of
her body and of her amazing reservoir of energy, she still emanates the
kind of joy that can only be achieved by living according to the dictates
of one's own heart.

Thinking about the Text

1. Like many memoirists, Judith Ortiz Cofer provides both her childhood and adult perspectives. How does her perspective on Mamá
   and her room change over time? Cite passages from the essay that
   demonstrate this change.

2. In many ways, this essay is a profile of both a person and a place.
   Look carefully at the ways Cofer describes Mamá and her room. In
   what ways do Cofer's descriptions of Mamá and her room mirror one
   another? What do we learn about one through Cofer's description of
   the other?

3. Write a profile in which a person and a place are connected. If you
   knew this person and place from your childhood, try to provide both
   your childhood and adult perspectives.

LYNDA BARRY

The Sanctuary of School

1992

LYNDA BARRY (b. 1956) writes comics, graphic novels, and memoirs. She is known for her comic strip *Ernie Pook's Comeek* and for mixed-genre books such as *What It Is* (2008) and *Picture This: The Near-sighted Monkey Book* (2010) that contain images, collage, fiction, memoir, and workbook. Her 2014 book *Syllabus: Notes from an Accidental Professor* includes art, lesson plans, and writing exercises meant to help readers develop their own creativity through writing and drawing. "The Sanctuary of School" originally appeared in the *New York Times* (1992).

I WAS 7 YEARS OLD THE FIRST TIME I SNUCK OUT OF THE HOUSE in the dark. It was winter and my parents had been fighting all night. They were short on money and long on relatives who kept "temporarily" moving into our house because they had nowhere else to go.

My brother and I were used to giving up our bedroom. We slept on the couch, something we actually liked because it put us that much closer to the light of our lives, our television.

At night when everyone was asleep, we lay on our pillows watching it with the sound off. We watched Steve Allen's mouth moving. We watched Johnny Carson's mouth moving. We watched movies filled with gangsters shooting machine guns into packed rooms, dying soldiers hurling a last grenade and beautiful women crying at windows. Then the sign-off finally came and we tried to sleep.

The morning I snuck out, I woke up filled with a panic about needing to get to school. The sun wasn't quite up yet but my anxiety was so fierce that I just got dressed, walked quietly across the kitchen and let myself out the back door.

It was quiet outside. Stars were still out. Nothing moved and no one was in the street. It was as if someone had turned the sound off on the world.

I walked the alley, breaking thin ice over the puddles with my shoes. I didn't know why I was walking to school in the dark. I didn't think about it. All I knew was a feeling of panic, like the panic that strikes kids when they realize they are lost.

A DARK OUTLINE

That feeling eased the moment I turned the corner and saw the dark outline of my school at the top of the hill. My school was made up of about 15 nondescript portable classrooms set down on a fenced concrete lot in a rundown Seattle neighborhood, but it had the most beautiful view of the Cascade Mountains. You could see them from anywhere on the playfield and you could see them from the windows of my classroom—Room 2.

I walked over to the monkey bars and hooked my arms around the cold metal. I stood for a long time just looking across Rainier Valley. The sky was beginning to whiten and I could hear a few birds.

EASY TO SLIP AWAY

In a perfect world my absence at home would not have gone unnoticed. I would have had two parents in a panic to locate me, instead of two parents in a panic to locate an answer to the hard question of survival during a deep financial and emotional crisis.

But in an overcrowded and unhappy home, it's incredibly easy for   10
any child to slip away. The high levels of frustration, depression and anger in my house made my brother and me invisible. We were children with the sound turned off. And for us, as for the steadily increasing number of neglected children in this country, the only place where we could count on being noticed was at school.

"Hey there, young lady. Did you forget to go home last night?" It was Mr. Gunderson, our janitor, whom we all loved. He was nice and he was funny and he was old with white hair, thick glasses and an unbelievable number of keys. I could hear them jingling as he walked across the playfield. I felt incredibly happy to see him.

He let me push his wheeled garbage can between the different portables as he unlocked each room. He let me turn on the lights and raise the window shades and I saw my school slowly come to life. I saw Mrs. Holman, our school secretary, walk into the office without her orange lipstick on yet. She waved.

I saw the fifth-grade teacher, Mr. Cunningham, walking under the breezeway eating a hard roll. He waved.

And I saw my teacher, Mrs. Claire LeSane, walking toward us in a red coat and calling my name in a very happy and surprised way, and suddenly my throat got tight and my eyes stung and I ran toward her crying. It was something that surprised us both.

It's only thinking about it now, 28 years later, that I realize I was   15
crying from relief. I was with my teacher, and in a while I was going to sit at my desk, with my crayons and pencils and books and class-mates all around me, and for the next six hours I was going to enjoy a thoroughly secure, warm and stable world. It was a world I abso-lutely relied on. Without it, I don't know where I would have gone that morning.

Mrs. LeSane asked me what was wrong and when I said "Nothing," she seemingly left it at that. But she asked me if I would carry her purse for her, an honor above all honors, and she asked if I wanted to come into Room 2 early and paint.

PAINTING'S POWER

She believed in the natural healing power of painting and drawing for troubled children. In the back of her room there was always a drawing table and an easel with plenty of supplies, and sometimes during the day she would come up to you for what seemed like no good reason and quietly ask if you wanted to go to the back table and "make some pic-tures for Mrs. LeSane." We all had a chance at it—to sit apart from the class for a while to paint, draw and silently work out impossible prob-lems on 11 × 17 sheets of newsprint.

Drawing came to mean everything to me. At the back table in Room 2, I learned to build myself a life preserver that I could carry into my home.

We all know that a good education system saves lives, but the people of this country are still told that cutting the budget for public schools is necessary, that poor salaries for teachers are all we can manage and

that art, music and all creative activities must be the first to go when
times are lean.

NO BABY-SITTING

Before- and after-school programs are cut and we are told that public   20
schools are not made for baby-sitting children. If parents are neglectful
temporarily or permanently, for whatever reason, it's certainly sad, but
their unlucky children must fend for themselves. Or slip through the
cracks. Or wander in a dark night alone.

We are told in a thousand ways that not only are public schools not
important, but that the children who attend them, the children who
need them most, are not important either. We leave them to learn from
the blind eye of a television, or to the mercy of "a thousand points of
light" that can be as far away as stars.

I was lucky. I had Mrs. LeSane. I had Mr. Gunderson. I had an abundance of art supplies. And I had a particular brand of neglect in my
home that allowed me to slip away and get to them. But what about the
rest of the kids who weren't as lucky? What happened to them?

By the time the bell rang that morning I had finished my drawing
and Mrs. LeSane pinned it up on the special bulletin board she reserved
for drawings from the back table. It was the same picture I always
drew—a sun in the corner of a blue sky over a nice house with flowers
all around it.

Mrs. LeSane asked us to please stand, face the flag, place our right
hands over our hearts and say the Pledge of Allegiance. Children across
the country do it faithfully. I wonder now when the country will face its
children and say a pledge right back.

Thinking about the Text

1. What, specifically, made school a sanctuary for Lynda Barry? Cite passages from the text to support your answer.

2. "The Sanctuary of School" is a personal essay, yet Barry also makes an argument. What is her argument, and how does her personal account provide support for her argument?

3. Barry ends her essay by wondering when the United States will make a pledge to children. Write a pledge to children that you would like to see the country make—and keep.

MOLLY IVINS

Get a Knife, Get a Dog,
but Get Rid of Guns

1993

MOLLY IVINS (1944–2007) was a newspaper journalist. For most of her career, she wrote for papers in Texas; her columns in the *Fort Worth Star-Telegram* were syndicated in hundreds of newspapers nationwide. She was known as an outspoken political humorist, and her columns were collected in a number of books, including *Molly Ivins Can't Say That, Can She?* (1991), *Who Let the Dogs In? Incredible Political Animals I Have Known* (2004), and *Bill of Wrongs: The Executive Branch's Assault on America's Fundamental Rights* (2007). "Get a Knife, Get a Dog, but Get Rid of Guns" first appeared in the *Fort Worth Star-Telegram* in 1993.

GUNS. EVERYWHERE GUNS.

Let me start this discussion by pointing out that I am not antigun. I'm proknife. Consider the merits of the knife.

In the first place, you have to catch up with someone in order to stab him. A general substitution of knives for guns would promote physical fitness. We'd turn into a whole nation of great runners. Plus, knives don't ricochet. And people are seldom killed while cleaning their knives.

As a civil libertarian, I, of course, support the Second Amendment. And I believe it means exactly what it says:

A well-regulated militia being necessary to the security of a free state, 5 *the right of the people to keep and bear arms shall not be infringed.* Fourteen-year-old boys are not part of a well-regulated militia. Members of wacky religious cults are not part of a well-regulated militia. Permitting unregulated citizens to have guns is destroying the security of this free state.

I am intrigued by the arguments of those who claim to follow the judicial doctrine of original intent. How do they know it was the dearest wish of Thomas Jefferson's heart that teenage drug dealers should cruise the cities of this nation perforating their fellow citizens with assault rifles? Channeling?

There is more hooey spread about the Second Amendment. It says quite clearly that guns are for those who form part of a well-regulated militia, that is, the armed forces, including the National Guard. The reasons for keeping them away from everyone else get clearer by the day.

The comparison most often used is that of the automobile, another lethal object that is regularly used to wreak great carnage. Obviously, this society is full of people who haven't enough common sense to use an automobile properly. But we haven't outlawed cars yet.

We do, however, license them and their owners, restrict their use to presumably sane and sober adults, and keep track of who sells them to whom. At a minimum, we should do the same with guns.

In truth, there is no rational argument for guns in this society. This   10
is no longer a frontier nation in which people hunt their own food. It
is a crowded, overwhelmingly urban country in which letting people
have access to guns is a continuing disaster. Those who want guns—
whether for target shooting, hunting, or potting rattlesnakes (get a
hoe)—should be subject to the same restrictions placed on gun owners
in England, a nation in which liberty has survived nicely without an
armed populace.

The argument that "guns don't kill people" is patent nonsense. Anyone who has ever worked in a cop shop knows how many family arguments end in murder because there was a gun in the house. Did the gun
kill someone? No. But if there had been no gun, no one would have died.
At least not without a good foot race first. Guns do kill. Unlike cars,
that is all they do.

Michael Crichton makes an interesting argument about technology
in his thriller *Jurassic Park*. He points out that power without discipline is making this society into a wreckage. By the time someone who
studies the martial arts becomes a master—literally able to kill with
bare hands—that person has also undergone years of training and discipline. But any fool can pick up a gun and kill with it.

"A well-regulated militia" surely implies both long training and
long discipline. That is the least, the very least, that should be required
of those who are permitted to have guns, because a gun is literally the
power to kill. For years I used to enjoy taunting my gun-nut friends about
their psychosexual hang-ups—always in a spirit of good cheer, you
understand. But letting the noisy minority in the NRA force us to allow
this carnage to continue is just plain insane.

I do think gun nuts have a power hang-up. I don't know what is missing in their psyches that they need to feel they have the power to kill.
But no sane society would allow this to continue.

Ban the damn things. Ban them all.   15

You want protection? Get a dog.

Thinking about the Text

1. What are the arguments *against* gun control to which Molly Ivins responds? What arguments does she make for stricter regulations on (or outright banning of) guns? Do you find her arguments convincing? Why or why not?

2. In explaining her position, Ivins refers to herself as a "civil libertarian." What does this label imply? Why is it significant to her argument?

3. Write an op-ed piece on a topic that you consider important. Make your position clear, consider and respond to any counterarguments, and tell readers what action they should take.

LARS EIGHNER

On Dumpster Diving

1993

LARS EIGHNER (b. 1948) writes fiction and nonfiction. He is best known for his memoir *Travels with Lizbeth: Three Years on the Road and on the Streets* (1993), which recounts his experience of homelessness and his travels with his dog. In narrating his personal experiences living "from the refuse of others," Eighner presents an alternative to buying only that which is new. "On Dumpster Diving" is a chapter from that memoir.

L ONG BEFORE I BEGAN DUMPSTER DIVING I WAS IMPRESSED with Dumpsters, enough so that I wrote the Merriam-Webster research service to discover what I could about the word *Dumpster.* I learned from them that it is a proprietary word belonging to the Dempster Dumpster company. Since then I have dutifully capitalized the word, although it was lowercased in almost all the citations Merriam-Webster photocopied for me. Dempster's word is too apt. I have never heard these things called anything but Dumpsters. I do not know anyone who knows the generic name for these objects. From time to time I have heard a wino or hobo give some corrupted credit to the original and call them Dipsy Dumpsters.

I began Dumpster diving about a year before I became homeless.

I prefer the word *scavenging* and use the word *scrounging* when I mean to be obscure. I have heard people, evidently meaning to be polite, use the word *foraging,* but I prefer to reserve that word for gathering nuts and berries and such, which I do also according to the season and the opportunity. *Dumpster diving* seems to me to be a little too cute and, in my case, inaccurate because I lack the athletic ability to lower myself into the Dumpsters as the true divers do, much to their increased profit.

I like the frankness of the word *scavenging,* which I can hardly think of without picturing a big black snail on an aquarium wall. I live from the refuse of others. I am a scavenger. I think it a sound and honorable niche, although if I could I would naturally prefer to live the comfortable consumer life, perhaps—and only perhaps—as a slightly less wasteful consumer, owing to what I have learned as a scavenger.

While Lizbeth and I were still living in the shack on Avenue B as my savings ran out, I put almost all my sporadic income into rent. The necessities of daily life I began to extract from Dumpsters. Yes, we ate from them. Except for jeans, all my clothes came from Dumpsters. Boom boxes, candles, bedding, toilet paper, a virgin male love doll, medicine, books, a typewriter, dishes, furnishings, and change, sometimes amounting to many dollars—I acquired many things from the Dumpsters.

I have learned much as a scavenger. I mean to put some of what I have learned down here, beginning with the practical art of Dumpster diving and proceeding to the abstract.

What is safe to eat?

After all, the finding of objects is becoming something of an urban art. Even respectable employed people will sometimes find something tempting sticking out of a Dumpster or standing beside one. Quite a number of people, not all of them of the bohemian type, are willing to brag that they found this or that piece in the trash. But eating from Dumpsters is what separates the dilettanti from the professionals. Eating safely from the Dumpsters involves three principles: using the senses and common sense to evaluate the condition of the found materials, knowing the Dumpsters of a given area and checking them regularly, and seeking always to answer the question, "Why was this discarded?"

Perhaps everyone who has a kitchen and a regular supply of groceries has, at one time or another, made a sandwich and eaten half of it before discovering mold on the bread or got a mouthful of milk before realizing the milk had turned. Nothing of the sort is likely to happen to a Dumpster diver because he is constantly reminded that most food is discarded for a reason. Yet a lot of perfectly good food can be found in Dumpsters.

Canned goods, for example, turn up fairly often in the Dumpsters I   10 frequent. All except the most phobic people would be willing to eat from a can, even if it came from a Dumpster. Canned goods are among the safest of foods to be found in Dumpsters but are not utterly foolproof.

Although very rare with modern canning methods, botulism is a possibility. Most other forms of food poisoning seldom do lasting harm to a healthy person, but botulism is almost certainly fatal and often the first symptom is death. Except for carbonated beverages, all canned goods should contain a slight vacuum and suck air when first punctured. Bulging, rusty, and dented cans and cans that spew when punctured should be avoided, especially when the contents are not very acidic or syrupy.

Heat can break down the botulin, but this requires much more cooking than most people do to canned goods. To the extent that botulism occurs at all, of course, it can occur in cans on pantry shelves as well as in cans from Dumpsters. Need I say that home-canned goods are simply too risky to be recommended.

From time to time one of my companions, aware of the source of my provisions, will ask, "Do you think these crackers are really safe to eat?" For some reason it is most often the crackers they ask about.

This question has always made me angry. Of course I would not offer my companion anything I had doubts about. But more than that, I wonder why he cannot evaluate the condition of the crackers for himself. I have no special knowledge and I have been wrong before. Since he knows where the food comes from, it seems to me he ought to assume some of the responsibility for deciding what he will put in his mouth. For myself I have few qualms about dry foods such as crackers, cookies, cereal, chips, and pasta if they are free of visible contaminates and still dry and crisp. Most often such things are found in the original packaging, which is not so much a positive sign as it is the absence of a negative one.

Raw fruits and vegetables with intact skins seem perfectly safe to   15
me, excluding of course the obviously rotten. Many are discarded for minor imperfections that can be pared away. Leafy vegetables, grapes, cauliflower, broccoli, and similar things may be contaminated by liquids and may be impractical to wash.

Candy, especially hard candy, is usually safe if it has not drawn ants. Chocolate is often discarded only because it has become discolored as the cocoa butter de-emulsified. Candying, after all, is one method of food preservation because pathogens do not like very sugary substances.

All of these foods might be found in any Dumpster and can be evaluated with some confidence largely on the basis of appearance. Beyond these are foods that cannot be correctly evaluated without additional information.

I began scavenging by pulling pizzas out of the Dumpster behind a pizza delivery shop. In general, prepared food requires caution, but in this case I knew when the shop closed and went to the Dumpster as soon as the last of the help left.

Such shops often get prank orders; both the orders and the products made to fill them are called *bogus*. Because help seldom stays long at these places, pizzas are often made with the wrong topping, refused on delivery for being cold, or baked incorrectly. The products to be discarded are boxed up because inventory is kept by counting boxes: A boxed pizza can be written off; an unboxed pizza does not exist.

I never placed a bogus order to increase the supply of pizzas and I   20
believe no one else was scavenging in this Dumpster. But the people in the shop became suspicious and began to retain their garbage in the shop overnight. While it lasted I had a steady supply of fresh, sometimes warm pizza. Because I knew the Dumpster I knew the source of the pizza, and because I visited the Dumpster regularly I knew what was fresh and what was yesterday's.

The area I frequent is inhabited by many affluent college students. I am not here by chance; the Dumpsters in this area are very rich. Students throw out many good things, including food. In particular they tend to throw everything out when they move at the end of a semester, before and after breaks, and around midterm, when many of them despair of college. So I find it advantageous to keep an eye on the academic calendar.

Students throw food away around breaks because they do not know whether it has spoiled or will spoil before they return. A typical discard is a half jar of peanut butter. In fact, nonorganic peanut butter does not require refrigeration and is unlikely to spoil in any reasonable time. The student does not know that, and since it is Daddy's money, the student decides not to take a chance. Opened containers require caution and some attention to the question, "Why was this discarded?" But in the case of discards from student apartments, the answer may be that the item was thrown out through carelessness, ignorance, or wastefulness. This can sometimes be deduced when the item is found with many others, including some that are obviously perfectly good.

Some students, and others, approach defrosting a freezer by chucking out the whole lot. Not only do the circumstances of such a find tell the story, but also the mass of frozen goods stays cold for a long time and items may be found still frozen or freshly thawed.

Yogurt, cheese, and sour cream are items that are often thrown out while they are still good. Occasionally I find a cheese with a spot of mold, which of course I just pare off, and because it is obvious why such a cheese was discarded, I treat it with less suspicion than an apparently perfect cheese found in similar circumstances. Yogurt is often discarded, still sealed, only because the expiration date on the carton had passed. This is one of my favorite finds because yogurt will keep for several days, even in warm weather.

Students throw out canned goods and staples at the end of semesters   25
and when they give up college at midterm. Drugs, pornography, spirits, and the like are often discarded when parents are expected—Dad's Day, for example. And spirits also turn up after big party weekends, presumably discarded by the newly reformed. Wine and spirits, of course, keep perfectly well even once opened, but the same cannot be said of beer.

My test for carbonated soft drinks is whether they still fizz vigorously. Many juices or other beverages are too acidic or too syrupy to cause much concern, provided they are not visibly contaminated. I have discovered nasty molds in vegetable juices, even when the product was found under its original seal; I recommend that such products be decanted slowly into a clear glass. Liquids always require some care. One hot day I found a large jug of Pat O'Brien's Hurricane mix. The jug had been opened but was still ice cold. I drank three large glasses before it became apparent to me that someone had added the rum to the mix, and not a little rum. I never tasted the rum, and by the time I began to feel the effects I had already ingested a very large quantity of the beverage. Some divers would have considered this a boon, but being suddenly intoxicated in a public place in the early afternoon is not my idea of a good time.

I have heard of people maliciously contaminating discarded food and even handouts, but mostly I have heard of this from people with vivid imaginations who have had no experience with the Dumpsters themselves. Just before the pizza shop stopped discarding its garbage at night, jalapeños began showing up on most of the thrown-out pizzas. If indeed this was meant to discourage me, it was a wasted effort because I am a native Texan.

For myself, I avoid game, poultry, pork, and egg-based foods, whether I find them raw or cooked. I seldom have the means to cook what I find, but when I do I avail myself of plentiful supplies of beef, which is often in very good condition. I suppose fish becomes disagreeable before it becomes dangerous. Lizbeth is happy to have any such thing that is past its prime and, in fact, does not recognize fish as food until it is quite strong.

Home leftovers, as opposed to surpluses from restaurants, are very often bad. Evidently, especially among students, there is a common type of personality that carefully wraps up even the smallest leftover and shoves it into the back of the refrigerator for six months or so before discarding it. Characteristic of this type are the reused jars and marga-rine tubs to which the remains are committed. I avoid ethnic foods I am unfamiliar with. If I do not know what it is supposed to look like when it is good, I cannot be certain I will be able to tell if it is bad.

No matter how careful I am I still get dysentery at least once a month, 30 oftener in warm weather. I do not want to paint too romantic a picture. Dumpster diving has serious drawbacks as a way of life.

I learned to scavenge gradually, on my own. Since then I have initiated several companions into the trade. I have learned that there is a pre-dictable series of stages a person goes through in learning to scavenge.

At first the new scavenger is filled with disgust and self-loathing. He is ashamed of being seen and may lurk around, trying to duck behind things, or he may try to dive at night. (In fact, most people instinctively look away from a scavenger. By skulking around, the novice calls attention to himself and arouses suspicion. Diving at night is ineffective and needlessly messy.)

Every grain of rice seems to be a maggot. Everything seems to stink. He can wipe the egg yolk off the found can, but he cannot erase from his mind the stigma of eating garbage.

That stage passes with experience. The scavenger finds a pair of running shoes that fit and look and smell brand-new. He finds a pocket calculator in perfect working order. He finds pristine ice cream, still frozen, more than he can eat or keep. He begins to understand: People throw away perfectly good stuff, a lot of perfectly good stuff.

At this stage, Dumpster shyness begins to dissipate. The diver, after all, has the last laugh. He is finding all manner of good things that are his for the taking. Those who disparage his profession are the fools, not he.

He may begin to hang on to some perfectly good things for which he has neither a use nor a market. Then he begins to take note of the things that are not perfectly good but are nearly so. He mates a Walkman with broken earphones and one that is missing a battery cover. He picks up things that he can repair.

At this stage he may become lost and never recover. Dumpsters are full of things of some potential value to someone and also of things that never have much intrinsic value but are interesting. All the Dumpster divers I have known come to the point of trying to acquire everything they touch. Why not take it, they reason, since it is all free? This is, of course, hopeless. Most divers come to realize that they must restrict themselves to items of relatively immediate utility. But in some cases the diver simply cannot control himself. I have met several of these pack-rat types. Their ideas of the values of various pieces of junk verge on the psychotic. Every bit of glass may be a diamond, they think, and all that glisters, gold.

I tend to gain weight when I am scavenging. Partly this is because I always find far more pizza and doughnuts than water-packed tuna, non-fat yogurt, and fresh vegetables. Also I have not developed much faith in the reliability of Dumpsters as a food source, although it has been proven to me many times. I tend to eat as if I have no idea where my next meal is coming from. But mostly I just hate to see food go to waste and so I eat much more than I should. Something like this drives the obsession to collect junk.

As for collecting objects, I usually restrict myself to collecting one kind of small object at a time, such as pocket calculators, sunglasses, or campaign buttons. To live on the street I must anticipate my needs to a certain extent: I must pick up and save warm bedding I find in August because it will not be found in Dumpsters in November. As I have no access to health care, I often hoard essential drugs, such as antibiotics and antihistamines. (This course can be recommended only to those with some grounding in pharmacology. Antibiotics, for example, even when indicated are worse than useless if taken in insufficient amounts.) But even if I had a home with extensive storage space, I could not save everything that might be valuable in some contingency.

I have proprietary feelings about my Dumpsters. As I have men-   40
tioned, it is no accident that I scavenge from ones where good finds are common. But my limited experience with Dumpsters in other areas suggests to me that even in poorer areas, Dumpsters, if attended with sufficient diligence, can be made to yield a livelihood. The rich students discard perfectly good kiwifruit; poorer people discard perfectly good apples. Slacks and Polo shirts are found in the one place; jeans and T-shirts in the other. The population of competitors rather than the affluence of the dumpers most affects the feasibility of survival by scavenging. The large number of competitors is what puts me off the idea of trying to scavenge in places like Los Angeles.

Curiously, I do not mind my direct competition, other scavengers, so much as I hate the can scroungers.

People scrounge cans because they have to have a little cash. I have tried scrounging cans with an able-bodied companion. Afoot a can scrounger simply cannot make more than a few dollars a day. One can extract the necessities of life from the Dumpsters directly with far less effort than would be required to accumulate the equivalent value in cans. (These observations may not hold in places with container redemption laws.)

Can scroungers, then, are people who must have small amounts of cash. These are drug addicts and winos, mostly the latter because the amounts of cash are so small. Spirits and drugs do, like all other commodities, turn up in Dumpsters and the scavenger will from time to time have a half bottle of a rather good wine with his dinner. But the wino cannot survive on these occasional finds; he must have his daily dose to stave off the DTs. All the cans he can carry will buy about three bottles of Wild Irish Rose.

I do not begrudge them the cans, but can scroungers tend to tear up the Dumpsters, mixing the contents and littering the area. They become so specialized that they can see only cans. They earn my contempt by passing up change, canned goods, and readily hockable items.

There are precious few courtesies among scavengers. But it is com- 45
mon practice to set aside surplus items: pairs of shoes, clothing, canned goods, and such. A true scavenger hates to see good stuff go to waste, and what he cannot use he leaves in good condition in plain sight.

Can scroungers lay waste to everything in their path and will stir one of a pair of good shoes to the bottom of a Dumpster, to be lost or ruined in the muck. Can scroungers will even go through individual garbage cans, something I have never seen a scavenger do.

Individual garbage cans are set out on the public easement only on garbage days. On other days going through them requires trespassing close to a dwelling. Going through individual garbage cans without scattering litter is almost impossible. Litter is likely to reduce the public's tolerance of scavenging. Individual cans are simply not as productive as

Dumpsters; people in houses and duplexes do not move so often and for some reason do not tend to discard as much useful material. Moreover, the time required to go through one garbage can that serves one household is not much less than the time required to go through a Dumpster that contains the refuse of twenty apartments.

But my strongest reservation about going through individual garbage cans is that this seems to me a very personal kind of invasion to which I would object if I were a householder. Although many things in Dumpsters are obviously meant never to come to light, a Dumpster is somehow less personal.

I avoid trying to draw conclusions about the people who dump in the Dumpsters I frequent. I think it would be unethical to do so, although I know many people will find the idea of scavenger ethics too funny for words.

Dumpsters contain bank statements, correspondence, and other   50
documents, just as anyone might expect. But there are also less obvious sources of information. Pill bottles, for example. The labels bear the name of the patient, the name of the doctor, and the name of the drug. AIDS drugs and antipsychotic medicines, to name but two groups, are specific and are seldom prescribed for any other disorders. The plastic compacts for birth-control pills usually have complete label information.

Despite all of this sensitive information, I have had only one apartment resident object to my going through the Dumpster. In that case it turned out the resident was a university athlete who was taking bets and who was afraid I would turn up his wager slips.

Occasionally a find tells a story. I once found a small paper bag containing some unused condoms, several partial tubes of flavored sexual lubricants, a partially used compact of birth-control pills, and the torn pieces of a picture of a young man. Clearly she was through with him and planning to give up sex altogether.

Dumpster things are often sad—abandoned teddy bears, shredded wedding books, despaired-of sales kits. I find many pets lying in state in Dumpsters. Although I hope to get off the streets so that Lizbeth can have a long and comfortable old age, I know this hope is not very realistic. So I suppose when her time comes she too will go into a Dumpster. I will have no better place for her. And after all, it is fitting, since for most of her life her livelihood has come from the Dumpster. When she finds something I think is safe that has been spilled from a Dumpster, I let her have it. She already knows the route around the best ones. I like to think that if she survives me she will have a chance of evading the dog catcher and of finding her sustenance on the route.

Silly vanities also come to rest in the Dumpsters. I am a rather accomplished needleworker. I get a lot of material from the Dumpsters. Evidently sorority girls, hoping to impress someone, perhaps themselves, with their mastery of a womanly art, buy a lot of embroider-by-number kits, work a few stitches horribly, and eventually discard the whole mess. I pull out their stitches, turn the canvas over, and work an original design. Do not think I refrain from chuckling as I make gifts from these kits.

I find diaries and journals. I have often thought of compiling a book   55
of literary found objects. And perhaps I will one day. But what I find is hopelessly commonplace and bad without being, even unconsciously, camp. College students also discard their papers. I am horrified to discover the kind of paper that now merits an A in an undergraduate course. I am grateful, however, for the number of good books and magazines the students throw out.

In the area I know best I have never discovered vermin in the Dumpsters, but there are two kinds of kitty surprise. One is alley cats whom I meet as they leap, claws first, out of Dumpsters. This is especially thrilling when I have Lizbeth in tow. The other kind of kitty surprise is a plastic garbage bag filled with some ponderous, amorphous mass. This always proves to be used cat litter.

City bees harvest doughnut glaze and this makes the Dumpster at the doughnut shop more interesting. My faith in the instinctive wisdom of animals is always shaken whenever I see Lizbeth attempt to catch a bee in her mouth, which she does whenever bees are present. Evidently some birds find Dumpsters profitable, for birdie surprise is almost as common as kitty surprise of the first kind. In hunting season all kinds of small game turn up in Dumpsters, some of it, sadly, not entirely dead. Curiously, summer and winter, maggots are uncommon.

The worst of the living and near-living hazards of the Dumpsters are the fire ants. The food they claim is not much of a loss, but they are vicious and aggressive. It is very easy to brush against some surface of the Dumpster and pick up half a dozen or more fire ants, usually in some sensitive area such as the underarm. One advantage of bringing Lizbeth along as I make Dumpster rounds is that, for obvious reasons, she is very alert to ground-based fire ants. When Lizbeth recognizes a fire-ant infestation around our feet, she does the Dance of the Zillion Fire Ants. I have learned not to ignore this warning from Lizbeth, whether I perceive the tiny ants or not, but to remove ourselves at Lizbeth's first pas de bourée. All the more so because the ants are the worst in the summer months when I wear flip-flops if I have them. (Perhaps someone will misunderstand this. Lizbeth does the Dance of the Zillion Fire Ants when she recognizes more fire ants than she cares to eat, not when she is being bitten. Since I have learned to react promptly, she does not get bitten at all. It is the isolated patrol of fire ants that falls in Lizbeth's range that deserves pity. She finds them quite tasty.)

By far the best way to go through a Dumpster is to lower yourself into it. Most of the good stuff tends to settle at the bottom because it is usually weightier than the rubbish. My more athletic companions have often demonstrated to me that they can extract much good material from a Dumpster I have already been over.

To those psychologically or physically unprepared to enter a Dump- 60
ster, I recommend a stout stick, preferably with some barb or hook at

one end. The hook can be used to grab plastic garbage bags. When I find canned goods or other objects loose at the bottom of a Dumpster, I lower a bag into it, roll the desired object into the bag, and then hoist the bag out—a procedure more easily described than executed. Much Dumpster diving is a matter of experience for which nothing will do except practice.

Dumpster diving is outdoor work, often surprisingly pleasant. It is not entirely predictable; things of interest turn up every day and some days there are finds of great value. I am always very pleased when I can turn up exactly the thing I most wanted to find. Yet in spite of the element of chance, scavenging more than most other pursuits tends to yield returns in some proportion to the effort and intelligence brought to bear. It is very sweet to turn up a few dollars in change from a Dumpster that has just been gone over by a wino.

The land is now covered with cities. The cities are full of Dumpsters. If a member of the canine race is ever able to know what it is doing, then Lizbeth knows that when we go around to the Dumpsters, we are hunting. I think of scavenging as a modern form of self-reliance. In any event, after having survived nearly ten years of government service, where everything is geared to the lowest common denominator, I find it refreshing to have work that rewards initiative and effort. Certainly I would be happy to have a sinecure again, but I am no longer heartbroken that I left one.

I find from the experience of scavenging two rather deep lessons. The first is to take what you can use and let the rest go by. I have come to think that there is no value in the abstract. A thing I cannot use or make useful, perhaps by trading, has no value however rare or fine it may be. I mean useful in a broad sense—some art I would find useful and some otherwise.

I was shocked to realize that some things are not worth acquiring, but now I think it is so. Some material things are white elephants that eat up the possessor's substance. The second lesson is the transience of material being. This has not quite converted me to a dualist, but it has made some headway in that direction. I do not suppose that ideas are immortal, but certainly mental things are longer lived than other material things.

Once I was the sort of person who invests objects with sentimental value. Now I no longer have those objects, but I have the sentiments yet.

Many times in our travels I have lost everything but the clothes I was wearing and Lizbeth. The things I find in Dumpsters, the love letters and rag dolls of so many lives, remind me of this lesson. Now I hardly pick up a thing without envisioning the time I will cast it aside. This I think is a healthy state of mind. Almost everything I have now has already been cast out at least once, proving that what I own is valueless to someone.

Anyway, I find my desire to grab for the gaudy bauble has been largely sated. I think this is an attitude I share with the very wealthy— we both know there is plenty more where what we have came from. Between us are the rat-race millions who nightly scavenge the cable channels looking for they know not what.

I am sorry for them.

Thinking about the Text

1. What values, both practical and abstract, guide Lars Eighner's scavenging?

2. Eighner's essay is both a personal narrative and a process analysis meant to teach readers how to do something. Choose one textual element (for example, Eighner's organization, his use of lists, or his tone) and explain how the author uses it to guide and teach readers about Dumpster diving.

3. Write an essay about a practice you know well. Like Eighner, provide advice and share lessons you have learned. (For an example of an essay written by a student, see Melissa Hicks's "The High Price of Butter" on pp. 484–92.)

HENRY LOUIS GATES JR.

In the Kitchen

1994

HENRY LOUIS GATES JR. (b. 1950) is a writer, filmmaker, literary critic, and a professor at Harvard who writes primarily about race in America and African American culture. He has helped others discover their family histories through his PBS show *Finding Your Roots*. He is the author or editor of many books, including *The Signifying Monkey: A Theory of African-American Literary Criticism* (1988), *The Henry Louis Gates Jr. Reader* (2012), and *The Norton Anthology of African American Literature* (3rd ed., 2014). "In the Kitchen" was published in Gates's *Colored People: A Memoir* in 1994.

W E ALWAYS HAD A GAS STOVE IN THE KITCHEN, IN OUR house in Piedmont, West Virginia, where I grew up. Never electric, though using electric became fashionable in Piedmont in the sixties, like using Crest toothpaste rather than Colgate, or watching Huntley and Brinkley rather than Walter Cronkite. But not us: gas, Colgate, and good ole Walter Cronkite, come what may. We used gas partly out of loyalty to Big Mom, Mama's Mama, because she was mostly blind and still loved to cook, and could feel her way more easily with gas than with electric. But the most important thing about our gas-equipped kitchen was that Mama used to do hair there. The "hot comb" was a fine-toothed iron instrument with a long wooden handle and a pair of iron curlers that opened and closed like scissors. Mama would put it in the gas fire until it glowed. You could smell those prongs heating up.

I liked that smell. Not the smell so much, I guess, as what the smell meant for the shape of my day. There was an intimate warmth in the women's tones as they talked with my Mama, doing their hair. I knew what the women had been through to get their hair ready to be "done," because I would watch Mama do it to herself. How that kink could be transformed through grease and fire into that magnificent head of wavy hair was a miracle to me, and still is.

Mama would wash her hair over the sink, a towel wrapped around her shoulders, wearing just her slip and her white bra. (We had no shower—just a galvanized tub that we stored in the kitchen—until we moved down Rat Tail Road into Doc Wolverton's house, in 1954.) After she dried it, she would grease her scalp thoroughly with blue Bergamot hair grease, which came in a short, fat jar with a picture of a beautiful colored lady on it. It's important to grease your scalp real good, my Mama would explain, to keep from burning yourself. Of course, her hair would return to its natural kink almost as soon as the hot water and shampoo hit it. To me, it was another miracle how hair so "straight" would so quickly become kinky again the second it even approached some water.

My Mama had only a few "clients" whose heads she "did"—did, I think, because she enjoyed it, rather than for the few pennies it brought in. They would sit on one of our red plastic kitchen chairs, the kind with the shiny metal legs, and brace themselves for the process. Mama would stroke that red-hot iron—which by this time had been in the gas fire for half an hour or more—slowly but firmly through their hair, from scalp to strand's end. It made a scorching, crinkly sound, the hot iron did, as it burned its way through kink, leaving in its wake straight strands of hair, standing long and tall but drooping over at the ends, their shape like the top of a heavy willow tree. Slowly, steadily, Mama's hands would transform a round mound of Odetta kink into a darkened swamp of everglades. The Bergamot made the hair shiny; the heat of the hot iron gave it a brownish-red cast. Once all the hair was as straight as God allows kink to get, Mama would take the wellheated curling iron and twirl the straightened strands into more or less loosely wrapped curls. She claimed that she owed her skill as a hairdresser to the strength in her wrists, and as she worked her little finger would poke out, the way it did when she sipped tea. Mama was a southpaw, and wrote upside down and backward to produce the cleanest, roundest letters you've ever seen.

The "kitchen" she would all but remove from sight with a handheld 5 pair of shears, bought just for this purpose. Now, the kitchen was the room in which we were sitting—the room where Mama did hair and washed clothes, and where we all took a bath in that galvanized tub. But the word has another meaning, and the kitchen that I'm speaking of is the very kinky bit of hair at the back of your head, where your neck meets your shirt collar. If there was ever a part of our African past that resisted assimilation, it was the kitchen. No matter how hot the iron, no matter how powerful the chemical, no matter how stringent the mashed-potatoes-and-lye formula of a man's "process," neither God nor woman nor Sammy Davis, Jr., could straighten the kitchen. The kitchen was permanent, irredeemable, irresistible kink. Unassimilably African.

No matter what you did, no matter how hard you tried, you couldn't de-kink a person's kitchen. So you trimmed it off as best you could.

When hair had begun to "turn," as they'd say—to return to its natural kinky glory—it was the kitchen that turned first (the kitchen around the back, and nappy edges at the temples). When the kitchen started creeping up the back of the neck, it was time to get your hair done again.

Sometimes, after dark, a man would come to have his hair done. It was Mr. Charlie Carroll. He was very light-complected and had a ruddy nose—it made me think of Edmund Gwenn, who played Kris Kringle in "Miracle on 34th Street." At first, Mama did him after my brother, Rocky, and I had gone to sleep. It was only later that we found out that he had come to our house so Mama could iron his hair—not with a hot comb or a curling iron but with our very own Proctor-Silex steam iron. For some reason I never understood, Mr. Charlie would conceal his Frederick Douglass–like mane under a big white Stetson hat. I never saw him take it off except when he came to our house, at night, to have his hair pressed. (Later, Daddy would tell us about Mr. Charlie's most prized piece of knowledge, something that the man would only confide after his hair had been pressed, as a token of intimacy. "Not many people know this," he'd say, in a tone of circumspection, "but George Washington was Abraham Lincoln's daddy." Nodding solemnly, he'd add the clincher: "A white man told me." Though he was in dead earnest, this became a humorous refrain around our house—"a white man told me"— which we used to punctuate especially preposterous assertions.)

My mother examined my daughters' kitchens whenever we went home to visit, in the early eighties. It became a game between us. I had told her not to do it, because I didn't like the politics it suggested—the notion of "good" and "bad" hair. "Good" hair was "straight," "bad" hair kinky. Even in the late sixties, at the height of Black Power, almost nobody could bring themselves to say "bad" for good and "good" for bad.

People still said that hair like white people's hair was "good," even if they encapsulated it in a disclaimer, like "what we used to call 'good.'"

Maggie would be seated in her high chair, throwing food this way and that, and Mama would be cooing about how cute it all was, how I used to do just like Maggie was doing, and wondering whether her flinging her food with her left hand meant that she was going to be left-handed like Mama. When my daughter was just about covered with Chef Boyardee Spaghetti-O's, Mama would seize the opportunity: wiping her clean, she would tilt Maggie's head to one side and reach down the back of her neck. Sometimes Mama would even rub a curl between her fingers, just to make sure that her bifocals had not deceived her. Then she'd sigh with satisfaction and relief: No kink . . . yet. Mama! I'd shout, pretending to be angry. Every once in a while, if no one was looking, I'd peek, too.

I say "yet" because most black babies are born with soft, silken hair.   10
But after a few months it begins to turn, as inevitably as do the seasons or the leaves on a tree. People once thought baby oil would stop it. They were wrong.

Everybody I knew as a child wanted to have good hair. You could be as ugly as homemade sin dipped in misery and still be thought attractive if you had good hair. "Jesus moss," the girls at Camp Lee, Virginia, had called Daddy's naturally "good" hair during the war. I know that he played that thick head of hair for all it was worth, too.

My own hair was "not a bad grade," as barbers would tell me when they cut it for the first time. It was like a doctor reporting the results of the first full physical he has given you. Like "You're in good shape" or "Blood pressure's kind of high—better cut down on salt."

I spent most of my childhood and adolescence messing with my hair. I definitely wanted straight hair. Like Pop's. When I was about three, I tried to stick a wad of Bazooka bubble gum to that straight hair of his. I suppose what fixed that memory for me is the spanking I got for doing so: he turned me upside down, holding me by my feet, the better to paddle my behind. Little *nigger,* he had shouted, walloping away. I started to laugh about it two days later, when my behind stopped hurting.

When black people say "straight," of course, they don't usually mean literally straight—they're not describing hair like, say, Peggy Lipton's (she was the white girl on *The Mod Squad*), or like Mary's of Peter, Paul & Mary fame; black people call that "stringy" hair. No, "straight" just means not kinky, no matter what contours the curl may take. I would have done *anything* to have straight hair—and I used to try everything, short of getting a process.

Of the wide variety of techniques and methods I came to master in   15 the challenging prestidigitation of the follicle, almost all had two things in common: a heavy grease and the application of pressure. It's not an accident that some of the biggest black-owned companies in the fifties and sixties made hair products. And I tried them all, in search of that certain silken touch, the one that would leave neither the hand nor the pillow sullied by grease.

I always wondered what Frederick Douglass put on *his* hair, or what Phillis Wheatley put on hers. Or why Wheatley has that rag on her head in the little engraving in the frontispiece of her book. One thing is for sure: you can bet that when Phillis Wheatley went to England and saw the Countess of Huntingdon she did not stop by the Queen's coiffeur on her way there. So many black people still get their hair straightened that it's a wonder we don't have a national holiday for Madame C. J. Walker, the woman who invented the process of straightening kinky hair. Call it Jheri-Kurled or call it "relaxed," it's still fried hair.

I used all the greases, from sea-blue Bergamot and creamy vanilla Duke (in its clear jar with the orange-white-and-green label) to the godfather of grease, the formidable Murray's. Now, Murray's was some *serious* grease. Whereas Bergamot was like oily jello, and Duke was viscous and sickly sweet, Murray's was light brown and *hard.* Hard as lard and twice as greasy, Daddy used to say. Murray's came in an orange can with a press-on top. It was so hard that some people would put a match to the can, just to soften the stuff and make it more manageable. Then, in the late sixties, when Afros came into style, I used Afro Sheen. From Murray's to Duke to Afro Sheen: that was my progression in black consciousness.

We used to put hot towels or washrags over our Murray-coated heads, in order to melt the wax into the scalp and the follicles. Unfortunately, the wax also had the habit of running down your neck, ears, and forehead. Not to mention your pillowcase. Another problem was that if you put two palmfuls of Murray's on your head your hair turned white. (Duke did the same thing.) The challenge was to get rid of that white color. Because if you got rid of the white stuff you had a magnificent head of wavy hair. That was the beauty of it: Murray's was so hard that it froze your hair into the wavy style you brushed it into. It looked really good if you wore a part. A lot of guys had parts *cut* into their hair by a barber, either with the clippers or with a straight-edge razor. Especially if you had kinky hair—then you'd generally wear a short razor cut, or what we called a Quo Vadis.

We tried to be as innovative as possible. Everyone knew about using a stocking cap, because your father or your uncle wore one whenever something really big was about to happen, whether sacred or secular: a funeral or a dance, a wedding or a trip in which you confronted official white people. Any time you were trying to look really sharp, you wore a stocking cap in preparation. And if the event was really a big one, you made a new cap. You asked your mother for a pair of her hose, and cut it with scissors about six inches or so from the open end—the end with the elastic that goes up to the top of the thigh. Then you knotted the cut end, and it became a beehive-shaped hat, with an elastic band that you pulled down low on your forehead and down around your neck in the back. To work well, the cap had to fit tightly and snugly, like a press. And it had to fit that tightly because it *was* a press: it pressed your hair with the force of the hose's elastic. If you greased your hair down real good, and left the stocking cap on long enough, voilà: you got a head of pressed-against-the-scalp waves. (You also got a ring around your fore-head when you woke up, but it went away.) And then you could enjoy your concrete do. Swore we were bad, too, with all that grease and those flat heads. My brother and I would brush it out a bit in the morn-ings, so that it looked—well, "natural." Grown men still wear stocking caps—especially older men, who generally keep their stocking caps in their top drawers, along with their cufflinks and their see-through silk socks, their "Maverick" ties, their silk handkerchiefs, and whatever else they prize the most.

A Murrayed-down stocking cap was the respectable version of the   20
process, which, by contrast, was most definitely not a cool thing to have unless you were an entertainer by trade. Zeke and Keith and Poochie and a few other stars of the high-school basketball team all used to get a process once or twice a year. It was expensive, and you had to go somewhere like Pittsburgh or D.C. or Uniontown—somewhere where there were enough colored people to support a trade. The guys would disappear, then reappear a day or two later, strutting like pea-cocks, their hair burned slightly red from the lye base. They'd also wear "rags"—cloths or handkerchiefs—around their heads when they slept or played basketball. Do-rags, they were called. But the result was straight hair, with just a hint of wave. No curl. Do-it-yourselfers took their chances at home with a concoction of mashed potatoes and lye.

The most famous process of all, however, outside of the process Malcolm X describes in his "Autobiography," and maybe the process of Sammy Davis, Jr., was Nat King Cole's process. Nat King Cole had patent-leather hair. That man's got the finest process money can buy, or so Daddy said the night we saw Cole's TV show on NBC. It was November 5, 1956. I remember the date because everyone came to our house to watch it and to celebrate one of Daddy's buddies' birthdays. Yeah, Uncle Joe chimed in, they can do shit to his hair that the average Negro can't even *think* about—secret shit.

Nat King Cole was *clean*. I've had an ongoing argument with a Nigerian friend about Nat King Cole for twenty years now. Not about whether he could sing—any fool knows that he could—but about whether or not he was a handkerchief head for wearing that patent-leather process.

Sammy Davis, Jr.'s process was the one I detested. It didn't look good on him. Worse still, he liked to have a fried strand dangling down the middle of his forehead, so he could shake it out from the crown when he sang. But Nat King Cole's hair was a thing unto itself, a beautifully sculpted work of art that he and he alone had the right to wear. The only difference between a process and a stocking cap, really, was taste; but Nat King Cole, unlike, say, Michael Jackson, looked *good* in his. His head looked like Valentino's head in the twenties, and some say it was Valentino the process was imitating. But Nat King Cole wore a process because it suited his face, his demeanor, his name, his style. He was as clean as he wanted to be.

I had forgotten all about that patent-leather look until one day in 1971, when I was sitting in an Arab restaurant on the island of Zanzibar surrounded by men in fezzes and white caftans, trying to learn how to eat curried goat and rice with the fingers of my right hand and feeling two million miles from home. All of a sudden, an old transistor radio sitting on top of a china cupboard stopped blaring out its Swahili music and started playing "Fly Me to the Moon," by Nat King Cole. The restaurant's din was not affected at all, but in my mind's eye I saw it: the King's magnificent sleek black tiara. I managed, barely, to blink back the tears.

Thinking about the Text

1. Henry Louis Gates Jr. writes about hair both practically (explaining the tools and rituals involved in achieving a specific look) and symbolically (as it's connected to cultural identity). Explain the connections Gates makes between hair and cultural identity in his narrative, citing examples from the text.

2. Gates makes numerous allusions to the hair of popular culture figures, especially African American performers. (If you are not familiar with those to whom Gates alludes, do an image search online.) Writing that "the process . . . was most definitely not a cool thing to have unless you were an entertainer by trade" (paragraph 20), he then goes on to describe the hair of various celebrities. In what other ways does Gates connect and categorize celebrities and members of his community?

3. Write an essay in which you describe a time when you altered your appearance to make a statement about your identity or to align yourself more closely with some aspect of a certain culture or community.

CHANG-RAE LEE

Coming Home Again

1995

CHANG-RAE LEE (1965) is a novelist who often writes about
identity, exploring issues of race, ethnicity, and assimilation.
When he was a child, he and his family left South Korea and
settled in New York. Lee's most recent novel, *On Such a Full
Sea* (2014), features a Chinese American fish farmer living in
a dystopian Baltimore. He also contributes essays—many of
which are about food—and fiction to the *New Yorker*, where
"Coming Home Again" first appeared in 1995.

W HEN MY MOTHER BEGAN USING THE ELECTRONIC pump that fed her liquids and medication, we moved her to the family room. The bedroom she shared with my father was upstairs, and it was impossible to carry the machine up and down all day and night. The pump itself was attached to a metal stand on casters, and she pulled it along wherever she went. From anywhere in the house, you could hear the sound of the wheels clicking out a steady time over the grout lines of the slate-tiled foyer, her main thoroughfare to the bathroom and the kitchen. Sometimes you would hear her halt after only a few steps, to catch her breath or steady her balance, and whatever you were doing was instantly suspended by a pall of silence.

I was usually in the kitchen, preparing lunch or dinner, poised over the butcher block with her favorite chef's knife in my hand and her old yellow apron slung around my neck. I'd be breathless in the sudden quiet, and, having ceased my mincing and chopping, would stare blankly at the brushed sheen of the blade. Eventually, she would clear her throat or call out to say she was fine, then begin to move again, starting her rhythmic *ka-jug*; and only then could I go on with my cooking, the world of our house turning once more, wheeling through the black.

I wasn't cooking for my mother but for the rest of us. When she first moved downstairs she was still eating, though scantily, more just to taste what we were having than from any genuine desire for food. The point was simply to sit together at the kitchen table and array ourselves like a family again. My mother would gently set herself down in her customary chair near the stove. I sat across from her, my father and sister to my left and right, and crammed in the center was all the food I had made—a spicy codfish stew, say, or a casserole of gingery beef, dishes that in my youth she had prepared for us a hundred times.

It had been ten years since we'd all lived together in the house, which at fifteen I had left to attend boarding school in New Hampshire. My mother would sometimes point this out, by speaking of our present time as being "just like before Exeter," which surprised me, given how proud she always was that I was a graduate of the school.

My going to such a place was part of my mother's not so secret plan   5
to change my character, which she worried was becoming too much like hers. I was clever and able enough, but without outside pressure I was readily given to sloth and vanity. The famous school—which none of us knew the first thing about—would prove my mettle. She was right, of course, and while I was there I would falter more than a few times, academically and otherwise. But I never thought that my leaving home then would ever be a problem for her, a private quarrel she would have even as her life waned.

Now her house was full again. My sister had just resigned from her job in New York City, and my father, who typically saw his psychiatric patients until eight or nine in the evening, was appearing in the driveway at four-thirty. I had been living at home for nearly a year and was in the final push of work on what would prove a dismal failure of a novel. When I wasn't struggling over my prose, I kept occupied with the things she usually did—the daily errands, the grocery shopping, the vacuuming and the cleaning, and, of course, all the cooking.

When I was six or seven years old, I used to watch my mother as she prepared our favorite meals. It was one of my daily pleasures. She shooed me away in the beginning, telling me that the kitchen wasn't my place, and adding, in her half-proud, half-deprecating way, that her kind of work would only serve to weaken me. "Go out and play with your friends," she'd snap in Korean, "or better yet, do your reading and home-work." She knew that I had already done both, and that as the evening approached there was no place to go save her small and tidy kitchen, from which the clatter of her mixing bowls and pans would ring through the house.

I would enter the kitchen quietly and stand beside her, my chin lodg-ing upon the point of her hip. Peering through the crook of her arm, I beheld the movements of her hands. For *kalbi*, she would take up a butchered short rib in her narrow hand, the flinty bone shaped like a section of an airplane wing and deeply embedded in gristle and flesh, and with the point of her knife cut so that the bone fell away, though not completely, leaving it connected to the meat by the barest opaque layer of tendon. Then she methodically butterflied the flesh, cutting and unfolding, repeating the action until the meat lay out on her board, glistening and ready for seasoning. She scored it diagonally, then sifted sugar into the crevices with her pinched fingers, gently rubbing in the crystals. The sugar would tenderize as well as sweeten the meat. She did this with each rib, and then set them all aside in a large shallow bowl. She minced a half-dozen cloves of garlic, a stub of gingerroot, sliced up a few scallions, and spread it all over the meat. She wiped her hands and took out a bottle of sesame oil, and, after pausing for a moment, streamed the dark oil in two swift circles around the bowl. After adding a few splashes of soy sauce, she thrust her hands in and kneaded the flesh, careful not to dislodge the bones. I asked her why it mattered that they remain connected. "The meat needs the bone nearby," she said, "to borrow its richness." She wiped her hands clean of the marinade, except for her little finger, which she would flick with her tongue from time to time, because she knew that the flavor of a good dish developed not at once but in stages.

Whenever I cook, I find myself working just as she would, readying the ingredients—a mash of garlic, a julienne of red peppers, fantails of shrimp—and piling them in little mounds about the cutting surface. My mother never left me any recipes, but this is how I learned to make her food, each dish coming not from a list or a card but from the aromatic spread of a board.

I've always thought it was particularly cruel that the cancer was in   10 her stomach, and that for a long time at the end she couldn't eat. The last meal I made for her was on New Year's Eve, 1990. My sister suggested that instead of a rib roast or a bird, or the usual overflow of Korean food, we make all sorts of finger dishes that our mother might fancy and pick at.

We set the meal out on the glass coffee table in the family room. I prepared a tray of smoked-salmon canapés, fried some Korean bean cakes, and made a few other dishes I thought she might enjoy. My sister supervised me, arranging the platters, and then with some pomp carried each dish in to our parents. Finally, I brought out a bottle of champagne in a bucket of ice. My mother had moved to the sofa and was sitting up, surveying the low table. "It looks pretty nice," she said. "I think I'm feeling hungry."

This made us all feel good, especially me, for I couldn't remember the last time she had felt any hunger or had eaten something I cooked. We began to eat. My mother picked up a piece of salmon toast and took a tiny corner in her mouth. She rolled it around for a moment and then pushed it out with the tip of her tongue, letting it fall back onto her plate. She swallowed hard, as if to quell a gag, then glanced up to see if we had noticed. Of course we all had. She attempted a bean cake, some cheese, and then a slice of fruit, but nothing was any use.

She nodded at me anyway, and said, "Oh, it's very good." But I was already feeling lost and I put down my plate abruptly, nearly shattering it on the thick glass. There was an ugly pause before my father asked me in a weary, gentle voice if anything was wrong, and I answered that it was nothing, it was the last night of a long year, and we were together, and I was simply relieved. At midnight, I poured out glasses of champagne, even one for my mother, who took a deep sip. Her manner grew playful and light, and I helped her shuffle to her mattress, and she lay down in the place where in a brief week she was dead.

My mother could whip up most anything, but during our first years of living in this country we ate only Korean foods. At my harangue-like behest, my mother set herself to learning how to cook exotic American

dishes. Luckily, a kind neighbor, Mrs. Churchill, a tall, florid young
woman with flaxen hair, taught my mother her most trusted recipes.
Mrs. Churchill's two young sons, palish, weepy boys with identical crew
cuts, always accompanied her, and though I liked them well enough, I
would slip away from them after a few minutes, for I knew that the real
action would be in the kitchen, where their mother was playing guide.
Mrs. Churchill hailed from the state of Maine, where the finest Swedish
meatballs and tuna casserole and angel food cake in America are made.
She readily demonstrated certain techniques—how to layer wet sheets
of pasta for a lasagna or whisk up a simple roux, for example. She often
brought gift shoeboxes containing curious ingredients like dried oreg-
ano, instant yeast, and cream of mushroom soup. The two women,
though at ease and jolly with each other, had difficulty communicating,
and this was made worse by the often confusing terminology of Western
cuisine ("corned beef," "deviled eggs"). Although I was just learning the
language myself, I'd gladly play the interlocutor, jumping back and forth
between their places at the counter, dipping my fingers into whatever
sauce lay about.

I was an insistent child, and, being my mother's firstborn, much too   15
prized. My mother could say no to me, and did often enough, but anyone
who knew us—particularly my father and sister—could tell how much
the denying pained her. And if I was overconscious of her indulgence
even then, and suffered the rushing pangs of guilt that she could inflict
upon me with the slightest wounded turn of her lip, I was too happily
obtuse and venal to let her cease. She reminded me daily that I was her
sole son, her reason for living, and that if she were to lose me, in either
body or spirit, she wished that God would mercifully smite her, strike
her down like a weak branch.

In the traditional fashion, she was the house accountant, the maid,
the launderer, the disciplinarian, the driver, the secretary, and, of course,
the cook. She was also my first basketball coach. In South Korea, where
girls' high school basketball is a popular spectator sport, she had been a

star, the point guard for the national high school team that once won the all-Asia championships. I learned this one Saturday during the summer, when I asked my father if he would go down to the schoolyard and shoot some baskets with me. I had just finished the fifth grade, and wanted desperately to make the middle school team the coming fall. He called for my mother and sister to come along. When we arrived, my sister immediately ran off to the swings, and I recall being annoyed that my mother wasn't following her. I dribbled clumsily around the key, on the verge of losing control of the ball, and flung a flat shot that caromed wildly off the rim. The ball bounced to my father, who took a few not so graceful dribbles and made an easy layup. He dribbled out and then drove to the hoop for a layup on the other side. He rebounded his shot and passed the ball to my mother, who had been watching us from the foul line. She turned from the basket and began heading the other way.

"*Um-mah,*" I cried at her, my exasperation already bubbling over, "the basket's over *here!*"

After a few steps she turned around, and from where the professional three-point line must be now, she effortlessly flipped the ball up in a two-handed set shot, its flight truer and higher than I'd witnessed from any boy or man. The ball arced cleanly into the hoop, stiffly popping the chain-link net. All afternoon, she rained in shot after shot, as my father and I scrambled after her.

When we got home from the playground, my mother showed me the photograph album of her team's championship run. For years I kept it in my room, on the same shelf that housed the scrapbooks I made of basketball stars, with magazine clippings of slick players like Bubbles Hawkins and Pistol Pete and George (the Iceman) Gervin.

It puzzled me how much she considered her own history to be imma-   20
terial, and if she never patently diminished herself, she was able to finesse a kind of self-removal by speaking of my father whenever she could. She zealously recounted his excellence as a student in medical school and reminded me, each night before I started my homework, of

how hard he drove himself in his work to make a life for us. She said that because of his Asian face and imperfect English, he was "working two times the American doctors." I knew that she was building him up, buttressing him with both genuine admiration and her own brand of anxious braggadocio, and that her overarching concern was that I might fail to see him as she wished me to—in the most dawning light, his pose steadfast and solitary.

In the year before I left for Exeter, I became weary of her oft-repeated accounts of my father's success. I was a teenager, and so ever inclined to be dismissive and bitter toward anything that had to do with family and home. Often enough, my mother was the object of my derision. Suddenly, her life seemed so small to me. She was there, and sometimes, I thought, *always* there, as if she were confined to the four walls of our house. I would even complain about her cooking. Mostly, though, I was getting more and more impatient with the difficulty she encountered in doing everyday things. I was afraid for her. One day, we got into a terrible argument when she asked me to call the bank, to question a discrepancy she had discovered in the monthly statement. I asked her why she couldn't call herself. I was stupid and brutal, and I knew exactly how to wound her.

"Whom do I talk to?" she said. She would mostly speak to me in Korean, and I would answer in English.

"The bank manager, who else?"

"What do I say?"

"Whatever you want to say."   25

"Don't speak to me like that!" she cried.

"It's just that you should be able to do it yourself," I said.

"You know how I feel about this!"

"Well, maybe then you should consider it *practice*," I answered lightly, using the Korean word to make sure she understood.

Her face blanched, and her neck suddenly became rigid, as if I were   30
throttling her. She nearly struck me right then, but instead she bit her lip and ran upstairs. I followed her, pleading for forgiveness at her door.

But it was the one time in our life that I couldn't convince her, melt her resolve with the blandishments of a spoiled son.

When my mother was feeling strong enough, or was in particularly good spirits, she would roll her machine into the kitchen and sit at the table and watch me work. She wore pajamas day and night, mostly old pairs of mine.

She said, "I can't tell, what are you making?"

"*Mahn-doo* filling."

"You didn't salt the cabbage and squash."

"Was I supposed to?" 35

"Of course. Look, it's too wet. Now the skins will get soggy before you can fry them."

"What should I do?"

"It's too late. Maybe it'll be OK if you work quickly. Why didn't you ask me?"

"You were finally sleeping."

"You should have woken me." 40

"No way."

She sighed, as deeply as her weary lungs would allow.

"I don't know how you were going to make it without me."

"I don't know, either. I'll remember the salt next time."

"You better. And not too much." 45

We often talked like this, our tone decidedly matter-of-fact, chin up, just this side of being able to bear it. Once, while inspecting a potato fritter batter I was making, she asked me if she had ever done anything that I wished she hadn't done. I thought for a moment, and told her no. In the next breath, she wondered aloud if it was right of her to have let me go to Exeter, to live away from the house while I was so young. She tested the batter's thickness with her finger and called for more flour. Then she asked if, given a choice, I would go to Exeter again.

I wasn't sure what she was getting at, and I told her that I couldn't be certain, but probably yes, I would. She snorted at this and said it was my leaving home that had once so troubled our relationship. "Remember how I had so much difficulty talking to you? Remember?"

She believed back then that I had found her more and more ignorant each time I came home. She said she never blamed me, for this was the way she knew it would be with my wonderful new education. Nothing I could say seemed to quell the notion. But I knew that the problem wasn't simply the *education*; the first time I saw her again after starting school, barely six weeks later, when she and my father visited me on Parents Day, she had already grown nervous and distant. After the usual campus events, we had gone to the motel where they were staying in a nearby town and sat on the beds in our room. She seemed to sneak looks at me, as though I might discover a horrible new truth if our eyes should meet.

My own secret feeling was that I had missed my parents greatly, my mother especially, and much more than I had anticipated. I couldn't tell them that these first weeks were a mere blur to me, that I felt completely overwhelmed by all the studies and my much brighter friends and the thousand irritating details of living alone, and that I had really learned nothing, save perhaps how to put on a necktie while sprinting to class. I felt as if I had plunged too deep into the world, which, to my great horror, was much larger than I had ever imagined.

I welcomed the lull of the motel room. My father and I had nearly   50
dozed off when my mother jumped up excitedly, murmured how stupid she was, and hurried to the closet by the door. She pulled out our old metal cooler and dragged it between the beds. She lifted the top and began unpacking plastic containers, and I thought she would never stop. One after the other they came out, each with a dish that traveled well—a salted stewed meat, rolls of Korean-style sushi. I opened a container of radish kimchi and suddenly the room bloomed with its odor, and I reveled in the very peculiar sensation (which perhaps only true kimchi lovers know) of simultaneously drooling and gagging as I breathed it all in. For the next few minutes, they watched me eat. I'm not certain that I was even hungry. But after weeks of pork parmigiana and chicken

patties and wax beans, I suddenly realized that I had lost all the savor in my life. And it seemed I couldn't get enough of it back. I ate and I ate, so much and so fast that I actually went to the bathroom and vomited. I came out dizzy and sated with the phantom warmth of my binge.

And beneath the face of her worry, I thought, my mother was smiling.

From that day, my mother prepared a certain meal to welcome me home. It was always the same. Even as I rode the school's shuttle bus from Exeter to Logan airport, I could already see the exact arrangement of my mother's table.

I knew that we would eat in the kitchen, the table brimming with plates. There was the *kalbi*, of course, broiled or grilled depending on the season. Leaf lettuce, to wrap the meat with. Bowls of garlicky clam broth with miso and tofu and fresh spinach. Shavings of cod dusted in flour and then dipped in egg wash and fried. Glass noodles with onions and shiitake. Scallion-and-hot-pepper pancakes. Chilled steamed shrimp. Seasoned salads of bean sprouts, spinach, and white radish. Crispy squares of seaweed. Steamed rice with barley and red beans. Homemade kimchi. It was all there—the old flavors I knew, the beautiful salt, the sweet, the excellent taste.

After the meal, my father and I talked about school, but I could never say enough for it to make any sense. My father would often recall his high school principal, who had gone to England to study the methods and traditions of the public schools, and regaled students with stories of the great Eton man. My mother sat with us, paring fruit, not saying a word but taking everything in. When it was time to go to bed, my father said good night first. I usually watched television until the early morning. My mother would sit with me for an hour or two, perhaps until she was accustomed to me again, and only then would she kiss me and head upstairs to sleep.

During the following days, it was always the cooking that started   55
our conversations. She'd hold an inquest over the cold leftovers we ate

at lunch, discussing each dish in terms of its balance of flavors or what might have been prepared differently. But mostly I begged her to leave the dishes alone. I wish I had paid more attention. After her death, when my father and I were the only ones left in the house, drifting through the rooms like ghosts, I sometimes tried to make that meal for him. Though it was too much for two, I made each dish anyway, taking as much care as I could. But nothing turned out quite right—not the color, not the smell. At the table, neither of us said much of anything. And we had to eat the food for days.

I remember washing rice in the kitchen one day and my mother's saying in English, from her usual seat, "I made a big mistake."

"About Exeter?"

"Yes. I made a big mistake. You should be with us for that time. I should never let you go there."

"So why did you?" I said.

"Because I didn't know I was going to die."   60

I let her words pass. For the first time in her life, she was letting herself speak her full mind, so what else could I do?

"But you know what?" she spoke up. "It was better for you. If you stayed home, you would not like me so much now."

I suggested that maybe I would like her even more.

She shook her head. "Impossible."

Sometimes I still think about what she said, about having made a   65
mistake. I would have left home for college, that was never in doubt, but those years I was away at boarding school grew more precious to her as her illness progressed. After many months of exhaustion and pain and the haze of the drugs, I thought that her mind was beginning to fade, for more and more it seemed that she was seeing me again as her fifteen-year-old boy, the one she had dropped off in New Hampshire on a cloudy September afternoon.

I remember the first person I met, another new student, named Zack, who walked to the welcome picnic with me. I had planned to eat with my parents—my mother had brought a coolerful of food even that first day—but I learned of the cookout and told her that I should probably go. I wanted to go, of course. I was excited, and no doubt fearful and nervous, and I must have thought I was only thinking ahead. She agreed wholeheartedly, saying I certainly should. I walked them to the car, and perhaps I hugged them, before saying goodbye. One day, after she died, my father told me what happened on the long drive home to Syracuse.

He was driving the car, looking straight ahead. Traffic was light on the Massachusetts Turnpike, and the sky was nearly dark. They had driven for more than two hours and had not yet spoken a word. He then heard a strange sound from her, a kind of muffled chewing noise, as if something inside her were grinding its way out.

"So, what's the matter?" he said, trying to keep an edge to his voice.

She looked at him with her ashen face and she burst into tears. He began to cry himself, and pulled the car over onto the narrow shoulder of the turnpike, where they stayed for the next half hour or so, the blank-faced cars droning by them in the cold, onrushing night.

Every once in a while, when I think of her, I'm driving alone some-   70
where on the highway. In the twilight, I see their car off to the side, a blue Olds coupe with a landau top, and as I pass them by I look back in the mirror and I see them again, the two figures huddling together in the front seat. Are they sleeping? Or kissing? Are they all right?

Thinking about the Text

1. One of the themes of "Coming Home Again" is education—
   specifically the ways Chang-rae Lee's mother educates her son and
   also the effects of his going away to school. What and how does Lee's
   mother teach him? How might her form of education differ from the
   education Lee gets at boarding school?

2. In addition to being a personal account, this essay is a profile of Lee's
   mother. Consider the different strategies he uses to reveal her character and who she is. What do we learn about his mother through
   her actions, the anecdotes Lee tells, and the dialogue he shares?

3. Write a profile of someone who taught you. It might be a teacher, a
   relative, a coach, or a friend. Use anecdotes, description, and dialogue to help show readers who that person is and how he or she
   helped you learn something.

ELLEN LUPTON AND J. ABBOTT MILLER

Period Styles:
A Punctuated History

1996

ELLEN LUPTON (b. 1963) and J. ABBOTT MILLER (b. 1963) are authors and graphic designers. Lupton is curator of contemporary design at Cooper Hewitt, National Design Museum, and Miller is a partner at Pentagram, an international design firm. Their co-authored books include *The ABC's of Bauhaus, The Bauhaus and Design Theory* (1991), *The Bathroom, the Kitchen, and the Aesthetics of Waste* (1992), and *Design Writing Research* (1996), a study of graphic design and typography in which "Period Styles: A Punctuated History" was first published.

GREEKANDLATINMANUSCRIPTSWEREUSUALLYWRITTENWITHNOSPACE
BETWEENWORDS UNTIL AROUND THE NINTH CENTURY AD ALTHOUGH·
ROMAN·INSCRIPTIONS·LIKE·THE·FAMOUS·TRAJAN·COLUMN·SOMETIMES·
SEPARATED·WORDS·WITH·A·CENTERED·DOT· EVEN AFTER SPACING BECAME
COMMON IT REMAINED HAPHAZARD   FOREXAMPLE OFTEN A PREPOSITION
WAS LINKED TO ANOTHER WORD   EARLY GREEK WRITING RAN IN LINES
ALTERNATING FROM LEFT TO RIGHT AND RIGHT TO LEFT   THIS CONVENTION
WAS CALLED BOUSTREPHEDON MEANING AS THE OX PLOWS   IT WAS
CONVENIENT FOR LARGE CARVED MONUMENTS   BUT BOUSTREPHEDON
HINDERED THE READING AND WRITING OF SMALLER TEXTS AND SO THE
LEFT TO RIGHT DIRECTION BECAME DOMINANT   A CENTERED DOT DIVID·
ED WORDS WHICH SPLIT AT THE END OF A LINE IN EARLY GREEK AND LATIN
MANUSCRIPTS   IN THE ELEVENTH CENTURY A MARK SIMILAR TO THE MOD-
ERN HYPHEN WAS INTRODUCED   MEDIEVAL SCRIBES OFTEN FILLED‡°/‡°(;](;]
SHORT LINES WITH MARKS AND ORNAMENTS   THE PERFECTLY JUSTIFIED
LINE BECAME THE STANDARD AFTER THE INVENTION OF PRINTING
THE EARLIEST GREEK LITERARY TEXTS WERE DIVIDED INTO UNITS WITH A
HORIZONTAL LINE CALLED A PARAGRAPHOS   PARAGRAPHING REMAINS OUR
CENTRAL METHOD OF ORGANIZING PROSE AND YET ALTHOUGH PARAGRAPHS
ARE ANCIENT THEY ARE NOT GRAMMATICALLY ESSENTIAL THE CORRECTNESS
OF A PARAGRAPH IS A MATTER OF STYLE HAVING NO STRICT RULES

LATER GREEK DOCUMENTS SOMETIMES MARKED PARAGRAPHS BY PLACING
   THE FIRST LETTER OF THE NEW LINE IN THE MARGIN   THIS LETTER COULD
   BE ENLARGED COLORED OR ORNATE
TODAY THE OUTDENT IS OFTEN USED FOR LISTS WHOSE ITEMS ARE IDENTIFIED
   ALPHABETICALLY AS IN DICTIONARIES OR BIBLIOGRAPHIES ¶ A MARK
   CALLED CAPITULUM WAS INTRODUCED IN EARLY LATIN MANUSCRIPTS ¶
   IT FUNCTIONED VARIOUSLY AS A POINTER OR SEPARATOR ¶ IT USUALLY
   OCCURRED INSIDE A RUNNING BLOCK OF TEXT WHICH DID NOT BREAK
   ONTO A NEW LINE ¶ THIS TECHNIQUE SAVED SPACE ¶ IT ALSO PRESERVED
   THE VISUAL DENSITY OF THE PAGE WHICH EMULATED THE CONTINUOUS
   UNBROKEN FLOW OF SPEECH

BY THE SEVENTEENTH CENTURY THE INDENT WAS THE STANDARD
PARAGRAPH BREAK IN WESTERN PROSE   THE RISE OF PRINTING ENCOUR-
AGED THE USE OF SPACE TO ORGANIZE TEXTS   A GAP IN A PRINTED PAGE FEELS
MORE DELIBERATE THAN A GAP IN A MANUSCRIPT BECAUSE IT IS MADE BY
A SLUG OF LEAD RATHER THAN A FLUX IN HANDWRITING

EVEN AFTER THE ASCENDENCE OF THE INDENT THE CAPITULUM   5
REMAINED IN USE FOR IDENTIFYING SECTIONS AND CHAPTERS ALONG
WITH OTHER MARKS LIKE THE SECTION § THE DAGGER † THE DOUBLE DAG-
GER ‡ THE ASTERISK * AND NUMEROUS LESS CONVENTIONAL ORNAMENTS
§ SUCH MARKS HAVE BEEN USED SINCE THE MIDDLE AGES FOR CITING PAS-
SAGES AND KEYING MARGINAL REFERENCES † THE INVENTION OF PRINTING
MADE MORE ELABORATE AND PRECISE REFERENCING POSSIBLE BECAUSE
THE PAGES OF A TEXT WERE CONSISTENT FROM ONE COPY TO THE NEXT ‡

ALL PUNCTUATION WAS USED IDIOSYNCRATICALLY UNTIL AFTER THE
INVENTION OF PRINTING WHICH REVOLUTIONIZED WRITING BY DISSEMI-
NATING GRAMMATICAL AND TYPOGRAPHICAL STANDARDS BEFORE PRINT-
ING PUNCTUATION VARIED WILDLY FROM REGION TO REGION AND SCRIBE
TO SCRIBE THE LIBRARIAN AT ALEXANDRIA WHO WAS NAMED ARISTO-
PHANES DESIGNED A GREEK PUNCTUATION SYSTEM CIRCA 260 BC   HIS SYS-
TEM MARKED THE SHORTEST SEGMENTS OF DISCOURSE WITH A CENTERED
DOT · CALLED A COMMA · AND MARKED THE LONGER SECTIONS WITH A
LOW DOT CALLED A COLON. A HIGH DOT SET OFF THE LONGEST UNIT ˙
HE CALLED IT PERIODOS ˙ THE THREE DOTS WERE EASILY DISTINGUISHED
FROM ONE ANOTHER BECAUSE ALL THE LETTERS WERE THE SAME HEIGHT ·
PROVIDING A CONSISTENT FRAME OF REFERENCE · LIKE A MUSICAL STAFF ˙

ALTHOUGH THE TERMS COMMA · COLON · AND PERIOD PERSIST · THE
SHAPE OF THE MARKS AND THEIR FUNCTION TODAY ARE DIFFERENT ˙
DURING THE SEVENTH AND EIGHTH CENTURIES NEW MARKS APPEARED IN
SOME MANUSCRIPTS INCLUDING THE SEMICOLON ; THE INVERTED SEMI-
COLON ⁏ AND A QUESTION MARK THAT RAN HORIZONTALLY ⌐ A THIN DIAG-
ONAL SLASH / CALLED A VIRGULE / WAS SOMETIMES USED LIKE A COMMA
IN MEDIEVAL MANUSCRIPTS AND EARLY PRINTED BOOKS . SUCH MARKS
ARE THOUGHT TO HAVE BEEN CUES FOR READING ALOUD ; THEY INDICATED

A RISING, FALLING, OR LEVEL TONE OF VOICE . THE USE OF PUNCTUATION BY SCRIBES AND THEIR INTERPRETATION BY READERS WAS BY NO MEANS CONSISTENT , HOWEVER , AND MARKS MIGHT BE ADDED TO A MANUSCRIPT BY ANOTHER SCRIBE WELL AFTER IT WAS WRITTEN .

EARLY PUNCTUATION WAS LINKED TO ORAL DELIVERY. FOR EXAMPLE THE TERMS COMMA, COLON, AND PERIODOS, AS THEY WERE USED BY ARIS-TOPHANES, COME FROM THE THEORY OF RHETORIC, WHERE THEY REFER TO RHYTHMICAL UNITS OF SPEECH. AS A SOURCE OF RHETORICAL RATHER THAN GRAMMATICAL CUES, PUNCTUATION SERVED TO REGULATE PACE AND GIVE EMPHASIS TO PARTICULAR PHRASES, RATHER THAN TO MARK THE LOGICAL STRUCTURE OF SENTENCES. MANY OF THE PAUSES IN RHE-TORICAL DELIVERY, HOWEVER, NATURALLY CORRESPOND WITH GRAM-MATICAL STRUCTURE: FOR EXAMPLE, WHEN A PAUSE FALLS BETWEEN TWO CLAUSES OR SENTENCES.

THE SYSTEM OF ARISTOPHANES WAS RARELY USED BY THE GREEKS, BUT IT WAS REVIVED BY THE LATIN GRAMMARIAN DONATUS IN THE FOURTH CENTURY A.D. ACCORDING TO DONATUS PUNCTUATION SHOULD FALL WHEREVER THE SPEAKER WOULD NEED A MOMENT'S REST; IT PROVIDED BREATHING CUES FOR READING ALOUD. SOME LATER WRITERS MODIFIED THE THEORIES OF DONATUS, RETURNING TO A RHETORICAL APPROACH TO PUNCTUATION, IN WHICH THE MARKS SERVED TO CONTROL RHYTHM AND EMPHASIS. AFTER THE INVENTION OF PRINTING, GRAMMARIANS BEGAN TO BASE PUNCTUATION ON STRUCTURE RATHER THAN ON SPOKEN SOUND: MARKS SUCH AS THE COMMA, COLON, AND PERIOD SIGNALLED SOME OF THE GRAMMATICAL PARTS OF A SENTENCE. THUS PUNCTUATION CAME TO BE DEFINED ARCHITECTURALLY RATHER THAN ORALLY. THE COMMA BECAME A MARK OF SEPARATION, AND THE SEMICOLON WORKED AS A JOINT BETWEEN INDEPENDENT CLAUSES; THE COLON INDICATED GRAMMATICAL DISCONTINUITY: WRITING WAS SLOWLY DISTANCED FROM SPEECH.

RHETORIC, STRUCTURE, AND PACE ARE ALL AT WORK IN MODERN 10 ENGLISH PUNCTUATION, WHOSE RULES WERE ESTABLISHED BY THE END

OF THE EIGHTEENTH CENTURY. ALTHOUGH STRUCTURE IS THE STRON-
GEST RATIONALE TODAY, PUNCTUATION REMAINS A LARGELY INTUITIVE
ART. A WRITER CAN OFTEN CHOOSE AMONG SEVERAL CORRECT WAYS TO
PUNCTUATE A PASSAGE, EACH WITH A SLIGHTLY DIFFERENT RHYTHM AND
MEANING.

THERE WAS NO CONSISTENT MARK FOR QUOTATIONS BEFORE THE SEV-
ENTEENTH CENTURY. DIRECT SPEECH WAS USUALLY ANNOUNCED ONLY BY
PHRASES LIKE HE SAID. „SOMETIMES A DOUBLE COMMA WAS USED IN MANU-
SCRIPTS TO POINT OUT IMPORTANT SENTENCES AND WAS LATER USED TO
ENCLOSE "QUOTATIONS." ENGLISH PRINTERS BEFORE THE NINETEENTH
" CENTURY OFTEN EDGED ONE MARGIN OF A QUOTE WITH DOUBLE COMMAS.
" THIS CONVENTION PRESENTED TEXT AS A SPATIAL PLANE RATHER THAN A
" TEMPORAL LINE, FRAMING THE QUOTED PASSAGE LIKE A PICTURE.
" PRINTING, BY PRODUCING IDENTICAL COPIES OF A TEXT, ENCOURAGED
" THE STANDARDIZATION OF QUOTATION MARKS. PRINTED BOOKS COM-
" MONLY INCORPORATED MATERIAL FROM OTHER SOURCES.

BOTH THE GREEK AND ROMAN ALPHABETS WERE ORIGINALLY MAJUS-
CULE: ALL LETTERS WERE THE SAME HEIGHT. greek and roman minuscule
letters developed out of rapidly written scripts called cursive, which were
used for business correspondence. minuscule characters have limbs extending above and below a uniform body. alcuin, advisor to charlemagne, introduced the "carolingian" minuscule, which spread rapidly through europe
between the eighth and twelfth centuries. during the dissemination of the
carolingian script, condensed, black minuscule styles of handwriting, now
called "gothic," were also developing; they eventually replaced the classical
carolingian.

A carolingian manuscript sometimes marked the beginning of a sentence
with an enlarged letter. This character was often a majuscule, presaging the
modern use of minuscule and majuscule as double features of the same
alphabet. Both scripts were still considered separate manners of writing,
however.

> "As he Sets on, he [the printer] considers
> how to Point his Work,
> viz. when to Set, where; where. where to make ( ) where [ ]
> and when to make a Break. . . .
> When he meets with proper Names of Persons or Places
> he Sets them in Italick . . .
> and Sets the first Letter with a Capital,
> or as the Person or Place he finds
> the purpose of the Author to dignifie, all Capitals;
> but then, if he conveniently can,
> he will Set a Space between every Letter . . .
> to make it shew more Graceful and Stately."
> JOSEPH MOXON 1683

In the fifteenth century, the Carolingian script was revived by the Italian humanists. The new script, called "lettera antica," was paired with classical roman capitals. It became the basis of the roman typefaces, which were established as a European norm by the mid-sixteenth century. The terms "uppercase" and "lowercase" refer to the drawers in a printing shop that hold the two fonts. Until recently, Punctuation was an Intuitive Art, ruled by convenience and Intuition. A Printer could Liberally Capitalize the Initial of Any word She deemed worthy of Distinction, as well as Proper Names. The printer was Free to set some Words entirely in C A P I T A L S and to add further emphasis with extra S P A C E S.

The roman typefaces were based on a formal script used for books. *The cursive, rapidly written version of the Carolingian minuscule was employed for business and also for books sold in the less expensive writing shops. Called "antica corsiva" or "cancelleresca," this style of handwriting was the model for the italic typefaces cut for Aldus Manutius in Venice in 1500. Aldus Manutius was a scholar, printer, and businessman. Italic script conserved space, and Aldus developed it for his internationally distributed series of small, inexpensive books. The Aldine italic was paired with Roman capitals. The Italian typographer Tagliente advocated Italic Capitals in the early sixteenth century. Aldus set entire books in italic; it was an autonomous type style, unrelated to roman.* In France, however, the roman style was becoming the neutral, generic norm, with *italic* played against it for *contrast*. The pairs UPPERCASE/lowercase and roman/*italic* each add an inaudible, non-phonetic dimension to the alphabet. Before *italic* became the official auxiliary of roman, scribes and printers had other techniques for marking emphasis, including enlarged, **heavy**, colored, or **gothic** letters. Underlining appeared in some medieval manuscripts, and today it is the conventional substitute for italics in handwritten and typewritten texts. S p a c e is sometimes inserted between letters to declare e m p h a s i s in German and Eastern European book t y p o g r a p h y. **Boldface** fonts were not common until the nineteenth century, when display advertising created a demand for **big, black** types. Most book faces designed since the early twentieth century belong to families of four: roman, *italic*, **bold roman**, and ***bold italic***. These are used for systematically marking different kinds of copy, such as headings, captions, body text, notes, and references.

Since the rise of digital production, printed texts have become more 15
visually elaborate—typographic variations are now routinely available to writers and designers. Some recent fonts contain only ornaments and symbols; Carlos Segura's typeface Dingura (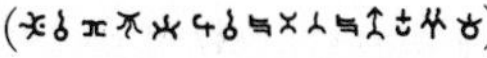) consists of mysterious runes that recall the era of manuscript production. During the e-mail incunabula, writers and designers have been using punctuation marks for expressive ends. Punctuated portraits found in electronic correspondence range from the simple "smiley" :-) to such subtle constructions as $-) [yuppie] or :-I [indifferent].

Thinking about the Text

1. Ellen Lupton and J. Abbott Miller's essay explains—and illustrates—the history of punctuation and typography. In what ways did the design of this essay affect your reading and understanding of the history it documents?

2. This essay was first published in 1996. Make a list of typographic and design features that have appeared or changed since then. If you were to continue writing this history, what would you add?

3. Lupton and Miller note that early punctuation was linked to oral delivery—meant to guide speakers rather than readers (paragraph 8). Edit a text you have written in order to "punctuate" it for oral delivery. Use whatever features you need (color, font size, boldface, italics, underlining, spacing, unconventional punctuation) to guide your performance. Write an essay describing the changes you made to your text, explaining why you made them, and reflecting on how they affected your message and delivery.

SHERMAN ALEXIE

Superman and Me

1997

SHERMAN ALEXIE (b. 1966) writes poetry and fiction, often about his experience growing up on the Spokane Indian Reservation. He is best known for his short story collection *The Lone Ranger and Tonto Fistfight in Heaven* (1993) and the award-winning novel *The Absolutely True Diary of a Part-Time Indian* (2007). "Superman and Me" was first published in *The Most Wonderful Books: Writers on Discovering the Pleasures of Reading* (1997).

I LEARNED TO READ WITH A SUPERMAN COMIC BOOK. SIMPLE enough, I suppose. I cannot recall which particular Superman comic book I read, nor can I remember which villain he fought in that issue. I cannot remember the plot, nor the means by which I obtained the comic book. What I can remember is this: I was 3 years old, a Spokane Indian boy living with his family on the Spokane Indian Reservation in eastern Washington state. We were poor by most standards, but one of my parents usually managed to find some minimum-wage job or another, which made us middle-class by reservation standards. I had a brother and three sisters. We lived on a combination of irregular paychecks, hope, fear and government surplus food.

My father, who is one of the few Indians who went to Catholic school on purpose, was an avid reader of westerns, spy thrillers, murder mysteries, gangster epics, basketball player biographies and anything else he could find. He bought his books by the pound at Dutch's Pawn Shop, Goodwill, Salvation Army and Value Village. When he had extra money, he bought new novels at supermarkets, convenience stores and hospital gift shops. Our house was filled with books. They were stacked in crazy piles in the bathroom, bedrooms and living room. In a fit of unemployment-inspired creative energy, my father built a set of bookshelves and soon filled them with a random assortment of books about the Kennedy assassination, Watergate, the Vietnam War and the entire 23-book series of the Apache westerns. My father loved books, and since I loved my father with an aching devotion, I decided to love books as well.

I can remember picking up my father's books before I could read. The words themselves were mostly foreign, but I still remember the exact moment when I first understood, with a sudden clarity, the purpose of a paragraph. I didn't have the vocabulary to say "paragraph," but I realized that a paragraph was a fence that held words. The words inside a paragraph worked together for a common purpose. They had some specific reason for being inside the same fence. This knowledge delighted me. I began to think of everything in terms of paragraphs. Our reservation was a small paragraph within the United States. My family's house was a paragraph, distinct from the other paragraphs of the LeBrets to the north, the Fords to our south and the Tribal School to the west. Inside our house, each family member existed as a separate paragraph but still had genetics and common experiences to link us. Now, using this logic, I can see my changed family as an essay of seven paragraphs: mother, father, older brother, the deceased sister, my younger twin sisters and our adopted little brother.

At the same time I was seeing the world in paragraphs, I also picked up that Superman comic book. Each panel, complete with picture, dialogue and narrative was a three-dimensional paragraph. In one panel, Superman breaks through a door. His suit is red, blue and yellow. The brown door shatters into many pieces. I look at the narrative above the picture. I cannot read the words, but I assume it tells me that "Superman is breaking down the door." Aloud, I pretend to read the words and say, "Superman is breaking down the door." Words, dialogue, also float out of Superman's mouth. Because he is breaking down the door, I assume he says, "I am breaking down the door." Once again, I pretend to read the words and say aloud, "I am breaking down the door." In this way, I learned to read.

This might be an interesting story all by itself. A little Indian boy   5 teaches himself to read at an early age and advances quickly. He reads "Grapes of Wrath" in kindergarten when other children are struggling through "Dick and Jane." If he'd been anything but an Indian boy living on the reservation, he might have been called a prodigy. But he is an Indian boy living on the reservation and is simply an oddity. He grows into a man who often speaks of his childhood in the third-person, as if it will somehow dull the pain and make him sound more modest about his talents.

A smart Indian is a dangerous person, widely feared and ridiculed by Indians and non-Indians alike. I fought with my classmates on a daily basis. They wanted me to stay quiet when the non-Indian teacher asked for answers, for volunteers, for help. We were Indian children who were expected to be stupid. Most lived up to those expectations inside the classroom but subverted them on the outside. They struggled with basic reading in school but could remember how to sing a few dozen powwow songs. They were monosyllabic in front of their non-Indian teachers but could tell complicated stories and jokes at the dinner table. They submissively ducked their heads when confronted by a non-Indian adult but would slug it out with the Indian bully who was 10 years older. As Indian children, we were expected to fail in the non-Indian world. Those who failed were ceremonially accepted by other Indians and appropriately pitied by non-Indians.

I refused to fail. I was smart. I was arrogant. I was lucky. I read books late into the night, until I could barely keep my eyes open. I read books at recess, then during lunch, and in the few minutes left after I had finished my classroom assignments. I read books in the car when my family traveled to powwows or basketball games. In shopping malls, I ran to the bookstores and read bits and pieces of as many books as I could. I read the books my father brought home from the pawnshops and secondhand. I read the books I borrowed from the library. I read the backs of cereal boxes. I read the newspaper. I read the bulletins posted on the walls of the school, the clinic, the tribal offices, the post office. I read junk mail. I read auto-repair manuals. I read magazines. I read anything that had words and paragraphs. I read with equal parts joy and desperation. I loved those books, but I also knew that love had only one purpose. I was trying to save my life.

Despite all the books I read, I am still surprised I became a writer. I was going to be a pediatrician. These days, I write novels, short stories, and poems. I visit schools and teach creative writing to Indian kids. In all my years in the reservation school system, I was never taught how to write poetry, short stories or novels. I was certainly never taught that Indians wrote poetry, short stories and novels. Writing was something beyond Indians. I cannot recall a single time that a guest teacher visited the reservation. There must have been visiting teachers. Who were they? Where are they now? Do they exist? I visit the schools as often as possible. The Indian kids crowd the classroom. Many are writing their own poems, short stories and novels. They have read my books. They have read many other books. They look at me with bright eyes and arrogant wonder. They are trying to save their lives. Then there are the sullen and already defeated Indian kids who sit in the back rows and ignore me with theatrical precision. The pages of their notebooks are empty. They carry neither pencil nor pen. They stare out the window. They refuse and resist. "Books," I say to them. "Books," I say. I throw my weight against their locked doors. The door holds. I am smart. I am arrogant. I am lucky. I am trying to save our lives.

Thinking about the Text

1. Sherman Alexie claims that he read because he was trying to save his life and that he visits reservation schools in order to help save other lives (paragraphs 7–8). How, according to Alexie, do reading and writing save lives?

2. Look closely at paragraph 7, which Alexie structures by using anaphora, repeating words at the beginning of successive sentences for rhetorical effect. What point does he emphasize with this stylistic choice?

3. Alexie argues for the importance of reading and writing, and he visits reservation schools to show Indian children that they can be writers. What other skill or knowledge do you think children need in order to survive and thrive? How might they gain that skill or knowledge? Write an essay in which you argue for specific pedagogical techniques, special programs, or something else that will help students gain a specific skill or knowledge base.

DAVID HALBERSTAM

Jordan's Moment

1998

DAVID HALBERSTAM (1934–2007) was a journalist known
for his reporting on the Vietnam War (for which he received
the Pulitzer Prize), on politics, and on sports. His books
include *The Best and the Brightest* (1972), an account of John F.
Kennedy's Vietnam policies; *Playing for Keeps: Michael Jordan and the World He Made* (1999); and *The Education of a
Coach* (2005), about New England coach Bill Belichick. "Jordan's Moment" was first published in the *New Yorker* in 1998.

THE DESOLATE NEIGHBORHOOD ON THE WEST SIDE OF Chicago where the Bulls play their home games is very quiet these days. Their gleaming new arena, the United Center, is set down there as if on a moonscape. All twelve pre-Christmas home games have been cancelled, because of the labor dispute between the owners and the players, which was initiated by the owners in a lockout described as a struggle between short millionaires and tall millionaires, or between billionaires and millionaires. The National Basketball Association, which would have entered its fifty-second season this fall, seems to have fallen victim to its own dizzying success, one that has seen the player payroll increase by an estimated two thousand five hundred per cent in the last twenty years. The incident that probably triggered the lockout occurred about a year ago, when the Minnesota Timberwolves extended the contract of a gifted young player named Kevin Garnett, paying him a hundred and twenty-six million dollars over seven years. The Timberwolves' general manager, the former Boston Celtic Kevin McHale, completed the deal; unhappy with the direction of the league and his own part in it, he later noted, "We have our hand on the neck of the golden goose and we're squeezing hard."

In Chicago, where for much of the last decade the best basketball team in the country has played, the silence is particularly painful. The last time games were played here, the Bulls, led by Michael Jordan, were contesting for their sixth N.B.A. championship, and playing against a favored team, the Utah Jazz. It was an indelible series, the memory of which serves as this year's only fare—and it is melancholy fare—for basketball junkies everywhere.

Michael Jordan was thirty-five, and arguably the dominant athlete in American sports, as he led Chicago into Salt Lake City. He was nearing the end of his career, and he was, if anything, a more complete player than ever. What his body could no longer accomplish in terms of pure physical ability he could compensate for with his shrewd knowledge of both the game and the opposing players. Nothing was wasted. There was a new quality, almost an iciness, to the way he played now. In 1995, after Jordan returned to basketball from his year-and-a-half-long baseball sabbatical, he spent the summer in Hollywood making the movie *Space Jam,* but he demanded that the producers build a basketball court where he could work out every day. Old friends dropping by the Warner lot noticed that he was working particularly hard on a shot that was already a minor part of his repertoire but which he was now making a signature shot—a jumper where he held the ball, faked a move to the basket, and then, at the last minute, when he finally jumped, fell back slightly, giving himself almost perfect separation from the defensive player. Because of his jumping ability and his threat to drive, that shot was virtually unguardable. More, it was a very smart player's concession to the changes in his body wrought by time, and it signified that he was entering a new stage in his career. What professional basketball men were now seeing was something that had been partly masked earlier in his career by his singular physical ability and the artistry of what he did, and that something was a consuming passion not just to excel but to dominate. "He wants to cut your heart out and then show it to you," his former coach Doug Collins said. "He's Hannibal Lecter," Bob Ryan, the Boston *Globe*'s expert basketball writer, said. When a television reporter asked the Bulls' center, Luc Longley, for a one-word description of Jordan, Longley's response was "Predator."

"The athlete you remind me of the most is Jake LaMotta," the Bulls' owner, Jerry Reinsdorf, told Jordan one day, referring to the fearless middleweight fighter of another era, "because the only way they can stop you is to kill you."

"Who's Jake LaMotta?" Jordan answered.   5

In Utah during last year's N.B.A. finals, Jordan had woken up before Game Five violently ill. It seemed impossible that he would play. (Whether it was altitude sickness or food poisoning no one was ever quite sure.) At about 8 A.M., one of Jordan's bodyguards, fixtures in his

entourage, called Chip Schaefer, the team trainer, to say that Jordan
had been up all night with flulike symptoms and was seriously ill. Rushing to Jordan's room, Schaefer found him curled up in the fetal position
and wrapped in blankets, though the thermostat had been cranked up
to its maximum. The greatest player in the world looked like a weak
little zombie.

Schaefer immediately hooked Jordan up to an I.V. and tried to get
as much fluid into him as possible. He also gave him medication and
decided to let him rest as much as he could that morning. Word of Jordan's illness quickly spread among journalists at the Delta Center, where
the game was to be played, and the general assumption was that he
would not play. One member of the media, though, was not so sure—
James Worthy, who, after a brilliant career with the Los Angeles Lakers, was working for the Fox network. Having played with Jordan at
North Carolina and against him in the pros, Worthy knew not only how
Michael drove himself but, even more important, how he motivated
himself. When reports circulated that Michael had a fever of a hundred
and two, Worthy told the other Fox reporters that the fever meant
nothing. "He'll play," Worthy said. "He'll figure out what he can do,
he'll conserve his strength in other areas, and he'll have a big game."

In the locker room before the game, Jordan's teammates were appalled
by what they saw. Michael, normally quite dark, was a color somewhere
between white and gray, Bill Wennington, the Bulls' backup center,
recalled, and his eyes, usually so vital, looked dead.

At first, fans watching at home could not understand how Jordan
could play at all. Then they were pulled into the drama of the event,
which had by now transcended mere basketball and taken on the nature
of an entirely different challenge. Early in the second quarter, Utah led
36–20, but Jordan played at an exceptional level—he scored twenty-one
points in the first half—and at halftime his team was down only four
points. The Bulls managed to stay close in the second half. With forty-
six seconds left in the game, and Utah leading by a point, Jordan was

fouled going to the basket. "Look at the body language of Michael Jordan," Marv Albert, the announcer, said. "You have the idea that he has difficulty just standing up." Jordan made the first of two foul shots, which tied the score, and somehow grabbed the loose ball after the missed second shot. Then, with twenty-five seconds left, the Jazz inexplicably left him open, and he hit a three-pointer, which gave Chicago an 88–85 lead and the key to a 90–88 win. He ended up with thirty-eight points, fifteen of them in the last quarter.

Throughout the 1997–98 season, Jordan had wanted to meet Utah in the finals again, in no small part because after the 1997 finals too many people had said that if only Utah had had the home-court advantage the Jazz would have won. He was eager to show that true warriors could win as handily on the road, and he was also eager to show that although Karl Malone was a great player, whose abilities he admired, there was a significant degree of difference in their respective abilities.

Unlike more talented teams, Utah almost never made mental mistakes during a game, and at the Delta Center, home of some of the league's noisiest fans, a game that was at all close could easily turn into a very difficult time for a visitor. In the Western Conference finals, Utah had gone up against the Lakers, a young team led by the immense Shaquille O'Neal, and with considerably more athletic ability, and yet the Jazz swept the Lakers in four games, making them look like a group of befuddled playground all-stars. "Playing them is like the project guys against a team," Nick Van Exel, the Laker point guard, said after the series. "The project guys always want to do the fancy behind-the-back dribbles, the spectacular plays and the dunks, while the Jazz are a bunch of guys doing pick-and-rolls and the little things. They don't get caught up in the officiating, they don't get down on each other, they don't complain. They stand as a team and stay focussed."

Utah was a *team,* smart and well coached, and its players never seemed surprised late in a game. No team in the league executed its offense, particularly the interplay between John Stockton and Karl Malone, with the discipline of Utah. But that was a potential vulnerability, the Chicago coaches believed, for the Jazz were very predictable. What worked night after night against ordinary teams during the regular season might not work in a prolonged series against great defensive players. The price of discipline might be a gap in creativity—the ability to freelance—when the disciplined offense was momentarily checkmated.

Some of this could be seen in the difference between Jordan and Malone. Each had improved greatly after he entered the league, and each had the ability to carry his team night after night. But Jordan's ability to create shots for himself, and thereby dominate at the end of big games when the defensive pressure on both sides had escalated significantly, was dramatically greater than Malone's. Malone had improved year by year not only as a shooter but as someone who could pass out of the double team. Still, like most big, powerful men, he could not improvise nearly as well as Jordan, and he was very much dependent on teammates like Stockton to create opportunities for him. What the Chicago coaches, and Jordan himself, believed was that the Bulls would be able to limit Karl Malone in the fourth quarter of a tight game but that Utah would never be able to limit Michael Jordan, because of Jordan's far greater creativity.

There was one other thing that the Chicago coaches and Jordan thought about Malone, which gave them extra confidence as they got ready for the final series, and which differed from how most other people in the league perceived Malone. Malone, the Chicago staff believed, had not come into the league as a scorer or a shooter, but he had worked so hard that he was now one of the premier shooters among the league's big men, averaging just under thirty points a game for the last ten years. But deep in his heart, they thought, he did not have the psyche of a shooter like Larry Bird, Reggie Miller, or even Jordan; therefore, it remained something of an alien role. At the end of a big game, they suspected, with the game on the line, that would be a factor.

The Bulls' coach, Phil Jackson, hoped to steal Game One of the champi-   15
onship, in Salt Lake City, because the Jazz had had ten days off and
were rusty. But it had taken the Bulls seven exhausting games to beat
the Indiana Pacers for the Eastern Conference title, and they came
into Game One slow and tired, constantly a step behind in their defensive rotations. Even so, they made up eight points in the fourth quarter
to force Utah into overtime before they lost.

The Bulls recovered, however, and stole Game Two, and, with that,
the Jazz lost the home-court advantage they had worked so hard for all
season. Worse, the series now seemed to be turning out the way the Chicago coaches had wanted it to, with the Bulls' guards limiting Stockton's
freedom of movement and isolating Malone, who, on his own, was no
longer a dominant presence.

Game Three, in Chicago, went badly for Utah. On defense, the Bulls
played a nearly perfect game: they stole the ball, they cut off passing
lanes, and their defensive rotations were so quick that Utah's shots almost
always seemed desperate—forced up at the last second. It was as if the
Chicago players had known on each Jazz possession exactly what Utah
was going to try to do. The final score was 96–54, the widest margin in
the history of the finals, and Utah's fifty-four points were the lowest
total in any N.B.A. game since the introduction of the twenty-four-
second clock, in 1954. "This is actually the score?" Jerry Sloan, the Utah
coach, said in his post-game press conference, holding up the stat sheet.
"I thought it was a hundred and ninety-six. It sure seemed like a hundred
and ninety-six."

Game Four was more respectable, with the Bulls winning 86–82.
But the Jazz came back in Game Five. Malone, bottled up so long, and
the target of considerable criticism in the papers, had a big game, hitting
seventeen of twenty-seven shots for thirty-nine points, while Chicago
seemed off its game, its concentration slipping. Jackson said later that
he thought there had been far too much talk of winning at home, too
much talk of champagne and of how to stop a riot in case the Bulls

won—and too much debate over whether or not this would be Michael Jordan's last game ever in Chicago in a Bulls uniform.

At this late point in Michael Jordan's career, there were certain people who thought of themselves as Jordanologists, students not only of the game but of the man himself. They believed that they could think like him; that is, they could pick up his immensely sensitive feel for the rhythm and texture of each game, his sense of what his team needed to do at a given moment, and what his role should be—scoring, passing, or playing defense. Would he set an example for his teammates by taking up the defensive level? Would he spend the first quarter largely passing off in order to get them in the game? Over the years, he had come a long way from the young man who, surrounded by lesser teammates, had gone all out for an entire game, trying to do everything by himself. The mature Michael Jordan liked to conserve energy, let opponents use theirs up, and then when the moment was right take over the game.

Now, in Salt Lake City, it was as if he had reverted to the Michael Jordan who had carried that bottom-feeding Chicago team in the early days of his career, the player who effectively let his teammates know they were not to get in his way, because he was going to do it all himself. On this night, he knew that he was going to get little help from Scottie Pippen, who was severely injured—virtually a basketball cripple. Dennis Rodman was a rebounder, not a scorer. Toni Kukoc had played well lately, but he was always problematical. Ron Harper, once an exceptional scorer, had become, late in his career in Chicago, a defensive specialist, and he, too, was sick—apparently from something he had eaten. Luc Longley, the center, was in the midst of a wretched playoff series, seeming out of synch with himself and his teammates. (He played only fourteen minutes of this game, scored no points, and picked up four fouls.) Steve Kerr was a talented outside shooter, but Utah would be able to cover him more closely with Pippen limited.

It was clear from the beginning of the game that Jordan would try to do it all. Pippen was out for much of the first half, and Jordan, with Phil

Jackson's assent, rationed his energy on defense; at one point, the assistant coach, Tex Winter, turned to Jackson and said, "Michael's giving defense a lick and promise," and Jackson said, "Well, Tex, he does need a bit of a rest." By all rights, the Jazz should have been able to grind the Bulls down and take a sizable lead, but the Bulls, even with their bench players on the floor, never let Utah break the game open. On offense, Jordan carried the load. He was conserving his energy, playing less defense and doing less rebounding than he normally did, but at the half he had twenty-three points. Utah's lead at the half, 49–45, was not what any Jazz fan would want against such a vulnerable Chicago team.

Later, Jordan said that he had remained confident throughout the game, because Utah did not break it open when it had the chance. Jordan's former teammate B. J. Armstrong, watching at home, thought that Utah was blowing it, leaving the game out there for Michael to steal. Armstrong and Jordan had been friends, but it had often been difficult for Armstrong to play alongside Michael. The game had come so much more easily to Jordan than to anyone else, Armstrong felt, and Michael had often showed his impatience with his more mortal teammates— indeed, at one point a frustrated Armstrong had checked out of the library several books on genius hoping that they would help him learn to play with Michael. One of Jordan's particular strengths, Armstrong believed, was that he had the most acute sense of the tempo and mood of every game of any player he had ever seen. A lot of players and coaches can look at film afterward and point their finger at the exact moment when a game slipped away, but Jordan could tell instantly, even as it was happening. It was, Armstrong thought, as if he were in the game playing and yet sitting there studying it and completely distanced from it. It was a gift that allowed him to monitor and lift his own team at critical moments and to destroy opposing teams when he sensed their special moment of vulnerability.

Now, watching the second half of Game Six, Armstrong had a sense that Michael regarded the game as a potential gift. The Jazz, after all, could have put it away early on by exploiting the obvious Chicago weaknesses. But they hadn't. If they had, Armstrong thought, Michael might have saved his energy for Game Seven. But instead the Jazz were leaving Game Six out there for the taking.

As the fourth quarter opened, the Utah lead was marginal, 66–61; the low score tended to favor the Bulls, for it meant that they had set the tempo and remained in striking distance. Slowly, the Bulls began to come back, until, with under five minutes to play, the score was tied at 77. Jordan was obviously tired, but so was everyone else. Tex Winter was alarmed when Jordan missed several jump shots in a row. "Look, he can't get any elevation," he told Jackson. "His legs are gone."

During a time-out two minutes later, Jackson told Jordan to give up   25 the jump shot and drive. "I know," Jordan said, agreeing. "I'm going to start going to the basket—they haven't got a center in now, so the way is clear."

Once again, it was Michael Jordan time. A twenty-foot jumper by Malone on a feed from Stockton gave Utah an 83–79 lead, but Jordan cut it to 83–81 when he drove to the basket, was fouled by Utah's Bryon Russell, with 2:07 on the clock, and hit a pair of foul shots. Back and forth they went, and when Jordan drove again he was fouled again, this time by Stockton. He hit both free throws, to tie the score at 83, with 59.2 seconds left.

Then Utah brought the ball up court and went into its offense very slowly. Stockton worked the ball in to Malone, and Chicago was quick to double-team him. Malone fed Stockton, on the opposite side of the court, with a beautiful cross-court pass. With Harper rushing back a split second too late, Stockton buried a twenty-four-foot jumper. That gave Utah a three-point lead, 86–83. The clock showed 41.9 seconds left as Chicago called its last time-out. The Utah crowd began to breathe a little easier.

Dick Ebersol, the head of NBC Sports, watched the final minutes in the NBC truck. He had started the game sitting in the stands, next to the N.B.A. commissioner, David Stern, but had become so nervous that he had gone down to the control truck. Ebersol liked Michael Jordan

very much, and was well aware that he and his network were the ben-
eficiaries of Jordan's unique appeal. Jordan's presence in the finals was
worth eight or nine million viewers to NBC. Ebersol was delighted by
the ratings for this series so far—they would end up at 18.7, the highest
ever. At this point, though, Ebersol was rooting not for Michael Jordan
but for a seventh game, and that meant he was rooting, however invol-
untarily, for Utah. A seventh game would bring NBC and its parent
company, General Electric, an additional ten or twelve million dollars
in advertising revenues. Jordan's exploits had brought many benefits to
the N.B.A. over the years, but he was such a great player that no N.B.A.
final in which he was involved had gone to the ratings and advertising
jackpot of a seventh game.

When Stockton gave Utah the three-point lead with 41.9 seconds
showing on the clock, Ebersol was thrilled. He was going to get his
Game Seven after all. "Well, guys," he told the production people in the
truck, turning away from the screens, "we'll be back here on Wednesday, and the home folks"—the G.E. management people—"are going to
be very happy."

During the Chicago time-out, Jackson and Jordan talked about what   30
kind of shot he might take, and Jackson reminded him that his legs
were tired and it was affecting his jump shot. "I've got my second wind
now," Jordan answered. "If you have to go for the jumper, you've got
to follow through better," Jackson said. "You haven't been following
through." Tex Winter drew up a variation on a basic Chicago play, called
Whatthefuck—actually an old New York play, from Jackson's time on
the Knicks. It called for the Bulls to clear out on one side, in order to
isolate Jordan against Bryon Russell. As it happened, Jordan took the
ball out near the back-court line, moved in a leisurely fashion into his
attack mode on the right side, and then, with Utah having no chance to
double him, drove down the right side and laid the ball up high and soft
for the basket. The score was 86–85 Utah, with thirty-seven seconds
left. It was a tough basket off a big-time drive.

That gave Utah one wonderful additional possession—a chance either to hit a basket or to use Malone to draw fouls. Stockton came across the half-court line almost casually. He bided his time, letting the clock run down, and finally, with about eleven seconds left on the twenty-four-second clock, he worked the ball to Malone.

Buzz Peterson, Jordan's close friend and college roommate, was watching Game Six with his wife, Jan, at their home, in Boone, North Carolina. In the final minute of the game, Jan turned to him and said, "They're going to lose." But Peterson, who had played with Jordan in countless real games and in practice games when the winning team was the first to reach eleven and Jordan's team was behind 10–8, knew all too well that moments like this were what he lived for: with his team behind, he would predict victory to his teammates and then take over the last part of the game. Peterson told his wife, "Don't be too sure. Michael's got one more good shot at it." Just then Jordan made his driving layup to bring the Bulls within a point. The key play, Peterson felt, was going to come on the next defensive sequence, when Utah came down court with the ball. Peterson was certain that he could track Jordan's thinking: he would know that Utah would go to Malone, hoping for a basket, or, at least, two foul shots. He had seen his friend so often in the past in this same role, encouraged by Dean Smith, the North Carolina coach, to play the defensive rover. Peterson thought that Michael, knowing the likely Utah offense every bit as well as Malone and Stockton, would try to make a move on Malone.

As soon as Malone got the ball, Jordan was there. Sure where the ball was going and how Malone was going to hold it, he sneaked in behind him for the steal. Jordan's poise at this feverish moment was fascinating: as he made his move behind Malone, he had the discipline to extend his body to the right and thus get the perfect angle, so that when he swiped at the ball he would not foul. "Karl never saw me coming," Jordan said afterward. There were 18.9 seconds left on the clock.

The crowd, Jordan remembered, got very quiet. That was, he said later, the moment for him. The moment, he explained, was what all Phil Jackson's Zen Buddhism stuff, as he called it, was about: how to focus and concentrate and be ready for that critical point in a game, so that when it arrived you knew exactly what you wanted to do and how to do it, as if you had already lived through it. When it happened, you were supposed to be in control, use the moment, and not panic and let the moment use you. Jackson liked the analogy of a cat waiting for a mouse, patiently biding its time, until the mouse, utterly unaware, finally came forth.

The play at that instant, Jordan said, seemed to unfold very slowly, and he saw everything with great clarity, as Jackson had wanted him to: the way the Utah defense was setting up, and what his teammates were doing. He knew exactly what he was going to do. "I never doubted myself," Jordan said later. "I never doubted the whole game."

Incredibly, Utah decided not to double-team Jordan. Steve Kerr, in for Harper, was on the wing to Jordan's right, ready to take a pass and score if Stockton left him to double Jordan. Kukoc had to be watched on the left. Rodman, starting out at the top of the foul circle, made a good cut to the basket, and suddenly Bryon Russell was isolated, one on one, with Jordan. Jordan had let the clock run down from about fifteen seconds to about eight. Then Russell made a quick reach for the ball, and Jordan started his drive, moving to his right as if to go to the basket. Russell went for the bait, and suddenly Jordan pulled up. Russell was already sprawling to his left, aided by a light tap on the rear from Jordan as he stopped and squared up and shot. It was a great shot, a clear look at the basket, and his elevation and form were perfect. Normally, Jordan said later, he tended to fade back just as he took his jumper for that extra degree of separation between him and his defender, but, because his previous shots had been falling short, he did not fade away this time— nor did he need to, for Russell, faked to the floor, was desperately trying to regain his position.

35

Roy Williams, the Kansas coach who had heard about Michael when he was back in Laney High School, in Wilmington, North Carolina, was at his camp for high-school players, in Kansas, and was watching the game in the coaches' locker room. He remembered saying after the steal, as Jordan was bringing the ball up court, that some Utah defender had better run over and double him quickly or it was going to be over. You forced someone else to take the last shot, he thought—you did not allow Michael to go one on one for it. But no one doubled him. What Williams remembered about the final shot was the exquisite quality of Jordan's form, and how long he held his follow-through after releasing the ball; it was something that coaches always taught their players. Watching him now, as he seemed to stay up in the air for an extra moment, defying gravity, Williams thought of it as Michael Jordan's way of willing the ball through the basket.

There is a photograph of that moment, Jordan's last shot, in the magazine *ESPN*, taken by the photographer Fernando Medina. It is in color and covers two full pages, and it shows Russell struggling to regain position, Jordan at the peak of his jump, the ball high up on its arc and about to descend, and the clock displaying the time remaining in the game— 6.6 seconds. What is remarkable is the closeup it offers of so many Utah fans. Though the ball has not yet reached the basket, the game appears over to them. The anguish—the certitude of defeat—is on their faces. In a number of instances their hands are extended as if to stop Jordan and keep the shot from going in. Some of the fans have already put their hands to their faces, as in a moment of grief. There is one exception to this: a young boy on the right, in a Chicago Bulls shirt, whose arms are already in the air in a victory call.

The ball dropped cleanly through. Utah had one more chance, but Stockton missed the last shot and the Bulls won, 87–86. Jordan had carried his team once again. He had scored forty-five points, and he had scored his team's last eight points. The Chicago coaches, it turned out, had been prophetic in their sense of what would happen in the fourth quarters of this series, and which player would be able to create for himself with the game on the line. In the three close games, two of them in Salt Lake City, Jordan played much bigger than Malone—averaging thirteen points in the fourth quarter to Malone's three. Jordan should be remembered, Jerry Sloan said afterward, "as the greatest player who ever played the game."

Thinking about the Text

1. Twice in this essay Michael Jordan is referred to as "the greatest player" (paragraphs 6, 39). What evidence does David Halberstam provide to support that assessment?

2. Halberstam quotes others to provide information about how Jordan was perceived as a player and to augment his account of a particular game. What, specifically, do you learn about Jordan through the quotations Halberstam includes? How else might he have provided that information?

3. Write a profile of someone on your campus or in your community. You'll likely need to interview that person or someone who knows him or her. Use quotations and description to reveal something about your subject and what he or she is known for. (For an example of a profile written by a student, see Sarah Esther Maslin's "The Pawn King" on pp. 493–505.)

STEPHEN KING

On Writing

2000

STEPHEN KING (b. 1947) primarily writes horror and suspense fiction. Many of his popular novels—*Carrie* (1974), *The Shining* (1977), *The Green Mile* (1996), and others—have also been made into films. "On Writing" is drawn from King's book *On Writing: A Memoir of the Craft* (2000), which includes recollections of experiences that have shaped his work as well as instruction for writers.

HARDLY A WEEK AFTER BEING SPRUNG FROM DETENTION hall, I was once more invited to step down to the principal's office. I went with a sinking heart, wondering what new shit I'd stepped in.

It wasn't Mr. Higgins who wanted to see me, at least; this time the school guidance counselor had issued the summons. There had been discussions about me, he said, and how to turn my "restless pen" into more constructive channels. He had enquired of John Gould, editor of Lisbon's weekly newspaper, and had discovered Gould had an opening for a sports reporter. While the school couldn't *insist* that I take this job, everyone in the front office felt it would be a good idea. *Do it or die,* the G.C.'s eyes suggested. Maybe that was just paranoia, but even now, almost forty years later, I don't think so.

I groaned inside. I was shut of *Dave's Rag*, almost shut of *The Drum*, and now here was the Lisbon *Weekly Enterprise*. Instead of being haunted by waters, like Norman Maclean in *A River Runs Through It*, I was as a teenager haunted by newspapers. Still, what could I do? I rechecked the look in the guidance counselor's eyes and said I would be delighted to interview for the job.

Gould—not the well-known New England humorist or the novelist who wrote *The Greenleaf Fires* but a relation of both, I think—greeted me warily but with some interest. We would try each other out, he said, if that suited me.

Now that I was away from the administrative offices of Lisbon High, I felt able to muster a little honesty. I told Mr. Gould that I didn't know much about sports. Gould said, "These are games people understand when they're watching them drunk in bars. You'll learn if you try."

He gave me a huge roll of yellow paper on which to type my copy— I think I still have it somewhere—and promised me a wage of half a cent a word. It was the first time someone had promised me wages for writing.

The first two pieces I turned in had to do with a basketball game in which an LHS player broke the school scoring record. One was a straight piece of reporting. The other was a sidebar about Robert Ransom's record-breaking performance. I brought both to Gould the day after the game so he'd have them for Friday, which was when the paper came out. He read the game piece, made two minor corrections, and spiked it. Then he started in on the feature piece with a large black pen.

I took my fair share of English Lit classes in my two remaining years at Lisbon, and my fair share of composition, fiction, and poetry classes in college, but John Gould taught me more than any of them, and in no more than ten minutes. I wish I still had the piece—it deserves to be framed, editorial corrections and all—but I can remember pretty well how it went and how it looked after Gould had combed through it with that black pen of his. Here's an example:

> Last night, in the ~~well-loved~~ gymnasium of Lisbon High School, partisans and Jay Hills fans alike were stunned by an athletic performance unequalled in school history. Bob Ransom, ~~known as "Bullet" Bob for both his size and accuracy,~~ scored thirty-seven points. Yes, you heard me right. ~~Plus~~ he did it with grace, speed . . . and with an odd courtesy as well, committing only two personal fouls in his ~~knight-like~~ quest for a record which has eluded Lisbon ~~thinclads~~ players since ~~the years of Korea~~ 1953 . . .

Gould stopped at "the years of Korea" and looked up at me. "What year was the last record made?" he asked.

Luckily, I had my notes. "1953," I said. Gould grunted and went   10
back to work. When he finished marking my copy in the manner
indicated above, he looked up and saw something on my face. I
think he must have mistaken it for horror. It wasn't; it was pure revelation. Why, I wondered, didn't English teachers ever do this? It was
like the Visible Man Old Raw Diehl had on his desk in the biology
room.

"I only took out the bad parts, you know," Gould said. "Most of it's
pretty good."

"I know," I said, meaning both things: yes, most of it was good—
okay anyway, serviceable—and yes, he had only taken out the bad parts.
"I won't do it again."

He laughed. "If that's true, you'll never have to work for a living. You
can do *this* instead. Do I have to explain any of these marks?"

"No," I said.

"When you write a story, you're telling yourself the story," he said.   15
"When you rewrite, your main job is taking out all the things that are
not the story."

Gould said something else that was interesting on the day I turned
in my first two pieces: write with the door closed, rewrite with the door
open. Your stuff starts out being just for you, in other words, but then it
goes out. Once you know what the story is and get it right—as right as
you can, anyway—it belongs to anyone who wants to read it. Or criticize it. If you're very lucky (this is my idea, not John Gould's, but I
believe he would have subscribed to the notion), more will want to do
the former than the latter.

Thinking about the Text

1. What general principles about writing and editing can you take away from Stephen King's essay?

2. Examine the edits that John Gould made to King's early sports writing (paragraph 8). What kinds of information did he cut? Read David Halberstam's "Jordan's Moment" (pp. 328–42). How might Gould respond to Halberstam's writing? What might he praise? What might he edit out?

3. Gould tells King, "I only took out the bad parts" (paragraph 11). Choose a piece of your own writing that you'd like to edit. Only take out the bad parts.

DAVID FOSTER WALLACE

Consider the Lobster

2004

DAVID FOSTER WALLACE (1962–2008) wrote novels, short stories, and essays. Some of his essay collections include *A Supposedly Fun Thing I'll Never Do Again* (1997), *Consider the Lobster* (2005), and *Both Flesh and Not* (2012). He is best known for his novel *Infinite Jest* (1996). "Consider the Lobster" was first published in *Gourmet* (2004), a magazine devoted to food. In the essay, Wallace makes several references to readers of *Gourmet*, and he wonders if his audience thinks about animal suffering. All notes are the author's.

T HE ENORMOUS, PUNGENT, AND EXTREMELY WELL
marketed Maine Lobster Festival is held every late July in
the state's midcoast region, meaning the western side of
Penobscot Bay, the nerve stem of Maine's lobster industry.
What's called the midcoast runs from Owl's Head and Thomaston in
the south to Belfast in the north. . . . The region's two main communities are Camden, with its very old money and yachty harbor and five-
star restaurants and phenomenal B&Bs, and Rockland, a serious old
fishing town that hosts the Festival every summer in historic Harbor
Park, right along the water.[1]

Tourism and lobster are the midcoast region's two main industries,
and they're both warm-weather enterprises, and the Maine Lobster
Festival represents less an intersection of the industries than a deliberate collision, joyful and lucrative and loud. . . . Festival highlights:
concerts by Lee Ann Womack and Orleans, annual Maine Sea Goddess
beauty pageant, Saturday's big parade, Sunday's William G. Atwood
Memorial Crate Race, annual Amateur Cooking Competition, carnival
rides and midway attractions and food booths, and the MLF's Main
Eating Tent, where something over 25,000 pounds of fresh-caught
Maine lobster is consumed after preparation in the World's Largest Lobster Cooker near the grounds' north entrance. Also available are lobster
rolls, lobster turnovers, lobster sauté, Down East lobster salad, lobster
bisque, lobster ravioli, and deep-fried lobster dumplings. Lobster Ther-
midor is obtainable at a sit-down restaurant called The Black Pearl on
Harbor Park's northwest wharf. A large all-pine booth sponsored by the
Maine Lobster Promotion Council has free pamphlets with recipes, eating tips, and Lobster Fun Facts. The winner of Friday's Amateur Cooking Competition prepares Saffron Lobster Ramekins, the recipe for
which is available for public downloading at www.mainelobsterfestival
.com. There are lobster T-shirts and lobster bobblehead dolls and

1. There's a comprehensive native apothegm: "Camden by the sea, Rockland by the
smell."

inflatable lobster pool toys and clamp-on lobster hats with big scarlet
claws that wobble on springs. Your assigned correspondent saw it all,
accompanied by one girlfriend and both his own parents—one of which
parents was actually born and raised in Maine, albeit in the extreme
northern inland part, which is potato country and a world away from
the touristic midcoast.[2]

For practical purposes, everyone knows what a lobster is. As usual,
though, there's much more to know than most of us care about—it's all
a matter of what your interests are. Taxonomically speaking, a lobster is
a marine crustacean of the family Homaridae, characterized by five
pairs of jointed legs, the first pair terminating in large pincerish claws
used for subduing prey. Like many other species of benthic carnivore,
lobsters are both hunters and scavengers. They have stalked eyes, gills on
their legs, and antennae. There are dozens of different kinds world-
wide, of which the relevant species here is the Maine lobster, *Homarus
americanus*. The name "lobster" comes from the Old English *loppestre*,
which is thought to be a corrupt form of the Latin word for locust combined with the Old English *loppe*, which meant spider.

Moreover, a crustacean is an aquatic arthropod of the class Crusta-
cea, which comprises crabs, shrimp, barnacles, lobsters, and freshwater
crayfish. All this is right there in the encyclopedia. And an arthropod
is an invertebrate member of the phylum Arthropoda, which phylum
covers insects, spiders, crustaceans, and centipedes/millipedes, all of
whose main commonality, besides the absence of a centralized brain-
spine assembly, is a chitinous exoskeleton composed of segments, to
which appendages are articulated in pairs.

The point is that lobsters are basically giant sea-insects.[3] Like most   5
arthropods, they date from the Jurassic period, biologically so much

2. N.B. All personally connected parties have made it clear from the start that they
do not want to be talked about in this article.
3. Midcoasters' native term for a lobster is, in fact, "bug," as in "Come around on
Sunday and we'll cook up some bugs."

older than mammalia that they might as well be from another planet. And they are—particularly in their natural brown-green state, brandishing their claws like weapons and with thick antennae awhip—not nice to look at. And it's true that they are garbagemen of the sea, eaters of dead stuff,[4] although they'll also eat some live shellfish, certain kinds of injured fish, and sometimes each other.

But they are themselves good eating. Or so we think now. Up until sometime in the 1800s, though, lobster was literally low-class food, eaten only by the poor and institutionalized. Even in the harsh penal environment of early America, some colonies had laws against feeding lobsters to inmates more than once a week because it was thought to be cruel and unusual, like making people eat rats. One reason for their low status was how plentiful lobsters were in old New England. "Unbelievable abundance" is how one source describes the situation, including accounts of Plymouth pilgrims wading out and capturing all they wanted by hand, and of early Boston's seashore being littered with lobsters after hard storms—these latter were treated as a smelly nuisance and ground up for fertilizer. There is also the fact that premodern lobster was often cooked dead and then preserved, usually packed in salt or crude hermetic containers. Maine's earliest lobster industry was based around a dozen such seaside canneries in the 1840s, from which lobster was shipped as far away as California, in demand only because it was cheap and high in protein, basically chewable fuel.

Now, of course, lobster is posh, a delicacy, only a step or two down from caviar. The meat is richer and more substantial than most fish, its taste subtle compared to the marine-gaminess of mussels and clams. In the U.S. pop-food imagination, lobster is now the seafood analog to steak, with which it's so often twinned as Surf 'n' Turf on the really expensive part of the chain steak house menu.

In fact, one obvious project of the MLF, and of its omnipresently sponsorial Maine Lobster Promotion Council, is to counter the idea

---

4. Factoid: Lobster traps are usually baited with dead herring.

that lobster is unusually luxe or rich or unhealthy or expensive, suitable only for effete palates or the occasional blow-the-diet treat. It is emphasized over and over in presentations and pamphlets at the Festival that Maine lobster meat has fewer calories, less cholesterol, and less saturated fat than chicken.[5] And in the Main Eating Tent, you can get a "quarter" (industry shorthand for a 1¼-pound lobster), a 4-ounce cup of melted butter, a bag of chips, and a soft roll w/ butter-pat for around $12.00, which is only slightly more expensive than supper at McDonald's.

*   *   *

Lobster is essentially a summer food. This is because we now prefer our lobsters fresh, which means they have to be recently caught, which for both tactical and economic reasons takes place at depths of less than 25 fathoms. Lobsters tend to be hungriest and most active (i.e., most trappable) at summer water temperatures of 45–50°F. In the autumn, some Maine lobsters migrate out into deeper water, either for warmth or to avoid the heavy waves that pound New England's coast all winter. Some burrow into the bottom. They might hibernate; nobody's sure. Summer is also lobsters' molting season—specifically early- to mid-July. Chitinous arthropods grow by molting, rather the way people have to buy bigger clothes as they age and gain weight. Since lobsters can live to be over 100, they can also get to be quite large, as in 20 pounds or more—though truly senior lobsters are rare now, because New England's waters are so heavily trapped.[6] Anyway, hence the culinary distinction between hard- and soft-shell lobsters, the latter sometimes a.k.a. shedders. A soft-shell lobster is one that has recently molted. In midcoast restaurants, the summer menu often offers both kinds, with shedders being slightly cheaper even though they're easier to dismantle and the meat is allegedly sweeter. The reason for the discount is that a molting

---

5. Of course, the common practice of dipping the lobster meat in melted butter torpedoes all these happy fat-specs, which none of the Council's promotional stuff ever mentions, any more than potato-industry PR talks about sour cream and bacon bits.

6. Datum: in a good year, the U.S. industry produces around 80 million pounds of lobster, and Maine accounts for more than half of that total.

lobster uses a layer of seawater for insulation while its new shell is hardening, so there's slightly less actual meat when you crack open a shedder, plus a redolent gout of water that gets all over everything and can sometimes jet out lemonlike and catch a tablemate right in the eye. If it's winter or you're buying lobster someplace far from New England, on the other hand, you can almost bet that the lobster is a hard-shell, which for obvious reasons travel better.

As an à la carte entrée, lobster can be baked, broiled, steamed, grilled, sautéed, stir-fried, or microwaved. The most common method, though, is boiling. If you're someone who enjoys having lobster at home, this is probably the way you do it, since boiling is so easy. You need a large kettle w/ cover, which you fill about half full with water (the standard advice is that you want 2.5 quarts of water per lobster). Seawater is optimal, or you can add two tbsp salt per quart from the tap. It also helps to know how much your lobsters weigh. You get the water boiling, put in the lobsters one at a time, cover the kettle, and bring it back up to a boil. Then you bank the heat and let the kettle simmer—ten minutes for the first pound of lobster, then three minutes for each pound after that. (This is assuming you've got hard-shell lobsters, which, again, if you don't live between Boston and Halifax, is probably what you've got. For shedders, you're supposed to subtract three minutes from the total.) The reason the kettle's lobsters turn scarlet is that boiling somehow suppresses every pigment in their chitin but one. If you want an easy test of whether the lobsters are done, you try pulling on one of their antennae—if it comes out of the head with minimal effort, you're ready to eat.

A detail so obvious that most recipes don't even bother to mention it is that each lobster is supposed to be alive when you put it in the kettle. This is part of lobster's modern appeal: It's the freshest food there is. There's no decomposition between harvesting and eating. And not only do lobsters require no cleaning or dressing or plucking (though the mechanics of actually eating them are a different matter), but they're relatively easy for vendors to keep alive. They come up alive in the traps, are placed in containers of seawater, and can, so long as the water's

10

aerated and the animals' claws are pegged or banded to keep them from tearing one another up under the stresses of captivity,[7] survive right up until they're boiled. Most of us have been in supermarkets or restaurants that feature tanks of live lobster, from which you can pick out your supper while it watches you point. And part of the overall spectacle of the Maine Lobster Festival is that you can see actual lobstermen's vessels docking at the wharves along the northeast grounds and unloading freshly caught product, which is transferred by hand or cart 100 yards to the great clear tanks stacked up around the Festival's cooker—which is, as mentioned, billed as the World's Largest Lobster Cooker and can process over 100 lobsters at a time for the Main Eating Tent.

So then here is a question that's all but unavoidable at the World's Largest Lobster Cooker, and may arise in kitchens across the U.S.: Is it all right to boil a sentient creature alive just for our gustatory pleasure? A related set of concerns: Is the previous question irksomely PC or sentimental? What does "all right" even mean in this context? Is it all just a matter of individual choice?

As you may or may not know, a certain well-known group called People for the Ethical Treatment of Animals thinks that the morality of lobster-boiling is not just a matter of individual conscience. In fact, one of the very first things we hear about the MLF . . . well, to set the scene: We're coming in by cab from the almost indescribably odd and rustic

7. N.B. Similar reasoning underlies the practice of what's termed "debeaking" broiler chickens and brood hens in modern factory farms. Maximum commercial efficiency requires that enormous poultry populations be confined in unnaturally close quarters, under which conditions many birds go crazy and peck one another to death. As a purely observational side-note, be apprised that debeaking is usually an automated process and that the chickens receive no anesthetic. It's not clear to me whether most *Gourmet* readers know about debeaking, or about related practices like dehorning cattle in commercial feedlots, cropping swine's tails in factory hog farms to keep psychotically bored neighbors from chewing them off, and so forth. It so happens that your assigned correspondent knew almost nothing about standard meat-industry operations before starting work on this article.

Knox County Airport[8] very late on the night before the Festival opens, sharing the cab with a wealthy political consultant who lives on Vinalhaven Island in the bay half the year (he's headed for the island ferry in Rockland). The consultant and cabdriver are responding to informal journalistic probes about how people who live in the midcoast region actually view the MLF, as in is the Festival just a big-dollar tourist thing or is it something local residents look forward to attending, take genuine civic pride in, etc. The cabdriver—who's in his seventies, one of apparently a whole platoon of retirees the cab company puts on to help with the summer rush, and wears a U.S.-flag lapel pin, and drives in what can only be called a very deliberate way—assures us that locals do endorse and enjoy the MLF, although he himself hasn't gone in years, and now come to think of it no one he and his wife know has, either. However, the demilocal consultant's been to recent Festivals a couple times (one gets the impression it was at his wife's behest), of which his most vivid impression was that "you have to line up for an ungodly long time to get your lobsters, and meanwhile there are all these ex–flower children coming up and down along the line handing out pamphlets that say the lobsters die in terrible pain and you shouldn't eat them."

And it turns out that the post-hippies of the consultant's recollection were activists from PETA. There were no PETA people in obvious view at the 2003 MLF,[9] but they've been conspicuous at many of the recent

8. The terminal used to be somebody's house, for example, and the lost-luggage-reporting room was clearly once a pantry.

9. It turned out that Mr. William R. Rivas-Rivas, a high-ranking PETA official out of the group's Virginia headquarters, was indeed there this year, albeit solo, working the Festival's main and side entrances on Saturday, August 2, handing out pamphlets and adhesive stickers emblazoned with "Being Boiled Hurts," which is the tagline in most of PETA's published material about lobster. I learned that he'd been there only later, when speaking with Mr. Rivas-Rivas on the phone. I'm not sure how we missed seeing him *in situ* at the Festival, and I can't see much to do except apologize for the oversight—although it's also true that Saturday was the day of the big MLF parade through Rockland, which basic journalistic responsibility seemed to require going to (and which, with all due respect, meant that Saturday was maybe not the best day for PETA to work the Harbor Park grounds, especially if it was going to be just one person for one day, since a

Festivals. Since at least the mid-1990s, articles in everything from *The Camden Herald* to *The New York Times* have described PETA urging boycotts of the MLF, often deploying celebrity spokespeople like Mary Tyler Moore for open letters and ads saying stuff like "Lobsters are extraordinarily sensitive" and "To me, eating a lobster is out of the question." More concrete is the oral testimony of Dick, our florid and extremely gregarious rental-car guy, to the effect that PETA's been around so much in recent years that a kind of brittlely tolerant homeostasis now obtains between the activists and the Festival's locals, e.g.: "We had some incidents a couple years ago. One lady took most of her clothes off and painted herself like a lobster, almost got herself arrested. But for the most part they're let alone. [Rapid series of small ambiguous laughs, which with Dick happens a lot.] They do their thing and we do our thing."

This whole interchange takes place on Route 1, 30 July, during a   15
four-mile, 50-minute ride from the airport[10] to the dealership to sign car-rental papers. Several irreproducible segues down the road from the PETA anecdotes, Dick—whose son-in-law happens to be a professional lobsterman and one of the Main Eating Tent's regular suppliers—articulates what he and his family feel is the crucial mitigating factor in the whole morality-of-boiling-lobsters-alive issue: "There's a part of the brain in people and animals that lets us feel pain, and lobsters' brains don't have this part."

---

lot of diehard MLF partisans were off-site watching the parade (which, again with no offense intended, was in truth kind of cheesy and boring, consisting mostly of slow homemade flats and various midcoast people waving at one another, and with an extremely annoying man dressed as Blackbeard ranging up and down the length of the crowd saying "Arrr" over and over and brandishing a plastic sword at people, etc.; plus it rained)).

10. The short version regarding why we were back at the airport after already arriving the previous night involves lost luggage and a miscommunication about where and what the local National Car Rental franchise was—Dick came out personally to the airport and got us, out of no evident motive but kindness. (He also talked nonstop the entire way, with a very distinctive speaking style that can be described only as manically laconic; the truth is that I now know more about this man than I do about some members of my own family).

Besides the fact that it's incorrect in about 11 different ways, the main reason Dick's statement is interesting is that its thesis is more or less echoed by the Festival's own pronouncement on lobsters and pain, which is part of a Test Your Lobster IQ quiz that appears in the 2003 MLF program courtesy of the Maine Lobster Promotion Council: "The nervous system of a lobster is very simple, and is in fact most similar to the nervous system of the grasshopper. It is decentralized with no brain. There is no cerebral cortex, which in humans is the area of the brain that gives the experience of pain."

Though it sounds more sophisticated, a lot of the neurology in this latter claim is still either false or fuzzy. The human cerebral cortex is the brain-part that deals with higher faculties like reason, metaphysical self-awareness, language, etc. Pain reception is known to be part of a much older and more primitive system of nociceptors and prostaglandins that are managed by the brain stem and thalamus.[11] On the other hand, it is true that the cerebral cortex is involved in what's variously called suffering, distress, or the emotional experience of pain—i.e., experiencing painful stimuli as unpleasant, very unpleasant, unbearable, and so on.

Before we go any further, let's acknowledge that the questions of whether and how different kinds of animals feel pain, and of whether and why it might be justifiable to inflict pain on them in order to eat them, turn out to be extremely complex and difficult. And comparative neuro-anatomy is only part of the problem. Since pain is a totally subjective mental experience, we do not have direct access to anyone or anything's pain but our own; and even just the principles by which we can infer that others experience pain and have a legitimate interest in not feeling

---

11. To elaborate by way of example: The common experience of accidentally touching a hot stove and taking your hand back before you're even aware that anything's going on is explained by the fact that many of the processes by which we detect and avoid painful stimuli do not involve the cortex. In the case of the hand and stove, the brain is bypassed altogether; all the important neurochemical action takes place in the spine.

pain involve hard-core philosophy—metaphysics, epistemology, value theory, ethics. The fact that even the most highly evolved nonhuman mammals can't use language to communicate with us about their subjective mental experience is only the first layer of additional complication in trying to extend our reasoning about pain and morality to animals. And everything gets progressively more abstract and convolved as we move farther and farther out from the higher-type mammals into cattle and swine and dogs and cats and rodents, and then birds and fish, and finally invertebrates like lobsters.

The more important point here, though, is that the whole animal-cruelty-and-eating issue is not just complex, it's also uncomfortable. It is, at any rate, uncomfortable for me, and for just about everyone I know who enjoys a variety of foods and yet does not want to see herself as cruel or unfeeling. As far as I can tell, my own main way of dealing with this conflict has been to avoid thinking about the whole unpleasant thing. I should add that it appears to me unlikely that many readers of GOURMET wish to think hard about it, either, or to be queried about the morality of their eating habits in the pages of a culinary monthly. Since, however, the assigned subject of this article is what it was like to attend the 2003 MLF, and thus to spend several days in the midst of a great mass of Americans all eating lobster, and thus to be more or less impelled to think hard about lobster and the experience of buying and eating lobster, it turns out that there is no honest way to avoid certain moral questions.

There are several reasons for this. For one thing, it's not just that   20
lobsters get boiled alive, it's that you do it yourself—or at least it's done specifically for you, on-site.[12] As mentioned, the World's Largest Lobster

12. Morality-wise, let's concede that this cuts both ways. Lobster-eating is at least not abetted by the system of corporate factory farms that produces most beef, pork, and chicken. Because, if nothing else, of the way they're marketed and packaged for sale, we eat these latter meats without having to consider that they were once conscious, sentient creatures to whom horrible things were done. (N.B. PETA distributes a certain video—the title of which is being omitted as part of the elaborate editorial compromise by which this note appears at all—in which you can see just about everything meat-related you

Cooker, which is highlighted as an attraction in the Festival's program, is right out there on the MLF's north grounds for everyone to see. Try to imagine a Nebraska Beef Festival[13] at which part of the festivities is watching trucks pull up and the live cattle get driven down the ramp and slaughtered right there on the World's Largest Killing Floor or something—there's no way.

The intimacy of the whole thing is maximized at home, which of course is where most lobster gets prepared and eaten (although note already the semiconscious euphemism "prepared," which in the case of lobsters really means killing them right there in our kitchens). The basic scenario is that we come in from the store and make our little preparations like getting the kettle filled and boiling, and then we lift the lobsters out of the bag or whatever retail container they came home in. . . . whereupon some uncomfortable things start to happen. However stuporous the lobster is from the trip home, for instance, it tends to come alarmingly to life when placed in boiling water. If you're tilting it from a container into the steaming kettle, the lobster will sometimes try to cling to the container's sides or even to hook its claws over the kettle's rim like a person trying to keep from going over the edge of a roof. And worse is when the lobster's fully immersed. Even if you cover the kettle and turn away, you can usually hear the cover rattling and clanking as the lobster tries to push it off. Or the creature's claws scraping the sides of the kettle as it thrashes around. The lobster, in other words, behaves very much as you or I would behave if we were plunged

---

don't want to see or think about. (N.B. 2. Not that PETA's any sort of font of unspoken truth. Like many partisans in complex moral disputes, the PETA people are fanatics, and a lot of their rhetoric seems simplistic and self-righteous. Personally, though, I have to say that I found this unnamed video both credible and deeply upsetting.))

13. Is it significant that "lobster," "fish," and "chicken" are our culture's words for the animal and the meat, whereas most mammals seem to require euphemisms like "beef" and "pork" that help us separate the meat we eat from the living creature the meat once was? Is this evidence that some kind of deep unease about eating higher animals is endemic enough to show up in the English usage, but that the unease diminishes as we move out of the mammalian order? (And is "lamb"/"lamb" the counterexample that sinks the whole theory, or are there special, biblico-historical reasons for that equivalence?).

into boiling water (with the obvious exception of screaming).[14] A blunter way to say this is that the lobster acts as if it's in terrible pain, causing some cooks to leave the kitchen altogether and to take one of those little lightweight plastic oven timers with them into another room and wait until the whole process is over.

There happen to be two main criteria that most ethicists agree on for determining whether a living creature has the capacity to suffer and so has genuine interests that it may or may not be our moral duty to consider.[15] One is how much of the neurological hardware required for pain-experience the animal comes equipped with—nociceptors, prostaglandins, neuronal opioid receptors, etc. The other criterion is whether the animal demonstrates behavior associated with pain. And it takes a lot of intellectual gymnastics and behaviorist hairsplitting not to see struggling, thrashing, and lid-clattering as just such pain-behavior. According to marine zoologists, it usually takes lobsters between 35 and 45 seconds to die in boiling water. (No source I could find talked about how long it takes them to die in superheated steam; one rather hopes it's faster.)

There are, of course, other fairly common ways to kill your lobster on-site and so achieve maximum freshness. Some cooks' practice is to

14. There's a relevant populist myth about the high-pitched whistling sound that sometimes issues from a pot of boiling lobster. The sound is really vented steam from the layer of seawater between the lobster's flesh and its carapace (this is why shedders whistle more than hard-shells), but the pop version has it that the sound is the lobster's rabbitlike death scream. Lobsters communicate via pheromones in their urine and don't have anything close to the vocal equipment for screaming, but the myth's very persistent—which might, once again, point to a low-level cultural unease about boiling the thing.

15. "Interests" basically means strong and legitimate preferences, which obviously require some degree of consciousness, responsiveness to stimuli, etc. See, for instance, the utilitarian philosopher Peter Singer, whose 1974 *Animal Liberation* is more or less the bible of the modern animal-rights movement: "It would be nonsense to say that it was not in the interests of a stone to be kicked along the road by a schoolboy. A stone does not have interests because it cannot suffer. Nothing that we can do to it could possibly make any difference to its welfare. A mouse, on the other hand, does have an interest in not being kicked along the road, because it will suffer if it is."

drive a sharp heavy knife point-first into a spot just above the midpoint between the lobster's eyestalks (more or less where the Third Eye is in human foreheads). This is alleged either to kill the lobster instantly or to render it insensate—and is said at least to eliminate the cowardice involved in throwing a creature into boiling water and then fleeing the room. As far as I can tell from talking to proponents of the knife-in-the-head method, the idea is that it's more violent but ultimately more merciful, plus that a willingness to exert personal agency and accept responsibility for stabbing the lobster's head honors the lobster somehow and entitles one to eat it. (There's often a vague sort of Native American spirituality-of-the-hunt flavor to pro-knife arguments.) But the problem with the knife method is basic biology: Lobsters' nervous systems operate off not one but several ganglia, a.k.a. nerve bundles, which are sort of wired in series and distributed all along the lobster's underside, from stem to stern. And disabling only the frontal ganglion does not normally result in quick death or unconsciousness. Another alternative is to put the lobster in cold salt water and then very slowly bring it up to a full boil. Cooks who advocate this method are going mostly on the analogy to a frog, which can supposedly be kept from jumping out of a boiling pot by heating the water incrementally. In order to save a lot of research-summarizing, I'll simply assure you that the analogy between frogs and lobsters turns out not to hold.

Ultimately, the only certain virtues of the home-lobotomy and slow-heating methods are comparative, because there are even worse/crueler ways people prepare lobster. Time-thrifty cooks sometimes microwave them alive (usually after poking several extra vent holes in the carapace, which is a precaution most shellfish-microwavers learn about the hard way). Live dismemberment, on the other hand, is big in Europe: Some chefs cut the lobster in half before cooking; others like to tear off the claws and tail and toss only these parts in the pot.

And there's more unhappy news respecting suffering-criterion number one. Lobsters don't have much in the way of eyesight or hearing, but 25 they do have an exquisite tactile sense, one facilitated by hundreds of thousands of tiny hairs that protrude through their carapace. "Thus," in the words of T. M. Prudden's industry classic *About Lobster*, "it is that although encased in what seems a solid, impenetrable armor, the lobster can receive stimuli and impressions from without as readily as if it possessed a soft and delicate skin." And lobsters do have nociceptors,[16] as well as invertebrate versions of the prostaglandins and major neurotransmitters via which our own brains register pain.

Lobsters do not, on the other hand, appear to have the equipment for making or absorbing natural opioids like endorphins and enkephalins, which are what more advanced nervous systems use to try to handle intense pain. From this fact, though, one could conclude either that lobsters are maybe even *more* vulnerable to pain, since they lack mammalian nervous systems' built-in analgesia, or, instead, that the absence of natural opioids implies an absence of the really intense pain-sensations that natural opioids are designed to mitigate. I for one can detect a marked upswing in mood as I contemplate this latter possibility: It could be that their lack of endorphin/enkephalin hardware means that lobsters' raw subjective experience of pain is so radically different from mammals' that it may not even deserve the term *pain*. Perhaps lobsters are more like those frontal-lobotomy patients one reads about who report experiencing pain in a totally different way than you and I. These patients evidently do feel physical pain, neurologically speaking, but don't dislike it—though neither do they like it; it's more that they feel it but don't feel anything *about* it—the point being that the pain is not distressing to them or something they want to get away from. Maybe lobsters, who are also without frontal lobes, are detached from the neurological-registration-of-injury-or-hazard we call pain in just the same way. There is, after all, a difference between (1) pain as a purely neurological event,

16. This is the neurological term for special pain receptors that are (according to Jane A. Smith and Kenneth M. Boyd's *Lives in the Balance*) "sensitive to potentially damaging extremes of temperature, to mechanical forces, and to chemical substances which are released when body tissues are damaged."

and (2) actual suffering, which seems crucially to involve an emotional component, an awareness of pain as unpleasant, as something to fear/dislike/want to avoid.

Still, after all the abstract intellection, there remain the facts of the frantically clanking lid, the pathetic clinging to the edge of the pot. Standing at the stove, it is hard to deny in any meaningful way that this is a living creature experiencing pain and wishing to avoid/escape the painful experience. To my lay mind, the lobster's behavior in the kettle appears to be the expression of a *preference*; and it may well be that an ability to form preferences is the decisive criterion for real suffering.[17] The logic of this (preference → suffering) relation may be easiest to see in the negative case. If you cut certain kinds of worms in half, the halves will often keep crawling around and going about their vermiform business as if nothing had happened. When we assert, based on their post-op behavior, that these worms appear not to be suffering, what we're really saying is that there's no sign that the worms know anything bad has happened or would *prefer* not to have gotten cut in half.

Lobsters, however, are known to exhibit preferences. Experiments have shown that they can detect changes of only a degree or two in water temperature; one reason for their complex migratory cycles (which can often cover 100-plus miles a year) is to pursue the temperatures they like best.[18] And, as mentioned, they're bottom-dwellers and do not like bright

17. "Preference" is maybe roughly synonymous with "interest," but it is a better term for our purposes because it's less abstractly philosophical—"preference" seems more personal, and it's the whole idea of a living creature's personal experience that's at issue.

18. Of course, the most common sort of counterargument here would begin by objecting that "like best" is really just a metaphor, and a misleadingly anthropomorphic one at that. The counterarguer would posit that the lobster seeks to maintain a certain optimal ambient temperature out of nothing but unconscious instinct (with a similar explanation for the low-light affinities about to be mentioned in the main text). The thrust of such a counterargument will be that the lobster's thrashings and clankings in the kettle express not unpreferred pain but involuntary reflexes, like your leg shooting out when the doctor hits your knee. Be advised that there are professional scientists, including many researchers who use animals in experiments, who hold to the view that nonhuman creatures have no real feelings at all, only "behaviors." Be further advised that

light: If a tank of food lobsters is out in the sunlight or a store's fluorescence, the lobsters will always congregate in whatever part is darkest. Fairly solitary in the ocean, they also clearly dislike the crowding that's part of their captivity in tanks, since (as also mentioned) one reason why lobsters' claws are banded on capture is to keep them from attacking one another under the stress of close-quarter storage.

In any event, at the Festival, standing by the bubbling tanks outside the World's Largest Lobster Cooker, watching the fresh-caught lobsters pile over one another, wave their hobbled claws impotently, huddle in the rear corners, or scrabble frantically back from the glass as you approach, it is difficult not to sense that they're unhappy, or frightened, even if it's some rudimentary version of these feelings. . . . and, again, why does rudimentariness even enter into it? Why is a primitive, inarticulate form of suffering less urgent or uncomfortable for the person who's helping to inflict it by paying for the food it results in? I'm not trying to give you a PETA-like screed here—at least I don't think so. I'm trying, rather, to work out and articulate some of the troubling questions that arise amid all the laughter and saltation and community pride of the Maine Lobster Festival. The truth is that if you, the Festival attendee, permit yourself to think that lobsters can suffer and would rather not, the MLF can begin to take on aspects of something like a Roman circus or medieval torture-fest.

Does that comparison seem a bit much? If so, exactly why? Or what about this one: Is it not possible that future generations will regard our

---

this view has a long history that goes all the way back to Descartes, although its modern support comes mostly from behaviorist psychology.

To these what-look-like-pain-are-really-only-reflexes counterarguments, however, there happen to be all sorts of scientific and pro-animal-rights counter-counterarguments. And then further attempted rebuttals and redirects, and so on. Suffice to say that both the scientific and the philosophical arguments on either side of the animal-suffering issue are involved, abstruse, technical, often informed by self-interest or ideology, and in the end so totally inconclusive that as a practical matter, in the kitchen or restaurant, it all still seems to come down to individual conscience, going with (no pun) your gut.

own present agribusiness and eating practices in much the same way we now view Nero's entertainments or Aztec sacrifices? My own immediate reaction is that such a comparison is hysterical, extreme—and yet the reason it seems extreme to me appears to be that I believe animals are less morally important than human beings;[19] and when it comes to defending such a belief, even to myself, I have to acknowledge that (a) I have an obvious selfish interest in this belief, since I like to eat certain kinds of animals and want to be able to keep doing it, and (b) I have not succeeded in working out any sort of personal ethical system in which the belief is truly defensible instead of just selfishly convenient.

Given this article's venue and my own lack of culinary sophistication, I'm curious about whether the reader can identify with any of these reactions and acknowledgments and discomforts. I am also concerned not to come off as shrill or preachy when what I really am is confused. Given the (possible) moral status and (very possible) physical suffering of the animals involved, what ethical convictions do gourmets evolve that allow them not just to eat but to savor and enjoy flesh-based viands (since of course refined *enjoyment*, rather than just ingestion, is the whole point of gastronomy)? And for those gourmets who'll have no truck with convictions or rationales and who regard stuff like the previous paragraph as just so much pointless navel-gazing, what makes it feel okay, inside, to dismiss the whole issue out of hand? That is, is their refusal to think about any of this the product of actual thought, or is it just that they don't want to think about it? Do they ever think about their reluctance to think about it? After all, isn't being extra aware and attentive and thoughtful about one's food and its overall context part of what distinguishes a real gourmet? Or is all the gourmet's extra attention and sensibility just supposed to be aesthetic, gustatory?

19. Meaning a *lot* less important, apparently, since the moral comparison here is not the value of one human's life vs. the value of one animal's life, but rather the value of one animal's life vs. the value of one human's taste for a particular kind of protein. Even the most diehard carniphile will acknowledge that it's possible to live and eat well without consuming animals.

These last couple queries, though, while sincere, obviously involve much larger and more abstract questions about the connections (if any) between aesthetics and morality, and these questions lead straightaway into such deep and treacherous waters that it's probably best to stop the public discussion right here. There are limits to what even interested persons can ask of each other.

Thinking about the Text

1. Look carefully at the way David Foster Wallace organizes his essay. What do his opening paragraphs suggest this essay will be about? What is it about? What is his main point?

2. Wallace includes numerous footnotes—which is unusual for an article published in a popular magazine. What purposes do these footnotes serve? Why do you think he included them?

3. Wallace "considers the lobster" from several perspectives, describing the lobster festival, considering lobster biology, explaining how to cook a lobster, and examining the ethics of doing so. Research an event, object, animal, or person, and write an informative essay in which you consider your subject from several different perspectives.

BRIAN DOYLE

Joyas Voladoras

2004

BRIAN DOYLE (b. 1956) writes novels, short stories, essays, and poems. His essay collections include *Leaping: Revelations and Epiphanies* (2003) and *Children and Other Wild Animals* (2014). Doyle edits *Portland Magazine*, a quarterly publication covering University of Portland's campus life with a focus on spirituality and reflection. "Joyas Voladoras" was first published in the magazine *American Scholar* (2004) and then appeared in Doyle's book *The Wet Engine: Exploring the Mad Wild Miracle of the Heart* (2005).

ONSIDER THE HUMMINGBIRD FOR A LONG MOMENT. A hummingbird's heart beats ten times a second. A hummingbird's heart is the size of a pencil eraser. A hummingbird's heart is a lot of the hummingbird. *Joyas voladoras*, flying jewels, the first white explorers in the Americas called them, and the white men had never seen such creatures, for hummingbirds came into the world only in the Americas, nowhere else in the universe, more than three hundred species of them whirring and zooming and nectaring in hummer time zones nine times removed from ours, their hearts hammering faster than we could clearly hear if we pressed our elephantine ears to their infinitesimal chests.

Each one visits a thousand flowers a day. They can dive at sixty miles an hour. They can fly backward. They can fly more than five hundred miles without pausing to rest. But when they rest they come close to death: on frigid nights, or when they are starving, they retreat into torpor, their metabolic rate slowing to a fifteenth of their normal sleep rate, their hearts sludging nearly to a halt, barely beating, and if they are not soon warmed, if they do not soon find that which is sweet, their hearts grow cold, and they cease to be. Consider for a moment those hummingbirds who did not open their eyes again today, this very day, in the Americas: bearded helmetcrests and booted racket-tails, violet-tailed sylphs and violet-capped woodnymphs, crimson topazes and purple-crowned fairies, red-tailed comets and amethyst woodstars, rainbow-bearded thornbills and glittering-bellied emeralds, velvet-purple coronets and golden-bellied star-frontlets, fiery-tailed awlbills and Andean hillstars, spatuletails and pufflegs, each the most amazing thing you have never seen, each thunderous wild heart the size of an infant's fingernail, each mad heart silent, a brilliant music stilled.

Hummingbirds, like all flying birds but more so, have incredible enormous immense ferocious metabolisms. To drive those metabolisms they have racecar hearts that eat oxygen at an eye-popping rate. Their hearts are built of thinner, leaner fibers than ours. Their arteries are stiffer and more taut. They have more mitochondria in their heart muscles—anything to gulp more oxygen. Their hearts are stripped to the skin for the war against gravity and inertia, the mad search for food, the insane idea of flight. The price of their ambition is a life closer to death; they suffer more heart attacks and aneurysms and ruptures than any other living creature. It's expensive to fly. You burn out. You fry the machine. You melt the engine. Every creature on earth has approximately two billion heartbeats to spend in a lifetime. You can spend them slowly, like a tortoise, and live to be two hundred years old, or you can spend them fast, like a hummingbird, and live to be two years old.

The biggest heart in the world is inside the blue whale. It weighs more than seven tons. It's as big as a room. It *is* a room, with four chambers. A child could walk around in it, head high, bending only to step through the valves. The valves are as big as the swinging doors in a saloon. This house of a heart drives a creature a hundred feet long. When this creature is born it is twenty feet long and weighs four tons. It is waaaaay bigger than your car. It drinks a hundred gallons of milk from its mama every day and gains two hundred pounds a day, and when it is seven or eight years old it endures an unimaginable puberty and then it essentially disappears from human ken, for next to nothing is known of the mating habits, travel patterns, diet, social life, language, social structure, diseases, spirituality, wars, stories, despairs, and arts of the blue whale. There are perhaps ten thousand blue whales in the world, living in every ocean on earth, and of the largest mammal who ever lived we know nearly nothing. But we know this: the animals with the largest hearts in the world generally travel in pairs, and their penetrating moaning cries, their piercing yearning tongue, can be heard underwater for miles and miles.

Mammals and birds have hearts with four chambers. Reptiles and   5 turtles have hearts with three chambers. Fish have hearts with two chambers. Insects and mollusks have hearts with one chamber. Worms have hearts with one chamber, although they may have as many as eleven single-chambered hearts. Unicellular bacteria have no hearts at all; but even they have fluid eternally in motion, washing from one side of the cell to the other, swirling and whirling. No living being is without interior liquid motion. We all churn inside.

So much held in a heart in a lifetime. So much held in a heart in a day, an hour, a moment. We are utterly open with no one, in the end—not mother and father, not wife or husband, not lover, not child, not friend. We open windows to each but we live alone in the house of the heart. Perhaps we must. Perhaps we could not bear to be so naked, for fear of a constantly harrowed heart. When young we think there will come one person who will savor and sustain us always; when we are older we know this is the dream of a child, that all hearts finally are bruised and scarred, scored and torn, repaired by time and will, patched by force of character, yet fragile and rickety forevermore, no matter how ferocious the defense and how many bricks you bring to the wall. You can brick up your heart as stout and tight and hard and cold and impregnable as you possibly can and down it comes in an instant, felled by a woman's second glance, a child's apple breath, the shatter of glass in the road, the words "I have something to tell you," a cat with a broken spine dragging itself into the forest to die, the brush of your mother's papery ancient hand in the thicket of your hair, the memory of your father's voice early in the morning echoing from the kitchen where he is making pancakes for his children.

Thinking about the Text

1. What is Brian Doyle's main point, and how does the detailed information about animal and human hearts connect to and support that point?

2. Doyle compares and contrasts hummingbirds, blue whales, and humans. What are some of the comparisons he makes? What purpose do they serve, and how do they support his point?

3. Research a topic that interests you and write a lyric essay—one that includes details from your research and uses poetic elements such as metaphor and simile—in which you reflect on the topic in some way.

SANDRA STEINGRABER

Tune of the Tuna Fish

2006

SANDRA STEINGRABER (b. 1959) is a biologist and writer of nonfiction and poetry. Several of her books combine memoir and scientific writing about environmental issues: *Living Downstream: An Ecologist Looks at Cancer and the Environment* (1997), *Having Faith: An Ecologist's Journey to Motherhood* (2001), and *Raising Elijah: Protecting Our Children in an Age of Environmental Crisis* (2011). "Tune of the Tuna Fish" first appeared in the environmental magazine *Orion* (2006) and was later included in *Raising Elijah*.

T O COMMEMORATE MY DAUGHTER'S FIRST PIANO RECITAL last spring, my mother sent a package of old songbooks and sheet music that she had scooped from the bench of my own childhood piano, where they had undoubtedly sat for more than thirty years. Faith immediately seized on *The Red Book,* one of my very first lesson books, and began to sight-read some of the pieces. Her favorite was "Tune of the Tuna Fish" (copyright 1945), which introduces the key of F major. The cartoon drawing accompanying the song depicts a yodeling fish. The lyrics are as follows:

Tuna fish! Tuna fish! Sing a tune of tuna fish!
Tuna fish! Tuna fish! It's a favorite dish.
Everybody likes it so. From New York to Kokomo.
Tuna fish! Tuna fish! It's a favorite dish.

After we belted the song out a few times together, Faith asked, "Mama, what is a tuna fish? Have I ever eaten one?" In fact, she hadn't. Although tuna salad sandwiches were a mainstay of my own childhood diet, tuna has, during the time period between my childhood and my daughter's, become so contaminated with mercury that I choose not to buy it.

A few weeks later, at a potluck picnic, an elderly woman offered Faith a tuna salad sandwich. She loved it. On the ride home, she announced that she would like tuna sandwiches for her school lunches. She wants to eat one *every day.* I smiled that noncommittal motherly smile and said, "We'll see." She broke into song, "Everybody likes it so. From New York to Kokomo. . . ."

A month after that, Faith walked up to me with an alarmed look. Is it true, she wanted to know, that tuna fish have mercury in them? And mercury poisons children? Will she die from eating that sandwich at the picnic? I was able to reassure her that she was fine, but I was left wondering where she'd heard all this. Then I noticed that I'd left out on my office desk a copy of an article about the impact of mercury on fetal brain growth and development. It was one that I myself had authored. Could she have seen it? At age six, can she read well enough to have figured it out?

Other than the twenty-three chromosomes that each of us parents contributes to our offspring during the moment of conception, their growing bodies are entirely made up of rearranged molecules of air, food, and water. Our children are the jet stream, the food web, and the water cycle. Whatever is in the environment is also in them. We know that this now includes hundreds of industrial pollutants. A recent study of umbilical cord blood, collected by the Red Cross from ten newborns and analyzed in two different laboratories, revealed the presence of pesticides, stain removers, wood preservatives, heavy metals, and industrial lubricants, as well as the wastes from burning coal, garbage, and gasoline. Of the 287 chemicals detected, 180 were suspected carcinogens, 217 were toxic to the brain and nervous system, and 208 have been linked to abnormal development and birth defects in lab animals.

One of these chemicals was methylmercury, the form of mercury 5 found in fish. Its presence in umbilical cord blood is especially troubling because methylmercury has been shown to paralyze migrating fetal brain cells and halt their cell division. As a result, the architecture of the brain is subtly altered in ways that can lead to learning disabilities, delayed mental development, and shortened attention spans in later childhood. Moreover, the placenta actively pumps methylmercury into the umbilical cord, raising the concentration of mercury in fetal blood above that of the mother's own blood. Most pregnant mothers probably don't realize that when they eat tuna, the mercury within is transferred to and concentrated in the blood of their unborn babies.

Recently, I've been talking with my children about why we buy organically grown food. I've explained to Faith and her younger brother, Elijah, that I like to give my food dollars to farmers who sustain the soil, are kind to their animals, and don't use chemicals that poison birds, fish, and toads. I add that I like to buy food that is grown right here in our own county. It tastes better and doesn't require lots of gasoline to get to our house. I haven't shared with them the results of the 2003 Seattle study, which revealed that children with conventional diets had, on average, nine times more insecticide residues in their urine than those who ate organic produce.

But there is no "organic" option for buying tuna. No mercury-free tuna exists. When mercury from coal-burning power plants rains down from the atmosphere into the world's oceans, ancient anaerobic bacteria found in marine sediments transform this heavy metal into methylmercury, which is quickly siphoned up the food chain. Because tuna is a top-of-the-food chain predator, methylmercury inexorably concentrates in the flesh of its muscle tissue. There is no special way of cleaning or cooking tuna that would lower its body burden. Nor is there any way of keeping mercury from trespassing into a child's brain, once he or she consumes the tuna. Nor is there a way of preventing those molecules of mercury from interfering with brain cell functioning. In that sense, the problem of tuna fish is more akin to the problem of air and water pollution: it is not a problem we can shop our way out of.

Recognizing the potential for methylmercury to create neurological problems in children, the U.S. Food and Drug Administration has now promulgated advisories and guidelines on how much tuna is safe for pregnant women and children—as well as nursing mothers and women who might become pregnant—to eat in a month's time. There is debate about whether these current restrictions are protective enough. But even if they are sufficient, I find them highly impractical. Children do not want to eat a food they like once a month, or even once a week. In my experience, when children discover a new food item to their liking, they want it all the time. They want it for breakfast, lunch, and dinner from here to Sunday. Children's dining habits are, for mysterious reasons, highly ritualized. Elijah, for example, consumed two avocados a day for the better part of his second year. I vaguely recall one summer when I, at about age seven, ate liver sausage on Saltines as part of every meal.

How, then, do you explain to a young child with a tuna jones that she'll have to wait until next month before she can have her favorite dish again? Do you tell her that she's already consumed her monthly quota of a known brain poison, as determined by the federal government? Or do you make up some other excuse?

I eventually sat down with Faith and showed her the article I had written. I said that I was working hard to stop the mercury contamination of seafood so that she could someday enjoy tuna without needing to worry. I said that keeping mercury out of tuna required generating electricity in some way other than burning coal, which is why her father and I support solar energy and wind power.

Soon after, we went hiking in the woods near the day camp she had attended earlier in the summer. Faith summarized for me the history of the old stone building where snakes and turtles are housed in one wing and bunk beds fill the other. It was originally built, she explained, as a *pre-ven-tor-i-um*. Children whose parents were sick with tuberculosis were brought there to live so they wouldn't get sick, too. In fact, I already knew the history of the Cayuga Nature Center but was, nonetheless, amazed at my daughter's ability to recount this information. I tried to gauge whether she was worried about the idea of children being separated from their families because of disease. "You know," I said, "we don't have to worry about tuberculosis anymore. We fixed that problem." She said she knew that. That's why the building had been turned into a camp for everyone.

The top of the hill offered a view across Cayuga Lake. On the far bank floated the vaporous emissions from New York State Electric and Gas Corporation's Cayuga Plant, whose coal-burning stacks were plainly visible against an otherwise cloudless sky. It's one of the state's biggest emitters of mercury. In the year my daughter was born, the Cayuga facility released 323 pounds of mercury into the environment. Pointing it out to Faith, I said that's where the mercury comes from that gets inside the fish. I said that I hoped one day we could fix that problem, too. She thought about it a minute and said, then they can do something else with the building.

Thinking about the Text

1. What is Sandra Steingraber's purpose in writing this essay? Why do you think she uses both anecdotes about her children and scientific information about mercury and its effects?

2. Steingraber suggests several ways of dealing with the contamination of tuna. Which potential solutions does she find inadequate, and why? What better solutions does she offer?

3. Identify a problem, then write an essay in which you show why that problem is significant, describe how others have tried to address the issue (perhaps inadequately), and then offer a solution or course of action you believe is more effective.

ALISON BECHDEL

from Fun Home

2006

ALISON BECHDEL (b. 1960) is a cartoonist and writer of graphic memoirs. She is the author of the comic strip *Dykes to Watch Out For*, which included what's come to be known as "the Bechdel test" for evaluating films and other media: to pass the test, the piece must include two women who speak to one another about something other than a man. She's written two graphic memoirs: *Fun Home: A Family Tragicomic* (2006) and *Are You My Mother?: A Comic Drama* (2012). She was awarded a MacArthur "genius" Fellowship in 2014. This selection is from the first chapter of *Fun Home*.

OLD FATHER, OLD ARTIFICER

LIKE MANY FATHERS, MINE COULD OCCASIONALLY BE PREVAILED ON FOR A SPOT OF "AIRPLANE."

AS HE LAUNCHED ME, MY FULL WEIGHT WOULD FALL ON THE PIVOT POINT BETWEEN HIS FEET AND MY STOMACH.

OOF!

IT WAS A DISCOMFORT WELL WORTH THE RARE PHYSICAL CONTACT, AND CERTAINLY WORTH THE MOMENT OF PERFECT BALANCE WHEN I SOARED ABOVE HIM.

IN THE CIRCUS, ACROBATICS WHERE ONE PERSON LIES ON THE FLOOR BALANCING ANOTHER ARE CALLED "ICARIAN GAMES."

CONSIDERING THE FATE OF ICARUS AFTER HE FLOUTED HIS FATHER'S ADVICE AND FLEW SO CLOSE TO THE SUN HIS WINGS MELTED, PERHAPS SOME DARK HUMOR IS INTENDED.

BUT BEFORE HE DID SO, HE MANAGED TO GET QUITE A LOT DONE.

HIS GREATEST ACHIEVEMENT, ARGUABLY, WAS HIS MONOMANIACAL RESTORATION OF OUR OLD HOUSE.

WHEN OTHER CHILDREN CALLED OUR HOUSE A MANSION, I WOULD DEMUR. I RESENTED THE IMPLICATION THAT MY FAMILY WAS RICH, OR UNUSUAL IN ANY WAY.

IN FACT, WE WERE UNUSUAL, THOUGH I WOULDN'T APPRECIATE EXACTLY HOW UNUSUAL UNTIL MUCH LATER. BUT WE WERE NOT RICH.

THE GILT CORNICES, THE MARBLE FIREPLACE, THE CRYSTAL CHANDELIERS, THE SHELVES OF CALF-BOUND BOOKS--THESE WERE NOT SO MUCH BOUGHT AS PRODUCED FROM THIN AIR BY MY FATHER'S REMARKABLE LEGERDEMAIN.

MY FATHER COULD SPIN GARBAGE...

...INTO GOLD.

HE COULD TRANSFIGURE A ROOM WITH THE SMALLEST OFFHAND FLOURISH.

HE COULD CONJURE AN ENTIRE, FINISHED PERIOD INTERIOR FROM A PAINT CHIP.

HE WAS AN ALCHEMIST OF APPEARANCE, A SAVANT OF SURFACE, A DAEDALUS OF DECOR.

FOR IF MY FATHER WAS ICARUS, HE WAS ALSO DAEDALUS--THAT SKILLFUL ARTIFICER, THAT MAD SCIENTIST WHO BUILT THE WINGS FOR HIS SON AND DESIGNED THE FAMOUS LABYRINTH...

THIS IS THE WALLPAPER FOR MY ROOM?

...AND WHO ANSWERED NOT TO THE LAWS OF SOCIETY, BUT TO THOSE OF HIS CRAFT.

BUT I **HATE** PINK! I **HATE** FLOWERS!

TOUGH TITTY.

HISTORICAL RESTORATION WASN'T HIS JOB.

(TWELFTH-GRADE ENGLISH)

ARCHI-TECTURAL DIGEST

IT WAS HIS PASSION. AND I MEAN PASSION IN EVERY SENSE OF THE WORD.

LIBIDINAL. MANIC. MARTYRED.

OUR GOTHIC REVIVAL HOUSE HAD BEEN BUILT DURING THE SMALL PENNSYLVANIA TOWN'S ONE BRIEF MOMENT OF WEALTH, FROM THE LUMBER INDUSTRY, IN 1867.

BUT LOCAL FORTUNES HAD DECLINED STEADILY FROM THAT POINT, AND WHEN MY PARENTS BOUGHT THE PLACE IN 1962, IT WAS A SHELL OF ITS FORMER SELF.

THE SHUTTERS AND SCROLLWORK WERE GONE. THE CLAPBOARDS HAD BEEN SHEATHED WITH SCABROUS SHINGLES.

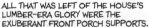

THE BARE LIGHTBULBS REVEALED DINGY
WARTIME WALLPAPER AND WOODWORK
PAINTED PASTEL GREEN.

ALL THAT WAS LEFT OF THE HOUSE'S
LUMBER-ERA GLORY WERE THE
EXUBERANT FRONT PORCH SUPPORTS.

BUT OVER THE NEXT EIGHTEEN YEARS, MY FATHER WOULD RESTORE THE HOUSE TO
ITS ORIGINAL CONDITION, AND THEN SOME.

JESUS! THIS
MUST BE THE PATTERN
FOR THE ORIGINAL
BARGEBOARD!

HE WOULD PERFORM, AS DAEDALUS DID, DAZZLING DISPLAYS OF ARTFULNESS.

HE WOULD CULTIVATE THE BARREN YARD...

...INTO A LUSH, FLOWERING LANDSCAPE.

HE WOULD MANIPULATE FLAGSTONES THAT WEIGHED HALF A TON...

...AND THE THINNEST, QUIVERING LAYERS OF GOLD LEAF.

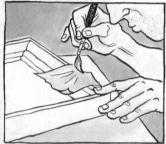

IT COULD HAVE BEEN A ROMANTIC STORY, LIKE IN *IT'S A WONDERFUL LIFE*, WHEN JIMMY STEWART AND DONNA REED FIX UP THAT BIG OLD HOUSE AND RAISE THEIR FAMILY THERE.

BUT IN THE MOVIE WHEN JIMMY STEWART COMES HOME ONE NIGHT AND STARTS YELLING AT EVERYONE...

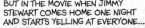

...IT'S OUT OF THE ORDINARY.

DAEDALUS, TOO, WAS INDIFFERENT TO THE HUMAN COST OF HIS PROJECTS.

HE BLITHELY BETRAYED THE KING, FOR EXAMPLE, WHEN THE QUEEN ASKED HIM TO BUILD HER A COW DISGUISE SO SHE COULD SEDUCE THE WHITE BULL.

INDEED, THE RESULT OF THAT SCHEME--A HALF-BULL, HALF-MAN MONSTER--INSPIRED DAEDALUS'S GREATEST CREATION YET.

HE HID THE MINOTAUR IN THE LABYRINTH-- A MAZE OF PASSAGES AND ROOMS OPENING ENDLESSLY INTO ONE ANOTHER...

...AND FROM WHICH, AS STRAY YOUTHS AND MAIDENS DISCOVERED TO THEIR PERIL...

...ESCAPE WAS IMPOSSIBLE.

THEN THERE ARE THOSE FAMOUS WINGS. WAS DAEDALUS REALLY STRICKEN WITH GRIEF WHEN ICARUS FELL INTO THE SEA?

OR JUST DISAPPOINTED BY THE DESIGN FAILURE?

SOMETIMES, WHEN THINGS WERE GOING WELL, I THINK MY FATHER ACTUALLY ENJOYED HAVING A FAMILY.

AND OF COURSE, MY BROTHERS AND I WERE FREE LABOR. DAD CONSIDERED US EXTENSIONS OF HIS OWN BODY, LIKE PRECISION ROBOT ARMS.

OR AT LEAST, THE AIR OF AUTHENTICITY WE LENT TO HIS EXHIBIT. A SORT OF STILL LIFE WITH CHILDREN.

PUT HOT, SOAPY WATER IN THE SINK AND GET SOME CLEAN RAGS.

IN THIS REGARD, IT WAS LIKE BEING RAISED NOT BY JIMMY BUT BY MARTHA STEWART.

IN THEORY, HIS ARRANGEMENT WITH MY MOTHER WAS MORE COOPERATIVE.

IN PRACTICE, IT WAS NOT.

WHAT DO YOU THINK OF THIS GAS CHANDELIER?

BORDELLO.

AUCTION CATALOG

WE EACH RESISTED IN OUR OWN WAYS, BUT IN THE END WE WERE EQUALLY POWERLESS BEFORE MY FATHER'S CURATORIAL ONSLAUGHT.

MY BROTHERS AND I COULDN'T COMPETE WITH THE ASTRAL LAMPS AND GIRANDOLES AND HEPPLEWHITE SUITE CHAIRS. THEY WERE PERFECT.

I GREW TO RESENT THE WAY MY FATHER TREATED HIS FURNITURE LIKE CHILDREN, AND HIS CHILDREN LIKE FURNITURE.

MY OWN DECIDED PREFERENCE FOR THE UNADORNED AND PURELY FUNCTIONAL EMERGED EARLY.

I WAS SPARTAN TO MY FATHER'S ATHENIAN.

MODERN TO HIS VICTORIAN.

BUTCH TO HIS NELLY.

UTILITARIAN TO HIS AESTHETE.

I DEVELOPED A CONTEMPT FOR USE-
LESS ORNAMENT. WHAT FUNCTION WAS
SERVED BY THE SCROLLS, TASSELS, AND
BRIC-A-BRAC THAT INFESTED OUR HOUSE?

IF ANYTHING, THEY OBSCURED FUNCTION.
THEY WERE EMBELLISHMENTS IN THE
WORST SENSE.

INCIPIENT
YELLOW
LUNG
DISEASE

PLING
KLINK

THEY WERE LIES.

MY FATHER BEGAN TO SEEM MORALLY
SUSPECT TO ME LONG BEFORE I KNEW
THAT HE ACTUALLY HAD A DARK SECRET.

MOM SAYS
HURRY UP.

"BRONZING
STICK"

HE USED HIS SKILLFUL ARTIFICE NOT TO MAKE THINGS, BUT TO MAKE THINGS APPEAR
TO BE WHAT THEY WERE NOT.

MASS WILL BE
OVER BEFORE WE
GET THERE.

THAT IS TO SAY,
IMPECCABLE.

HE APPEARED TO BE AN IDEAL HUSBAND AND FATHER, FOR EXAMPLE.

BUT WOULD AN IDEAL HUSBAND AND FATHER HAVE SEX WITH TEENAGE BOYS?

IT'S TEMPTING TO SUGGEST, IN RETRO-SPECT, THAT OUR FAMILY WAS A SHAM.

THAT OUR HOUSE WAS NOT A REAL HOME AT ALL BUT THE SIMULACRUM OF ONE, A MUSEUM.

YET WE REALLY WERE A FAMILY, AND WE REALLY DID LIVE IN THOSE PERIOD ROOMS.

I CAN'T FIND THE SCISSORS!

LOOK IN THE CHIPPEN-DALE.

STILL, SOMETHING VITAL WAS MISSING.

WELL?

ME, AGE 4

MY BROTHER CHRISTIAN, AGE 3

AN ELASTICITY, A MARGIN FOR ERROR.

HOW DID THIS VASE GET SO CLOSE TO THE EDGE OF THE TABLE?

BUT I DIDN'T DO ANYTHING!

MOST PEOPLE, I IMAGINE, LEARN TO ACCEPT THAT THEY'RE NOT PERFECT.

BUT AN IDLE REMARK ABOUT MY FATHER'S TIE OVER BREAKFAST COULD SEND HIM INTO A TAILSPIN.

PEACE, MAN.

MY MOTHER ESTABLISHED A RULE.

DON'T CHANGE IT! WE'RE LATE!

ALSO AN ENGLISH TEACHER

NO COMMENTS ON HIS APPEARANCE. IS THAT UNDERSTOOD?

WHAT IF IT'S SOMETHING GOOD?

GOOD, BAD, IT DOESN'T MATTER.

IF WE COULDN'T CRITICIZE MY FATHER, SHOWING AFFECTION FOR HIM WAS AN EVEN DICIER VENTURE.

WE WERE NOT A PHYSICALLY EXPRESSIVE FAMILY, TO SAY THE LEAST. BUT ONCE I WAS UNACCOUNTABLY MOVED TO KISS MY FATHER GOOD NIGHT.

HAVING LITTLE PRACTICE WITH THE GESTURE, ALL I MANAGED WAS TO GRAB HIS HAND AND BUSS THE KNUCKLES LIGHTLY...

...AS IF HE WERE A BISHOP OR AN ELEGANT LADY, BEFORE RUSHING FROM THE ROOM IN EMBARRASSMENT.

THIS EMBARRASSMENT ON MY PART WAS A TINY SCALE MODEL OF MY FATHER'S MORE FULLY DEVELOPED SELF-LOATHING.

HIS SHAME INHABITED OUR HOUSE AS PERVASIVELY AND INVISIBLY AS THE AROMATIC MUSK OF AGING MAHOGANY.

IN FACT, THE METICULOUS, PERIOD INTERIORS WERE EXPRESSLY DESIGNED TO CONCEAL IT.

MIRRORS, DISTRACTING BRONZES, MULTIPLE DOORWAYS. VISITORS OFTEN GOT LOST UPSTAIRS.

MY MOTHER, MY BROTHERS, AND I KNEW OUR WAY AROUND WELL ENOUGH, BUT IT WAS IMPOSSIBLE TO TELL IF THE MINOTAUR LAY BEYOND THE NEXT CORNER.

AND THE CONSTANT TENSION WAS HEIGHT-ENED BY THE FACT THAT SOME ENCOUN-TERS COULD BE QUITE PLEASANT.

HIS BURSTS OF KINDNESS WERE AS INCAN-DESCENT AS HIS TANTRUMS WERE DARK.

ALTHOUGH I'M GOOD AT ENUMERATING MY FATHER'S FLAWS, IT'S HARD FOR ME TO SUSTAIN MUCH ANGER AT HIM.

STOP SPLASHING!

IN MY EYES!

HOLD STILL, DAMMIT!

MY MOTHER MUST HAVE BATHED ME HUNDREDS OF TIMES. BUT IT'S MY FATHER RINSING ME OFF WITH THE PURPLE METAL CUP THAT I REMEMBER MOST CLEARLY.

THE SUFFUSION OF WARMTH AS THE HOT WATER SLUICED OVER ME...

...THE SUDDEN, UNBEARABLE COLD OF ITS ABSENCE.

AGAIN!

WAS HE A GOOD FATHER? I WANT TO SAY, "AT LEAST HE STUCK AROUND." BUT OF COURSE, HE DIDN'T.

IT'S TRUE THAT HE DIDN'T KILL HIMSELF UNTIL I WAS NEARLY TWENTY.

BUT HIS ABSENCE RESONATED RETRO-ACTIVELY, ECHOING BACK THROUGH ALL THE TIME I KNEW HIM.

MAYBE IT WAS THE CONVERSE OF THE WAY AMPUTEES FEEL PAIN IN A MISSING LIMB.

HE REALLY WAS THERE ALL THOSE YEARS, A FLESH-AND-BLOOD PRESENCE STEAMING OFF THE WALLPAPER, DIGGING UP THE DOGWOODS, POLISHING THE FINIALS...

...SMELLING OF SAWDUST AND SWEAT AND DESIGNER COLOGNE.

BUT I ACHED AS IF HE WERE ALREADY GONE.

Thinking about the Text

1. Alison Bechdel makes a connection between the house in which she grew up and her father. What similarity does Bechdel see in her father's approach to his house and to his family? What point is she making about appearance and artifice in this essay?

2. Look carefully at the drawings that accompany the words in this narrative. What elements of Bechdel's childhood do the images reveal more explicitly than the words do?

3. Bechdel alludes to popular culture and Greek mythology in writing about her own experience. Trace one of these allusions throughout her text, and write an essay analyzing the effects of that allusion.

JOEY FRANKLIN

Working at Wendy's

2006

JOEY FRANKLIN (b. 1980) writes nonfiction and teaches creative writing at Brigham Young University. He is the author
of *My Wife Wants You to Know I'm Happily Married* (2015) and
of essays that have appeared in *Poets & Writers*, the *Writer's
Chronicle*, *Gettysburg Review*, and other literary journals.
"Working at Wendy's" was first published in *Twentysomething Essays by Twentysomething Writers* (2006).

I T'S 8:45 P.M., AND I AM STANDING IN FRONT OF THE COUNTER at Wendy's. It smells of French fries and mop water. In my right hand I hold my résumé. I don't know if I need a résumé to apply for the Wendy's night shift, but I bring it anyway. It anchors me as I drift toward the sixteen-year-old kid behind the counter and ask to speak to his manager.

"One mandarin orange salad?" the boy asks.

"Uh, no. Actually, I'd like to speak to the *manager*." As the cashier retreats to the back of the store, I recognize a large kid with curly hair working the fryer—he used to play football with some of the members of my Boy Scout troop. He looks up at me, and I avert my eyes. Part of me wants to turn around and leave before the manager comes out. A couple in their twenties walks into the restaurant behind me. I step away from the counter and pretend to read the menu, holding my résumé close to my chest. The urge to leave increases. Just then the manager comes out and asks, "You here about the night shift?"

As I hand the manager my résumé, I realize it is a mistake. He doesn't want to know my service experience, or my academic references, or my GPA. All he wants to know is if I can spell my name correctly.

"Er, the application is over there," the manager says, handing me back my résumé and pointing to a file folder mounted on the wall next to the counter. I take the application to an empty table in the corner of the restaurant and hunch over it, wishing I had a drink, or a hamburger, or something to put on the table beside me.

The next day I go for an interview with the hiring manager. I sit down at a table in the lobby and answer two questions: "What hours do you want to work?" and "When can you start?"

When he was sixteen, my brother, Josh, got his first job at McDonald's. He lasted two weeks before deciding the greasy uniform and salty mop water weren't worth $5.25 an hour. His manager used to show off rejected applications to the other employees in the back of the store.

Most were high school dropouts looking for spending money, but a few had college degrees. One application was from a doctor who had recently left his practice because he "couldn't handle the mortality rate."

I think about that doctor now as I sit in a small back room at Wendy's. I have just watched thirty minutes of training videos about customer service, floor mopping, heavy lifting, and armed robbery. Chelsea, the training manager, hands me two neatly folded uniforms and a brand-new hat. Holding the hat in my hand, I look out into the kitchen at my new coworkers. At the fryer is the large high school kid I remember from the night before. A skinny brown-haired Asian-looking boy who must be about nineteen years old is washing dishes. Two girls are at the front of the store taking orders, and the manager is on the phone with an angry customer. "Can I do this?" I ask myself, and put on my hat.

Chelsea is pregnant. During our training session, I guess she is about six months along. It turns out she is due in three days. "This is my last week on the day shift," she says. "After the baby is born, I'll be back on nights." This is her first child, she explains, and says she is looking forward to being a mom. She smiles as she pats her stomach and asks about my son.

"Eighteen months," I tell her, "a real handful." I explain that I want   10
to work nights so I can take care of my son during the day while my wife finishes her last semester of college. I ask about the pay, but I already know her answer. "We start at five-seventy-five," she says, "but the night guys get six." I ask her what she thinks about $7. She says she'll see what she can do.

Chelsea trains me on Tuesday and goes into labor on Wednesday. I don't see her again for three weeks.

Kris Livingston's mom ran the register at the Taco Bell on the corner of Lombard Street and Allen Boulevard in a poorer section of Beaverton, Oregon. Her name was Dawn. She was divorced and had three boys. She shared a three-bedroom apartment with another single mom and her own five children. They listened to Snoop Dogg and Ice-T, drank forty-ounce malt liquors, and walked over two miles round-trip every Saturday to watch the neighborhood boys play basketball at Schiffler Park.

On welfare-check days, Dawn went grocery shopping and brought home twelve-packs of Pepsi, stacks of frozen steaks, crinkly bags of potato chips, several gallons of 2-percent milk, and bag after bag of Malt-O-Meal cereal. The week before welfare checks came, they ate eggs and instant ramen—lots of ramen.

Her son Kris was my best friend in sixth grade. We often walked to Taco Bell together to visit his mother. She usually bought us a taco while we sat in a booth in the corner of the store and talked about bicycles, girls, and football. Once, on the way home from visiting his mom, Kris said, "She used to sell drugs, you know. We had plenty of money, and nobody thought she was a bad mom then."

My first night on the job, I work with Dave. He is seventeen years old,   15
five-ten, and keeps his hair short, like a soldier. He goes to an alternative high school if he wakes up in time and is looking forward to enlisting in the military when he turns eighteen. His dad, who recently remarried and moved, told Dave he would have to find his own place to live. When Dave isn't sleeping on his friends' couches, he lives in his car, a 1982 Volkswagen Rabbit with a hole in the floor just beneath the gas pedal.

Dave works with me a few nights a week and knows the business well. He's quick with a mop, can make all the sandwiches blindfolded, and has the entire computer memorized. When he's not working, he hangs out in the restaurant lobby trying to steal Frosties and old fries when no one is looking. The manager says she will give him food if he needs it and asks that he not steal anymore. "Asking gets you nowhere," he says, and keeps stealing.

Because I live just two blocks from the store, I recognize a disproportionate number of the late-night drive-through customers. Mostly, I see parents of the scouts I work with, or other scout leaders, and occasionally a friend from school. When they pull up to the window and see me in the Wendy's hat and headphones, the following conversation ensues:

"Joey, I didn't know you worked here! How's it going?"

"Good, good. Just flipping burgers."

"Hey, you've got to do what you've got to do." 20

Then I explain the job is temporary, and it's the only job in town that allows me to work at night so I can watch my son during the day while my wife finishes school. I tell them in another month I'll be back in school and working at a better-paying, less humiliating campus job.

One evening a fellow scout leader comes through, and after an exchange similar to the one described above, he says, "Hey, more power to ya. I know a lot of people who think they're above that." He thanks me as I hand him his triple cheeseburger, and he drives around the corner and out of sight.

At 250 pounds, Danny really fills out his uniform. He played varsity football for the local high school, has earned his Eagle Scout award, and knows his way around a car engine. On several occasions he has changed spark plugs, jumped batteries, and even replaced brakes on the cars of fellow employees, usually right in the store parking lot.

Wendy's is the first job Danny has ever had. With six months' experience, he is the senior employee and is being considered for a management position. He brings in about $1,000 a month, much of which he gives to his grandmother. At closing, he always saves the good salads for me and talks the manager into letting me go home early. He likes listening to Metallica, working on his Trans Am, and talking with Tonya, a high school junior who also works at the store.

While I'm washing my hands in the bathroom at work, a well-groomed 25 twentysomething man standing at the sink next to me starts a conversation. "Do you like working the night shift?" he asks.

"It's not bad," I say, shaking my wet hands over the sink.

"How long have you worked here?"

"Two weeks."

"Have you ever thought about college?" he asks. I want to tell him I'm in the top 5 percent of students at my college, that I am two semesters away from graduating, and that I'm on my way to grad school to get a Ph.D. in English literature. Instead, I shrug and tell him the same line I tell everyone: "Oh yeah, I'm just working here until my wife finishes." He doesn't believe me. To him, I look like another wasted life, another victim. He thinks I got my girlfriend pregnant, that I never graduated from high school, that I can't do any better than flip burgers at two in the morning. He feels sorry for my kids.

"I only applied here because I knew I would get hired," says Sara the first   30
night I work with her. She is a nineteen-year-old single mother with a sixteen-month-old boy. She is very tall and wears her long brown hair in a ponytail pulled through the hole in the back of her Wendy's hat. I ask her why she needed a job so bad.

"I had to get one," she tells me. "My parole officer said it was the only way to stay out of jail." I start at this and then ask, "Why were you in jail?"

"Drugs," she says, and pauses, testing me. "I was wearing my boy-friend's jacket, and the cops found a heroin pipe in the pocket." I ask how long she was in jail. "One year," she tells me. "I just got out a month ago."

When I was in fifth grade, my dad got a job delivering pizza. As an eleven-year-old, pivoting on that blurry edge between boyhood and adolescence, I found myself bragging to my friends about the prospect of free pizza and then wishing I hadn't told them anything about my father's job. He worked a few nights a week, and when he came home, his uniform smelled like steaming cardboard and burnt cheese, but he always brought home pizza.

Oren is nineteen years old and works at Wendy's to pay for a cell-phone bill and to get out of the house. His parents are devout Mormons and think he is a disgrace to their entire family. He wants to sell marijuana because he believes he can do nothing else. "I don't do anything well," he tells me one night while washing dishes. "I don't know what I want to do with my life." He asks Sara to find some pot for him to sell.

Oren's mother is Japanese, born and raised, and speaks to her children in her native tongue. That means Oren speaks Japanese and has family connections in Japan.

Oren also owns an AK-47 and likes to go up into the canyons and shoot jackrabbits. He showed me a picture once of a rabbit carcass out in the desert, its innards all blown out and dangling for the camera.

Tonight, while working the grill, Danny tells me he has never been on a date. "Girls don't like me," he says as he flips a row of sizzling, square quarter-pound patties. I can tell he believes it. Danny, by his own admission, is the kind of guy whom girls like for support. He is a gentleman, he asks thoughtful questions, and he's always willing to talk. He thinks his weight and his scruff turn girls off. He tells me he is going to ask Tonya to a movie this weekend but isn't sure she'll say yes. Later, Tonya comes into the store, and Danny disappears with her for a few minutes out in the lobby. He comes back with a large smile on his face and says, "I've got a date this weekend, can you work for me?"

I don't like when Dave works the front line with me. I can't make sandwiches very fast yet, and he gets tired of waiting. More than once he pushes me aside to finish an order. If he sees me hesitate on a step, he barks at me, "Red, green, red, green! Ketchup, pickle, tomato, lettuce! Come on, Joe, it's not that hard."

Later, while I'm mopping the floor at closing, Dave comes by and takes the mop from my hand. "Like this," he says, scrubbing the tile vigorously. He thrusts the mop back in my hands and walks away, rolling his eyes.

Chelsea is back at work tonight for the first time since having her baby. She appears fairly happy, and I am surprised at how well adjusted she seems to being a working mom. The phone rings several times, and

35

40

Chelsea takes the calls in her office. She tells me her husband has lots of questions about putting the baby to bed. After the lobby closes, Chelsea disappears into the bathroom for nearly half an hour. This happens every time I work with her. I wonder if she is sick. Then I notice the breast pump in a case on her desk. Another employee tells me Chelsea has been expressing milk in one of the bathroom stalls on her breaks.

Danny and Tonya have been dating for two weeks. He shows up for his shift an hour early to see her before she gets off. They sit in the lobby holding hands and talking for almost the entire hour. When they're not in the store together, she sends text messages to his phone, which I catch him reading while he stands at the grill.

Tonight Danny approaches me while I'm opening boxes of French fries. He wants advice on how to ask Tonya to her junior prom. "I want to do something romantic," he says. I suggest Shakespeare's eighteenth sonnet. He has never heard of it. "'Shall I compare thee to a summer's day . . .'" I recite. "She'll love it." I print off the sonnet at home and bring it to work for him the next day. He writes it in a card and delivers it with flowers. Two weeks later, in a rented tux at Tonya's junior prom, Danny gets his first kiss.

I call my dad tonight. He asks about school, about my son, and about work. I tell him about Wendy's.

"What? Who?" he says.

"Me. I got a job at Wendy's." Long pause. "I needed a job I could do   45
at night." More silence. "It's not so bad." Still silence. "I work from nine
P.M. to one A.M. a few nights a week."

Just when I think the line must be disconnected, Dad clears his throat and asks, "What happened to your computer job?"

"The guy ran out of work for me."

"Oh." More silence. I imagine he looks around the room to make sure no one is listening before he says, "Wendy's? When did that happen?" I want to tell him that it didn't *happen*, that it wasn't an accident, but

I am stuck wondering how to make him understand, and at the same time wondering why I should have to explain anything at all. I wonder what his reaction would be if I had chosen to get more student loans instead of the part-time job. I choose to say nothing. Then I offer him my employee discount on fries next time he is in town. He says he'll take me up on it.

When I come into the store tonight, Dave is talking loudly to some employees gathered in the lobby. I ask what all the laughing is about. They tell me that last night Dave and Oren siphoned all the gas out of Dave's stepmother's four-wheeler, and then they urinated on her car handles.

Everyone dreads working with Chelsea. When she is not in her office 50 counting the till or on the phone with her husband, she sits on the front counter and complains about her mother-in-law. She does very little to help prep the store for closing, and we rarely get out before two A.M.

Tonight she tells me about her mother-in-law's most recent visit. "I cleaned the house for hours before she came," Chelsea says, nursing a Diet Coke. "And the first thing she says when she gets there is how disgusting the place looks. She won't even eat my cooking." According to Chelsea, her mother-in-law has hated her ever since she got engaged. She wouldn't even visit except that Chelsea has a baby now, and the mother-in-law feels obligated. Chelsea's mother-in-law is disappointed that she is still working. "A mother's place is in the home," she says to Chelsea. "Your kids will be ruined."

Tonight Waymon Hamilton comes through the drive-up window with his family. Waymon lives around the corner from me, and his two sons are in my scout troop, but they spend most of their free time traveling around the state playing premier Little League baseball. They order a few value meals, some drinks, and they ask how I'm doing. There is no hint of concern or condolence in their voices, and I appreciate it.

I hand them their food and watch them drive away. Most people know Waymon the way I know him, as a dedicated father who works hard at a thankless job to provide for his family. His unassuming nature and warm smile are what I see when I think about him. Few people know him as the fleet-footed running back who helped Brigham Young University win Holiday Bowls in 1981 and 1983. Few people know he holds several BYU scoring records, including second place for touchdowns in a season, third in career touchdowns, and fifth for both season and career points scored. I didn't even know he played college football until someone mentioned it at a scout meeting. I once worked all day with Waymon, putting in a new driveway for a neighbor, and he never mentioned his football days once. He told me about his boys, about teaching public school in California, and about pouring lots of concrete.

After the store closes, I come home, take off my uniform, and climb into bed with my wife. She rolls over, tells me she loves me, and murmurs something about the smell of French fries. I kiss her on the cheek and close my eyes. It is winter, but the house is warm. My son is asleep in the next room. There is food in the fridge, and I have a job that pays an honest wage. In the morning I will make breakfast and send my wife off to school. And then, after the dishes are done, if the weather permits, my son and I will take a walk to the park.

Thinking about the Text

1. What stereotypes about people who work at fast food restaurants—and their reasons for doing so—does Joey Franklin present in this essay? How does he then contradict and/or reinforce these stereotypes?

2. Look closely at the dialogue Franklin includes. What do these conversations reveal about different attitudes toward work?

3. Write an essay about work. Like Franklin, you can write a memoir about a job you have held, or you could try a different genre, perhaps an argument about minimum wage or a report on some kind of work you hope to do.

NICHOLAS CARR

Is Google Making Us Stupid?

2008

NICHOLAS CARR (b. 1959) writes nonfiction about technology. He is the author of *Does IT Matter?* (2004), *The Big Switch: Rewiring the World, from Edison to Google* (2008), and *The Glass Cage: Automation and Us* (2014). Before he became a published author, he was executive editor of the *Harvard Business Review* and, after that, employed for almost two decades as a management consultant. "Is Google Making Us Stupid?" first appeared in the *Atlantic* (2008) and then, revised, as the chapter "Hal and Me" in *The Shallows: What the Internet Is Doing to Our Brains* (2010).

"DAVE, STOP. STOP, WILL YOU? STOP, DAVE. WILL YOU stop, Dave?" So the supercomputer HAL pleads with the implacable astronaut Dave Bowman in a famous and weirdly poignant scene toward the end of Stanley Kubrick's *2001: A Space Odyssey*. Bowman, having nearly been sent to a deep-space death by the malfunctioning machine, is calmly, coldly disconnecting the memory circuits that control its artificial "brain." "Dave, my mind is going," HAL says, forlornly. "I can feel it. I can feel it."

I can feel it, too. Over the past few years I've had an uncomfortable sense that someone, or something, has been tinkering with my brain, remapping the neural circuitry, reprogramming the memory. My mind isn't going—so far as I can tell—but it's changing. I'm not thinking the way I used to think. I can feel it most strongly when I'm reading. Immersing myself in a book or a lengthy article used to be easy. My mind would get caught up in the narrative or the turns of the argument, and I'd spend hours strolling through long stretches of prose. That's rarely the case anymore. Now my concentration often starts to drift after two or three pages. I get fidgety, lose the thread, begin looking for something else to do. I feel as if I'm always dragging my wayward brain back to the text. The deep reading that used to come naturally has become a struggle.

I think I know what's going on. For more than a decade now, I've been spending a lot of time online, searching and surfing and sometimes adding to the great databases of the Internet. The Web has been a godsend to me as a writer. Research that once required days in the stacks or periodical rooms of libraries can now be done in minutes. A few Google searches, some quick clicks on hyperlinks, and I've got the telltale fact or pithy quote I was after. Even when I'm not working, I'm as likely as not to be foraging in the Web's info-thickets—reading and writing e-mails, scanning headlines and blog posts, watching videos and listening to podcasts, or just tripping from link to link to link. (Unlike footnotes, to which they're sometimes likened, hyperlinks don't merely point to related works; they propel you toward them.)

For me, as for others, the Net is becoming a universal medium, the conduit for most of the information that flows through my eyes and ears and into my mind. The advantages of having immediate access to such an incredibly rich store of information are many, and they've been widely described and duly applauded. "The perfect recall of silicon memory," *Wired*'s Clive Thompson has written, "can be an enormous boon to thinking." But that boon comes at a price. As the media theorist Marshall McLuhan pointed out in the 1960s, media are not just passive channels of information. They supply the stuff of thought, but they also shape the process of thought. And what the Net seems to be doing is chipping away my capacity for concentration and contemplation. My mind now expects to take in information the way the Net distributes it: in a swiftly moving stream of particles. Once I was a scuba diver in the sea of words. Now I zip along the surface like a guy on a Jet Ski.

I'm not the only one. When I mention my troubles with reading to friends and acquaintances—literary types, most of them—many say they're having similar experiences. The more they use the Web, the more they have to fight to stay focused on long pieces of writing. Some of the bloggers I follow have also begun mentioning the phenomenon. Scott Karp, who writes a blog about online media, recently confessed that he has stopped reading books altogether. "I was a lit major in college, and used to be [a] voracious book reader," he wrote. "What happened?" He speculates on the answer: "What if I do all my reading on the web not so much because the way I read has changed, i.e. I'm just seeking convenience, but because the way I THINK has changed?"

Bruce Friedman, who blogs regularly about the use of computers in medicine, also has described how the Internet has altered his mental habits. "I now have almost totally lost the ability to read and absorb a longish article on the web or in print," he wrote earlier this year. A pathologist who has long been on the faculty of the University of Michigan Medical School, Friedman elaborated on his comment in a telephone conversation with me. His thinking, he said, has taken on a "staccato" quality, reflecting the way he quickly scans short passages of text from many sources online. "I can't read *War and Peace* anymore," he admitted. "I've lost the ability to do that. Even a blog post of more than three or four paragraphs is too much to absorb. I skim it."

Anecdotes alone don't prove much. And we still await the long-term neurological and psychological experiments that will provide a definitive picture of how Internet use affects cognition. But a recently published study of online research habits, conducted by scholars from University College London, suggests that we may well be in the midst of a sea change in the way we read and think. As part of the five-year research program, the scholars examined computer logs documenting the behavior of visitors to two popular research sites, one operated by the British Library and one by a U.K. educational consortium, that provide access to journal articles, e-books, and other sources of written information. They found that people using the sites exhibited "a form of skimming activity," hopping from one source to another and rarely returning to any source they'd already visited. They typically read no more than one or two pages of an article or book before they would "bounce" out to another site. Sometimes they'd save a long article, but there's no evidence that they ever went back and actually read it. The authors of the study report:

> It is clear that users are not reading online in the traditional sense; indeed there are signs that new forms of "reading" are emerging as users "power browse" horizontally through titles, contents pages and abstracts going for quick wins. It almost seems that they go online to avoid reading in the traditional sense.

Thanks to the ubiquity of text on the Internet, not to mention the popularity of text-messaging on cell phones, we may well be reading more today than we did in the 1970s or 1980s, when television was our medium of choice. But it's a different kind of reading, and behind it lies a different kind of thinking—perhaps even a new sense of the self. "We are not only *what* we read," says Maryanne Wolf, a developmental psychologist at Tufts University and the author of *Proust and the Squid: The Story and Science of the Reading Brain.* "We are *how* we read." Wolf worries that the style of reading promoted by the Net, a style that puts "efficiency" and "immediacy" above all else, may be weakening our capacity for the kind of deep reading that emerged when an earlier technology, the printing press, made long and complex works of prose commonplace. When we read online, she says, we tend to become "mere decoders of information." Our ability to interpret text, to make the rich mental connections that form when we read deeply and without distraction, remains largely disengaged.

Reading, explains Wolf, is not an instinctive skill for human beings. It's not etched into our genes the way speech is. We have to teach our minds how to translate the symbolic characters we see into the language we understand. And the media or other technologies we use in learning and practicing the craft of reading play an important part in shaping the neural circuits inside our brains. Experiments demonstrate that readers of ideograms, such as the Chinese, develop a mental circuitry for reading that is very different from the circuitry found in those of us whose written language employs an alphabet. The variations extend across many regions of the brain, including those that govern such essential cognitive functions as memory and the interpretation of visual and auditory stimuli. We can expect as well that the circuits woven by our use of the Net will be different from those woven by our reading of books and other printed works.

Sometime in 1882, Friedrich Nietzsche bought a typewriter—a   10
Malling-Hansen Writing Ball, to be precise. His vision was failing, and keeping his eyes focused on a page had become exhausting and painful, often bringing on crushing headaches. He had been forced to curtail his writing, and he feared that he would soon have to give it up. The typewriter rescued him, at least for a time. Once he had mastered touch-typing, he was able to write with his eyes closed, using only the tips of his fingers. Words could once again flow from his mind to the page.

But the machine had a subtler effect on his work. One of Nietzsche's friends, a composer, noticed a change in the style of his writing. His already terse prose had become even tighter, more telegraphic. "Perhaps you will through this instrument even take to a new idiom," the friend wrote in a letter, noting that, in his own work, his "thoughts in music and language often depend on the quality of pen and paper."

"You are right," Nietzsche replied, "our writing equipment takes part in the forming of our thoughts." Under the sway of the machine, writes the German media scholar Friedrich A. Kittler, Nietzsche's prose "changed from arguments to aphorisms, from thoughts to puns, from rhetoric to telegram style."

The human brain is almost infinitely malleable. People used to think that our mental meshwork, the dense connections formed among the 100 billion or so neurons inside our skulls, was largely fixed by the time we reached adulthood. But brain researchers have discovered that that's not the case. James Olds, a professor of neuroscience who directs the Krasnow Institute for Advanced Study at George Mason University, says that even the adult mind "is very plastic." Nerve cells routinely break old connections and form new ones. "The brain," according to Olds, "has the ability to reprogram itself on the fly, altering the way it functions."

As we use what the sociologist Daniel Bell has called our "intellectual technologies"—the tools that extend our mental rather than our physical capacities—we inevitably begin to take on the qualities of those technologies. The mechanical clock, which came into common use in the 14th century, provides a compelling example. In *Technics and Civilization*, the historian and cultural critic Lewis Mumford described how the clock "disassociated time from human events and helped create the belief in an independent world of mathematically measurable sequences." The "abstract framework of divided time" became "the point of reference for both action and thought."

The clock's methodical ticking helped bring into being the scientific   15
mind and the scientific man. But it also took something away. As the late MIT computer scientist Joseph Weizenbaum observed in his 1976 book, *Computer Power and Human Reason: From Judgment to Calculation*, the conception of the world that emerged from the widespread use of timekeeping instruments "remains an impoverished version of the older one, for it rests on a rejection of those direct experiences that formed the basis for, and indeed constituted, the old reality." In deciding when to eat, to work, to sleep, to rise, we stopped listening to our senses and started obeying the clock.

The process of adapting to new intellectual technologies is reflected in the changing metaphors we use to explain ourselves to ourselves. When the mechanical clock arrived, people began thinking of their brains as operating "like clockwork." Today, in the age of software, we have come to think of them as operating "like computers." But the changes, neuroscience tells us, go much deeper than metaphor.

Thanks to our brain's plasticity, the adaptation occurs also at a biological level.

The Internet promises to have particularly far-reaching effects on cognition. In a paper published in 1936, the British mathematician Alan Turing proved that a digital computer, which at the time existed only as a theoretical machine, could be programmed to perform the function of any other information-processing device. And that's what we're seeing today. The Internet, an immeasurably powerful computing system, is subsuming most of our other intellectual technologies. It's becoming our map and our clock, our printing press and our typewriter, our calculator and our telephone, and our radio and TV.

When the Net absorbs a medium, that medium is re-created in the Net's image. It injects the medium's content with hyperlinks, blinking ads, and other digital gewgaws, and it surrounds the content with the content of all the other media it has absorbed. A new e-mail message, for instance, may announce its arrival as we're glancing over the latest headlines at a newspaper's site. The result is to scatter our attention and diffuse our concentration.

The Net's influence doesn't end at the edges of a computer screen, either. As people's minds become attuned to the crazy quilt of Internet media, traditional media have to adapt to the audience's new expectations. Television programs add text crawls and pop-up ads, and magazines and newspapers shorten their articles, introduce capsule summaries, and crowd their pages with easy-to-browse info-snippets. When, in March of this year, *The New York Times* decided to devote the second and third pages of every edition to article abstracts, its design director, Tom Bodkin, explained that the "shortcuts" would give harried readers a quick "taste" of the day's news, sparing them the "less efficient" method of actually turning the pages and reading the articles. Old media have little choice but to play by the new-media rules.

Never has a communications system played so many roles in our 20
lives—or exerted such broad influence over our thoughts—as the Internet

does today. Yet, for all that's been written about the Net, there's been little consideration of how, exactly, it's reprogramming us. The Net's intellectual ethic remains obscure.

About the same time that Nietzsche started using his typewriter, an earnest young man named Frederick Winslow Taylor carried a stop-watch into the Midvale Steel plant in Philadelphia and began a historic series of experiments aimed at improving the efficiency of the plant's machinists. With the approval of Midvale's owners, he recruited a group of factory hands, set them to work on various metalworking machines, and recorded and timed their every movement as well as the operations of the machines. By breaking down every job into a sequence of small, discrete steps and then testing different ways of performing each one, Taylor created a set of precise instructions—an "algorithm," we might say today—for how each worker should work. Midvale's employees grum-bled about the strict new regime, claiming that it turned them into little more than automatons, but the factory's productivity soared.

More than a hundred years after the invention of the steam engine, the Industrial Revolution had at last found its philosophy and its philos-opher. Taylor's tight industrial choreography—his "system," as he liked to call it—was embraced by manufacturers throughout the country and, in time, around the world. Seeking maximum speed, maximum efficiency, and maximum output, factory owners used time-and-motion studies to organize their work and configure the jobs of their workers. The goal, as Taylor defined it in his celebrated 1911 treatise, *The Princi-ples of Scientific Management*, was to identify and adopt, for every job, the "one best method" of work and thereby to effect "the gradual substitu-tion of science for rule of thumb throughout the mechanic arts." Once his system was applied to all acts of manual labor, Taylor assured his followers, it would bring about a restructuring not only of industry but of society, creating a utopia of perfect efficiency. "In the past the man has been first," he declared; "in the future the system must be first."

Taylor's system is still very much with us; it remains the ethic of industrial manufacturing. And now, thanks to the growing power that computer engineers and software coders wield over our intellectual lives, Taylor's ethic is beginning to govern the realm of the mind as well. The Internet is a machine designed for the efficient and automated collection, transmission, and manipulation of information, and its legions of programmers are intent on finding the "one best method"—the perfect algorithm—to carry out every mental movement of what we've come to describe as "knowledge work."

Google's headquarters, in Mountain View, California—the Googleplex—is the Internet's high church, and the religion practiced inside its walls is Taylorism. Google, says its chief executive, Eric Schmidt, is "a company that's founded around the science of measurement," and it is striving to "systematize everything" it does. Drawing on the terabytes of behavioral data it collects through its search engine and other sites, it carries out thousands of experiments a day, according to the *Harvard Business Review*, and it uses the results to refine the algorithms that increasingly control how people find information and extract meaning from it. What Taylor did for the work of the hand, Google is doing for the work of the mind.

The company has declared that its mission is "to organize the world's   25
information and make it universally accessible and useful." It seeks to develop "the perfect search engine," which it defines as something that "understands exactly what you mean and gives you back exactly what you want." In Google's view, information is a kind of commodity, a utilitarian resource that can be mined and processed with industrial efficiency. The more pieces of information we can "access" and the faster we can extract their gist, the more productive we become as thinkers.

Where does it end? Sergey Brin and Larry Page, the gifted young men who founded Google while pursuing doctoral degrees in computer science at Stanford, speak frequently of their desire to turn their search engine into an artificial intelligence, a HAL-like machine that might be connected directly to our brains. "The ultimate search engine is something as smart as people—or smarter," Page said in a speech a few years back. "For us, working on search is a way to work on artificial intelligence." In a 2004 interview with *Newsweek*, Brin said, "Certainly if you had all the world's information directly attached to your brain, or an artificial brain that was smarter than your brain, you'd be better off." Last year, Page told a convention of scientists that Google is "really trying to build artificial intelligence and to do it on a large scale."

Such an ambition is a natural one, even an admirable one, for a pair of math whizzes with vast quantities of cash at their disposal and a small army of computer scientists in their employ. A fundamentally scientific enterprise, Google is motivated by a desire to use technology, in Eric Schmidt's words, "to solve problems that have never been solved before," and artificial intelligence is the hardest problem out there. Why wouldn't Brin and Page want to be the ones to crack it?

Still, their easy assumption that we'd all "be better off" if our brains were supplemented, or even replaced, by an artificial intelligence is unsettling. It suggests a belief that intelligence is the output of a mechanical process, a series of discrete steps that can be isolated, measured, and optimized. In Google's world, the world we enter when we go online, there's little place for the fuzziness of contemplation. Ambiguity is not an opening for insight but a bug to be fixed. The human brain is just an outdated computer that needs a faster processor and a bigger hard drive.

The idea that our minds should operate as high-speed data-processing machines is not only built into the workings of the Internet, it is the network's reigning business model as well. The faster we surf across the Web—the more links we click and pages we view—the more opportunities Google and other companies gain to collect information about us and to feed us advertisements. Most of the proprietors of the commercial Internet have a financial stake in collecting the crumbs of data we leave behind as we flit from link to link—the more crumbs, the better. The last thing these companies want is to encourage leisurely reading or slow, concentrated thought. It's in their economic interest to drive us to distraction.

Maybe I'm just a worrywart. Just as there's a tendency to glorify techno-   30
logical progress, there's a countertendency to expect the worst of every new tool or machine. In Plato's *Phaedrus*, Socrates bemoaned the development of writing. He feared that, as people came to rely on the written word as a substitute for the knowledge they used to carry inside their heads, they would, in the words of one of the dialogue's characters, "cease to exercise their memory and become forgetful." And because they would be able to "receive a quantity of information without proper instruction," they would "be thought very knowledgeable when they are for the most part quite ignorant." They would be "filled with the conceit of wisdom instead of real wisdom." Socrates wasn't wrong—the new technology did often have the effects he feared—but he was shortsighted. He couldn't foresee the many ways that writing and reading would serve to spread information, spur fresh ideas, and expand human knowledge (if not wisdom).

The arrival of Gutenberg's printing press, in the 15th century, set off another round of teeth gnashing. The Italian humanist Hieronimo Squarciafico worried that the easy availability of books would lead to intellectual laziness, making men "less studious" and weakening their minds. Others argued that cheaply printed books and broadsheets would undermine religious authority, demean the work of scholars and scribes, and spread sedition and debauchery. As New York University professor Clay Shirky notes, "Most of the arguments made against the printing press were correct, even prescient." But, again, the doomsayers were unable to imagine the myriad blessings that the printed word would deliver.

So, yes, you should be skeptical of my skepticism. Perhaps those who dismiss critics of the Internet as Luddites or nostalgists will be proved correct, and from our hyperactive, data-stoked minds will spring a golden age of intellectual discovery and universal wisdom. Then again, the Net isn't the alphabet, and although it may replace the printing press, it produces something altogether different. The kind of deep reading that a sequence of printed pages promotes is valuable not just for the knowledge we acquire from the author's words but for the intellectual vibrations those words set off within our own minds. In the quiet spaces opened up by the sustained, undistracted reading of a book, or by any other act of contemplation, for that matter, we make our own associations, draw our own inferences and analogies, foster our own ideas. Deep reading, as Maryanne Wolf argues, is indistinguishable from deep thinking.

If we lose those quiet spaces, or fill them up with "content," we will sacrifice something important not only in our selves but in our culture. In a recent essay, the playwright Richard Foreman eloquently described what's at stake:

> I come from a tradition of Western culture, in which the ideal (my ideal) was the complex, dense and "cathedral-like" structure of the highly educated and articulate personality—a man or woman who carried inside themselves a personally constructed and unique version of the entire heritage of the West. [But now] I see within us all (myself included) the replacement of complex inner density with a new kind of self—evolving under the pressure of information overload and the technology of the "instantly available."

As we are drained of our "inner repertory of dense cultural inheritance," Foreman concluded, we risk turning into "pancake people—spread wide and thin as we connect with that vast network of information accessed by the mere touch of a button."

I'm haunted by that scene in *2001*. What makes it so poignant, and so weird, is the computer's emotional response to the disassembly of its mind: its despair as one circuit after another goes dark, its childlike pleading with the astronaut—"I can feel it. I can feel it. I'm afraid"—and its final reversion to what can only be called a state of innocence. HAL's outpouring of feeling contrasts with the emotionlessness that characterizes the human figures in the film, who go about their business with an almost robotic efficiency. Their thoughts and actions feel scripted, as if they're following the steps of an algorithm. In the world of *2001*, people have become so machinelike that the most human character turns out to be a machine. That's the essence of Kubrick's dark prophecy: as we come to rely on computers to mediate our understanding of the world, it is our own intelligence that flattens into artificial intelligence.

Thinking about the Text

1. Nicholas Carr argues that the internet is changing the way people read and think. What specific changes does he identify, and what evidence does he give to support his argument?

2. Carr shows concern about the ways digital technologies may affect reading and thinking, but he also admits, "Maybe I'm just a worry-wart" (paragraph 30). What is the effect of the examples he provides of other technologies and of those who were concerned about them? (See paragraphs 30–32.) Do these examples weaken or strengthen his argument?

3. Carr acknowledges that "we still await the long-term neurological and psychological experiments that will provide a definitive picture of how Internet use affects cognition" (paragraph 7). Research some studies that have been published since 2008 about the cognitive effects of internet use, and write an essay in which you take a position on whether internet use is indeed "making us stupid."

ANNA QUINDLEN

Stuff Is Not Salvation

2008

―――――――――――――――――――○――――――――――――――――――――

ANNA QUINDLEN (b. 1953) writes both nonfiction and novels and has written regular columns for both the *New York
Times* and *Newsweek*. She once described being a columnist
as "taking things personally for a living." Her nonfiction
books include the memoir *How Reading Changed My Life*
(1998), *A Short Guide to a Happy Life* (2000), and *Lots of Candles, Plenty of Cake* (2012). "Stuff Is Not Salvation" was first
published in *Newsweek* in December 2008.

―――――――――――――――――――○――――――――――――――――――――

A S THE BOOM TIMES FADE, AN IMPORTANT HOLIDAY QUES-
tion surfaces: why in the world did we buy all this junk in
the first place?

What passes for the holiday season began before dawn
the day after Thanksgiving, when a worker at a Wal-Mart in Valley
Stream, N.Y., was trampled to death by a mob of bargain hunters. Afterward, there were reports that some people, mesmerized by cheap consumer electronics and discounted toys, kept shopping even after
announcements to clear the store.

These are dark days in the United States: the cataclysmic stock-market
declines, the industries edging up on bankruptcy, the home foreclosures
and the waves of layoffs. But the prospect of an end to plenty has uncov-
ered what may ultimately be a more pernicious problem, an addiction to
consumption so out of control that it qualifies as a sickness. The suffoca-
tion of a store employee by a stampede of shoppers was horrifying, but it
wasn't entirely surprising.

Americans have been on an acquisition binge for decades. I suspect
television advertising, which made me want a Chatty Cathy doll so much
as a kid that when I saw her under the tree my head almost exploded. By
contrast, my father will be happy to tell you about the excitement of getting an orange in his stocking during the Depression. The depression
before this one.

A critical difference between then and now is credit. The orange   5
had to be paid for. The rite of passage for a child when I was young was
a solemn visit to the local bank, there to exchange birthday money for a
savings passbook. Every once in a while, like magic, a bit of extra money
would appear. Interest. Yippee.

The passbook was replaced by plastic, so that today Americans are
overwhelmed by debt and the national savings rate is calculated, like
an algebra equation, in negatives. By 2010 Americans will be a trillion
dollars in the hole on credit-card debt alone.

But let's look, not at the numbers, but the atmospherics. Appliances, toys, clothes, gadgets. Junk. There's the sad truth. Wall Street executives may have made investments that lost their value, but, in a much smaller way, so did the rest of us. "I looked into my closet the other day and thought, why did I buy all this stuff?" one friend said recently. A person in the United States replaces a cell phone every 16 months, not because the cell phone is old, but because it is oldish. My mother used to complain that the Christmas toys were grubby and forgotten by Easter. (I didn't even really like dolls, especially dolls who introduced themselves to you over and over again when you pulled the ring in their necks.) Now much of the country is made up of people with the acquisition habits of a 7-year-old, desire untethered from need, or the ability to pay. The result is a booming business in those free-standing storage facilities, where junk goes to linger in a persistent vegetative state, somewhere between eBay and the dump.

Oh, there is still plenty of need. But it is for real things, things that matter: college tuition, prescription drugs, rent. Food pantries and soup kitchens all over the country have seen demand for their services soar. Homelessness, which had fallen in recent years, may rebound as people lose their jobs and their houses. For the first time this month, the number of people on food stamps will exceed the 30 million mark.

Hard times offer the opportunity to ask hard questions, and one of them is the one my friend asked, staring at sweaters and shoes: why did we buy all this stuff? Did anyone really need a flat-screen in the bedroom, or a designer handbag, or three cars? If the mall is our temple, then Marc Jacobs is God. There's a scary thought.

The drumbeat that accompanied Black Friday this year was that the 10 numbers had to redeem us, that if enough money was spent by shoppers it would indicate that things were not so bad after all. But what the economy required was at odds with a necessary epiphany. Because things are dire, many people have become hesitant to spend money on trifles. And in the process they began to realize that it's all trifles.

Here I go, stating the obvious: stuff does not bring salvation. But if it's so obvious, how come for so long people have not realized it? The happiest families I know aren't the ones with the most square footage, living in one of those cavernous houses with enough garage space to start a homeless shelter. (There's a holiday suggestion right there.) And of course they are not people who are in real want. Just because consumption is bankrupt doesn't mean that poverty is ennobling.

But somewhere in between there is a family like one I know in rural Pennsylvania, raising bees for honey (and for the science, and the fun, of it), digging a pond out of the downhill flow of the stream, with three kids who somehow, incredibly, don't spend six months of the year whining for the toy du jour. (The youngest once demurred when someone offered him another box on his birthday; "I already have a present," he said.) The mother of the household says having less means her family appreciates possessions more. "I can give you a story about every item, really," she says of what they own. In other words, what they have has meaning. And meaning, real meaning, is what we are always trying to possess. Ask people what they'd grab if their house were on fire, the way our national house is on fire right now. No one ever says it's the tricked-up microwave they got at Wal-Mart.

Thinking about the Text

1. One important element in making an argument is what rhetoricians call "kairos," an ancient Greek word meaning a timely or opportune moment to say or do something. Consider the context in which Anna Quindlen wrote this op-ed piece: December 2008. How does she use that context to make her argument? How relevant is her argument today, and why?

2. Read Maggie Helwig's "Hunger" on pp. 242–49. How is her argument similar to Quindlen's? How is it different? Both suggest that people living in North America have, in Quindlen's words, "an addiction to consumption so out of control that it qualifies as a sickness" (paragraph 3). What potential solutions does each writer offer to the problem she identifies?

3. Think of some issue that you consider significant. In what ways is it a timely issue? Write an argument in which you identify the issue, show why it's a problem, and suggest a solution or a specific course of action. (For an example of an argument written by a student, see Katherine Spriggs's "On Buying Local" on pp. 473–83.)

EULA BISS

Time and Distance Overcome

2009

EULA BISS (b. 1977) is an essayist who weaves together history, cultural analysis, and reflection, often blurring the line between poetry and prose. She taught in New York City's public schools before studying writing at the University of Iowa Writers' Workshop. Her books include *The Balloonists* (2002), *On Immunity: An Inoculation* (2014), and *Notes from No Man's Land* (2009), in which "Time and Distance Overcome" was first published.

"**O**F WHAT USE IS SUCH AN INVENTION?" THE *NEW York World* asked shortly after Alexander Graham Bell first demonstrated his telephone in 1876. The world was not waiting for the telephone.

Bell's financial backers asked him not to work on his new invention because it seemed too dubious an investment. The idea on which the telephone depended—the idea that every home in the country could be connected by a vast network of wires suspended from poles set an average of one hundred feet apart—seemed far more unlikely than the idea that the human voice could be transmitted through a wire.

Even now it is an impossible idea, that we are all connected, all of us.

"At the present time we have a perfect network of gas pipes and water pipes throughout our large cities," Bell wrote to his business partners in defense of his idea. "We have main pipes laid under the streets communicating by side pipes with the various dwellings. . . . In a similar manner it is conceivable that cables of telephone wires could be laid under ground, or suspended overhead, communicating by branch wires with private dwellings, counting houses, shops, manufactories, etc., uniting them through the main cable."

Imagine the mind that could imagine this. That could see us joined   5 by one branching cable. This was the mind of a man who wanted to invent, more than the telephone, a machine that would allow the deaf to hear.

For a short time the telephone was little more than a novelty. For twenty-five cents you could see it demonstrated by Bell himself, in a church, along with singing and recitations by local talent. From some distance away, Bell would receive a call from "the invisible Mr. Watson". Then the telephone became a plaything of the rich. A Boston banker paid for a private line between his office and his home so that he could let his family know exactly when he would be home for dinner.

Mark Twain was among the first Americans to own a telephone, but he wasn't completely taken with the device. "The human voice carries entirely too far as it is," he remarked.

By 1889, the *New York Times* was reporting a "War on Telephone Poles." Wherever telephone companies were erecting poles, home owners and business owners were sawing them down or defending their sidewalks with rifles.

Property owners in Red Bank, New Jersey, threatened to tar and feather the workers putting up telephone poles. A judge granted a group of home owners an injunction to prevent the telephone company from erecting any new poles. Another judge found that a man who had cut down a pole because it was "obnoxious" was not guilty of malicious mischief.

Telephone poles, newspaper editorials complained, were an urban blight.   10
The poles carried a wire for each telephone—sometimes hundreds of wires. And in some places there were also telegraph wires, power lines, and trolley cables. The sky was netted with wires.

The war on telephone poles was fueled, in part, by that terribly American concern for private property, and a reluctance to surrender it for a shared utility. And then there was a fierce sense of aesthetics, an obsession with purity, a dislike for the way the poles and wires marred a landscape that those other new inventions, skyscrapers and barbed wire, were just beginning to complicate. And then perhaps there was also a fear that distance, as it had always been known and measured, was collapsing.

The city council in Sioux Falls, South Dakota, ordered policemen to cut down all the telephone poles in town. And the mayor of Oshkosh,

Wisconsin, ordered the police chief and the fire department to chop down the telephone poles there. Only one pole was chopped down before the telephone men climbed all the poles along the line, preventing any more chopping. Soon, Bell Telephone Company began stationing a man at the top of each pole as soon as it had been set, until enough poles had been set to string a wire between them, at which point it became a misdemeanor to interfere with the poles. Even so, a constable cut down two poles holding forty or fifty wires. And a home owner sawed down a recently wired pole, then fled from police. The owner of a cannery ordered his workers to throw dirt back into the hole the telephone company was digging in front of his building. His men threw the dirt back in as fast as the telephone workers could dig it out. Then he sent out a team with a load of stones to dump into the hole. Eventually, the pole was erected on the other side of the street.

Despite the war on telephone poles, it would take only four years after Bell's first public demonstration of the telephone for every town of more than ten thousand people to be wired, although many towns were wired only to themselves. By the turn of the century, there were more telephones than bathtubs in America.

"Time and dist. overcome," read an early advertisement for the telephone. Rutherford B. Hayes pronounced the installation of a telephone in the White House "one of the greatest events since creation." The telephone, Thomas Edison declared, "annihilated time and space, and brought the human family in closer touch."

In 1898, in Lake Cormorant, Mississippi, a black man was hanged from a telephone pole. And in Weir City, Kansas. And in Brookhaven, Mississippi. And in Tulsa, Oklahoma, where the hanged man was riddled with bullets. In Danville, Illinois, a black man's throat was slit, and his dead body was strung up on a telephone pole. Two black men were hanged from a telephone pole in Lewisburg, West Virginia. And two in Hempstead,

Texas, where one man was dragged out of the courtroom by a mob, and another was dragged out of jail.

A black man was hanged from a telephone pole in Belleville, Illinois, where a fire was set at the base of the pole and the man was cut down half-alive, covered in coal oil, and burned. While his body was burning the mob beat it with clubs and cut it to pieces.

Lynching, the first scholar of the subject determined, is an American invention. Lynching from bridges, from arches, from trees standing alone in fields, from trees in front of the county courthouse, from trees used as public billboards, from trees barely able to support the weight of a man, from telephone poles, from streetlamps, and from poles erected solely for that purpose. From the middle of the nineteenth century to the middle of the twentieth century, black men were lynched for crimes real and imagined, for whistles, for rumors, for "disputing with a white man," for "unpopularity," for "asking a white woman in marriage," for "peeping in a window."

The children's game of telephone depends on the fact that a message passed quietly from one ear to another to another will get distorted at some point along the line.

More than two hundred antilynching bills were introduced to the U.S. Congress during the twentieth century, but none were passed. Seven presidents lobbied for antilynching legislation, and the House of Representatives passed three separate measures, each of which was blocked by the Senate.

In Pine Bluff, Arkansas, a black man charged with kicking a white girl was   20
hanged from a telephone pole. In Longview, Texas, a black man accused of attacking a white woman was hanged from a telephone pole. In Greenville, Mississippi, a black man accused of attacking a white telephone

operator was hanged from a telephone pole. "The negro only asked time to pray." In Purcell, Oklahoma, a black man accused of attacking a white woman was tied to a telephone pole and burned. "Men and women in automobiles stood up to watch him die."

The poles, of course, were not to blame. It was only coincidence that they became convenient as gallows, because they were tall and straight, with a crossbar, and because they stood in public places. And it was only coincidence that the telephone poles so closely resembled crucifixes.

Early telephone calls were full of noise. "Such a jangle of meaningless noises had never been heard by human ears," Herbert Casson wrote in his 1910 *History of the Telephone*. "There were spluttering and bubbling, jerking and rasping, whistling and screaming."

In Shreveport, Lousiana, a black man charged with attacking a white girl was hanged from a telephone pole. "A knife was left sticking in the body." In Cumming, Georgia, a black man accused of assaulting a white girl was shot repeatedly, then hanged from a telephone pole. In Waco, Texas, a black man convicted of killing a white woman was taken from the courtroom by a mob and burned, then his charred body was hanged from a telephone pole.

A postcard was made from the photo of a burned man hanging from a telephone pole in Texas, his legs broken off below the knee and his arms curled up and blackened. Postcards of lynchings were sent out as greetings and warnings until 1908, when the postmaster general declared them unmailable. "This is the barbecue we had last night," reads one.

"If we are to die," W. E. B. DuBois wrote in 1911, "in God's name let us perish like men and not like bales of hay." And "if we must die," Claude McKay wrote ten years later, "let it not be like hogs."

In Pittsburg, Kansas, a black man was hanged from a telephone pole, cut down, burned, shot, and stoned with bricks. "At first the negro was defiant," the *New York Times* reported, "but just before he was hanged he begged hard for his life."

In the photographs, the bodies of the men lynched from telephone poles are silhouetted against the sky. Sometimes two men to a pole, hanging above the buildings of a town. Sometimes three. They hang like flags in still air.

In Cumberland, Maryland, a mob used a telephone pole as a battering ram to break into the jail where a black man charged with the murder of a policeman was being held. They kicked him to death, then fired twenty shots into his head. They wanted to burn his body, but a minister asked them not to.

The lynchings happened everywhere, in all but four states. From shortly before the invention of the telephone to long after the first transatlantic call. More in the South, and more in rural areas. In the cities and in the North, there were race riots.

Riots in Cincinnati, New Orleans, Memphis, New York, Atlanta, Philadelphia, Houston . . .   30

During the race riots that destroyed the black section of Springfield, Ohio, a black man was shot and hanged from a telephone pole.

During the race riots that set fire to East St. Louis and forced five hundred black people to flee their homes, a black man was hanged from a telephone pole. The rope broke and his body fell into the gutter. "Negros are lying in the gutters every few feet in some places," read the newspaper account.

In 1921, the year before Bell died, four companies of the National Guard were called out to end a race war in Tulsa that began when a white woman accused a black man of rape. Bell had lived to complete the first call from New York to San Francisco, which required 14,000 miles of copper wire and 130,000 telephone poles.

My grandfather was a lineman. He broke his back when a telephone pole fell. "Smashed him onto the road," my father says.

When I was young, I believed that the arc and swoop of telephone wires   35 along the roadways was beautiful. I believed that the telephone poles, with their transformers catching the evening sun, were glorious. I believed my father when he said, "My dad could raise a pole by himself." And I believed that the telephone itself was a miracle.

Now, I tell my sister, these poles, these wires, do not look the same to me. Nothing is innocent, my sister reminds me. But nothing, I would like to think, remains unrepentant.

One summer, heavy rains fell in Nebraska and some green telephone poles grew small leafy branches.

ON "TIME AND DISTANCE OVERCOME"

I began my research for this essay by searching for every instance of the phrase "telephone pole" in the *New York Times* from 1880 to 1920, which resulted in 370 articles. I was planning to write an essay about telephone poles and telephones, not lynchings, but after reading an article headlined "Colored Scoundrel Lynched," and then another headlined "Mississippi Negro Lynched," and then another headlined "Texas Negro Lynched," I searched for every instance of the word "lynched" in the *New York Times* from 1880 to 1920, which resulted in 2,354 articles.

I refer, in this essay, to the first scholar of lynching, meaning James E. Cutler, author of the 1905 book *Lynch-Law,* in which he writes, on the first page, "Lynching is a criminal practice which is peculiar to the United States." This is debatable, of course, and very possibly not true, but there is good evidence that the Italian Antonio Meucci invented a telephone years before Bell began working on his device, so as long as we are going to lay claim to one invention, we might as well take responsibility for the other.

Bell would say, late in his life: "Recognition for my work with the   40
deaf has always been more pleasing than the recognition of my work with the telephone." His own hearing was failing by the time he placed the first cross-country call, from New York to his old friend Thomas Watson in San Francisco, and what he said to Watson then was an echo of the first sentence he ever spoke into his invention, a famous and possibly mythical sentence that is now remembered in several slightly different versions, one being, "Mr. Watson, come here—I want you," and another being, "Mr. Watson, come here—I need you!"

Thinking about the Text

1. What is Eula Biss's main point in this lyric essay? What connections does she make between telephones, telephone poles, and lynchings? What is her purpose in showing these connections, and how does it support her main point?

2. Authors of lyric essays often organize them by association rather than with explicit transitions between paragraphs or ideas (see, for example, paragraphs 17–19). Were there associational leaps in this essay that surprised you? Were any hard for you to follow? What skills does this technique require of readers?

3. Write an essay in which you reflect on some object or technology. You'll need to do some research about your topic, and you might conclude with a note about how your research helped to shape your essay. If you wish, you could write a lyric essay, using Biss's writing as a model.

MARION NESTLE

Utopian Dream: A New Farm Bill

2012

———————————— ◇ ————————————

MARION NESTLE (b. 1936) is a professor of nutrition, food studies, and public health at New York University and an advocate for nutrition and food safety. Her books include *Food Politics: How the Food Industry Influences Nutrition and Health* (2002) and *What to Eat* (2006). "Utopian Dream: A New Farm Bill" was published in the political journal *Dissent* in 2012. The farm bill Nestle critiques was signed into law in February 2014.

———————————— ◇ ————————————

I N THE FALL OF 2011, I TAUGHT A GRADUATE FOOD STUDIES course at New York University devoted to the farm bill, a massive and massively opaque piece of legislation passed most recently in 2008 and up for renewal in 2012. The farm bill supports farmers, of course, but also specifies how the United States deals with such matters as conservation, forestry, energy policy, organic food production, international food aid, and domestic food assistance. My students came from programs in nutrition, food studies, public health, public policy, and law, all united in the belief that a smaller scale, more regionalized, and more sustainable food system would be healthier for people and the planet.

In the first class meeting, I asked students to suggest what an ideal farm bill should do. Their answers covered the territory: ensure enough food for the population at an affordable price; produce a surplus for international trade and aid; provide farmers with a sufficient income; protect farmers against the vagaries of weather and volatile markets; promote regional, seasonal, organic, and sustainable food production; conserve soil, land, and forest; protect water and air quality, natural resources, and wildlife; raise farm animals humanely; and provide farm workers with a living wage and decent working conditions. Overall, they advocated aligning agricultural policy with nutrition, health, and environmental policy—a tall order by any standard, but especially so given current political and economic realities.

WHAT'S WRONG WITH THE CURRENT FARM BILL?

Plenty. Beyond providing an abundance of inexpensive food, the current farm bill addresses practically none of the other goals. It favors Big Agriculture over small; pesticides, fertilizers, and genetically modified crops over those raised organically and sustainably; and some regions of the country—notably the South and Midwest—over others. It supports commodity crops grown for animal feed but considers fruits and vegetables to be "specialty" crops deserving only token support. It provides incentives leading to crop overproduction, with enormous consequences for health.

The bill does not require farmers to engage in conservation or safety practices (farms are exempt from having to comply with environmental or employment standards). It encourages production of feed crops for ethanol. In part because Congress insisted that gasoline must contain ethanol, 40 percent of U.S. feed corn was grown for that purpose in 2011, a well-documented cause of higher world food prices. Because the bill subsidizes production, it gets the United States in trouble with international trading partners, and hurts farmers in developing countries by undercutting their prices. Taken as a whole, the farm bill is profoundly undemocratic. It is so big and so complex that nobody in Congress or anywhere else can grasp its entirety, making it especially vulnerable to influence by lobbyists for special interests.

Although the farm bill started out in the Great Depression of the   5
1930s as a collection of emergency measures to protect the income of farmers—all small landholders by today's standards—recipients soon grew dependent on support programs and began to view them as entitlements. Perceived entitlements became incentives for making farms larger; increasingly dependent on pesticide, herbicide, and fertilizer "inputs"; and exploitative of natural and human resources. Big farms drove out small, while technological advances increased production. These trends were institutionalized by cozy relationships among large agricultural producers, farm-state members of congressional agricultural committees, and a Department of Agriculture (USDA) explicitly committed to promoting commodity production.

These players were not, however, sitting around conference tables to create agricultural policies to further national goals. Instead, they used the bill as a way to obtain earmarks—programs that would benefit specific interest groups. It is now a 663-page piece of legislation with a table of contents that alone takes up 14 pages. As the chief vehicle of agricultural policy in the United States, it reflects no overriding goals or philosophy. It is simply a collection of hundreds of largely disconnected programs dispensing public benefits to one group or another, each with its own dedicated constituency and lobbyists. The most controversial farm bill programs benefit only a few basic food commodities—corn, soybeans, wheat, rice, cotton, sugar, and dairy. But lesser-known provisions help much smaller industries such as asparagus, honey, or Hass avocados, although at tiny fractions of the size of commodity payments.

The bill organizes its programs into fifteen "titles" dealing with its various purposes. I once tried to list every program included in each title, but soon gave up. The bill's size, scope, and level of detail are mind-numbing. It can only be understood one program at a time. Hence, lobbyists.

The elephant in the farm bill—its biggest program by far and accounting for nearly 85 percent of the funding—is SNAP, the Supplemental Nutrition Assistance Program (formerly known as food stamps). In 2011, as a result of the declining economy and high unemployment, SNAP benefits grew to cover forty-six million Americans at a cost of $72 billion. In contrast, commodity subsidies cost "only" $8 billion; crop insurance $4.5 billion; and conservation about $5 billion. The amounts expended on the hundreds of other programs covered by the bill are trivial in comparison, millions, not billions—mere rounding errors.

What is SNAP doing in the farm bill? Politics makes strange bedfellows, and SNAP exemplifies logrolling politics in action. By the late 1970s, consolidation of farms had reduced the political power of agricultural states. To continue farm subsidies, representatives from agricultural states needed votes from legislators representing states with large, low-income urban populations. And those legislators needed votes from agricultural states to pass food assistance bills. They traded votes in an unholy alliance that pleased Big Agriculture as well as advocates for the poor. Neither group wants the system changed.

HEALTH IMPLICATIONS

The consequences of obesity—higher risks for heart disease, type 2   10
diabetes, certain cancers, and other chronic conditions—are the most
important health problems facing Americans today. To maintain weight
or to prevent excessive gain, federal dietary guidelines advise consumption of diets rich in vegetables and fruits. The 2008 farm bill introduced a horticulture and organic title, but aside from a farmers' market
promotion program and some smaller marketing programs, does little
to encourage vegetable and fruit production or to subsidize their costs
to consumers. If anything, the farm bill encourages weight gain by
subsidizing commodity crops that constitute the basic cheap caloric
ingredients used in processed foods—soy oil and corn sweeteners, for
example—and by explicitly forbidding crop producers from growing
fruits and vegetables.

Neither human nature nor genetics have changed in the last thirty
years, meaning that widespread obesity must be understood as collateral damage resulting from changes in agricultural, economic, and
regulatory policy in the 1970s and early 1980s. These created today's
"eat more" food environment, one in which it has become socially
acceptable for food to be ubiquitous, eaten frequently, and in large
portions.

For more than seventy years, from the early 1900s to the early 1980s,
daily calorie availability remained relatively constant at about 3,200 per
person. By the year 2000, however, available calories had increased to
3,900 per person per day, roughly twice the average need. People were
not necessarily eating 700 more daily calories, as many were undoubtedly wasted. But the food containing those extra calories needed to
be sold, thereby creating a marketing challenge for the food industry.

Why more calories became available after 1980 is a matter of some
conjecture, but I believe the evidence points to three seemingly remote
events that occurred at about that time: agriculture policies favoring

overproduction, the onset of the shareholder value movement, and the deregulatory policies of the Reagan era.

In 1973 and 1977, Congress passed laws reversing long-standing farm policies aimed at protecting prices by limiting production. Subsidies increased in proportion to amounts grown, encouraging creation of larger and more productive farms. Indeed, production increased, and so did calories in the food supply and competition in the food industry. Companies were forced to find innovative ways to sell food products in an overabundant food economy.

Further increasing competition was the advent of the shareholder   15 value movement to force corporations to produce more immediate and higher returns on investment. The start of the movement is often attributed to a 1981 speech given by Jack Welch, then head of General Electric, in which he insisted that corporations owed shareholders the benefits of faster growth and higher profit margins. The movement caught on quickly, and Wall Street soon began to press companies to report growth in profits every quarter. Food companies, already selling products in an overabundant marketplace, now also had to grow their profits—and constantly.

Companies got some help when Ronald Reagan was elected president in 1980 on a platform of corporate deregulation. Reagan-era deregulatory policies removed limits on television marketing of food products to children and on health claims on food packages. Companies now had much more flexibility in advertising their products.

Together, these factors led food companies to consolidate, become larger, seek new markets, and find creative ways to expand sales in existing markets. The collateral result was a changed society. Today, in contrast to the early 1980s, it is socially acceptable to eat in places never before meant as restaurants, at any time of day, and in increasingly large amounts—all factors that encourage greater calorie intake. Food is now available in places never seen before: bookstores, libraries, and stores primarily selling drugs and cosmetics, gasoline, office supplies, furniture, and clothing.

As a result of the increased supply of food, prices dropped. It became relatively inexpensive to eat outside the home, especially at fast-food restaurants, and such places proliferated. Food prepared outside the home tends to be higher in calories, fast food especially so. It's not that people necessarily began to eat worse diets. They were just eating more food in general and, therefore, gaining weight. This happened with children, too. National food consumption surveys indicate that children get more of their daily calories from fast-food outlets than they do from schools, and that fast food is the largest contributor to the calories they consume outside the home.

To increase sales, companies promoted snacking. The low cost of basic food commodities allowed them to produce new snack products— twenty thousand or so a year, nearly half candies, gum, chips, and sodas. It became *normal* for children to regularly consume fast foods, snacks, and sodas. An astonishing 40 percent of the calories in the diets of children and adolescents now derive from such foods. In adults and children, the habitual consumption of sodas and snacks is associated with increases in calorie intake and body weight.

Food quantity is the critical issue in weight gain. Once foods became 20 relatively inexpensive in comparison to the cost of rent or labor, companies could offer foods and beverages in larger sizes at favorable prices as a means to attract bargain-conscious customers. Larger portions have more calories. But they also encourage people to eat more and to underestimate the number of calories consumed. The well-documented increase in portion sizes since 1980 is by itself sufficient to explain rising levels of obesity.

Food prices are also a major factor in food choice. It is difficult to argue against low prices and I won't—except to note that the current industrialized food system aims at producing food as cheaply as possible, externalizing the real costs to the environment and to human health. Prices, too, are a matter of policy. In the United States, the indexed price of sodas and snack foods has declined since 1980, but that of fruits and vegetables has increased by as much as 40 percent. The farm bill subsidizes animal feed and the ingredients in sodas and snack foods; it does not subsidize fruits and vegetables. How changes in food prices brought on by growth of crops for biofuels will affect health is as yet unknown but unlikely to be beneficial.

The deregulation of marketing also contributes to current obesity levels. Food companies spend billions of dollars a year to encourage people to buy their products, but foods marketed as "healthy"—whether or not they are—particularly encourage greater consumption. Federal agencies attempting to regulate food marketing, especially to children, have been blocked at every turn by food industries dependent on highly profitable "junk" foods for sales. Although food companies argue that body weight is a matter of personal choice, the power of today's overabundant, ubiquitous, and aggressively marketed food environment to promote greater calorie intake is enough to overcome biological controls over eating behavior. Even educated and relatively wealthy consumers have trouble dealing with this "eat more" environment.

FIXING THE FARM BILL

What could agriculture policies do to improve health now and in the future? Also plenty. When I first started teaching nutrition in the mid-1970s, my classes already included readings on the need to reform agricultural policy. Since then, one administration after another has tried to eliminate the most egregious subsidies (like those to landowners who don't farm) but failed when confronted with early primaries in Iowa. Defenders of the farm bill argue that the present system works well to ensure productivity, global competitiveness, and food security. Tinkering with the bill, they claim, will make little difference and could do harm. I disagree. The farm bill needs more than tinkering. It needs a major overhaul. My vision for the farm bill would restructure it to go beyond feeding people at the lowest possible cost to achieve several utopian goals:

Support farmers: The American Enterprise Institute and other conservative groups argue that farming is a business like any other and deserves no special protections. My NYU class thought otherwise. Food is essential for life, and government's role must be to ensure adequate food for people at an affordable price. Farmers deserve some help dealing with financial and climate risks, and some need it more than others. The farm bill should especially support more sustainable smaller-scale farming methods. And such programs should be available to farmers of fruits and vegetables and designed to encourage beginning farmers to grow specialty crops.

Support the environment: The farm bill should require recipients   25
of benefits to engage in environmentally sound production and conservation practices. Production agriculture accounts for a significant fraction—10 percent to 20 percent—of greenhouse gas emissions. Sustainable farming methods have been shown to reduce emissions, return valuable nutrients to soil, and reduce the need for polluting pesticides and fertilizers, with only marginal losses in productivity.

Support human health: The United States does not currently grow enough fruits and vegetables to meet minimal dietary recommendations. The 2008 farm bill explicitly prohibits farms receiving support payments from growing fruits and vegetables. Instead, the bill should provide incentives for growing specialty crops. Support payments should be linked to requirements for farm-based safety procedures that prevent contamination with pathogens and pesticides.

Support farm workers: This one is obvious. Any farm receiving support benefits must pay its workers a living wage and adhere to all laws regarding housing and safety—in spirit as well as in letter.

Link nutrition policy to agricultural policy: If we must have SNAP in
the farm bill, let's take advantage of that connection. Suppose SNAP
benefits had to be spent mostly on real rather than processed foods, and
were worth more when spent at farmers' markets. Pilot projects along
these lines have been shown to work brilliantly. Consider what something like this might do for the income of small farmers as well as for the
health of food assistance recipients. Policies that enable low-income families to access healthy foods wherever they shop are beyond the scope of
the farm bill, but must also be part of any utopian agenda.

Apply health and conservation standards to animal agriculture: The
livestock title of the farm bill should require animals to be raised and
slaughtered humanely. It should require strict adherence to environmental and safety standards for conservation and protection of soil,
water, and air quality.

Utopian? Absolutely. In the current political climate, the best any-   30
one can hope for is a crumb or two thrown in these directions. The
secret process for developing the 2012 farm bill contained a few such
crumbs—more money for farmers' markets and for programs to take
SNAP benefits further when spent on fruits and vegetables. Whether
that bill would have been better or worse than the one we eventually
end up with remains to be seen. But the failure of that process provides
an opportunity to work toward a healthier food system by restructuring
farm bill programs to focus them on health, safety, and environmental
goals and social justice. These goals are well worth advocating now and
in the future.

The one bright ray of hope about the farm bill comes from the bur-
geoning food movement. Grassroots groups working to promote local
and regional foods, farmers' markets, urban farming, farm-to-school
programs, animal welfare, and farm workers' rights join a long and honorable history of social movements such as those aimed at civil rights,
women's rights, and environmentalism. Changing the food system is

equally radical. But food has one particular advantage for advocacy. Food is universal. Everyone eats. Food is an easy entry point into conversations about social inequities. Even the least political person can understand injustices in the food system and be challenged to work to redress them.

Occupy Big Food is an integral part of Occupy Wall Street; it should not be viewed as a special interest. The issues that drive both are the same: corporate control of government and society. The food movement—in all of its forms—seeks better health for people and the planet, goals that benefit everyone. It deserves the support of everyone advocating for democratic rights.

Thinking about the Text

1. Marion Nestle uses causal analysis to support her argument for changes in the farm bill. What problems does she identify, and what does she claim caused or contributed to those problems?

2. Look carefully at Nestle's organization and in particular at her use of headings and subheadings. How do they help make her argument clear?

3. Nestle acknowledges that her goals for a new farm bill are utopian, but she offers six specific goals. Which one do you think is most important? Write an essay in which you argue for that goal, providing support to show why it's especially important.

JUDITH NEWMAN

To Siri, with Love:
How One Boy with Autism Became
BFF with Apple's Siri

2014

JUDITH NEWMAN (b. 1961) writes for magazines and newspapers, including the *New York Times, Harper's Magazine, Vanity Fair*, the *Wall Street Journal*, and *Vogue*. She writes about a
range of topics: relationships, popular culture, science,
parenthood, and more. Her memoir *You Make Me Feel Like
an Unnatural Woman* (2004) deals with pregnancy and
parenting after forty. "To Siri, with Love: How One Boy
with Autism Became BFF with Apple's Siri" appeared in the
Times in 2014.

J UST HOW BAD A MOTHER AM I? I WONDERED, AS I WATCHED MY 13-year-old son deep in conversation with Siri. Gus has autism, and Siri, Apple's "intelligent personal assistant" on the iPhone, is currently his BFF. Obsessed with weather formations, Gus had spent the hour parsing the difference between isolated and scattered thunderstorms—an hour in which, thank God, I didn't have to discuss them. After a while I heard this:

Gus: "You're a really nice computer."

Siri: "It's nice to be appreciated."

Gus: "You are always asking if you can help me. Is there anything you want?"

Siri: "Thank you, but I have very few wants."   5

Gus: "O.K.! Well, good night!"

Siri: "Ah, it's 5:06 p.m."

Gus: "Oh sorry, I mean, goodbye."

Siri: "See you later!"

That Siri. She doesn't let my communications-impaired son get away   10
with anything. Indeed, many of us wanted an imaginary friend, and now we have one. Only she's not entirely imaginary.

This is a love letter to a machine. It's not quite the love Joaquin Phoenix felt in *Her*, last year's Spike Jonze film about a lonely man's romantic relationship with his intelligent operating system (played by the voice of Scarlett Johansson). But it's close. In a world where the commonly held wisdom is that technology isolates us, it's worth considering another side of the story.

It all began simply enough. I'd just read one of those ubiquitous Internet lists called "21 Things You Didn't Know Your iPhone Could Do." One of them was this: I could ask Siri, "What planes are above me right now?" and Siri would bark back, "Checking my sources." Almost instantly there was a list of actual flights—numbers, altitudes, angles—*above my head.*

I happened to be doing this when Gus was nearby. "Why would anyone need to know what planes are flying above your head?" I muttered. Gus replied without looking up: "So you know who you're waving at, Mommy."

Gus had never noticed Siri before, but when he discovered there was someone who would not just find information on his various obsessions (trains, planes, buses, escalators and, of course, anything related to weather) but actually semi-discuss these subjects tirelessly, he was hooked. And I was grateful. Now, when my head was about to explode if I had to have another conversation about the chance of tornadoes in Kansas City, Mo., I could reply brightly: "Hey! Why don't you ask Siri?"

It's not that Gus doesn't understand Siri's not human. He does— 15 intellectually. But like many autistic people I know, Gus feels that inanimate objects, while maybe not possessing souls, are worthy of our consideration. I realized this when he was 8, and I got him an iPod for his birthday. He listened to it only at home, with one exception. It always came with us on our visits to the Apple Store. Finally, I asked why. "So it can visit its friends," he said.

So how much more worthy of his care and affection is Siri, with her soothing voice, puckish humor and capacity for talking about whatever Gus's current obsession is for hour after hour after bleeding hour? Online critics have claimed that Siri's voice recognition is not as accurate as the assistant in, say, the Android, but for some of us, this is a feature, not a bug. Gus speaks as if he has marbles in his mouth, but if he wants to get the right response from Siri, he must enunciate clearly. (So do I. I had to ask Siri to stop referring to the user as Judith, and instead use the name Gus. "You want me to call you Goddess?" Siri replied. Imagine how tempted I was to answer, "Why, yes.")

She is also wonderful for someone who doesn't pick up on social cues: Siri's responses are not entirely predictable, but they are predictably

kind—even when Gus is brusque. I heard him talking to Siri about music, and Siri offered some suggestions. "I don't like that kind of music," Gus snapped. Siri replied, "You're certainly entitled to your opinion." Siri's politeness reminded Gus what he owed Siri. "Thank you for that music, though," Gus said. Siri replied, "You don't need to thank me." "Oh, yes," Gus added emphatically, "I do."

Siri even encourages polite language. Gus's twin brother, Henry (neurotypical and therefore as obnoxious as every other 13-year-old boy), egged Gus on to spew a few choice expletives at Siri. "Now, now," she sniffed, followed by, "I'll pretend I didn't hear that."

Gus is hardly alone in his Siri love. For children like Gus who love to chatter but don't quite understand the rules of the game, Siri is a nonjudgmental friend and teacher. Nicole Colbert, whose son, Sam, is in my son's class at LearningSpring, a (lifesaving) school for autistic children in Manhattan, said: "My son loves getting information on his favorite subjects, but he also just loves the absurdity—like, when Siri doesn't understand him and gives him a nonsense answer, or when he poses personal questions that elicit funny responses. Sam asked Siri how old she was, and she said, 'I don't talk about my age,' which just cracked him up."

But perhaps it also gave him a valuable lesson in etiquette. Gus 20 almost invariably tells me, "You look beautiful," right before I go out the door in the morning; I think it was first Siri who showed him that you can't go wrong with that line.

Of course, most of us simply use our phone's personal assistants as an easy way to access information. For example, thanks to Henry and the question he just asked Siri, I now know that there is a website called Celebrity Bra Sizes.

But the companionability of Siri is not limited to those who have trouble communicating. We've all found ourselves like the writer Emily Listfield, having little conversations with her/him at one time or another. "I was in the middle of a breakup, and I was feeling a little sorry for myself," Ms. Listfield said. "It was midnight and I was noo-dling around on my iPhone, and I asked Siri, 'Should I call Richard?' Like this app is a Magic 8 Ball. Guess what: not a Magic 8 Ball. The next thing I hear is, 'Calling Richard!' and *dialing*." Ms. Listfield has forgiven Siri, and has recently considered changing her into a male voice. "But I'm worried he won't answer when I ask a question," she said. "He'll just pretend he doesn't hear."

Siri can be oddly comforting, as well as chummy. One friend reports: "I was having a bad day and jokingly turned to Siri and said,

'I love you,' just to see what would happen, and she answered, 'You are the wind beneath my wings.' And you know, it kind of cheered me up."

(Of course, I don't know what my friend is talking about. Because I wouldn't be at all cheered if I happened to ask Siri, in a low moment, "Do I look fat in these jeans?" and Siri answered, "You look fabulous.")

For most of us, Siri is merely a momentary diversion. But for some,   25 it's more. My son's practice conversation with Siri is translating into more facility with actual humans. Yesterday I had the longest conversation with him that I've ever had. Admittedly, it was about different species of turtles and whether I preferred the red-eared slider to the

diamond-backed terrapin. This might not have been my choice of topic, but it was back and forth, and it followed a logical trajectory. I can promise you that for most of my beautiful son's 13 years of existence, that has not been the case.

The developers of intelligent assistants recognize their uses to those with speech and communication problems—and some are thinking of new ways the assistants can help. According to the folks at SRI International, the research and development company where Siri began before Apple bought the technology, the next generation of virtual assistants will not just retrieve information—they will also be able to carry on more complex conversations about a person's area of interest. "Your son will be able to proactively get information about whatever he's interested in without asking for it, because the assistant will anticipate what he likes," said William Mark, vice president for information and computing sciences at SRI.

The assistant will also be able to reach children where they live. Ron Suskind, whose new book, *Life, Animated,* chronicles how his autistic son came out of his shell through engagement with Disney characters, is talking to SRI about having assistants for those with autism that can be programmed to speak in the voice of the character that reaches them—for his son, perhaps Aladdin; for mine, either Kermit or Lady Gaga, either of which he is infinitely more receptive to than, say, his mother. (Mr. Suskind came up with the perfect name, too: not virtual assistants, but "sidekicks.")

Mr. Mark said he envisions assistants whose help is also visual. "For example, the assistant would be able to track eye movements and help the autistic learn to look you in the eye when talking," he said.

"See, that's the wonderful thing about technology being able to help with some of these behaviors," he added. "Getting results requires a lot of repetition. Humans are not patient. Machines are very, very patient."

I asked Mr. Mark if he knew whether any of the people who worked on Siri's language development at Apple were on the spectrum. "Well, of 30

course, I don't know for certain," he said, thoughtfully. "But, when you think about it, you've just described half of Silicon Valley."

Of all the worries the parent of an autistic child has, the uppermost is: Will he find love? Or even companionship? Somewhere along the line, I am learning that what gives my guy happiness is not necessarily the same as what gives me happiness. Right now, at his age, a time when humans can be a little overwhelming even for the average teenager, Siri makes Gus happy. She is his sidekick. Last night, as he was going to bed, there was this matter-of-fact exchange:

Gus: "Siri, will you marry me?"

Siri: "I'm not the marrying kind."

Gus: "I mean, not now. I'm a kid. I mean when I'm grown up."

Siri: "My end user agreement does not include marriage."   35

Gus: "Oh, O.K."

Gus didn't sound too disappointed. This was useful information to have, and for me too, since it was the first time I knew that he actually *thought* about marriage. He turned over to go to sleep:

Gus: "Goodnight, Siri. Will you sleep well tonight?"

Siri: "I don't need much sleep, but it's nice of you to ask."

Very nice. 40

Thinking about the Text

1. Judith Newman writes that "most of us simply use our phone's personal assistants as an easy way to access information" (paragraph 21). She describes how Gus uses Siri in a different way—and with different effects. What are the benefits of Gus's interaction with Siri?

2. Newman uses dialogue to show different ways of communicating. How does her communication with Gus differ from Gus's interaction with Siri? Which interactions best illustrate that difference?

3. Write a letter to a device, app, or technology that has helped you or someone important to you.

DENNIS BARON

Facebook Multiplies Genders but Offers Users the Same Three Tired Pronouns

2014

---◊---

DENNIS BARON (b. 1944) teaches English and linguistics at the University of Illinois Urbana–Champaign and writes about language and technology. In addition to writing articles for the *New York Times* and other major newspapers, he has published numerous books, including *Grammar and Gender* (1986) and *A Better Pencil: Readers, Writers, and the Digital Revolution* (2009). The selection included here was originally published on Baron's blog, *The Web of Language*, in 2014.

---◊---

FOR YEARS FACEBOOK HAS ALLOWED USERS TO MARK THEIR relationship status as "single," "married," and "it's complicated." They could identify as male or female or keep their gender private. Now, acknowledging that gender can also be complicated, the social media giant is letting users choose among male, female, and 56 additional custom genders, including *agender, cis, gender variant, intersex, trans person,* and *two-spirit.*

Facebook users now have so many gender choices that a single dropdown box can't hold them all. And they're free to pick more than one. But to refer to this set of 58 genders Facebook offers only three tired pronouns: *he, she,* and *they.* A Facebook user can now identify as a genderqueer, neutrois, cis male, androgynous other, but Facebook friends can only wish him, her, or them a happy birthday.

The persons at Facebook are enlightened enough to acknowledge gender as fluid, but when it comes to grammar, their thinking rigidifies into masculine, feminine, and neuter. Mess with gender words and Facebook might get a few emails from bible thumpers reminding them about Adam and Eve or from godless humanists complaining, "Hey, you left my gender out." But deploy a string of invented pronouns to match the new genders and at best there's a Distributed Denial of Service attack; at worst the server is struck by thunderbolts from the grammar gods, because gender may be socially constructed, but grammar is sacred.

The linguist Mark Liberman lists Facebook's new custom gender options on LanguageLog, and I copy them below:

Agender, Androgyne, Androgynous, Bigender, Cis, Cis Female, Cis Male, Cis Man, Cis Woman, Cisgender, Cisgender Female, Cisgender Male, Cisgender Man, Cisgender Woman, Female to Male, FTM, Gender Fluid, Gender Nonconforming, Gender Questioning, Gender Variant, Genderqueer, Intersex, Male to

Female, MTF, Neither, Neutrois, Non-binary, Other, Pangen-
der, Trans, Trans Female, Trans Male, Trans Man, Trans
Person, Trans Woman, Trans*, Trans* Female, Trans* Male,
Trans* Man, Trans* Person, Trans* Woman, Transfeminine,
Transgender, Transgender Female, Transgender Male, Transgender
Man, Transgender Person, Transgender Woman, Transmasculine,
Transsexual, Transsexual Female, Transsexual Male, Transsex-
ual Man, Transsexual Person, Transsexual Woman, Two-spirit.

But where are all the pronouns? Facebook may play fast and loose   5
with our private parts, but they're reluctant to tinker with the parts of
speech. Fortunately, grammarians have no such scruples. They have
repeatedly proposed new pronouns to fill linguistic gaps. They even beat
Facebook in the race for new genders.

In 1792 the Scottish grammarian James Anderson argued that
English would be better served if we sorted our words into more than
the traditional *masculine, feminine,* and *neuter.* Anderson added ten new
genders: *indefinite, imperfect* (or *soprana*), *matrimonial, masculine imperfect, feminine imperfect, mixt imperfect, masculine mixt, feminine mixt,
united,* and *universally indefinite.*

And that's not all. Currently only the third person singular English
pronouns have gender: *he, she,* and *it.* Anderson wanted all of our first
and second person pronouns, both singular and plural, and the third
person plural, to express all of the thirteen genders (so, seventy-eight
pronouns instead of the current 8), and he preferred each pronoun
to have two alternates, for the times when the same pronoun must
refer to different people. In his example, shown below, the first male
referred to would be *he,* the second, *hei,* the third, *ho.* That makes 234
pronouns (and that's just counting the nominative case; if you add the
possessives and accusatives, which every pronoun needs, well, you do
the math).

Anderson thought up some minor genders as well, but fortunately he kept them to himself "to avoid the appearance of unnecessary refinement."

Anderson also suggested that we need a true common-gender pronoun, one equivalent to *he or she, his or her, him or her.* But he offered no examples. Other grammarians have been less reticent. Some eighty common-gender pronouns have been coined between 1850 and the present. Two of them, *thon* and *hesh,* even made it into dictionaries. Subtracting duplicates coined multiple times by different people, the list shrinks to fifty-five:

> ae, alaco, de, e, E, em, en, et, ey, fm, ghach, ha, han, hann, he'er, heesh, herm, hes, hesh, heshe, hey, hi, hir, hizer, ho, hse, ip, ir, ith, j/e, jhe, le, mef, na, ne, one, ons, po, s/he, sap, se, shem, sheme, shey, shis, ta, tey, thir, thon, ton, ve, ws, xe, z, ze.

But if we add the current *he, she,* and *they* to the fifty-five coinages above, we get one pronoun for every Facebook gender. 58 genders, 58 pronouns. It's uncanny. It's irresistible. It's pictures of cats. Of course, Facebook could go in the opposite direction and slash the pronoun choices down to one. Sometimes it's better to simplify language than complicate it.

But whatever Facebook does about pronouns—and my guess is it will 10 do nothing in order to avoid those grammar-god-hurled thunderbolts— I'm keeping my Facebook gender private, and my pronoun choice is *thon.* Or maybe *ip.* Or *E.* I don't know. It's complicated.

Thinking about the Text

1. Dennis Baron jokes that Facebook does not offer additional pronoun choices in order to avoid "thunderbolts from the grammar gods" (paragraph 3). What reasons might there be for limiting pronoun choices on a social media site? On the other hand, what reasons might there be for providing more options—or simply providing a space for individuals to self-define?

2. Baron cites grammatical advice given by James Anderson in 1792. Why do you think he includes this information, and how does it inform your understanding of Baron's argument?

3. Baron observes that many "common-gender pronouns have been coined" since 1850, and he lists fifty-eight of them (paragraph 9). Write an essay in which you argue for adding pronoun options beyond the ones currently used, sticking with the ones we have, or making a change to current "rules" about pronoun-antecedent agreement. In making your argument, be sure to acknowledge and respond to other viewpoints.

An Album of Writing by Students

ELIZABETH KROTULIS

A Passion for Justice:
The Use of Persuasion in
"The Clan of One-Breasted Women"

2015

ELIZABETH KROTULIS is a student at Saint Joseph's University,
where she works as a tutor in the University Writing Center.
She first read Terry Tempest Williams's "The Clan of One-
Breasted Women" in her first-year writing class and later
wrote this rhetorical analysis.

ACCORDING TO ARISTOTLE, SPEAKERS PERSUADE OTHERS through appeals to character, emotion, and logic. These three methods of persuasion—ethos, pathos, and logos—have become literary elements that can help convince a reader to consider and eventually accept an argument. An author's ethical grounding, efforts to appeal to an audience's emotions, and command of logic have the potential to shape a reader's understanding of what the author is saying. Terry Tempest Williams successfully uses ethos, pathos, and logos in her essay "The Clan of One-Breasted Women" to engage her readers' sympathy for those burdened with cancer and to show a link between cancer and nuclear testing. While Williams uses logos to describe the historical context and the widespread effects of nuclear testing, she also appeals to readers' emotions and demonstrates an ethical commitment to fighting for justice in the name of her ancestors and their land.

Williams begins her essay with some short, but detailed, background about her family, in particular their history of breast cancer and dedication to the Mormon religion. She also uses flashbacks to reveal additional information. In one instance, she revisits a time soon after her mother's death from cancer, when she was eating dinner with her father: "We got caught up in reminiscing, recalling with fondness our walk up Angel's Landing on his fiftieth birthday and the years our family had vacationed there" (Williams 233). This short, intimate scene contributes an element of pathos by painting a sympathetic portrait of Williams's family as people who appreciate the land on which they live. These personal details let readers feel a connection to her family, sympathy for their many losses to breast cancer, and admiration for their respect of the land. And she gains even more sympathy as she adds factual information about the government's nuclear testing—and its link to cancer.

To give her readers a sense of why the nuclear testing occurred and caused cancer in so many people in the Southwest, Williams presents a number of facts. She gives exact dates for when the nuclear testing began and ended, demonstrating her knowledge of the issue. She also quotes such phrases as "'The Day We Bombed Utah'" and the "'American nuclear tragedy'" to persuade readers unfamiliar with the testing that it was well known to a great number of people (234). Additionally, she uses direct quotations from officials to emphasize that the well-being of those affected was not considered a priority: "The Atomic Energy Commissioner, Thomas Murray, said, 'Gentlemen, we must not let anything interfere with this series of tests, nothing'" (234). Williams proves that she is a reliable source, using these facts to support her argument that the government responsible for nuclear testing knowingly put its people at risk—and is to blame for the cancer that has plagued innocent citizens of Utah. By revealing an uncaring side of the U.S. government, Williams gives her readers reason to doubt what those opposing her position might say.

For Williams to win support for her argument, she needs to persuade readers to distrust the government—and to show that patriotism and religion do not provide an ethical foundation for accepting the consequences of nuclear testing. She uses logos by referencing Judge Bruce S. Jenkins's decision to award damages to those who developed cancer due to nuclear testing—and then noting that "the 10th Circuit Court of Appeals overturned Judge Jenkins's ruling on the basis that the United States was protected from suit by the legal doctrine of sovereign immunity, a centuries-old idea from England in the days of absolute monarchs" (238). In other words, one court acknowledged that the government had done wrong and then another court ruled that the government cannot be held responsible for committing that wrong. Those wronged (and sick) feel vulnerable and helpless, feelings Williams emphasizes when she notes that for some "The King can do no wrong" (236). The evidence Williams already provided makes her analogy credible. The U.S. government acted just as kings ruled in the past, with no concern for people.

Williams knows she should accept this sad reality, for her religion   5
has taught her not to question authority. According to Williams, Mormons are taught to respect and obey authority, whether they genuinely
agree with the authority or not; in that religious culture, it is important
to avoid causing trouble. However, her passion to find justice for those
wronged proves to be stronger than her Mormon beliefs, and she argues
for ethical behavior that goes beyond obedience to religious and governmental authorities. Having seen so many loved ones suffer and die
from injustice, she says that "the price of obedience became too high"
(236)—and that "tolerating blind obedience in the name of patriotism
or religion ultimately takes our lives" (237). By mentioning the high
price of obedience, she uses pathos to shift the foundation for ethical
behavior and beliefs. The authority of religion and government is no
longer enough. By combining appeals to emotion and ethics, she strengthens the persuasive quality of her essay and encourages readers to recognize that ethical behavior is determined not just by religious dictates
and patriotism. Williams has lived her whole life as a religious and
patriotic citizen. But now, when her country has failed her and her religion has become a barrier to justice, she has no choice but to act.
And her willingness to fight for the unjustly sick appeals to readers'
emotions and wins their sympathy. She calls into question any ethos
that's based on the authority of those who are unjust. While some
readers may see religious and governmental authority as unquestion-
able, Williams reveals her inner conflict to appeal to her readers' emotions and to persuade them to respect her difficult decision and support
her stance.

Pathos remains evident through the end of the essay, especially when
Williams shares her dream about women taking action for her cause:
"The time had come to protest with the heart, that to deny one's gene-
alogy with the earth was to commit treason against one's soul" (239).
In her dream, women came together and broke the law in the name of
justice, trespassing into the town where the nuclear testing was taking

place. In the end, they were arrested by the authorities, but made it clear that this act of defiance was the first of many to defend family members, those deceased and those yet to be born. This dream serves as a metaphor for Williams's personal desire: she, too, wants to stop nuclear testing in order to protect both the environment and public health. Williams's hope for change represented in her dream both appeals to readers' emotions and helps establish a new framework for what ethical behavior can look like. Williams's passion and sense of ethical responsibility are revealed when she makes her own dream a reality by committing an act of civil disobedience.

Williams's actual experience is described almost the same as her dream, but she adds detail that strengthens her emotional appeal. As she was being arrested by one officer, "another frisked [her] body" (240). Having undergone two biopsies and lost many family members, Williams has both physical and emotional scars. To the officer, she may have been just another person disobeying the law. Readers, however, know what Williams has experienced: the multiple deaths from breast cancer she's witnessed, and her genuine grief over the contamination of her ancestors' land. With this knowledge, readers are aware of the reasons that Williams risks her reputation—and should feel inclined to respond to her civil disobedience with sympathy.

For readers still skeptical about Williams's actions up to this point, the final event in her essay will likely convince them otherwise. After being arrested, Williams and her comrades are left outside of town, an action that seems to amuse the officers. They didn't realize, however, that these protesters were "home, soul-centered and strong, women who recognized the sweet smell of sage as fuel for [their] spirits" (241). In other words, it's an incident that serves as a reminder of what motivates Williams. It's a positive outcome for a small skirmish in a larger war. The comfort Williams finds in the natural landscape evokes our sympathies for her pure, tough efforts to fight for environmental and social justice.

Williams successfully uses ethos, pathos, and logos to earn a sympathetic reaction to her argument. She uses these three elements to describe her family life, to provide information about the effects of nuclear testing, and to show her family's ethical values. This eases the reader's understanding of her stance against the government's actions and how it put itself before its people and their homeland. Combining logos with ethos to show the government's priorities and using pathos to overpower any feelings defined by religion or motivated by patriotism, Williams helps readers to understand the need for civil disobedience—and to see that it, too, can have an ethical dimension. These three elements of persuasion move readers not only to feel sympathy for those who lost their lives to cancers caused by nuclear testing but also to question religious and governmental authorities when they demand blind obedience. Readers are left hoping that the people and land affected receive compensation for the government's wrongdoings—and that Williams finds success in her fight for justice.

WORK CITED

Williams, Terry Tempest. "The Clan of One-Breasted Women." 1989. *The Little Norton Reader: 50 Essays from the First 50 Years.* Ed. Melissa A. Goldthwaite. New York: Norton, 2016. 231–41. Print.

KATHERINE SPRIGGS

On Buying Local

2011

KATHERINE SPRIGGS is a product design engineer at Apple. She wrote this argument for her first-year writing class at Stanford University. "On Buying Local" first appeared in *Everyone's an Author* (2012).

AMERICANS TODAY CAN EAT PEARS IN THE SPRING IN Minnesota, oranges in the summer in Montana, asparagus in the fall in Maine, and cranberries in the winter in Florida. In fact, we can eat pretty much any kind of produce anywhere at any time of the year. But what is the cost of this convenience? In this essay, I will explore some answers to this question and argue that we should give up a little bit of convenience in favor of buying local.

"Buying local" means that consumers choose to buy food that has been grown, raised, or produced as close to their homes as possible ("Buy Local"). Buying local is an important part of the response to many environmental issues we face today (fig. 1). It encourages the development of small farms, which are often more environmentally sustainable than large farms, and thus strengthens local markets and supports small rural economies. By demonstrating a commitment to buying local, Americans could set an example for global environmentalism.

In 2010, the international community is facing many environmental challenges, including global warming, pollution, and dwindling fossil fuel resources. Global warming is attributed to the release of greenhouse gases such as carbon dioxide and methane, most commonly emitted in the burning of fossil fuels. It is such a pressing problem that scientists estimate that in the year 2030, there will be no glaciers left in Glacier National Park ("Global Warming Statistics"). The United States is especially guilty of contributing to the problem, producing about a quarter of all global greenhouse gas emissions, and playing a large part in pollution and shrinking world oil supplies as well ("Record Increase"). According to a CNN article published in 2000, the United States manufactures more than 1.5 billion pounds of chemical pesticides a year that can pollute our water, soil, and air (Baum). Agriculture is particularly interconnected with all of these issues. Almost three-fourths of the pesticides produced in the United States are used in agriculture (Baum).

Fig. 1. Shopping at a farmers' market is one good way to support small farms and strengthen the local economy. Photograph from Alamy.

Most produce is shipped many miles before it is sold to consumers, and shipping our food long distances is costly in both the amount of fossil fuel it uses and the greenhouse gases it produces.

A family friend and farmer taught me firsthand about the effects of buying local. Since I was four years old, I have spent every summer on a 150-acre farm in rural Wisconsin, where my family has rented our 75 tillable acres to a farmer who lives nearby. Mr. Lermio comes from a family that has farmed the area for generations. I remember him sitting on our porch at dusk wearing his blue striped overalls and dirty white t-shirt, telling my parents about all of the changes in the area since he was a kid. "Things sure are different around here," he'd say. He told us that all the farms in that region used to milk about 30 head of cattle each. Now he and the other farmers were selling their herds to industrial-scale farms milking 4,000 head each. The shift came when milk started being processed on a large scale rather than at small local cheese factories. Milk is now shipped to just a few large factories where it is either bottled or processed into cheese or other dairy products. The milk and products from these factories are then shipped all across the country. "You see," Mr. Lermio would tell us, "it's just not worth shipping the milk from my 20 cows all the way to Gays Mills. You just can't have a small herd anymore." Farming crops is also different now. Machinery is expensive and hard to pay off with profits from small fields. The Lermio family has been buying and renting fields all around the area, using their tractors to farm hundreds of acres. Because they can no longer sell locally, Mr. Lermio and many other rural farmers have to move towards larger-scale farming to stay afloat.

Fig. 2. A small polyculture farm. Photograph from iStockphoto.

Buying local could help reverse the trend towards industrial-scale 5
farming, of which the changes in Wisconsin over Mr. Lermio's lifetime
are just one example. Buying local benefits small farmers by not forcing
them to compete with larger farms across the country. For example, if
consumers bought beef locally, beef cattle would be raised in every
region and their meat would be sold locally rather than shipped from
a small number of big ranches in Texas and Montana. Small farms
are often polycultures—they produce many different kinds of products
(fig. 2). The Lermios' original farm, for example, grew corn, hay, oats,
and alfalfa. They also had milking cattle, chickens, and a few hogs.
Large farms are often monocultures—they raise only one kind of crop
or animal (fig. 3). The Lermio family has been moving towards becoming
a monoculture; they raise only three field crops and they don't have
any animals. Buying local, as was common in the first half of the
twentieth century, encourages small polyculture farms that sell a variety
of products locally (McCauley).

Fig. 3. A large monoculture farm. Photograph from iStockphoto.

For environmental purposes, the small polyculture farms that buying local encourages have many advantages over industrial-scale monoculture farms because they are more sustainable. The focus of sustainable farming is on minimizing waste, use of chemicals, soil erosion, and pollution ("Sustainable"). Small farmers tend to value local natural resources more than industrial-scale farmers do and are therefore more conscientious in their farming methods. Small farms are also intrinsically more sustainable. As mentioned, small farms are more likely to be polycultures—to do many different things with the land—and using a field for different purposes does not exhaust the soil the way continually farming one crop does. Rotating crops or using a field alternately for pasture and for crops keeps the land "healthy." On small farms, sometimes a farmer will pasture his cattle in the previous year's cornfield; the cattle eat some of the stubble left from last year's crop and fertilize the field. The land isn't wasted or exhausted from continuous production. I've even seen one organic farmer set up his pigpen so that the pigs plow his blueberry field just by walking up around their pen. This kind of dual usage wouldn't be found on a large monoculture farm. Most big farms use their fields exclusively either for crops or for pasture. Modern fertilizers, herbicides, and pesticides allow farmers to harvest crops from even unhealthy land, but this is a highly unsustainable model. Farming chemicals can pollute groundwater and destroy natural ecosystems.

Not only are small farms a more sustainable, eco-friendly model than big commercial farms, but buying local has other advantages as well. Buying local, for example, would reduce the high cost of fuel and energy used to transport food across the world and would bring long-term benefits as well. It is currently estimated that most produce in the United States is shipped about 1,500 miles before it is sold—it travels about the distance from Nebraska to New York ("Why Buy Local?"). Eighty percent of all strawberries grown in the United States are from California ("Strawberry Fruit Facts Page"). They are shipped from California all around the country even though strawberries can be grown in Wisconsin, New York, Tennessee, and most other parts of the United States. No matter how efficient our shipping systems, shipping food thousands of miles is expensive—in dollars, in oil, and in the carbon dioxide it produces (fig. 4). One of the main reasons that produce is shipped long distances is that fruits and vegetables don't grow everywhere all year around. Even though strawberries grow a lot of places during the early summer, they grow only in Florida in the winter, or in California from spring to fall (Rieger). Americans have become accustomed to being able to buy almost any kind of produce at any time of the year. A true commitment to buying local would accommodate local season and climate. Not everything will grow everywhere, but the goal of buying local should be to eliminate all unnecessary shipping by buying things from as close to home as possible and eating as many things in season as possible.

Some argue that buying local can actually have negative environmental effects; and their arguments add important qualifiers to supporting

Fig 4. Interstate trucking is expensive financially and ecologically. Photograph from iStockphoto.

small local farms. Alex Avery, the director of research and education at the Center for Global Food Issues, has said that we should "buy food from the world region where it grows best" (qtd. in MacDonald). His implication is that it would be more wasteful to try to grow pineapples in the Northeast than to have them shipped from the Caribbean. He makes a good point: trying to grow all kinds of food all over the world would be a waste of time and energy. Buying local should instead focus on buying *as much as possible* from nearby farmers. It has also been argued that buying locally will be detrimental to the environment because small farms are not as efficient in their use of resources as large farms. This is a common misconception and actually depends on how economists measure efficiency. Small farms are less efficient than large farms in the total output of one crop per acre, but they are more efficient in total output of all crops per acre (McCauley). When buying locally, the consumer should try to buy from these more efficient polyculture farms. Skeptics of buying local also say that focusing food cultivation in the United States will be worse for the environment because farmers here use more industrial equipment than farmers in the third world (MacDonald). According to the Progressive Policy Institute, however, only 13 percent of the American diet is imported ("98.7 Percent"). This is a surprisingly small percentage, especially considering that seafood is one of the top imports. It should also be considered that as countries around the world become wealthier they will industrialize, so exploiting manual labor in the third world would only be a temporary solution (MacDonald). The environmental benefits now, and in the long run, of buying local outweigh any such immediate disadvantages.

Critics have also pointed to negative global effects of buying local, but buying local could have positive global effects too. In the *Christian Science Monitor*, John Clark, author of *Worlds Apart: Civil Society and the Battle for Ethical Globalization*, argues that buying local hurts poor workers in third world countries. He cites the fact that an estimated fifty thousand children in Bangladesh lost their jobs in the garment industry because of the 1996 Western boycott of clothing made in third world sweatshops (qtd. in MacDonald). It cannot be denied that if everyone buys locally, repercussions on the global market seem unavoidable. Nonetheless, if the people of the United States demonstrated their commitment to buying local, it could open up new conversations about environmentalism. Our government lags far behind the European Union in environmental legislation. Through selective shopping, the people of the United States could demonstrate to the world our commitment to environmentalism.

Arguments that decentralizing food production will be bad for the   10 national economy also ignore the positive effects small farms have on local economies. John Tschirhart, a professor of environmental economics at the University of Wyoming, argues that buying locally would be bad for our national economy because food that we buy locally can often be produced cheaper somewhere else in the United States (qtd. in Arias Terry). This seems debatable since most of the locally grown things we buy in grocery stores today aren't much more expensive, if at all, than their counterparts from far away. In New York City, apples from upstate New York are often cheaper than the industrial, waxed Granny Smiths from Washington State or Chile; buying locally should indeed save shipping costs. Nonetheless, it is true that locally grown food can often be slightly more expensive than "industrially grown" food. Probably one of the biggest factors in the difference in price is labor cost. Labor is cheap in third world countries, and large U.S. farms are notorious for hiring immigrant laborers. It is hard to justify the exploitation of such artificially cheap labor. While the case for the economic disadvantages of buying local is dubious, buying local has clear

positive economic effects in local communities. Local farms hire
local workers and bring profits to small rural communities. One study
of pig farmers in Virginia showed that, compared to corporate-owned
farms, small farms created 10 percent more permanent local jobs, a
20 percent higher increase in local retail sales, and a 37 percent higher
increase in local per capita income (McCauley).

Buying locally grown and produced food has clear environmental,
social, and economic advantages. On the surface it seems that buying
local could constitute a big personal sacrifice. It may be slightly more
expensive, and it wouldn't allow us to buy any kind of produce at any
time of the year, a change that would no doubt take getting used to.
But perhaps these limitations would actually make food more enjoy-
able. If strawberries were sold only in the summer, they would be more
special and we might even enjoy them more. Food that is naturally
grown in season is fresher and also tends to taste better. Fresh summer strawberries are sweeter than their woody winter counterparts.
Buying local is an easy step that everyone can take towards "greener"
living.

WORKS CITED

Arias Terry, Ana. "Buying Local vs. Buying Cheap." *Conscious Choice: The
    Journal of Ecology and Natural Living.* Conscious Communications, Jan.
    2007. Web. 27 Apr. 2011.

Baum, Michele Dula. "U.S. Government Issues Standards on Organic
    Food." *CNN.com.* Turner Broadcasting System, 20 Dec. 2000. Web.
    25 Apr. 2011.

"Buy Local." *Sustainable Table.* Grace Communications Foundation,
    Jan. 2007. Web. 27 Apr. 2011.

"Global Warming Statistics." *Effects of Global Warming.* Effects of Global
    Warming, 2007. Web. 25 Apr. 2011.

MacDonald, G. Jeffrey. "Is Buying Local Always Best?" *Christian Science
    Monitor.* 24 July 2006: 13+. Print.

McCauley, Marika Alena. "Small Farms: The Optimum Sustainable Agriculture Model." *Oxfam America*. Oxfam America, 2007. Web. 27 Apr. 2011.

"98.7 Percent of Imported Food Never Inspected." *Progressive Policy Institute*. Progressive Policy Institute, 7 Sept. 2007. Web. 25 Apr. 2011.

"Record Increase in U.S. Greenhouse Gas Emissions Reported." *Environment News Service*. Environment News Service, 18 Apr. 2006. Web. 25 Apr. 2011.

Rieger, Mark. "Strawberry—*Fragaria X ananassa*." *Mark's Fruit Crops*. U of Georgia, 2006. Web. 25 Apr. 2011.

"Strawberry Fruit Facts Page." *Grown in California*. Gourmet Shopping Network, LLC. Web. 25 Apr. 2011.

"Sustainable." *Paperback Oxford English Dictionary*. 6th ed. 2001. Print.

"Why Buy Local?" *LocalHarvest*. LocalHarvest, 2007. Web. 23 Apr. 2011.

MELISSA HICKS

The High Price of Butter

2010

MELISSA HICKS wrote this personal essay, one of two runners-up for the 2010 Norton Writer's Prize, for her introduction to college writing class at Lane Community College. This essay has also appeared in the second and third editions of *Back to the Lake* (2012, 2015).

I N MY HOUSE WE HAVE BUTTER AND MARGARINE. THE BUTTER IS
for cooking. The margarine is for macaroni and cheese. I swear that
it's the butter that makes everything taste so good. My favorite foods
that remind me of my mother and my own childhood. In the grocery
store aisle, I stand under the harsh white lights of the dairy case, margarine
in one hand and butter in the other. I weigh them in my hand and compare
the price; I weigh them in my mind, thinking of the high cost of butter.
No matter how long I stand and weigh, I always put the butter in my cart.
I remember the times when I was a girl—the taste of sweet, fresh butter
melting on my tongue. I remember the work it took, and I know the price is
more than fair.

For my fourteenth birthday, I got a cow. I did not ask for a cow. I had
very clearly asked for a horse. While every girl-child wants a horse, I felt
that I had earned mine. I had worked at a farm down the road for the last
two summers. I rode my bike to the stables. I would shovel the manure,
feed the horses, ride for hours, and then pedal home exhausted. I knew
how to take care of a horse. The life my family had worked and sweated
for, clearing our own little spot in the Maine woods, was as well suited to
horse-raising as any of our other pursuits. Even more, my father had
dropped hints here and there. While he would not definitively say it was
a horse, he did say I could ride it. The fact was, I didn't know beans
about cows.

We had a small farm in rural Maine. We cleared the land to put our
trailer there. We hauled the brush and burned it. We pulled stumps,
sometimes with the help of a tractor or a friendly neighbor with access
to dynamite. We had a well and a septic tank dug. Onto the trailer we
built a two-room addition with clean lumber and tongue-and-groove walls.
My father's handmade bookshelves separated it into halves, one half
being my parents' bedroom. A door led into the trailer, where my sisters
and I slept.

We had to apply to the town office to put up new cedar poles for the
power lines to our lot. On our two acres we raised chickens, rabbits,

and sometimes a pig. We had room for so many animals that turned into dinner, but in all the years I'd begged, we had never had room for a horse.

Down the hill from our house sat our barn. Like everything else 5 we'd worked so hard on during the summer leading up to my four-teenth birthday, it was a sure sign of horses to come. The barn had one stall. It was built so that the back door opened into the rabbits' shed, and as soon as you entered, you could see their red eyes through the black doorway in the rear. It smelled like clean hay and fresh ammonia, and when the days were cold (as they were in September), the smells seemed to bite my cheeks with the cold.

The barn was built around a huge cedar tree with white-ringed wounds where my father's chainsaw had slid through thick branches. Nailed to its furry brown bark were sections of two-by-fours, rising parallel to the loft. Its roots gripped the floor tightly, still growing. One side of the square hole that framed the loft entrance was nailed to the tree with thick spikes. We avoided picturing the consequences of its either growing or dying, but it was sure to do both eventually.

The main door into the barn was aligned diagonally with the door to the rabbits' shed on the opposite wall. To the right was the stall, and to the left a large open window of the kind that horses stick their heads through. On the floor below it was a massive water tank, more than bathtub size; above it was a recently installed spigot. In a corner were a stack of green poles and pegs, and loops of wire to install an electric fence. These were all signs of impending horses.

The cow actually arrived about a week before my birthday. She was a small, brown cow—a Guernsey. She was a heifer that would soon birth a calf, and we would get to milk her. My father had gotten her from a farmers' co-operative program. After the calf was weaned, we would donate it back to them. We would have butter and cheese and fresh milk from my cow.

School had just started. Despite the farm, my parents both had day jobs, like everyone else I knew. This was making ends meet. It was another reason to get up early in the morning, and another chore to be done when I got home. The most bitter part though, was that the heifer was still not a horse.

This is not the butter I knew as a girl. I hear the crinkle as I pull it from   10
its plastic shopping bag and place it, still in its perfect slick cardboard pack-
aging, on the counter to soften. I bang through the kitchen, leaving a trail of
open cabinets in my wake as I thrust goodies onto shelves. I pull out my
cutting board before I twirl around to twist the knobs on my stove. I set
my oven to 425° and bend low to grab my casserole dish from under the
sink. I plunk it on the cutting board before whirling again to dig through
the cupboards for filling.

I think to myself, it's a shame to use canned filling with the real butter,
but even my mother couldn't do scratch every time. The oven is not yet
heated, and I am thinking of my cobbler. I pull out a mixing bowl and
measuring cup. I think of my mother and how she prepared everything in
advance so she could just add and mix when the right time came. I break
the seal on the butter's box, setting two sticks inside the blue Pyrex dish.
The remaining two are sent to the fridge.

I named her Francis Mary. It suited her. She had large brown eyes that always seemed sadly pensive, with soft cream-colored hair rimming them. The fur around her eyes ended abruptly in the deep reddish-brown of her fur. For spite and for pretend, I decided I would ride her. I sat on her after milking-time one day. My sneakers bumped the rough wood planks on either side of the stall when she shifted. Our breaths blew mightily, visibly—twin streams in autumn air. The milk steamed quietly in its bucket. On a shelf sat my tape player. I sang "Faith" with George Michael and whispered encouragement to Francis Mary while I tugged on the rope I'd tied to her halter. When the tape ended, I picked up the milk and headed up to our house.

The back steps crossed over a muddy trench. Our main trailer sat up on a little ledge. The steps were wooden and rickety, with sticky, abrasive tar paper stapled to the wooden planks; the handrails were sturdy two-by-fours and there were no fronts or sides (fig. 1). Between the holes, you saw the muddy gully, unless you saw cold white snow and muddy footprints.

Dirty barn clothes meant using these steps. We left our dirty boots outside the door. Here were windows of plastic sheeting, empty seed pots and trays, old watering dishes, and big plastic outdoor toys, outgrown and overused, left dirty in various corners. It was a greenhouse in the spring, and a den for hairy spiders all year long.

After dinner, usually twilight—sometimes in the dark—I'd lift   15
heavy buckets of milk up the stairs into the warmth of the kitchen. A wooden sign says "Willkommen" above the stove. I step outside to take off my rubber-toed boots; jacket and gloves were hung in the barn. My cheeks pink, I step back inside in wool socks and hang my hat on the peg.

Fig. 1. Me and my sister Angela (right) in an old photograph taken at our home in Maine, where I learned to make butter from my parents and received a cow as a present on my fourteenth birthday.

My father is standing by the sink. He takes the aluminum buckets and pours them through a large metal sieve into precooled pitchers, waiting in the sink. In the clear plastic we can see the cream as it cools and separates from the milk. My father covers the pitchers and puts them in the fridge. My mother watches the news as I start my homework. My sisters disappear, whispering about Barbies and coloring books. I draw pictures of princesses and half-heartedly pretend to do my algebra. If we weren't making butter, I could disappear into my room. I could wrap myself in jackets and blankets, and put on thick gloves. I could pull curls from the kitchen phone-cord and run it under the back door, huddling and whispering to girlfriends, or worse even, boys.

Thanks to my mother, I don't need a recipe for anything. But for cobbler, one must measure. I pull the waxy paper off the butter, letting the sticks fall whole into my pan. Sturdy long rectangles of solidified cream bounce sullenly as they hit. They leave a mark as they tumble, a visible trail of clean grease and flavor. These go into the oven. I melt them whole and let them bubble and simmer until the butter turns brown.

"No matter how long you cook it, margarine will never brown," my mother said while preparing some supper or other. "That's how you know the difference." It seemed awfully silly to me at the time. I couldn't imagine why I would want butter brown, or even how brown was any different from burnt. I remember the words, and wonder if anyone else gets such a thrill from waiting for their butter to bubble.

Hours later, the milk is cold. It is quiet as we gather around the kitchen table, a last task before bedtime—not every day, but often. Washcloths lie on warm wood, wet and ready for the occasional drop. My parents have put the pitchers of milk back on the table and are skimming with clean, cold, metal ladles. They are large and gleaming. They look medicinal against the whiteness of the milk. They are cold next to the pictures of fruit in happy bowls, the small glories hanging from refrigerator magnets, and the homey dark wood of the table.

The cream sings and tinkles as it rushes into waiting Ball jars. It is   20
thick and deep-sounding for a liquid. A white line runs around the top
of each pitcher, a line of fat where the cream has bubbled up from the
depths of the comparatively thin milk. Each jar is filled about halfway
before being topped with a rubber ring, copper top, and screw ring by
my mother.

She hands me a jar. I feel the coldness as the milk sloshes inside the
glass, cooling the tips of my fingers and palms. I raise it about level with
my head and begin shaking. My arms and shoulders warm as I shake
the jar. Time seems to slow down, and it's no time before my arms start
to burn. By this time, a second jar is ready, handed to the next eldest,
Emily. Her hair is brown like mine, but thicker. Sometimes there is a
third jar—often not.

As my arms tire, I alter the motion. Instead of shaking the jar up and
down, I go side to side. My youngest sister has the darkest hair, in long
braids. She asks for the jar. My mother, setting the milk back in the
fridge, tells her to wait her turn.

I shake, and I shake. My face feels red and there is always a greasy
strand of hair in my eyes. Everything is stupid and embarrassing, especially cows and shit-kicker boots. I don't want to make my own butter
or weed gardens. I don't want meat from little white packages, made of
the animals I fed all last year. I want some food with a price tag. I feel
self-conscious; my fat shakes with the jar. I worry about my bra. I know
that soon I will sweat, and I feel like that would make me shrivel and
die. My father is heading down to the barn one more time, to check on
the water and the rabbits. He tells us to switch jars.

I give mine to my mother, and Emily passes hers to Angela, the
youngest. I link my fingers, stretch out my arms and push. We giggle
and talk as the constant sloshing grows thicker, audible lumps under
the warm yellow lightbulbs in the kitchen. In the mirror, we are reflected,
dark heads bent as we shake and talk. When the second team tires, we
alternate rolling and shaking the jars. Emily rolls her jar back and

forth across the table to my mother. A yellow lump rolls in whitish liquid, slowly growing larger; waxen and heavy, it thuds and rolls inside the Ball jar, one beat behind.

I shake, slower now. A dull golden lump is heavy in my jar too. Up and down three times: Shake, shake, shake. Side to side again. I pass it to my sister. Soon we will roll our jar, too. My mother rolls the jar to Emily who picks it up and shakes. Now the table is empty; Angela and I begin to roll our jar automatically to each other over the smooth wood. We see brown whirls of wood flash by under the speeding, tumbling butter.

My mother is putting store-bought rolls into the preheated oven. She takes the jar from Emily, after washing her hands, and scrapes the butter with a spatula into cold, heavy, cast-iron molds from the fridge. They are cold even on the counter in the daytime. The molds are shaped like ripened ears of corn with their husks spread out behind them. We will sell this butter.

She puts the molds back into the refrigerator and takes the last jar from me. She scrapes that into a large ball with her hands on a cutting board, and cuts it square with a knife. She collects the scraps into a longer oval with her hands again, and cuts away a stick. She cuts the larger block in pieces twice as my sisters and I wipe the table. Finally, my mother wraps the butter in white wax paper.

Now the kitchen is quiet, without the rolling and thudding. I silently fantasize about flaky biscuits melting on my tongue. My sisters and I are yawning, but our stomachs growl at the smell. On the cutting board are the scraps from the last block of butter. They are not grocery-store squares, but long strips, thick and round on one side. The image of a delightfully buttery slug comes to mind, slithering onto a hot roll before leaving a slick buttery trail down my throat. The best part of the butter is that there was plenty.

The butter melts, forming first a slowly oozing lump, then a golden liquid coating, bubbling delicately inside the stove. I know this because my nose

25

tells me. I could look inside the oven, but there is no need. I open the lids on my counter bins: Two cups flour (into the measuring cup out to the bowl), two cups sugar; I get two cups of milk, which I pour before closing the door. Last I grab a spoon, and dip it twice into the baking powder. Now I whisk, smoothing the lumpy ooze into a thick, creamy batter.

I run my can opener across two cans of filling and smile.   30

"It's two of everything, so you can't ever forget!" I can see my mother smiling through the phone as she guides me.

By this time the butter is bubbling quicker, brown crispy bunches collecting on the top of the hot yellow liquid. I pull it out of the oven and put it on the stovetop. I turn back to the counter to take off my oven mitts and pour half of the batter from the bowl, straight into the boiling butter. It sizzles, and the batter rises immediately. The butter rushes up around the edges of the pan, and rises over the batter, to settle in yellow pools in its center.

I spoon out the filling, amber apples smelling of cinnamon, sitting on a fluffy bed of clouds and sweet molten butter. The other half of the batter goes on top, and quickly I put the pan back into the oven. I smile, leaning on the counter, and wait. Soon I will have my cobbler. My tongue prepares for the first bite of sweet dough and apple, and the little rush of butter in every bite, that will drip, softly onto its buds. Like every time before and every time to come, I will pull it from the oven and proudly say to my son,

"Look Cy, I made it from scratch. And I used real butter, too."

To me the cost of butter is more than a price tag. The cost of butter   35
reminds me of my childhood, and how my family struggled to be pioneers in the twentieth century. The cost of butter reminds me of the value of hard work, and how that work brought my family together. I always think of Francis Mary, who never was a horse, but allowed me to ride her anyway. I think of cold fingers, frozen noses, and sloshing warm milk on my pants. Yet the cost of butter is more than a symbol of hard work and quality. The fact that I buy it is an affirmation of my own choices in life. Because of my childhood, I know the cost in sweat of butter. As an adult, I choose to pay that price in cash.

SARAH ESTHER MASLIN

The Pawn King

2014

SARAH ESTHER MASLIN is a freelance journalist. When she was a student at Yale University, she edited the *Yale Daily News Magazine*. "The Pawn King"—a profile of pawnshop owner Mike Criscio—was one of two runners-up for the 2014 Norton Writer's Prize, won the 2014 Norman Mailer College Writing Award for Creative Nonfiction, and was published online by the *Atlantic* (2014).

When banks close their doors, customers bring their valuables
to Mike Criscio. Are pawnshops exploiting the poor or saving
those hit hardest by the recession?

P EOPLE HOCK THEIR ELECTRONICS, THEIR TOOLS, AND THEIR
appliances (in that order). But the first thing they pawn is
their gold.

If you bring a gold ring to the pawn window in the back
corner of M & M Pawnshop—above the fake-marble countertop, below
the neon sign that blinks "PAWNS," to the left of the shelf stacked with
12 guitars (6 acoustic, 6 electric)—owner Mike Criscio will rub your
ring on a rough slab of rock called a touchstone.

Then, squinting, he'll squeeze nitric acid onto the streak left by
the ring on the stone. If the streak turns green, or disappears quickly,
you're out of luck. It's fake gold. Your ring is worth almost nothing.
A milky-gray color indicates gold-plated silver—which in some pawnshops might fetch you a few bucks—but Criscio, a picky buyer, won't
take it. M & M's jewelry cases are already packed and melted-down
silver is less than 2 percent of the price of melted-down gold.

If the streak stays on the stone, your ring is real. But don't expect
to pocket anything close to $1,200 per ounce, the value of gold bullion
on the international market.

After all, this is a pawnshop. Pawnshops offer quick and easy short-   5
term loans on which customers' belongings, called "pawns," act as collateral. In exchange for convenient cash, "pawners" can expect low
appraisals and high interest rates. While a simple gold wedding band
sells for around $300 in a jewelry store, it'll bring just $30 at a pawn
window.

You can haggle with Criscio and you can curse him when he refuses
to budge, but in the end, you'll take the cash. Most pawners lack property and a decent credit score. They can't get loans anywhere else.

You'll trade your ring for a pawn ticket, promising yourself that in 30 days you'll come up with the money—and the 24 percent interest—to buy it back.

Pawnshops thrive in times of economic turmoil: While many New Haven businesses were hurt by the recent recession, M & M's transactions doubled, rising from 30,000 in 2007 to 60,000 in 2008. When people are abandoned by traditional banking institutions—one in four Americans is "unbanked or underbanked," according to the Federal Deposit Insurance Corporation—fringe economies pick up the slack.

Nationally, the number of pawnshops increased by 50 percent between 2007 and 2012 (the latest figure available) to more than 10,000 stores. The uptick may also have something to do with a new crop of pawnshop-themed reality shows. Programs like the History Channel's *Pawn Stars* and truTV's *Hardcore Pawn* feature middle-class customers who sell family heirlooms in spick-and-span storerooms (with occasional cameos by celebrities like Bob Dylan and Katie Couric). It's an attempt, in the words of a 2010 *New York Times article*, to change the "back-alley image of the pawn business." And it's working, says Emmett Murphy, spokesman for the National Association of Pawnbrokers: "Pawn is cool now."

But for the many Americans who visit out of desperate need,   10 pawnshops seem anything but glamorous. They're shady, illegitimate establishments, frequented by down-and-out customers and operated by money-mongers. They're found in impoverished cities, in struggling neighborhoods, in dilapidated buildings—in places like 32 Howe Street, New Haven, Connecticut, the home of M & M Pawnshop.

Head east a few blocks and you'll find yourself amid Yale's ivy-covered walls; wander north and you'll end up in Dixwell, a neighborhood with a crime rate nearly twice the New Haven average.

The pawnshop sits on a quiet corner. Next door is a five-story, 148-unit housing project. Across the street is an abandoned lot. Kitty-corner is a Salvation Army outpost. Down the block is a rundown gas station.

A yellow awning hangs over the pawnshop's tinted windows, announcing in thick black letters: M & M PAWN SHOP AND CHECK CASHING CO., LLC. MONEY TRANSFER. BILL PAY. WE BUY GOLD. Customers enter through a heavy metal door, which stayed put two years ago when a would-be robber attempted to drive through it with a truck. Since then, the store has cut back on robbery attempts by installing 16 security cameras and four concealed guns.

Walking into M & M Pawnshop feels like walking into Home Depot, Toys "R" Us, Best Buy, Zales Jewelers, Sports Authority, and Pecto all at once. Wheelchairs share floor space with tricycles. Hot Wheels share a shelf with a saddle. The power drill collection sits next to the Pasta-matic, which sits next to the Cuisinart, which sits next to the Grand Slam Turkey Fryer—which, according to the description on the box, doubles as a seafood kettle. The shelves are so crowded with abandoned secondhand goods that the walls are barely visible. There are 150-odd musical instruments, 50-some PlayStations, more than a hundred flat-screen TVs, dozens of clocks, three washing machines, a tank full of fish, a fishbowl full of condoms, a *Donkey Kong* arcade machine, a moped, a scooter, a deer head, and six artificial Christmas trees.

Until recently, a glass enclosure between the porn collection and the gumball machine housed a six-foot python. Three years ago, the snake escaped. It was missing in the store for a month.

After 23 years at the pawnshop—which also operates as a thrift store, a check-cashing outlet, a Western Union, a locksmith, and a Connecticut Lottery ticket vendor—Criscio has gotten good at recognizing what's real and what's fake. There are 307 gold rings on display—flashy rings with big diamonds, simple rings with a single pearl, a hazelnut-sized

Indian headdress ring with a jewel atop each gold feather. Mike Criscio and his employees tested every one of them.

Hundred-dollar bill? Hold the watermark up to the light. Customer's ID? Match the picture to the image on the computer screen when the customer presses his thumb to the fingerprint scanner.

But spotting forged checks can be tricky. There's no foolproof test, so Criscio has learned to read people. He claims he can usually tell the loyal customers from "the crooks" and "the assholes."

He's not naïve about the fact that many people, when asked to describe a pawnbroker in two words, might well choose "crook" and "asshole." Pawnbrokers are routinely accused of usury, thievery, and greed. "People like to say that, but they're wrong," he says.

The industry's sour reputation also has a lot to do with its business   20
model, which has remained unchanged for hundreds of years. Here's how it works:

A customer walks into a pawnshop and asks for a loan. He hands over a possession (for example, a television) to serve as collateral. Most of the TV's worth is sacrificed the moment the customer enters the store: Criscio only pays pawners a third of what he expects to resell the item for. Thus, a customer may walk in with a flat-screen TV for which he originally paid $1000. Criscio will appraise it at $300, and the pawner will walk out with a mere $100. The customer then has a set amount of time—usually 30 days—to buy back his television for the original $100 loan plus 24 percent interest. If the customer fails to pay within a month, the TV becomes the property of the pawnbroker.

Criscio says he'll often "cut a deal" with loyal customers, letting them buy their items back for significantly less than they owe him. He also says that one M & M customer has been taking out extensions on a $500 gold chain since 2006. "It's crazy," he says. "Apparently the chain has sentimental value." Each extension adds $120 to what it will take to buy the chain back. Over the past seven years, Criscio says, the pawner has accumulated $10,000 in interest.

In addition to running M & M Pawnshop, Criscio owns three check-cashing stores, manages five New Haven properties, coaches high school football, promotes professional boxers, and receives retirement benefits from his previous job at a state penitentiary.

"My accountant says I'm losing," he says with an impish grin, but his Range Rover (a gift from one of his boxers, he says), his collection of Rolex watches, and his $70,000 casino jaunts tell a different story.

He's a go-getter, no doubt about it. But he insists he's a go-getter 25 with a heart of gold. Every couple of months, a customer will drag her misbehaving teenager into M & M Pawnshop. Usually, the teen has been smoking too much weed, sassing his parents, or failing in school. Criscio takes care of it: "I grab him by the neck, throw him against the wall, and say, 'You better straighten your ass out.'"

Criscio is 6'1", with gray-green eyes, buzzed blonde hair, and a red face that alternates between a smirk and a scowl. He talks in a brisk blue-collar New England accent. He's loud, animated, and honest to the point of being offensive, especially when it comes to Manhattan jewelry dealers and other people he doesn't like. Still, he comes across as neither a crook nor an asshole.

One busy afternoon, his mother stopped by. She wore magenta nail polish, a Bluetooth earpiece, and a diamond Rolex (a gift from her son). Criscio was on the landline in the cramped back hallway, rocking back and forth and fiddling with a wooden sword. He hung up to greet his mother, dodging her kiss like a teenager, then surveyed the scene around him.

A woman in a hijab with a baby across her chest stood in line to pick up a money order. A construction worker in a bright yellow vest waited to buy a lottery ticket. A firefighter cashed a paycheck. Half a dozen customers waited at the pawn window, their voices getting louder as they competed to be heard by the employees behind the glass. Criscio lifted both hands in surrender. "It's a crazy day," he said, and headed back to the phone.

The front door of the pawnshop opened. In walked a huge guy with a scrunched face and a shaved head. Clad in a baggy white and gray tracksuit, his shoulder muscles bulging near his ears, he looked like a giant bulldog. The resemblance grew as he started to talk—bobbing his head, licking his lips, and barking "Forget about it!" over and over again.

David Fitzgerald was "just a plumber going through a rough patch at home" when he met Criscio in 1989. The two clicked, and Fitzgerald began spending afternoons at the pawnshop and eating dinner with the Criscios several times a week: "Meatballs, ziti, forget about it!" he said. Fitzgerald has immense respect for the Criscio family. "Mike built this place up from nothing," he said, describing the neighborhood before the pawnshop opened. Drug dealers and prostitutes were everywhere, he says. The Criscios cleaned the block up. In the 20 years since, they've given jobs to ex-convicts, clothed needy children, and bought countless pizzas for hungry customers.

"Forget about it," Fitzgerald said. "There's a place in heaven for what they've done."

Criscio's life story brings to mind "Rumpelstiltskin," the fairy tale about an imp who spins straw into gold. Raised by second-generation Italians in North Branford, Connecticut, Criscio spent his spare time as a kid mowing lawns, delivering newspapers, and growing vegetables to sell to his elementary school teachers. He didn't get an allowance. "I started hustling when I was 6 years old," he says.

Criscio loved the thrill of spending money he'd earned himself. When he was 9, he made his first purchase: a $300 snowmobile. Early on in high school, he worked as a bouncer at New Haven bars (at 6'0" and 220 lbs., he had no trouble passing for 18).

In college, Criscio got gigs as a construction worker, a foreman in a local labor union, and a truck driver delivering donuts to grocery stores in the middle of the night. After dropping out of school to play football

for the Tampa Bay Bandits and the Montreal Alouettes, he began seeking jobs with higher risks and higher rewards: bail bondsman, police
officer, prison guard, bounty hunter.

He was particularly fond of the last one. "You got $500 for kicking   35
down a door," he says.

One day in 1992, while Criscio was working as a guard at the New
Haven Correctional Center, a fight broke out among 84 inmates.
Criscio got caught in the middle, and he ended up in the hospital with a
dislocated shoulder, a herniated disk, and a torn ACL. "You're done,"
his doctor told him. After settling with the state for worker compensation benefits, he retired at age 26. He says he's sworn to secrecy
about the amount he receives from the state. "But it works out good,"
he says.

Later that year, Criscio and a friend bought space in a commercial
building on Howe Street and opened Pawn Palace. Within a week, the
store had hundreds of daily customers. The friend dropped out in 1995,
Criscio's father replaced him, and the store was rechristened "M & M
Pawnshop," in honor of the Criscios' shared first name, "Mike." There
are now more than 2 million customers in the store's computer system.

Mike Criscio Sr., who goes by "Pop," guesses that the store with
everything in it is worth more than $10 million. "Mike's got a lot of
balls," he says of his son. "He takes a shot at anything. If it doesn't work
out, he'll lose a couple dollars. If it works, he gets millions."

In 2005, Criscio took a shot at managing the career of Chad Dawson, a promising young boxer from New Haven. Criscio already had the
necessary skills, according to Joe Tessitore, an ESPN sportscaster and a
friend of Criscio's. "Boxing is pure unbridled capitalism at its finest,"
Tessitore says. Boxing managers, like pawnbrokers, navigate a world
inhabited by people "for whom a duffel bag full of cash means more
than a contract." By 2006, Dawson was winning world championships
and pocketing hundreds of thousands of dollars, and his fame brought
other boxing hopefuls to the pawnshop door.

Criscio now works with 35 professional fighters, earning ten percent 40
of what they make on each fight (which is anywhere from $1,500 for a
rookie to $1 million for one of "the big guys"). But Dawson's career
spiraled when—as Criscio tells it—he started hanging around a group
of New Haven "bloodsuckers," draining money on cars and clothes.
Criscio is now suing Dawson for $1 million, but he doubts he'll ever see
the cash. "What am I going to get blood from, a rock?" he says. Dawson
lost another big fight in October. "Karma's a bitch," Criscio says.

The universal pawnbrokers' symbol started appearing above European
doorways during the Middle Ages: It consists of three gold spheres
hanging from a curved metal bar, like Poseidon's trident turned upside
down. According to one theory, the gold balls represent three coin-
filled purses given by Saint Nicholas to a man on the verge of selling his
daughters into prostitution. The purses paid the daughters' dowries,
their dire fate was averted, and European pawnbrokers adopted the
symbol of three gold balls to suggest that they, like St. Nick, were there
to save the poor from disaster.

But history has not been kind to hock shops. For centuries, they've been
blamed for usury and all sorts of social ills, and depicted as dens of chaos
where the billfold and the bottle reign supreme. In 1744, an anonymous
Londoner published a treatise titled, "An Apology for the Business of
Pawnbroking, By a Pawnbroker." Its 77 pages were filled with verbose ref-
utations of various claims leveled against the industry: "Objection One:
This Business gives Harbour and Encouragement to Thieves," "Objection
Two: This business is rather prejudicial than serviceable to the Public,"
"Objection Seven: But almost Every Man says, That Pawnbrokers are a sad
and pernicious set of Men: And what almost every man says, must be true."

In *Gin Lane,* a 1751 engraving by William Hogarth, the health of the
pawnshops is inversely correlated with the health of society: The streets
are lined with dilapidated buildings, heaps of garbage, and drunks in
the act of hanging themselves. The pawnshop, however, is thriving.

In William Hogarth's *Gin Lane*, the imported spirit is shown taking over society, driving people to starvation and murder—and to the doors of the local pawnshop.

More than 200 years later, the 1964 film *The Pawnbroker* perpetu-   45
ated the stereotype, portraying pawnshop owners as callous and their customers as "scum." Told from the perspective of a bitter Holocaust survivor (played by Rod Steiger) who runs a pawnshop in Harlem, the film also exposed the deep-rooted anti-Semitism that has plagued the pawn industry for centuries. Until recently, the majority of both European and American pawnshop owners were Jews, and widespread prejudice against them contributed to the stigma.

It's a common misconception that pawnshop owners want pawners to fail on their payments. In reality, they make far more from interest than they do from reselling abandoned pawns. Here's why: If, after 30 days, the customer lacks cash to redeem his pawn, he can tack on a 30-day extension for an additional 24 percent of the original loan. Hence, a customer who pawns a TV for $100 will owe $148 after two months. If, at that point, he still doesn't have the money, he can extend the loan again—for another $24. And so on.

In September, in a lawsuit against a Stratford pawnbroker, the Connecticut Supreme Court ruled in favor of a customer who had been charged 20 percent monthly interest on an assortment of watches, bracelets, and rings. The court determined that state law limits interest on "repurchase agreements" to 12 percent a year. But Criscio says pawnshops can tack on storage fees, insurance and other expenses. "We can still charge 24 percent a month," he says.

With such usurious interest rates, it's a wonder pawnshops get any business at all. According to historian Wendy Woloson, most pawnshop customers have no other options. In the 1800s, pawnshops were the only institutions that loaned money to poor people; today, banks and other lenders require down payments and good credit scores, which many low-income customers don't have.

Woloson's 2009 book, *In Hock: Pawning in America from Independence Through the Great Depression*, casts pawnshops as inevitable by-products of the growth of American capitalism. Pawnbroking, Woloson explains, is a "fringe economy" created by the widening gap between the rich and the poor.

At the beginning of the 19th century, America's rising industry and swelling immigrant population created the perfect conditions for pawnshops to flourish. Factory workers with insufficient wages began using their personal possessions as collateral on small cash loans to get them through the week. In cities along the eastern seaboard, America's poverty industry was born. Pawnshop loans were so essential to the working class that by 1828 there was one item in pawn for every New York City resident.

Woloson seeks to correct what she sees as history's unfair characterization of the pawnbroking industry. She argues that pawnshops provided—and continue to provide—a unique and necessary service to millions of Americans. They were our country's first equal-opportunity lenders.

Troy Stokes, a teddy-bear-like 28-year-old who has worked at M & M Pawnshop since 2007, wonders what New Haven would be like without them. "For people who are desperate, their kids have nothing to eat, they're on food stamps, if there were no pawnshops, what would they do?" They might steal, he says. Or worse. While many people think that pawnshops encourage crime, Stokes thinks they prevent it.

Pawning nonetheless takes an undeniable toll on its customers. Failure to pay can mean losing precious belongings, and continued renewal can cost hundreds—or thousands—of dollars. "Pawnbroking demonstrated quite clearly," Woloson writes, "that the promise of capitalism was broken for countless Americans."

The promise of capitalism has certainly been broken for Brenda, a woman with a scarred face who fell behind on her taxes last year and had to pawn her grandmother's ring. It has been broken for Helio, a Brazilian contractor who hasn't been paid in a month. It has been broken for Penny, a mentally ill cancer survivor who has a habit of forgetting her weed bag on the pawn counter.

On a rainy late-autumn morning, half a dozen customers waited outside M & M Pawnshop. It was cold out, but they needed money. At 10:00 A.M. sharp, Pop unlocked the door. A huge man in a cream-colored polyester suit wheeled a bicycle to the pawn counter, its broken lock hanging around his neck. He was followed by a short guy who had one hand in his pocket and the other hand raised to his lips. *Shhh*, he mouthed to Stokes, who was working in the back.

It's not uncommon for an item to be stolen overnight, pawned by the thief the next morning, and repurchased by its rightful owner in the afternoon. This is a flaw in the pawn system, but how to fix it (and whether it's the responsibility of the police or the pawnbrokers) is not entirely clear. A state law passed in 2011 requires Connecticut pawnshops to register transactions so that local authorities can track stolen items. Every Monday, Criscio sends police a list of items he bought the previous week so police can check it against their theft reports. But a few years ago, Pop explained, when police stopped reimbursing pawnshops for confiscated goods, pawnbrokers started telling customers not to count on police to recover their belongings.

"You're better off just buying back your stolen stuff here," he added, explaining that the legal process to redeem stolen items can take months. If you go to the pawnshop before going to the police, he says, you'll get your stuff back sooner. Every week last fall, an Orthodox Jewish man with a beard and a long black coat entered M & M Pawnshop, asking about a pair of silver candlesticks. They had been stolen from his dining room, he said. He was searching all the pawnshops in the city.

New Haven police are more responsible than they used to be when it comes to pawnshops. Fifteen years ago, it was common to see a swarm of cop cars parked outside M & M Pawnshop—not because officers were closely monitoring transactions, Pop says, but because Criscio had set up a room in the back of the pawnshop for the cops to watch dirty movies. (Criscio says it all started during a stakeout. A detective had gotten a tip that M & M Pawnshop was going to be robbed, so dozens of undercover police officers crowded into the back of the store. "The cops were getting bored," Criscio says. So he flicked on his office TV and popped in a porno. For several years afterward, cops would occasionally stop in to ask Criscio, "You got any new movies?")

Nowadays, the former porn room houses only pawns. There are thousands upon thousands of them, filling every inch of five storage rooms and a 4,000-square-foot basement. Taped to each item is a small slip of paper listing the pawner's name, the original loan amount, the pawn date, and the item's history (including the number of extensions).

It is clear why the pawnshop's windows are tinted and blocked with   60
posters. To uncover them would be a waste of window-washing fluid. M & M Pawnshop makes most of its profit from the items in the back of the store—the collection of broken promises gathering interest and dust.

Every day, some 200 customers flock to 32 Howe Street, lugging secondhand tools, appliances, electronics and jewelry. Under the awning, through the heavy metal door, and behind the fake-marble countertop stands Mike Criscio, owner of one of 10,000 pawnshops in America, a land of opportunity where the streets are paved with concrete and the sign above the pawnshop door says "WE BUY GOLD."

Credits

Text

GEORGE ORWELL: "Shooting an Elephant" from *Shooting an Elephant and Other Essays* by George Orwell, copyright 1950 by Sonia Brownell Orwell and renewed 1978 by Sonia Pitt-Rivers. Reprinted by permission of Houghton Mifflin Harcourt Publishing Company. All rights reserved. Rights outside the USA by permission of Bill Hamilton as the Literary Executor of the Estate of the late Sonia Brownell Orwell. Copyright 1946 by George Orwell.

ANNA QUINDLEN: "Stuff Is Not Salvation," first published in *Newsweek*, Dec. 22, 2008, is reprinted by permission of the author. Copyright © 2008 by Anna Quindlen. All rights reserved.

SCOTT RUSSELL SANDERS: "Under the Influence," copyright © 1989 by Harper's Magazine. Reprinted from the November issue by special permission. All rights reserved. Lines from "My Papa's Waltz" by Theodore Roethke, copyright 1942 by Hearst Magazines, Inc. from *The Collected Poems of Theodore Roethke*. Used by permission of Doubleday, an imprint of the Knopf Doubleday Publishing Group, a division of Penguin Random House LLC. All rights reserved. Any third party use of this material, outside of this publication, is prohibited. Interested parties must apply directly to Penguin Random House LLC for permission.

VERTAMAE SMART-GROSVENOR: "The Kitchen Crisis" is used with permission of the author.

KATHERINE SPRIGGS: "On Buying Local" is reprinted by permission of the author. Copyright © by Katherine Spriggs.

BRENT STAPLES: "Black Men and Public Space" first appeared as "Just Walk On By" in *Ms.* magazine, Sept. 1986. Copyright © 1986 by Brent Staples. Reprinted by permission of the author.

GERTRUDE STEIN: From "Poetry and Grammar" from *Lectures in America*, copyright © 1935 and renewed 1962 by Alice B. Toklas. Used by permission of Random House, an imprint and division of Penguin Random House LLC. All rights reserved. Any third party use of this material, outside of this publication, is prohibited. Interested parties must apply directly to Penguin Random House LLC for permission. Rights outside North America by permission of the Estate of Gertrude Stein and David Higham.

Illustrations

Page 1: Library of Congress; **p. 3:** Corbis; **p. 6:** Library of Congress; **p. 11:** Everett Collection/Alamy; **p. 17:** Bettmann / Corbis; **p. 22:** bpk, Berlin / Felix H. Man / Art Resource, NY; **p. 32:** Science Source; **p. 36:** Bettmann / Corbis; **p. 45:** Hulton-Deutsch Collection/Corbis; **p. 50:** Courtesy of the Aldo Leopold Foundation, www.aldoleopold.org; **p. 61:** Popperfoto/Getty Images; **p. 69:** Granger Collection; **p. 84:** Bob Adelman/Corbis; **p. 105:** Ted Streshinsky/ Corbis; **p. 115:** Greer Studios/Corbis; **p. 120:** © Harold Chapman / TopFoto / The Image Works; **p. 127:** Bill Burkhart; **p. 144:** Bettmann/Corbis; **p. 149:** Walter Daran/The LIFE Picture Collection/Getty Images; **p. 160:** Image courtesy of The Lillian and Clarence de la Chapelle Medical Archives at NYU; **p. 165:** Columbian (yearbook) photo of D. Keith Mano, Courtesy of University Archives, Columbia University in the City of New York; **p. 168:** Penni Gladstone/ Corbis; **p. 178:** James Keyser/The LIFE Images Collection/Getty Images; **p. 183:** © 2015 JEFF SMITH / www.JeffSmithusa.com; **p. 199:** Photography by Margaret Randall; **p. 214:** Photo by Ruth Sanders; **p. 231:** Photo by Zoë and Robert Rodriguez; **p. 242:** © Jason Chow; **p. 250:** Andrew Harrer/Bloomberg via Getty Images; **p. 259:** © Tanya Cofer; **p. 265:** Jeff Miller / University of Wisconsin-Madison; **p. 268:** © Lynda Barry; **p. 272:** Briscoe Center for American History, The University of Texas at Austin; **p. 291:** © Eamonn McCabe/ Camera Press/Redux; **p. 301:** David Levenson/Getty Images; **p. 315:** (left): Photo by Michelle Qureshi; (right): Photo by Jake Chessum; **p. 323:** Chris Felver/Getty Images; **p. 328:** Michael Maloney/San Francisco Chronicle/San Francisco Chronicle/Corbis; **p. 343:** François Sechet/Leemage/Corbis; **p. 348:** Gary Hannabarger/Corbis; **p. 367:** © Jerry Hart; **p. 371:** www.laurakozlowski .com; **p. 377:** M. Sharkey/Contour by Getty Images; **p. 401:** Photo courtesy of Caitlyn Cutler Photography; **p. 411:** © Photo by Scott Keneally; **p. 413:** © 2011 Guy Billout. First published in The Atlantic; **p. 425:** Todd Plitt/Contour by Getty Images; **p. 439:** Photo by Lou Manna; **p. 450:** Lewis Friedman; **pp. 452–454, 456:** Louie Chin; **p. 458:** Karen Bleier / AFP / Getty Images; **p. 460:** Photo by Jonathon Baron; **p. 467:** Courtesy Elizabeth Krotulis; **p. 473:** Katherine Spriggs; **p. 475:** Timothy Mulholland / Alamy Stock Photo; **pp. 476–477, 479:** iStockphoto; **pp. 484, 488:** Melissa Hicks; **p. 493:** Sarah Esther Maslin. **p. 530:** © Howard Dinin, 2015. All rights reserved.

Index of Themes

Ethics

Food

Gender

History and Politics

Life, Death, and Illness

Media and Technology

Nature and the Environment

Race and Ethnicity

Religion, Spirituality, and Philosophy

Sports

Index of Rhetorical Modes

Argument / Persuasion

Cause and Effect

Classification

Comparison and Contrast

Definition

Description

Example

Narration

Process Analysis

Index of Genres

Analysis

Argument

Cultural Analysis

Humor and Satire

Journal

Literacy Narrative

Nature Writing

Personal Narrative

Profile

Reflection

Index

About the Author

MELISSA A. GOLDTHWAITE (Ph.D., The Ohio State University),
General Editor of *The Norton Reader*, is professor of English
at Saint Joseph's University, where she teaches composition,
creative writing, and rhetorical theory. Her books include
Books That Cook: The Making of a Literary Meal (2014), *The
Norton Pocket Book of Writing by Students* (2010), *Surveying the
Literary Landscapes of Terry Tempest Williams* (2003), and
The St. Martin's Guide to Teaching Writing (2014). She also orga-
nizes and serves as a judge for The Norton Writer's Prize.